East Asian Capitalism

East Asian Capitalism

Diversity, Continuity, and Change

Edited by
Andrew Walter and Xiaoke Zhang

OXFORD
UNIVERSITY PRESS

OXFORD

UNIVERSITY PRESS

Great Clarendon Street, Oxford OX2 6DP,
United Kingdom

Oxford University Press is a department of the University of Oxford.
It furthers the University's objective of excellence in research, scholarship,
and education by publishing worldwide. Oxford is a registered trade mark of
Oxford University Press in the UK and in certain other countries

British Library Cataloguing in Publication Data

Data available

Library of Congress Cataloging in Publication Data

Data available

ISBN 978–0–19–964309–7

Printed in Great Britain by
MPG Books Group, Bodmin and King's Lynn

Links to third party websites are provided by Oxford in good faith and
for information only. Oxford disclaims any responsibility for the materials
contained in any third party website referenced in this work.

Acknowledgements

In the research and preparation of this volume, we have accumulated debts to various individuals and institutions. As editors, we wish to thank the contributors for their cooperation and efficiency, which made the editing of the volume more agreeable than can be the case with such collective and inter-disciplinary projects. We are grateful to the following people for having made extensive and constructive comments on the thematic and country chapters: Ann Booth, Jenny Corbett, Bob Hancké, Jeff Henderson, and Richard Whitley. Thanks are also due to the anonymous reviewers whose suggestions and criticisms helped to improve the central arguments and analytical coherence of the volume. While organizing the workshop in June 2010 from which this volume was born, we received and gratefully acknowledge financial support from the Institute of Asia-Pacific Studies of the University of Nottingham, the London School of Economics, and the Japan Foundation. Finally, David Musson and Emma Lambert at OUP provided a generous mixture of advice and guidance at crucial points. Any remaining errors and omissions are ours alone.

Andrew Walter
Xiaoke Zhang
September 2011

Acknowledgements

Contents

Contents

List of Figures

List of Tables

List of Contributors

Shaun Breslin is Professor of Politics and International Studies and Director of the Centre for the Study of Globalisation and Regionalisation at the University of Warwick. He is also co-editor of *The Pacific Review* and Associate Fellow of the Chatham House Asia Programme, and of LSE Ideas. He has authored books on China and the global political economy, Mao Zedong, centre–local relations in China, and comparative government and politics (joint authored) and edited or co-edited volumes on China's international relations, online Chinese nationalism, comparative regionalism, and regional environmental governance. He has published over seventy articles and book chapters, primarily on the political economy of contemporary China.

Richard W. Carney is Research Fellow at the Department of International Relations, Australian National University. His research primarily focuses on the politics and the origins of financial institutions. He is the author of *Contested Capitalism: The Political Origins of Financial Institutions* (Routledge, 2009) as well as the editor of *Lessons from the Asian Financial Crisis* (Routledge, 2009). His articles have appeared or are forthcoming in the *Journal of Financial Economics*, *Journal of East Asian Studies*, *Business and Politics*, and *New Political Economy*. He was a Jean Monnet fellow at the European University Institute and he has been a visiting professor at INSEAD. His current research examines the rise of state capitalism in East Asia.

Frederic C. Deyo is Professor of Sociology at the State University of New York, Binghamton. He is the author of *Dependent Development and Industrial Order: An Asian Case Study* (Praeger, 1981) and *Beneath the Miracle: Labour Subordination in the New Asian Industrialism* (University of California Press, 1989), and the editor of *The Political Economy of the New Asian Industrialism* (Cornell University Press, 1987), *Social Reconstructions of the World Automobile Industry* (Macmillan, 1996), and *Economic Governance and the Challenge of Flexibility in East Asia* (Rowman and Littlefield, 2001). He has published more then forty journal articles and book chapters on labour markets and industrial relations in East Asia. He is currently completing a study of the labour impact of neo-liberal reform in China, Thailand, South Korea, and the Philippines.

Karl J. Fields is Professor of Politics and Government and Director of Asian Studies at the University of Puget Sound in Tacoma, Washington, DC. His research interests include various topics of East Asian comparative political economy, including government–business relations, economic reform, and regional integration. His books include *Enterprise and the State in Korea and Taiwan* (Cornell, 1995) and *Cases in Comparative Politics* (Norton, 2010).

Edmund Terence Gomez is Professor at the Faculty of Economics and Administration, University of Malaya. He is the author and editor of more than ten books on the political economy of capitalist development in East Asia. His recent publications include *Malaysia's Political Economy* (Cambridge University Press, 1999), *Chinese Business in Southeast Asia* (Routledge, 2001), *Political Business in East Asia* (Routledge, 2002), and *The State of Malaysia* (Routledge, 2004).

Masahiro Kotosaka is a DPhil candidate in Management Studies at Saïd Business School, Oxford University. His research project aims to reconcile different theories of multinational enterprises and explain how firms make make-or-buy and location decisions concurrently in the globalized business environment. Before joining Oxford's Doctoral Programme, he spent eight years running IT and retail business ventures and working as a management consultant with McKinsey & Company, first in Tokyo and then in Frankfurt.

Ching Kwan Lee is Professor of Sociology at the University of California, Los Angeles. She is the author of *Against the Law: Labour Protests in China's Rustbelt and Sunbelt* (University of California Press, 2007) and *Gender and the South China Miracle: Two Worlds of Factory Women* (University of California Press, 1998). She is the co-editor of *Reclaiming Chinese Society: New Social Activism* (Routledge, 2009) and *Re-envisioning the Chinese Revolution: Politics and Poetics of Collective Memory in Reform China* (Stanford University Press, 2007). Her articles have appeared in *American Sociological Review*, *British Journal of Industrial Relations*, *China Quarterly*, *Modern China*, and other journals. She is currently working on two research projects: one on labour, property, and land rights politics in China and the other examines Chinese investment and labour practices in Zambia's copper mining and construction industries.

Thomas B. Pepinsky is Assistant Professor in the Department of Government at Cornell University, where he is also the Director of the International Political Economy Program and Associate Director of the Cornell Modern Indonesia Project. His research lies at the intersection of comparative politics and international political economy, with a focus on emerging markets in Southeast Asia. He is the author of *Economic Crises and the Breakdown of Authoritarian Regimes* (Cambridge University Press, 2009), as well as articles that appear or are forthcoming in the *American Journal of Political Science*, *World Politics*, *Political Research Quarterly*, *Studies in Comparative International Development*, *Journal of Democracy*, and several other journals and edited volumes. His current research interests include comparative responses to the Great Meltdown of 2008–9, the political economy of financial development in Southeast Asia, and political Islam in Indonesia.

Mari Sako is Professor of Management Studies at Saïd Business School, University of Oxford. Before taking up her current position, she taught at the Industrial Relations Department of the London School of Economics for ten years. Her publications include *How the Japanese Learn to Work* (Routledge, 1989), *Prices, Quality and Trust* (Cambridge University Press, 1992), *Japanese Labour and Management in Transition* (Routledge, 1997), *Are Skills the Answer?* (Oxford University Press, 1999), and *Shifting Boundaries of the Firm* (Oxford University Press, 2006). She was a principal researcher for the MIT International Motor Vehicle Program during 1993–2006, working on modularization, outsourcing, and supplier parks in the global automotive industry. She is also a senior fellow of the ESRC-EPSRC Advanced Institute of Management in Britain. More recently, as a member of the Novak Druce Centre for Professional Services at Saïd Business School, she has been researching about the globalization of law firms, the outsourcing and off-shoring of professional services and their impact on the professions.

Wataru Takahashi is Professor in the Research Institute for Economics and Business Administration, Kobe University, and Former Director-General, Institute for Monetary and Economic Studies, the Bank of Japan. He has been a visiting professor at the Chinese Academy of Social Sciences, Keio, Kyoto and Tokyo Universities, and the Tianjin University of Science and Technology. He has published extensively on financial markets, reforms, and crises in Japan, China, and many other East Asian countries.

Andrew Walter is Reader in International Political Economy in the London School of Economics and Political Science. His main research interests include the political economy of international money and finance and the political economy of finance in East Asia. His previous books include *China, the United States and Global Order* (Cambridge University Press, 2011, with Rosemary Foot), *Analyzing the Global Political Economy* (Princeton University Press, 2009, with Gautam Sen), and *Governing Finance: East Asia's Adoption of Global Standards* (Cornell University Press, 2008). His current research is concerned with the political consequences of financial crises.

Xiaoke Zhang is Professor in Manchester Business School, the University of Manchester. His major research interests are in comparative political economy, with a regional focus on East Asia. He is the author of *The Changing Politics of Finance in Korea and Thailand* (Routledge, 2002) and *The Political Economy of Capital Market Reforms in Southeast Asia* (Palgrave-Macmillan, 2010), and the co-editor of *International Financial Governance under Stress* (Cambridge University Press, 2003). His research articles have appeared in *Review of International Political Economy*, *International Political Science Review*, *Journal of Public Policy*, *Studies in Comparative International Development*, and many other refereed international journals. He is currently working on dominant coalitions and financial market changes in East Asia and on institutional diversity within China's emergent capitalism.

Part One
Introduction

1

Debating East Asian Capitalism: Issues and Themes

Andrew Walter and Xiaoke Zhang

Since the middle of the twentieth century, capitalism has worked tremendously well in much of East Asia. The remarkable development of first Japan and then South Korea (henceforth Korea), Singapore, and Taiwan into world-class economies in defiance of an array of political and social challenges both at home and abroad earned them the hyperbole of the East Asian miracle. The extraordinary episodes of high growth since the 1970s in the Southeast Asian resource-based countries, specifically Indonesia, Malaysia, and Thailand, displayed striking similarities in terms of policy settings and economic outcomes. China and Vietnam, the two nominally socialist countries, made serious and sustained efforts to turn their economic systems in an unequivocally capitalist direction during the final two decades of the twentieth century, achieving equally remarkable growth outcomes. East Asian capitalism also appeared to be highly resilient, rebounding quickly from the global downturn of the early 1980s, the more challenging Asian crisis of the late 1990s, and most recently the global financial crisis of the late 2000s. By comparison to those of many other developing and emerging market countries, the experiences of capitalist development in many East Asian economies have been exemplary and enviable.

However, the same forces that have made East Asian capitalism so dynamic for so long have inevitably brought with them formidable and ever-present challenges. The continuous process of capital accumulation and the perennial reconstitution of markets as the organizing principle of the economy have unleashed constant political, demographic, and economic pressures. The strains of capitalist development have been acutely manifest in widening income gaps, persistent corruption, environmental degradation, and governance failures across the region. Internal social and political conflicts have

3

Table 1.1. Decade growth outcomes, selected Asian countries

	Average annual change in real GDP per capita (%)		
	1980s	1990s	2000s
China	8.3	8.8	9.3
Hong Kong	5.7	2.1	3.6
India	3.3	3.5	5.5
Indonesia	3.1	2.8	4.1
Japan	3.2	1.2	0.8
Korea	8.5	5.7	4.0
Malaysia	3.0	4.4	2.7
Philippines	−0.8	0.6	2.3
Singapore	5.0	4.4	3.1
Taiwan	6.3	5.4	3.2
Thailand	5.5	4.1	3.3
Vietnam	3.9	5.6	5.8
Average	4.6	4.0	4.0
Standard deviation	2.6	2.2	2.1

Source: IMF, World Economic Outlook Database, April 2010.

threatened in some cases to relegate some countries to a second tier character-ized by mediocre innovation performances, relatively high sociopolitical instability, and economic stagnation (Table 1.1).

Although there is no trend decline in average regional growth rates since the 1980s, underlining the point about resilience since the Asian crisis, slower growth since the 1980s is observable in the most advanced Asian economies. Among this top tier, some reduction in growth rates should have been ex-pected given their successful catch-up. But with the exception of Japan, per capita growth in this category (Hong Kong, Korea, Singapore, and Taiwan) remains impressive given their now relatively high levels of per capita income.[1] There are arguably more worrying cases of slowing growth in the middle tier, notably Malaysia and Thailand, along with persistently mediocre growth out-comes in the Philippines. These latter cases are increasingly at odds with the picture of continuing economic dynamism presented by countries as diverse as China, India, Indonesia, and Vietnam. Thus, although the average dispersion of growth outcomes in the region has actually fallen since 1980, there has been a growing divergence in growth performance between the most advanced countries and China, with attendant domestic and international implications.

Some have argued that growth slowdowns in the top and middle tiers of Asian economies indicate a deeper, structural problem with Asian capitalism (Islam and Chowdhury, 2000; Akhand and Gupta, 2005). In this view, globalization has

---

[1] Average per capita income levels (measured using purchasing power parity) in 2010 are very similar to those in the United States for Hong Kong and Singapore, and are about two-thirds of the US level for Japan, Korea, and Taiwan (IMF, World Economic Database, April 2010).

disrupted the existing configuration of business, financial, and industrial systems in some countries and eroded the broad institutional framework that underpinned past economic success. A number of East Asian governments have tried to balance external and domestic pressures for institutional reform in recent years. But it remains unclear whether patterns of institutional reform in the region and their relationship to growth outcomes exhibit any general tendencies, and what are the dominant forces behind the changes that have taken place.

An appropriate point of departure for examining these questions is the varieties of capitalism (VoC) approach (Soskice, 1999; Hall and Soskice, 2001; Hall and Gingerich, 2009) that has gained considerable currency in recent years. This approach claims to be firm-centred and prioritizes institutionalized relationships between firms, employees, and shareholders as the key determinants of national economic performances. Focusing on the process of economic policy adjustment in developed countries during the 1980s and 1990s, it distinguishes between two ideal types: liberal market economies (LMEs) and coordinated market economies (CMEs). While firms develop and manage relations with other actors through arms-length competitive markets in LMEs, they are said to do so primarily through non-market or strategic coordination in CMEs. These two distinct capitalist forms rest on institutional complementarities by which different spheres of the political economy are mutually reinforcing. The resultant comparative institutional advantages not only mediate national responses to globalization—thereby reinforcing the tendencies towards systemic divergence—but also render such responses path dependent. In the case of 'mixed market economies' (MMEs) in which neither market nor strategic forms of coordination predominate, the VoC approach predicts that globalization is more likely to be institutionally destabilizing, promoting convergence towards one or other of the two ideal types (Hancké et al., 2007b: 6–7).

Recent critiques and revisions of the VoC approach have converged on two key themes. First, the reductive tendency of the approach to posit a binary division of capitalism into two 'equilibrium' varieties has raised serious doubts about whether that division can accommodate the actual diversity of capitalism at the sub-national, national, and transnational levels (Howell, 2003; Thelen, 2004; Crouch, 2005; Hay, 2005). Alternative conceptual frameworks have thus been developed to identify more fine-grained and complex typologies of capitalism not only in advanced industrial societies (Amable, 2003; Boyer, 2005; Hancké et al., 2007b: 24–8; Whitley, 2007; Streeck, 2009) but also in emerging market countries (Nölke and Vliegenthart, 2009; Schneider, 2009). The downside of this proliferation of additional capitalist varieties is that it dilutes the relative parsimony of the original VoC approach without providing a typology on which national and regional specialists can agree.

The second theme that has arisen from the debate over the VoC approach concerns its core concepts of institutional complementarities and coordination.

Many complain that the VoC framework is unable to explain fundamental institutional change except through recourse to the role of exogenous forces in 'critical junctures' (Howell, 2003; Crouch, 2005; Streeck and Thelen, 2005; Mahoney and Thelen, 2010). The functionalism inherent in the VoC approach also assumes that institutional outcomes are economically determined without clearly specifying the 'selection mechanism' for national success or failure (Streeck, 2009). Recent revisionist literatures have instead highlighted the potential importance of endogenous processes of incremental change, of more open-ended possibilities for institutional evolution, and of the role of political coalitions, states, and policy discourses in such processes (Culpepper, 2005; Hall, 2006; Schmidt, 2009; Streeck, 2009; Mahoney and Thelen, 2010). These issues are addressed in the final section of this chapter.

Throughout the post-1945 period, some East Asian countries managed to resolve, in a wide variety of ways and at different points in time, the political, policy, and institutional barriers to rapid growth. But just as in the developed world, these successful countries have not converged on a single institutional framework, notably including the period since 1980 when the globalization of production and finance has accelerated. This outcome raises important questions about whether successful East Asian economies collectively or singularly represent different models of capitalism that are distinct from the standard typologies, what patterns of institutional evolution in the region can be discerned, and whether the causes of these institutional changes are similar or distinctive compared to that which has occurred in the developed world.

This volume brings together conceptual and empirical analyses of the evolving patterns of East Asian capitalism against the backdrop of global market integration and periodic economic crises since the 1980s. More specifically, it seeks to provide an interdisciplinary account of variations, changes, or continuities in institutional structures that govern financial systems, industrial relations, and product markets and shape the evolution of national political economies. The geographical focus of the volume is China, Japan, Korea, Indonesia, the Philippines, Malaysia, Taiwan, and Thailand. This focus is inevitably selective, but it provides a lens through which the changing varieties of capitalist development in East Asia generally can be understood.

In line with this analytical focus, the volume has three different yet interrelated objectives. First, building on extant comparative institutional analyses, it provides a typology of East Asian capitalism that identifies key institutional domains to be included in cross-national comparisons and establishes guiding principles for categorizing political economies across the region. Second, an analytical framework is required to elucidate the nature and mode of institutional changes in East Asian countries over the past two decades. The volume provides such a framework by establishing the theoretical criteria for identifying observable changes and illuminating the trajectory and pattern of these changes both within and across the key institutional spheres of the East Asian political economy. And finally, the volume advances theoretical propositions concerning the potential causes of these institutional changes. While particular chapters emphasize different causal variables, collectively they constitute a coherent effort to theorize the changing varieties of East Asian capitalism.

The balance of this chapter is divided into five sections. The first delineates the major contributions of this volume to current debates about the changing dynamics of East Asian capitalism. The second section provides a typology of capitalist varieties in East Asia. The third and fourth sections suggest a conceptual framework for illustrating the properties and patterns of institutional changes and identify the key causal variables of changes respectively. The fifth and final section concludes by discussing the organization of the volume.

Key Contributions

The study of capitalist development in East Asia has centred on several prominent theoretical paradigms that have ebbed and flowed though the past decades. Early analyses (Pye, 1967; Myrdal, 1968) couched in the terms of modernization theory held traditional cultural orientations culpable for hindering the emergence of modernizing social, political, and institutional environments conducive to entrepreneurship and industrialization in East Asia. The rapid growth of Korea, Taiwan, and Singapore in the 1960s and 1970s delivered a serious blow to modernization theory and saw the resurgence of the neoclassical perspective as canonical accounts of capitalist dynamism in East Asia (Little et al., 1970; Chen, 1979; Balassa, 1981). The basis of economic success was considered to be the outward-looking and market-oriented policy settings in which government intervention was limited and entrepreneurs were freed to pursue their natural comparative advantage. In the 1980s, these neoclassical accounts were challenged by a developmental state literature that attributed rapid industrialization in some parts of East Asia to the growth-promoting role of the state. This literature emphasized state strength and capacity as the crucial determinants of cross-national variations in the trajectory of capitalist development (Johnson, 1987; Amsden, 1989; Wade, 1990). Since the 1990s, this statist approach has been revised to take account of changes in state structures and development strategies across the region.[2] However, this literature has for the most part developed in isolation from the literature on comparative capitalism, prompting some to call for more

---

[2] Revisionist efforts are represented in Clark and Roy (1997); Weiss (1998, 2003); Boyd and Ngo (2005); and Underhill and Zhang (2005).

attention to be given to understanding the changing varieties of capitalist institutions in the Asian region (Haggard, 2004).

As noted earlier, most studies on the varied and changing configurations of national capitalism in the context of globalization have focused on advanced industrial societies. To the extent that attention has been paid to developing and emerging market countries, this has mainly centred on East Central Europe (Feldmann, 2007; King, 2007; Lane and Myant, 2007; Mykhnenko, 2007; Nölke and Vliegenthart, 2009) and Latin America (Huber, 2003; Schneider, 2009). Given the continuing dramatic shift in the centre of gravity of the global economy towards the East Asian region (Quah, 2010), the lack of attention to this part of the world is both striking and worrying. This volume seeks to fill this crucial analytical lacuna by making three important contributions to current theoretical and policy debates in the comparative political economy of capitalism: it shifts the empirical focus away from Asian development strategies to the varieties of capitalist institutions; it develops a holistic approach to exploring the interactions between dominant spheres of Asian political economies; and it analyses changes in the institutions of East Asian capitalism.

As noted earlier, scholarly efforts to develop a typology of capitalist diversity have not to date effectively balanced analytical parsimony with empirical diversity. Authors uncomfortable with the North Atlantic-centrism of the VoC literature[3] have often described East Asian capitalism in a largely undifferentiated manner, portraying the institutional similarities across the region as sufficient to justify such encompassing terms as 'state-led' (Wade, 1990), 'network' (Fruin, 1999), 'relationship-based' (Rajan and Zingales, 1998), or simply 'Asian' capitalism (Amable, 2003). This tendency is also visible in work by some other authors who stress the resilience of East Asian capitalism in the face of globalization (Johnson, 1998; Rhodes and Higgott, 2000). At the other extreme, a significant body of region-specific literature has denied the existence of a single East Asian model, preferring to stress the great diversity of the political economies of the region (Beeson, 1999; Carney et al., 2009; Tipton, 2009).

There is an obvious tension here between the desire to formulate parsimonious theories of institutional change or resilience and the need to be sufficiently attentive to the significant differences among Asian political economies. In an attempt to overcome this problem, some authors have distinguished Asian political economies on the basis of business systems (Whitley, 1992; Safarian and Dobson, 1996; Orrù et al., 1997; Carney et al., 2009), financial institutions (Haggard et al., 1993; Ghosh, 2006), labour markets and industrial relations (Deyo, 1989; Rowley and Benson, 2000; Warner, 2002), and welfare regimes

---

[3] When dealing with the important Japanese case, the VoC literature generally placed Japan in the CME category, underplaying the greater coordinating role of the state compared to the paradigmatic German case.

(Ramesh, 2000; Holliday and Wilding, 2003; Walker and Wong, 2005). The difficulty with such studies from our perspective is that each focuses narrowly on only one among a number of important institutional spheres. This evades the questions of institutional complementarities and of the possibility of identifying broader patterns of capitalist organization.

Another line of approach has similarities with the VoC literature in its emphasis on the persistence of long-established differences in national economic architectures arising from such factors as the timing of industrialization, trajectories of economic development, and patterns of state intervention (Weiss, 2003; Holliday, 2005; Chang, 2006; Mo and Okimoto, 2006). This literature has been concerned with identifying the elements of continuity in the responses of national political economies to external pressures for change, particularly those associated with the crisis of the late 1990s. While these historical institutionalist analyses provide an important corrective to market-driven explanations that presume rapid institutional convergence (e.g. Rajan and Zingales, 1998), they underplay significant changes in a range of institutional spheres of the East Asian political economy in recent decades (Vogel, 2006; Yeung, 2006; Peng and Wong, 2008; Zhang, 2009). Just as the VoC literature has sometimes overlooked the profound changes that have occurred in some of its paradigmatic cases,[4] this empirical literature has shown that theory can also be an obstacle to recognizing and understanding institutional change in East Asia, as will be shown in the following section.

A Typology of East Asian Capitalism

This section delineates the defining features of key institutional dimensions that underpin modern capitalist economies, develops some guiding principles for explaining the organization of these dimensions that generates the systemic logic of economic activity, and describes the different configurations of key institutional domains across capitalist models in East Asia.

Developing a typology of capitalist models, even within a region, that is both conceptually parsimonious and sufficiently empirically encompassing is difficult. The difficulty is compounded by the lack of widely accepted theoretical criteria for identifying key institutional spheres that characterize political economies and for ascertaining the number of distinct models of national capitalisms (Jackson and Deeg, 2008). However, we suggest that there is a considerable degree of consensus among both the VoC and the Asian institutionalist literature that business systems, financial market architectures, and

---

[4] For an analysis of the nature and implications of the changes in the German system since the 1980s, see Streeck (2009).

labour market regimes are all crucial components of capitalist political economies. We also argue that there is a growing consensus that the roles of politics and the state require much greater attention than they were initially given in the VoC approach (Hancké et al., 2007b).

Institutional Domains

This study prioritizes business, financial, and labour market organizations as core components of a typology of evolving capitalist models. Note that although the VoC approach places considerable emphasis on the importance of institutional complementarities across these domains within both LMEs and CMEs for different kinds of innovation, production strategies, and welfare provision, the analysis of these claimed complementarities is not a major concern here. However, it is important to recognize that business, financial, and labour market organizations all interact to shape both how economic inputs are turned into outputs and societal organization more generally.

Business systems pertain to the ways in which intra-firm and inter-firm relations are coordinated to carry out production and exchange. Business systems play a linchpin role in calibrating the character of financial and labour institutions in a given political economy (Whitley, 1999; McNally, 2007). This is reflected in both the comparative capitalism literature and in studies on the politics of East Asian development (MacIntyre, 1994; Gomez, 2002). Furthermore, economic performance is a crucial function of intra-firm relations and inter-firm alliances that affect the orientation of industrial policies (Haggard, 2004; Root, 2006). Finally, given the importance of business systems in influencing other institutional arrangements and development outcomes, a focus on such systems is likely to provide an analytically useful means to capture change since firms are often key agents of institutional innovation and recombination (Crouch, 2005).

Intra-firm relations and inter-firm alliances interact to shape the national configuration of business systems (Safarian and Dobson, 1996; Whitley, 1999; Redding, 2005). Intra-firm relations are reflected in the distribution of power between managers and shareholders and between controlling and minority shareholders. They define the extent to which ownership is concentrated and owners are directly involved in corporate management. Intra-firm relations are also shaped by the forms of manager–employee interactions and the degrees of employee influence over work-organization decisions. These two key aspects of intra-firm relations—ownership structure and work management—have varied across East Asia, producing different policy and industrialization patterns (McVey, 1992; Whitley, 1992, 1999; Fields, 1995). Inter-firm relations include alliances or networks between firms from different industries and may foster long-term and reciprocal business partnerships and develop functional competencies. In East Asia, such inter-firm networks have differed in terms of their breadth and longevity, with inter-firm ties being broad and long-lived in Japan, Korea, and Taiwan but narrow and temporary in many Southeast Asian countries.

The second institutional dimension in our typology is financial regimes. Financial systems channel savings into investments and are central to many of the key contributions to the VoC debate (Rajan and Zingales, 2003*b*; Culpepper, 2005). These have emphasized not only the dominant forms of industrial financing and the terms on which such financing is provided but also corporate governance patterns and financial regulatory regimes. National financial systems across East Asia, despite cross-country variations, have been generally described as bank based. Bank-centred financial markets, the privileged position of states in market regulation, and the dominant role of debt instruments in external corporate financing comprise fundamental elements of this system. They have influenced both the development trajectories of East Asian economies and other socio-economic institutions, above all business systems (Haggard et al., 1993; Haggard and Lee, 1995). More recently, financial market liberalization and integration have brought about crucial changes to East Asian bank-based financial systems of East Asia, but have not necessarily preordained convergence towards the Anglo-American model of capitalism (Walter, 2008; Zhang, 2009).

Financial systems are the short-hand expression for two interrelated institutional components: financial market structures and corporate governance patterns (Allen and Gale, 2000; Hölzl, 2006). In the comparative capitalism literature, these two institutional components of the financial system are considered to reinforce each other (Hölzl, 2006; Hall and Gingerich, 2009). Market structures are reflected in the relative importance of capital markets versus banks and non-bank financial institutions. Corporate governance patterns that derive from and reinforce financial market structures define corporate decision-making processes through which conflicts of interest between different groups within a firm can be managed. National financial systems are thus distinguished between bank-based and capital market-oriented market structures, and between insider- and outsider-oriented corporate governance regimes.

The third institutional dimension in our typology is labour market systems. The organization of work is central to every capitalist economy. Prior to the 1980s, poorly institutionalized industrial relations, politically weak unions, and family-centred welfare provision were widely regarded as defining features of labour market systems in many East Asian countries. These features were in turn seen as a function of state strategies and discourses, growth-first development imperatives, and productivist social policies that favoured business priorities (Deyo, 1989; Pempel, 2002; Holliday and Wilding, 2003). Over the past two decades, labour market institutions across East Asia—as elsewhere—have been experiencing crucial changes and new strains as a result of intensified market competition, the globalization of production, and in some cases democratization. Although expressed in different ways in different East Asian political economies, these changes and strains are manifest in the political ascendancy of unions, improved labour power and rights, labour market liberalization, and increased roles of states in welfare provision.

This volume uses the term labour market systems to denote a mix of employment relations, union organization, and welfare provision at the national level. In comparative literatures on developed (Crouch, 1993; Bamber and Lansbury, 1998) and East Asian countries (Frenkel and Kuruvilla, 2002; Kuruvilla and Erickson, 2002), employment relations are examined and compared along such key dimensions as the strength of labour unions, the structure of collective bargaining, the patterns of industrial conflict, and the institutions of skill development. While the essential features of employment relations are comparable across countries, there are considerable and enduring variations in the ways in which these relations are governed. National patterns of governance are primarily contingent upon the differential roles of employers, employees, labour unions, and the state in creating and changing industrial relations institutions. Frenkel and Peetz (1998) identify four broad models of labour market governance in East Asia: state unilateralism, state–employer domination, state–union corporatism, and national tripartite arrangements. Other scholars (Kuruvilla and Erickson, 2002) follow the same principle but adopt a more disaggregated approach to developing a largely country-based typology of industrial relations models.

Welfare regimes are a key institutional domain of the political economy that impacts labour market development and influences economic performance. The country-specific features of welfare regimes impinge upon industrial relations by influencing wage structures and labour utilization strategies. They exert shaping influence on economic activity by giving rise to high labour costs that may lead firms to push for industrial upgrading and technological innovations or reduce national competitiveness and hamper employment growth in labour-intensive sectors. Cross-country variations in welfare regimes are also likely to generate the different patterns of employment policies as reflected in gender gaps in earnings and unemployment duration. Holliday (2000, 2005) suggests that East Asian welfare regimes do not fit into Esping-Anderson's famous three-fold typology and can be better described as productivist welfare capitalism that subordinates social policy to development imperatives.[5] Several authors have challenged this encompassing depiction and argued that institutional variations in the welfare

[5] Esping-Anderson's typology (1990) of liberal, conservative, and social democratic welfare states distinguished between the degree and mode of welfare provision.

systems of East Asia have emerged due to pressures both exogenous and endogenous to these institutions. Kwon (2005*b*) makes a distinction between selective and inclusive developmental welfare states, for instance; following Esping-Anderson, Ramesh (2003) divides East Asian welfare regimes into a liberal variant (Singapore), a liberal–conservative orientation (Taiwan), and a nascent conservatism (Korea).

It should be noted that variations in the national configurations of business systems, financial architectures, and labour markets are shaped by different policy and regulatory regimes. National regulatory frameworks and reforms can affect the nature and direction of institutional changes in product, financial, and labour markets. Competition policies and antitrust legislation can reconfigure both intra-firm and inter-firm relations, for instance; financial market structures and corporate governance patterns are contingent upon regulatory practices and rules; labour markets and industrial relations also reflect policy and legislative reforms. Much will depend, of course, on the extent to which policy and legislation are effectively implemented and whether they are supported by key societal groups (Walter, 2008). Both exogenous and endogenous pressures can lead to changes in these policy and regulatory frameworks that in turn transform the contours of key capitalist institutions in East Asia. The analytical approach adopted in this study thus treats policy reforms and regulatory rules as crucial intervening variables that can serve to reproduce or to reshape business, financial, and labour institutions.

These three dimensions for comparing national capitalist models in East Asia and their respective key institutional components are summarized in Table 1.2. Together, they cover much of the ground that prominent comparative studies on capitalist varieties examine. The general discussion and characterization of these institutional dimensions are meant to be suggestive rather than exhaustive. The primary purpose is to demonstrate how and why they are conceptually and empirically relevant to a viable typology of capitalism.

Table 1.2. Institutional dimensions of comparative capitalism

	Business systems	Financial architectures	Labour market regimes
Key components	1. Intra-firm relations and coordination 2. Manager–worker interactions 3. Inter-firm alliances and networks	1. Financial market structures 2. Corporate governance patterns	1. Employment relations 2. Union organization and strength 3. Degrees and modes of welfare provision

Guiding Principles

In existing comparative literatures, different principles are used to construct typologies of capitalism. As already noted, the standard VoC typology is based on the principle of coordination, delineating the relative extent of market coordination versus strategic coordination (Hall and Soskice, 2001). While most scholars accept the importance of this distinction, even those sympathetic to the VoC approach have accepted that it omits something important.

A number of scholars have emphasized the importance of governance (Weiss, 1998; Boyer, 2005; Hancké et al., 2007b: 23–4), arguing for closer attention than in the VoC approach to politics and the distribution of political power. Höpner (2007), too, distinguishes between 'coordination' and 'organization', in which the latter refers to various social and political institutions that authoritatively override market processes and outcomes. Along similar lines, Streeck (2009: 153–5) defines organization as a core component of capitalism, signifying the presence of 'Durkheimian (political) institutions' that impose collective obligations on actors that they would not voluntarily accept.[6] 'Coordination', by contrast, which reduces transactions costs, can be promoted by voluntaristic 'Williamsonian' institutions internal and external to market actors and which are present in both CMEs and LMEs. Höpner's and Streeck's notion of organization is close to what Dahrendorf defined as 'plan rationality', which had 'as its dominant feature precisely the setting of substantive social norms. Planners determine in advance who does what and who gets what' (Dahrendorf, 1968: 219). Johnson (1982: 18–26) also drew on this in distinguishing between 'plan rational' (Asian) and 'plan ideological' (communist) developmental states, a distinction that Henderson (2011) develops in arguing for the important role of authoritative political intervention in many Asian developmental states to discipline firms and to shape economic outcomes. Schmidt (2009) also argues for closer attention to the varying role of the state in capitalist economies, claiming that a third 'state-influenced' market economy model is required to capture the essence of successful national capitalisms in France and parts of East Asia. Finally, along similar though less statist lines, some recent comparative studies (Nölke and Vliegenthart, 2009; Schneider, 2009) emphasize hierarchies—of various corporate, class, and political kinds—as key mechanisms of resource allocation in emerging market economies.[7]

Thus, there seems to be widespread agreement that the original VoC approach omits an important non-market dimension of some capitalist economies, in which political, corporate, and social hierarchies of power allocate resources,

---

[6] For Streeck, 'disorganized' capitalism signifies the absence of such institutions.

[7] Strikingly, neither draws upon Oliver Williamson's classic distinction between markets and hierarchies as allocation mechanisms (see Williamson, 1975).

constrain market activity, and enforce rules and social norms. A recognition of this dimension of capitalism is also consistent with our empirical understanding of East Asian political economies over the past half-century in two important ways. First, there is general agreement that governments in East Asia have been more actively involved in guiding economic outcomes than most of their counterparts in North America and Western Europe (World Bank, 1993; Stiglitz and Yusuf, 2001), though of course its nature and levels have varied significantly across the region (MacIntyre, 1994; Jomo, 2001). Although state intervention has been significantly reduced in all East Asian countries since the 1980s, such cross-country variations have persisted to some degree. Second, key social groups and hierarchies have also been important mechanisms for governing economic activity, particularly business and labour. The concepts of 'embedded autonomy' (Evans, 1995), 'governed interdependence' (Weiss, 1998), and 'state-market condominium' (Underhill and Zhang, 2005) indicate that the state organization of economic activity in the region takes place within broad social contexts and is shaped and mediated by various societal institutions (Doner, 1992; Clark and Roy, 1997). Thus, the state organization of the economy must be viewed in close relation to the social coordination of private market behaviour to explain the trajectory of capitalist development.

Table 1.3 characterizes heuristically the different ways in which these two governance mechanisms interact with each other and the resultant configurations of economic organization. When extensive state involvement exists alongside well-organized social groups (Cell I), economic activity is coordinated through mutually dependent and negotiated or co-governed relations. On the other hand, where state intervention in the economy is comparatively modest and weakly organized social groups play an ineffective role in market processes (Cell VI), the organization of economic activity tends to be atomistic, fluid, and individualized. Due to the lack of coordination and monitoring capabilities on the part of the state and key social groups, powerful individuals or small members of associates control the commanding heights of the economy, giving rise to the personalized character of market governance.

Table 1.3. Variations in the national modes of economic governance

		Social coordination of economic action	
		Strong	Weak
State organization of the economy	Extensive	I Co-governed	II State-led
	Modest	III Networked	IV Personalized

In the case of poorly organized and fragmented social groups coexisting with a well-organized state that moulds most components of economic activity through a myriad of interventions (Cell II), the mode of economic management is heavily state led. This generates a top-down governance structure in which multiple socio-economic actors and institutions are connected hierarchically to each other through the subordination of economic action to centralized authority. Finally, where state intervention is limited but the role of highly organized social groups in coordinating market behaviour is crucial (Cell III), economic governance is based on a multiplicity of socio-economic ties or networks among a broad array of organizational stakeholders—firms, unions, banks, and government agencies. Such networks are shaped as much by informal norms of reciprocity as by formal relations permeating business, financial, and labour institutions and facilitate coordination both within and between them.

A Four-Fold Typology

In line with each of the four kinds of economic organization, the three institutional domains—business systems, financial architectures, and labour market regimes—take on different characteristics, leading to four VoC, as detailed in Table 1.4. In the co-governed mode of economic activity, intra-firm relations are typified by concentrated ownership and non-participatory management structures. To the extent that business groups are highly horizontally integrated, this may suppress the development of networks across industrial sectors. The financial system relies largely on indirect finance through bank loans, reflecting the desire of the state to harness financial markets for industrial policy purposes and of business groups to retain ownership control. These structural features of business and financial systems facilitate the insider pattern of corporate governance in which owner-managers dominate. The development imperatives of the state and the political power of private business lead to relatively weak unions and limited collective bargaining. However, to compensate labour for repressive industrial relations policies, the state may institute employment protection and welfare programmes, invariably confined to regular workers in large firms. As important, government–private partnerships and long-term employment promote and encourage extensive vocational training.

When the state-led mode of market governance prevails, a significant role for state-owned enterprises (SOEs) is normal. However, ownership structures in many SOEs may be more fragmented than this implies, as various national and local government agencies may have significant ownership stakes or other means of exerting influence. Privately owned firms, many of which are small and medium sized, generally also have concentrated ownership. In both SOEs and private firms that feature top-down patterns of work organization,

Table 1.4. Core features of East Asian varieties of capitalism

	Co-governed	State-led	Networked	Personalized
Business systems				
Intra-firm relations	Concentrated ownership	State ownership in SOEs; ownership concentration in private firms	Modestly high ownership concentration	Ownership and management centralized
Manager–worker interdependence	Low; little employee participation	Top-down patterns of work organization	Extensive managerial delegation to workers	Very low/zero employee influence
Inter-firm alliance	Medium to low (if vertical integration is high)	Rare and sporadic	Extensive, institutionalized and facilitated by industrial associations	Limited or primarily based on personal linkages
Financial architectures				
Financial regulation	State guided but with business influence	Heavily state controlled	State influenced but significant business inputs and influences	State controlled but heavy private influence
Market structures	Largely bank based but better developed capital markets	Dominance of debt finance	Bank based but more important capital markets	Relation-oriented finance; poorly developed equity markets
Corporate governance	Insider model	Highly bureaucratized in SOEs; insider practices in private firms	Stakeholder/ insider dominated	Insider model; dominated by owner-managers
Labour market regimes				
Union organization	Relatively weak	Strong but controlled in SOEs; weak in private firms	Relatively powerful	Fragmented and very weak
Employment relations	Limited collective bargaining; longer term employment; strong vocational training	Limited bargaining; long-term employment and relatively strong training in SOEs; limited and weak in private firms	Firm-based bargaining but with informal coordination through national organizations; internal labour markets characterized by long-term/lifelong employment and firm-specific training	No/little collective bargaining; unstable and short-term employment; very weak in-firm training
Welfare provision	Employment protection and welfare benefits confined to workers in large firms	Public funded and quite extensive in SOEs; limited in private firms	Public and private funded; benefits varied across sectors and firms	Better welfare provision in SOEs; public funded but very limited in private firms
National cases (1980s)	Korea, Taiwan	China, Malaysia, Indonesia	Japan	Philippines, Thailand

employees have little influence over strategic decision processes. By the same token, inter-firm alliances and cross-sector coordination among state and private firms are rare and sporadic, albeit for different reasons. Given extensive state controls over financial market regulation, debt financing through banks is predominant and equity financing is weakly developed. Corporate governance in SOEs may be highly bureaucratized and dictated by purposes other than wealth maximization, whereas corporate governance in private firms is imbued with insider practices. While SOE unions may have dense memberships and may be relatively well organized, they are more an instrument of state policy than a negotiating partner. In line with the poorly organized private business sector, unions in privately owned firms tend to be highly fragmented and lack any effective workplace organization. Welfare provision and in-firm training may be quite extensive in SOEs but remain limited and weak in privately owned firms.

The networked variety of capitalism is closely associated with highly developed and mutually dependent intra-firm and inter-firm relations. While ownership in firms or business groups may be relatively concentrated, mainly through cross-shareholdings, management structures are likely to be more collective, with consensus building running across hierarchical levels. Similarly, work organization may exhibit high levels of interdependence between employers and employees and of managerial delegation to workers. Equally important, firms maintain close alliances with each other both within and between different sectors; such alliances are often facilitated by coherently organized business associations. In this densely networked business system, stakeholders rather than shareholders matter. The dominance of bank finance and the lack of hostile takeovers foster an insider model of corporate governance. Mirroring highly organized private business and bottom-up management structures, unions may be influential at workplace and even national levels. While wage bargaining may be firm based, informal coordination on bargaining through national labour and employer organizations is more likely. Close interactions between stakeholders encourage the growth of internal labour markets, particularly in large firms. Often characterized by long-term and even lifetime employment and firm-specific training, they generate employment stability but functional flexibility.

The fourth and final variety of capitalism features, first and foremost, highly personalized intra-firm relations, with ownership and management concentrated in the hands of individual founding owners and family members. The degree of managerial trust of workers is very low and employee participation in decision-making virtually non-existent. Business-to-business coordination is limited; to the extent that firms develop inter-firm or cross-sector relations, these are typically based on personal linkages rather than on long-term, institutionalized, and mutually dependent networks. Capital markets are poorly developed, due both to the desire of business elites to maintain family control and the weak ability of a poorly organized state to promote market growth. Large firms often obtain formal and informal finance through family-owned institutions, political connections, or personal relations. Relationship-oriented finance and high ownership concentration encourage an insider pattern of corporate governance. Finally, unions have little influence at work-place and national levels, partly because they are weakly organized and partly because there may be restrictions on union formation and activity. In line with weak unions, collective bargaining, largely firm based, is limited and ineffective. Employment relations tend to be unstable and short-term and are unlikely to be mediated by weak unions. Neither workers nor employers thus have any strong incentives to invest in specific skills and encourage vocational training. Likewise, weakly organized states and business are unable to promote skills development and improve innovation performances.

The representative country cases provided in Table 1.4 conform broadly, though not exactly, to the core defining features of each of the four VoC and serve to illustrate major institutional differences between them. It is important to note that these classifications reflect the institutional configurations of national capitalist models that prevailed in the 1980s against which the country chapters that follow set their points of empirical departure for analys-ing the changing varieties of East Asian capitalism. This four-fold typology based on the dynamics of market governance provides a conceptual frame-work for examining capitalist development generally and in East Asia in particular. Equally crucially, it helps distinguish varieties of institutional underpinning of capitalism not only within different regions but also between different countries within the same region.

Defining Institutional Change

In asking how capitalist political economies evolve, it is important to be clear about what they are. Capitalism is a system in which actors motivated by self-interest operating through markets and enjoying extensive (but incomplete) private property rights play a dominant role in the allocation of economic resources. But narrowly economic definitions of capitalism overlook that it is also an extensively institutionalized, social order (Streeck, 2009: 3). As we have emphasized, market actors and transactions depend upon and are shaped by a variety of institutions, which are 'patterns of human action and relationship that persist and reproduce themselves over time, independently of the iden-tity of the biological individuals performing within them' (Crouch, 2005: 10). These institutions include at one end of the (national) spectrum the formal political institutions associated with the state and at the other end institutions such as the firm (conceived of as a non-market hierarchy) and the family, with associations of various actors occupying an intermediate position. This also suggests that political economies might, for example, evolve towards lower levels of state intervention, without being any less 'institutionalized' at the sub-state level or without continuing to rely upon the extensive coordination of actor behaviour through non-state institutions (Höpner, 2007).

As is often pointed out, there are also many institutions of a relatively informal kind in which norms rather than binding rules are the most important constraints—these may be norms related to political leadership transition, to patriarchy within families, to age-related deference, etc. (Helmke and Levitsky, 2004). Generally, even formal, rule-based institutions also operate according to a variety of informal behavioural norms. Institutional change might therefore occur in relation to formal rules and/or informal norms. For example, US-style formal rules relating to corporate governance that strengthen minority shareholder rights might be adopted in an economy formerly characterized by more opaque norms that privileged insider owner-managers. But if formal enforcement mechanisms are weak and informal norms remain intact, actual corporate behaviour may remain relatively unchanged (Walter, 2008).

Another important distinction is between revolutionary and gradual change, with some recent studies arguing that relatively little attention has been devoted to the latter. In this view, institutional change can accumulate over time in ways that neither individual actors nor social scientists may expect and that lead eventually to very different institutional forms (Mahoney and Thelen, 2010). Actors may gradually redefine their relationship to institutions, which can be thereby reconfigured or even sidelined (e.g. this may have happened to the legally established church in countries such as the United Kingdom over the past century). This suggests that institutional change may not even require innovation in formal rules and processes, as it may occur when actors gradually 'recombine' and reinterpret existing institutions in novel ways. In an earlier work, Streeck and Thelen (2005) distinguish five different forms of incremental institutional change: displacement, when actors defect from old to new institutions; layering, when old institutions coexist alongside new ones but in which support gradually shifts towards the latter; drift, when institutions fall into neglect; conversion, when institutions are put to new purpose; and exhaustion, when institutions suffer from decreasing returns.

Conceived of in this way, institutions as social processes are in a constant process of dynamic evolution and change is likely to be the norm rather than the exception, contrary to the assumptions of the VoC approach. Although they can create powerful constraints and 'path dependence', there may be more than one path open to social actors and institutional evolution more contingent than either actors believe or some theories allow. Indeed, some individual actors may be in a state of permanent tension with institutions, choosing whether to follow, break, challenge, recombine, or innovate around associated norms and rules (Crouch, 2005: 19). This also implies that although institutions are often conceived as constraints upon the behaviour of individual actors, they can also empower individual actors. They are also endogenous, sometimes being the direct object of social and political innovation (Hall, 2010). Although the scope for actor autonomy in breaking out of or modifying established institutions should not be exaggerated, it may be especially prominent under capitalism, in which entrepreneurs seek to use, avoid, or sometimes undermine institutions for self-interested purposes. Given their extensive dependence on the self-interest of particular actors, capitalist social orders, as Marx, Schumpeter, and Polanyi among others emphasized, may thus have natural endogenous tendencies towards institutional change and destabilization. Financial innovation is perhaps the most conspicuous example of this in recent years (Tett, 2009), though it is not unique, as Sako's (2006) and Streeck's (2009) accounts of evolving Japanese and German manufacturing since the 1980s show.

There is also no reason why institutional change might not proceed more rapidly in some domains than in others. More extensive options for creating global production and supply chains might result in relatively rapid change in business sector relations with labour without disrupting financial market systems. Of course, the opposite might also be true: it is difficult to generalize about the kinds of areas in which rapid change is most likely. This also raises the interesting questions of whether and how much change in one area (e.g. finance) might spill over into change in others (such as labour markets or business innovation systems), and how these interrelationships affect any institutional complementarities that may have existed.

In sum, identifying and measuring change in capitalist political economies and social orders generally remains one of the most difficult of all enterprises in the social sciences and is likely to remain so. We cannot give a general answer to the question of precisely *how* path-dependent institutional evolution is, or to the question of when institutional change is gradual or 'fundamental', or when its effects are marginal or deep. These questions are left to the individual authors, who make different judgements about particular cases.

Explaining Institutional Change

This section briefly outlines a framework for explaining the dynamic evolution of capitalist political economies, keeping the above considerations in mind. This framework is not intended to be exhaustive, nor is it rigidly applied in each empirical chapter. Rather, it maps out the main competing explanations of institutional change in capitalist political economies, upon which subsequent chapters draw in different ways. In the concluding chapter, we pull together the findings of the case study chapters and assess their collective theoretical implications in the light of this framework.

The causes of institutional change can be categorized in different ways. Distinctions are commonly made between 'endogenous' and 'exogenous' causes (often approximating to internal/external or domestic/international distinctions); between market-based, social and political causes; and between material and ideational causes. All of these distinctions are artificial and involve oversimplifications of some kind. The distinction between domestic and international factors is especially problematic given the growing importance of transactional actors and forces (MNCs, some advocacy coalitions, policy discourses) in many countries since at least the mid-twentieth century. The endogenous–exogenous distinction is also often dependent upon the particular theoretical framework being deployed (what is exogenous for an economist may often not be for a sociologist). 'Exogenous shocks' such as wars or global recessions are in any case always intermediated by domestic institutions and economic structures. Nor are they simply material in nature, as they must always be interpreted by social actors. National politicians often try to frame economic recessions as 'global' in origin and hence as beyond their control, whereas reformers often propose alternative narratives that locate their sources and/or particular effects in dysfunctional national institutions. Sometimes, too, solely national, 'endogenous' crises may be reframed by political entrepreneurs as grave 'competitiveness' crises to facilitate the building of reform coalitions (Streeck, 2009: 164).

Hence, while we recognize that economic factors such as sustained growth underperformance may ultimately be important contributors to institutional change and economic crises provide opportunities for reformers and insurrectionaries, they are certainly not sufficient causes and probably not even necessary ones given the importance of incremental change. As regards their insufficiency, all economic forces are crucially intermediated by social and political institutions and by policy discourses. For these reasons, we divide the main explanations of institutional change into change coalitions, state action, and policy discourses.

The ability of actors to bring together different kinds of individuals and social movements into change coalitions is often seen as a crucial determinant of institutional change (Mahoney and Thelen, 2010). Economic shocks, such as deep recessions and marked relative economic decline of the kind that has plagued countries in recent times such as Zimbabwe and North Korea, will not result in institutional change unless such coalitions succeed in overcoming the various obstacles to change noted by Hall (2010: 207–13): uncertainty about the consequences of change, standard collective action dilemmas, deep power asymmetries, veto-player opposition, intra-coalition distributional conflicts, etc. The relative ease with which such obstacles can be overcome will be shaped by social norms as well as by the way in which political institutions channel, shape, and block the exercise of power, including the access of coalitional actors to the media, to policymakers, to political parties, and to the means of organized violence. This simply underlines the point already made that institutions have multiple interpretations and that political actors must act in circumstances not of their own choosing, though they may opportunistically take advantage of existing institutions (or new combinations or interpretations of them) to achieve change. That the existing institutional framework is not entirely deter-mining is underlined by the point that change coalitions may include transna-tional actors, who have more exit options and often have access to different kinds of institutions and resources. At different points in time and in different places, foreign states, international institutions, powerful individuals, MNCs, NGOs, and other transnational social movements may align with domestic actors in change coalitions or with their opponents.

State action and capacity can also be an important source of institutional change, not least because of the resources that states can command. Successful state action of this kind requires 'capacity', which depends upon a minimum degree of organizational efficiency and resources as well as some level of autonomy from social interests that oppose change or who prefer an alterna-tive path of reform. Again, existing national political institutions and rules on the one hand and the density of social networks and associations on the other are both likely to affect the prospects for such state-led change. However, the distinction between state action and societal coalitions is not always easy to make, since relevant state actors include leaders, political parties, and bureau-cracies: all of whom may be influenced or penetrated by some social interests. The literature on the 'embeddedness' of East Asian states is relevant here (Evans, 1995), though so too are classic developed country cases of successful institutional change such as Britain under Thatcher from 1979 (King and Wood, 1999; Crouch, 2005: 143–50). There, government and party institu-tions that concentrated power in the hands of a highly ideological leader and her allies helped to overcome resistance from various social groups, notably organized labour, but this case also shows that the successful mobilization of a supporting coalition of business and voters who responded to a powerful narrative of the causes of and solutions to British economic and social under-performance were important. State capacity to enforce institutional change and the new rules and behavioural norms that they bring can also increase the credibility of institutional change and thereby convince opportunists and other potential supporters to join change coalitions. Substantial state capacity can also reduce the gap mentioned above that frequently emerges between formal institutional change and real actor behaviour.

As for the third cause of institutional change, policy discourses, we have already noted that they are likely to be important components of successful change coalition formation and authoritative state-led reform. The ability of institutional entrepreneurs to construct a credible narrative about the short-comings of existing institutions and to reduce uncertainties about the con-sequences of reform is likely to be crucial in both respects. Such narratives can draw upon new scientific findings or upon new ideas linking institutions and social outcomes, as well as upon supporting material facts. In the right cir-cumstances, credible narratives of this kind may alter actors' perceived inter-ests and facilitate the reconstruction of political coalitions. As Jabko (2006) has shown, political entrepreneurs often draw strategically and selectively upon such ideas and the epistemic actors associated with them. The source of such ideas may be foreign and may be actively or more passively promoted by international organizations and social movements; they can also be asso-ciated with particularly successful foreign countries. But the case for the emulation of foreign institutional models must generally be made explicitly, which will include assessments of their likely impact for a variety of social groups. This case is likely to be easier if these ideas resonate with existing social norms and if a credible case can be made that foreign-born practices will fit with other social norms and institutions that have higher levels of support (Cortell and Davis, 2000: 23–4; Acharya, 2009). All of this suggests that most kinds of 'structural' forces, from globalization and regional integration to economic crises, need not be determinant or have simple linear implications. Even 'crises' are, in the end, social constructions that may or may not be interpreted in ways that result in successful institutional change (Blyth, 2002; Widmaier et al., 2007).

As the above discussion implies, we do not expect these three factors causing institutional change to be easily separated in practice. Indeed, there are good reasons to believe that they are likely to be mutually reinforcing, so that it would be surprising if there were not elements of all three in cases of successful institutional change. This means that discovering ultimate causes of change is always likely to be difficult. As noted earlier, capitalist political economies are likely to have tendencies towards endogenous change and instability, and gradual and sometimes imperceptible change may accumulate to a tipping point when proximate factors (such as deep recessions) result in fundamental change.

Organization of the Book

The chapters that follow elaborate the central theoretical and empirical issues raised here. This chapter has presented a panoramic view of capitalist development across East Asia and provides a foundation for understanding cross-national variations in institutional practices in individual countries. The remaining chapters are organized around the major empirical concerns of the book through division into three parts. The first part focuses on the changing nature of business–government relations that calibrates the character of other institutional arrangements in the national political economy. The second part assembles chapters on changes and variations in financial market structures and corporate governance patterns. The third and final part brings together chapters that address the evolution of labour relations systems. The concluding chapter picks up the major themes of the book, provides a synoptic analysis of institutional changes in national capitalism, and assesses the value of causal propositions by drawing upon the contributions to this book and other prominent empirical studies. It also explores the implications of the main findings of the book for future research on capitalist development in East Asia and beyond.

The country chapters do not employ a rigid common methodology to maximize comparability across the different cases nor do they attempt to provide a unified approach to accounting for changes and variations in key institutional domains that govern financial, product, and labour markets. The empirical facts and causal processes remain too contested for unity of this kind to be a realistic goal. However, the individual contributions take the key institutional features of national capitalism around the late 1980s as their respective points of departure and set their empirical analyses against the typology of East Asian capitalism developed in this chapter. More importantly, while the country chapters encompass a range of different cases, specific issues, and diverse methodologies, they are all structured around the two dominant themes of the book—the continuities and changes in the institutional underpinnings of capitalist development and the main driving forces behind them. These two themes run through the three parts of the book and facilitate an integrated analysis of how changing institutional practices in business, financial, and labour systems interact with each other and affect the evolution of capitalist political economies in the region.

Part Two
Business–Government Relations and Development Strategies

2

Government–Industry Relations in China: A Review of the Art of the State[1]

Shaun Breslin

Assessments of the nature of state–business relations in China are heavily influenced by the starting point of the observer. Those who compare China today with previous eras of Chinese Communist Party (CCP) control, seeking to understand change from a historical perspective, often point to what we might call the retreat of the state. Fiscal and monetary policy has largely replaced old-style state planning while privatization, mergers, and closures have resulted in the loss of millions of state-sector jobs and the non-state sector emerging as the primary source of economic growth. But when the basis of comparison is with other places, rather than with other times, then the tendency is to focus on the strength and pervasiveness of the state, rather than its weakness and limitations. Despite the rise of the private sector, the Chinese state retains control of key industries and resources and thus shapes the nature of the market that non-state actors operate in. In addition, while a clear space has been created for the private sector and for foreign economic actors, the parameters of those spaces (and what can occur within them) remain subject to the will of the state.

Of course, there is no contradiction in these two positions—it is just that they tend to result in different emphases and different ways of approaching the topic. This chapter attempts to provide a synthesis of sorts between the two positions. It is more influenced by the former approach than the latter, considering first the main drivers of economic strategy in China and then tracing the way in which the old state-planned system was reformed to

[1] This chapter was completed during a fellowship at the Centre for Non-Traditional Security Studies at the S. Rajaratnam School of International Studies at Nanyang Technological University in Singapore, and the author is grateful for their support.

become a state-led one in the 1980s and 1990s. But it also accepts that the state still has a very important (though different) role to play, and that the state's direction, and at times direct control of economic affairs, is stronger than in most comparator economies. Economic reform in China has created a 'market' system and increased the space for market actors; but it is not a free market. It has also created a 'capitalist' system of sorts, but it is not a neo-liberal one. The state plays a crucial role in regulating and controlling the market in ways that mark it out as substantially different from the 'co-governed', 'networked', and 'personalized' models of capitalisms outlined in Chapter 1 of this volume. In addition, the space in which the market operates is conditional on it serving perceived developmental interests—and when it does not, then the nature of that space can be quickly altered (as was the case in 2009).

Moreover, this chapter suggests that analysing who gets what through the financial system is crucial. As the experience of previous generations of developmental states has shown, studying finance is crucial to understanding how states protect and support key domestic industries and actors and mobilize economic activity to attain its developmental goals. But in the Chinese case, it is also crucial for understanding how different levels of the state interact with the economy and with each other. Indeed, to fully understand the nature of state–enterprise relations, we also need to rethink what we mean by 'the State'. It is a term that conjures up images of a unified effort—a single central state agency planning, owning, and controlling economic activity in a coordinated way. In contemporary China, state power is not so absolute—the state has different fragmented sources and centres of power which can at times compete with each other in the market (both the domestic and global markets). Furthermore, state entities are often one step (or more) removed from direct involvement in the market, either through indirect relations with private actors or through the establishment of secondary 'marketized' entities (or both). The form of capitalism that has materialized in China is one where state actors, often at the local level, remain central to the functioning of an economic system through control over key enterprises, indirect control over allocation of finance, and residual control over access to (local) markets.

China's economic system continues to evolve, and the situation is very different today from the form of state leadership that emerged from the initial transition from socialism in the 1980s. Indeed, tracing these changes forms a key part of this chapter. Increasingly, China seems to share many of the features and the underlying goals of national systems of political economy—not only the capitalist developmental states of post-war Asia but also early forms of strong state-led projects like the American System of the 1820s, in Germany under Bismarck, and in post-Meiji Japan.

Reforming State–Enterprise Relations

Motivations and Interests

When China's leaders embarked on relatively moderate economic reform after 1978, they were not working from any coherent plan or following a blueprint for a transition towards capitalism (however defined). Rather, the hallmark of China's transition was incrementalism (Zheng, 1999) and experimentalism (Heilmann, 2009), as reform-minded leaders tried to develop policies that first worked (in terms of increasing incomes and growth) and secondly were acceptable to more conservative leaders and those who stood to lose from the transition from socialism. Scholars of the early days of reform (White, 1984; Ash, 1988; Hamrin, 1990) paint a picture of a leadership somewhat swept along by the tide of events, trying to 'scramble repeatedly to "put out fires" and prevent disastrous outcomes' (Naughton, 1985: 244).

From the onset, policy change was driven by a combination of regime survival, ideological concerns and preferences, and the (perceived) interests of key societal groups. At the onset of reform, the Cultural Revolution had drained much of the faith in the party that the Chinese people had invested over previous decades. The need to rebuild legitimacy through a change from a politically mobilized to an economically mobilized society was the very basis of the loosening of state control in the first place. Today, despite continued high growth over a couple of decades, the leadership still does not take its tenure in power for granted, and remains sensitive (at times seeming perhaps ultra-sensitive) to potential challenges that might undermine its power. Achieving growth of 8 per cent per annum to maintain employment and ward off social unrest has become something of a shibboleth of party rule; and maintaining the means of controlling the economy in order to achieve this goal has been an important determinant of how state–economy relations have evolved.

Ideological concerns also remain important—but in a much changed way. Early policy debates were heavily influenced by competing conceptions of what economic reform was meant to achieve, and how far it should go in introducing market mechanisms and undermining state ownership (Hamrin, 1984; Bachman, 1986; Dittmer, 1990). Opposition to widespread privatization also conditioned both the way in which the state retreated from direct owner-ship in some economic sectors in the 1990s and remained the dominant actor in others. Today, the rejection of any role for the private has become a fringe activity associated with a small group of Maoist revivalists. But criticism of the logic of unbridled market capitalism and the 'market mystifications of neo-liberalism' (Wang, 2004: 49–50) remain strong and loud. Those who see liberalization and privatization as the source of growing inequality and unemployment are often referred to under the umbrella term of 'the New Left'. But in many respects, it is nationalism that has become the dominant and conditioning discourse, with liberalizing reforms often seen as privileging foreign interests over domestic ones and undermining China's ability to control its own economic destiny (Han, 2000).

Policy is also influenced by the interests of key societal groups. Before WTO (World Trade Organization) entry at least, the task of reform seemed to be to open up new opportunities whilst protecting those who stood to lose from the de-socialization of the economy (Lau et al., 2000). New non-state sectors emerged, but alongside the existing state sector rather than replacing it. With the effective introduction of privatization in the mid-1990s, business interests took on a new importance. The result is a symbiotic relationship (at the very least) between state elites and many of the new economic elites; they have effectively co-opted each other into an alliance that, for the time being, mutually reinforces each other's power and influence (not to mention personal fortunes).

Keeping the State, Introducing the Non-State

In combination, these three factors help explain the way in which state power and influence has been transformed in the post-Mao era. The first changes after 1978 saw the state loosen its control over farmers, allowing them to produce what they wanted once their obligations to the state had been met. Although the state (through the collective) retained ownership of the land, its monopoly on the pricing and distribution of agricultural produce was broken for the first time in decades (Zweig, 1997). By 1984, these reforms had spread into urban industrial sectors, and became formalized with the official classification of China as 'socialist commodity economy'. The state was still meant to take the leading role in guiding the drive towards industrialization and economic modernization, but individual enterprises would take responsibility for profits and losses and for responding to the economic demands of the people. In order to do this, the state began to cut the number of goods that were produced under mandatory plans and state set prices, allowing the 'law of value' to take a greater role (Cheng, 1985).

Non-state-controlled economic activity was playing an increasingly significant role in three ways. First, the drive to encourage foreign investment led to a change in policy to allow for wholly foreign-owned enterprises. Second, family-run activities with no more than five (later seven) employees under the title of 'individual ownership' (getihu 个体户) had become an integral part of the boom in small-scale service industries (hairdressers, small restaurants, etc.). In some parts of China, most notably Wenzhou (Liu, 1992), effectively private forms of activity had come to dominate the local economy well before its formal acceptance as a legitimate (within constraints) form of ownership in 1988. Third, by the end of the 1980s, small and medium-sized Township and Village Enterprises (TVEs) were producing a quarter of industrial production and brought in around a third of China's foreign exchange (Zweig, 1997: 254). Owned by local governments, TVEs are not strictly speaking 'private' and would probably be considered to be part of the 'public' sector in most parts of the world (Guo, 1998). Nevertheless, they were very different from state-owned enterprises (SOEs) in the way they operated and were considered to be a different form of economic entity.

The Retreat of the State?

Identifying turning points is always a bit of an arbitrary task. But Deng Xiaoping's support for quasi-capitalist development in his tour of southern China in 1992 (*the nanxun* 南巡) provides some sort of symbol of a new turn in policy where the private sector became not so much tolerated as progressively actively encouraged. In October 1993, the Chinese economy was once again redefined; this time as a 'socialist market economy' where the law of value and non-state forms of ownership would play an ever greater role, but SOEs would remain the dominant sector in the national economy.

For Yao Yang (2004), the process of *gaige* 改革 or 'reform' had run its course. It was deemed no longer possible to reform the system to make it work better; it was instead time to 'fundamentally change the system itself, gaizhi 改制.' The basic idea was captured by the slogan *zhuada fangxiao* 抓大放小—'grasp the big, let go of the small'. Large SOEs would be consolidated to create even larger internationally competitive enterprise groups (*qiye jituan* 企业集团) as the bedrock of the economy. These large conglomerates were to be the major recipients of state capital and would occupy key strategic sectors and those related to state security. Smaller and less efficient SOEs were also encouraged to merge, become efficient and competitive, and free themselves (or more correctly, be cut loose) from state ownership and support (Xiao, 1998) through 'shareholding transformation' (*gufenhua* 股份化)—a term that was more politically acceptable than calling it 'privatization' (*siyouhua* 私有化) (Oi, 2005). Whatever you call it, the scale of this ownership transition was remarkable. From 1996, 80 per cent of firms owned by county level and lower forms of government were privatized in less than two years (Zhao, 1999: 26), with virtually all of them gone by 2002 (Lin, 2008a: 4). From the announcement of *zhuada fangxiao* in 1995 to China's WTO entry at the end of 2001, there was a 40 per cent reduction in the number of workers in the state sector (46 million workers losing their jobs), and a 60 per cent reduction in workers in collectively owned urban enterprises (18.6 million). A further 34 million state sector workers registered as 'laid off' (Giles et al., 2003: 1). Conversely, by the end of the millennium, the broadly defined non-state sector accounted for 63 per cent of GDP, 80 per cent of growth, and was pretty much the only source of net new jobs (Fan, 2000).

In name at least, 'planning' disappeared altogether as the State Development Planning Commission merged with the Structural Reform Office of the State Council and the administrative and regulatory functions of the State Economic and Trade Commission to form the National Development and Reform Commission (NDRC). Indeed, when the 11th Five Year Plan was announced in 2005, the term *jihua* 计划 or 'plan' was replaced by *guihua gangyao* 规划纲要 or 'outline programme'. For NDRC minister, Ma Kai, the task of replacing state planning with a 'socialist market economy' was complete (People's Daily, 2005).

THE RETREAT OF THE STATE FROM THE PROVISION OF HEALTH, EDUCATION, AND WELFARE

The relative retreat of the state from direct economic ownership in many sectors had an important knock-on effect on the provision of basic social services. Prior to the onset of reform, China did not have a national social welfare system, with health, education, and welfare delivered by the workplace in urban China. So the closure of SOEs not only resulted in the loss of jobs but also threatened access to a range of non-income benefits and guarantees that workers in the state sector had enjoyed for decades. As Yep (2004) and Chou (2006) demonstrate, local governments in the countryside were often simply unable to cover basic costs through the normal budgetary process—particularly after they were stopped from raising money through the agricultural tax and by charging ad hoc fees on services provided by the central government. As a result, many local governments turned to marketization and the shedding of local state agencies to the private sector (Li, 2007).

The government's commitment to spreading welfare provision across the country is reported on an almost daily basis. Insurance schemes have been piloted in various places and more and more people are involved in schemes that include some combination of state, company, and individual contributions. The amount that these schemes cover, though, remains relatively low; for example, the cost of treatment for serious illness in the most modern hospitals falls overwhelmingly on the individual, and the amount and length of unemployment benefit is limited. As of 2010, roughly 167 million migrant workers were not eligible for any social security at all because they had not been resident in the same place for six months (Xin, 2010).

At the very least, we can say with confidence that we have witnessed 'the retreat of a public good regime' (Lin, 2008b: 11) through the process of state restructuring.

Redefining the State's Economic Role

So the story of Chinese state–enterprise reforms seems to be one of the state stepping back from its control of the economy and a concomitant rise of market forces and non-state actors. But despite this, the main conclusion of Kroeber and Yao's overview (2008) of privatization for *The Financial Times* was that 'economic power remains firmly concentrated in the hands of the state'. To explain this apparent contradiction, we need to look at what the state still owns, how state actors are also market actors, and give an analysis of what the state can control though mechanisms other than formal ownership.

The Nature of State Ownership

SIZE AND SCALE

The first and most obvious point to make is that state ownership remains significant, and the withdrawal from state ownership seems to have peaked in 2003–4. In April 2003, a new organization, SASAC (State-owned Assets Supervision and Administration Commission) took over responsibility for the state's interests in remaining SOEs as a shareholder rather than as direct manager/owner/planner.[2] The idea was to give enterprises the freedom to behave as commercial agents free from bureaucratic control, but without losing overall state ownership of key enterprises. This means that successful SOEs were left in a position where they could not only behave as market actors but also retain the benefits that accrue from being part of the state sector. Although ongoing mergers of SOEs mean that the number of central SASAC-controlled enterprises continued to diminish after 2004, we are left with a core of SOEs that seem destined to be at the heart of the state system for the foreseeable future. Moreover, as Naughton (2009*b*) notes, 2004 also marked the transition from SOEs being a drain on state finances towards a new era of profitability for the residual central state sector—though as we shall see, the way in which these profits were assured owes more to the preferential treatment that SOEs still received than it does to their competitive market performance.

So the state sector may not be as large as it once was, but it is still large by most international comparisons. Perhaps surprisingly, getting reliable and agreed figures for the number of enterprises by ownership type in China is not particularly easy (or maybe not surprising when you think of the size of the country). To be sure, the SASAC website (www.sasac.gov.cn) shows that

---

[2] The central SASAC is a commission of the State Council and looks after those enterprises where the owner is the central government. Most of China's SOEs are under local government ownership and under local, rather than central, SASAC control.

the central SASAC directly owns 125 entities (as of August 2011). But these are often large industrial groups which in turn are parents of numerous other smaller companies. In addition, when state firms go 'public', the state typically retains a majority holding so that they in some ways appear to be market actors whilst still also being part of the state sector (Garnaut et al., 2006: 41–2).

As a result, Rae (2008: 13) has argued that it is 'generally impossible to determine the exact ownership structure of Chinese business corporations. This includes those that claim to be privately owned' (Rae, 2008: 13). But this has not stopped people trying, and the best attempts have been made by Naughton (2006: 7–9), who calculates that firms under the ownership of central SASAC own about a third of the value of all shares on the Shenzhen and Shanghai markets, and just under a fifth of the value of the Hong Kong market. In a later study, Naughton (2009: 14) calculated that 'today's companies preside over a staggering 16,870 subsidiaries of all kinds'.

Moreover, the vast majority of SOEs are owned by provincial and municipal level SASACs, not by the centre. Some of these locally owned companies are very large entities indeed; the Shanghai Automotive Industry Corporation and Hai'er, China's leading manufacturer of white goods (owned by Qingdao city), are two examples of locally owned companies that now have a global reach and profile. Just like the centrally owned SOEs, large and smaller local state enterprises are also major shareholders themselves—typically of companies that were spun off from state enterprises during the period of privatization and restructuring—and constitute 'the largest group of controlling shareholders of listed companies in China' (Chen et al., 2009: 173).

We should note, though, that while more enterprises are ultimately owned by the state than appears at first sight, they do not serve the social functions that SOEs used to in the past and the directly owned SOEs still do today to a certain (lesser) extent. Employees do not receive the same welfare provision or security and are treated as if they were part of the non-state sector.

With this in mind, we can interpret the official figures with an interrogative eye. One of the most authoritative sources on the size of the state sector was the Second National Economic Census which concluded in December 2008 (the first was in 2004)—though this only covers the secondary and tertiary sectors, and SOEs remain dominant in the missing primary sector. One of the key findings of this census was the increase in the number of registered and licensed self-employed workers (up 30 per cent from 2004 to nearly 29 million). Over the same period, the number of SOEs had decreased by 20 per cent leaving the distribution as in Table 2.1.

THE COMMANDING HEIGHTS

Having said that the size of the residual state sector is still important (and bigger than might appear at first sight), the type of enterprises that the state

Table 2.1. Distribution of Chinese enterprises by ownership, 2008

	Number of corporations	Percent of total
Domestic-funded corporations	4,774,000	96.3
State-owned	143,000	2.9
Collective-owned	192,000	3.9
Share-holding cooperatives	64,000	1.3
Limited-liability corporations	551,000	11.1
Of which solely state funded	11,000	0.2
Of which other funded	540,000	10.9
Share-holding corporations Ltd.	97,000	2.0
Private	3,966,000	72.5
Other domestic corporations	119,000	2.4
Corporations with funds from Hong Kong, Macao, and Taiwan	84,000	1.7
Foreign-funded enterprises	102,000	2.0
Total	4,959,000	100.0

Source: National Bureau of Statistics in China (2009) 'Communiqué on Major Data of the Second National Economic Census', 25 December 2009 (available at http://www.stats.gov.cn/english/newsandcomingevents/t20091225_402610168.htm).

still owns is probably more important than the simple number of them. Smaller enterprises, those that were loss making in competitive sectors, and even those making a profit but with very low margins and therefore vulnerable to increased competition, have been let go. But via SASAC, the central government retains ownership (if not direct day-to-day control) of large enterprises that dominate key sectors and produce significant profits (Wildau, 2008). If we add the large locally owned enterprises, in 2007 almost 70 per cent of China's top 500 enterprises were state owned (Xiao et al., 2009: 159). State sector reform has left the central state as owners of key enterprises in 'strategically important sectors' (战略重要部分 *zhanlue zhongyao bufen*), defined by SASAC Chairman Li Rongrong as 'the vital arteries of the national economy and essential to national security' (China Daily, 2006).[3] The state also retains a controlling share in 'pillar' sectors of the economy.[4]

Theoretically, these sectors should have become open to private investment following the 2005 '36 guidelines', but as of 2010, little concrete seems to have been done to remove state monopolies. A 2011 report by the Chinese think tank, Tianzi (known as Unirule in English), suggested that the vast majority of the profits of these SOEs in 2010 resulted from their monopoly situation. They also received very preferential financial treatment, easy access to bank loans at

---

[3] Armaments, electrical power and distribution, oil and chemicals, telecommunications, coal, aviation, and shipping.

[4] Machinery, automobiles, IT, construction, steel, base metals, chemicals, land surveying, and R&D (Mattlin, 2009).

a third of the market interest rate, massively subsidized rent on land (which would have soaked up 63 per cent of their overall profits had they paid the market rate), a tax rate less than half of that for private companies, tax breaks on energy resources to the sum of RMB 497.7 billion between 2001 and 2009, fiscal subsidies of RMB 194.3 billion from 2007 to 2009, and other direct injections of capital from the central government when required. Moreover, the profits that they make are not redistributed through the financial system to help the rest of society but are largely retained by the enterprises themselves. According to the report, they only remitted 2.2 per cent of their profits to the state in 2010—and remitted none at all from 1994 to 2007 (Unirule, 2011).

China's most important research and development academies and institutes also remain under central SASAC control. When added to the government-funded research undertaken at universities and in the Chinese Academy of Science (which has ministerial standing), then the state remains responsible for R&D and training in a way that Gabriele (2009: 17) argues goes way beyond the 'normal' public sector research activities of other states and societies.

At the local level, many SOEs are smaller companies that do not necessarily have a national presence, but which are nevertheless the linchpin of local economies. These companies have access to finance and markets (including market information) that are not afforded to 'outsiders'—including outsiders from other local authorities within China itself. Individually, these SOEs are clearly not as powerful and significant as the major centrally owned conglomerates. But when considered as a whole, they can be seen as key determinants of daily economic activity in much of China.

Supporting and Promoting

State-led development in Japan, South Korea, and elsewhere occurred without the state directly owning key industrial enterprises, but instead by supporting and promoting targeted sectors and companies in other ways. In addition to the residual importance of state ownership outlined above, China has followed in the footsteps of earlier developmental states by using an array of indirect levers of control and influence. For example, China's leaders are keen to emulate their predecessors and support 'national champions' in the global economy. Most of these putative champions are large companies that remain under degrees of state ownership and benefit from 'normal' levels of state support (most notably policy-inspired financial support for global activities through the China Development Bank). But strong state support is also open to private national champions, such as Huawei, as China's leaders seek to promote China's economic profile overseas. Like many private companies, Huawei was established by people who had previously worked within the official system—in this case in the People's Liberation Army—and its supposed links with the military have frequently been articulated when it has come into contact with foreign governments and/or competitor companies (*Economist*, 2011).

The state also protects domestic producers in key sectors by limiting the level of external participation. 'The Catalogue Guiding Foreign Investment in Industry' sets out those economic sectors where foreign investment is encouraged, prohibited, and restricted. In the wake of China's WTO entry, the catalogue was revised three times to open previously closed sectors, but restrictions and caveats still limit what foreigners can do. Prohibited sectors include those deemed to be essential for national defence, key economic pillars, and essential services. The catalogue also prohibits investment in those areas that the leadership perceives could damage its monopoly on political power—the dissemination of news and information, publishing and entertainment, and 'social investigation' (Breslin, 2006).

In some sectors, injections of foreign capital are welcome, but only if the foreign interests remain subordinate to national interests and national development objectives are not distorted. This includes the production and processing of staple foods (most notably grain), medical and pharmaceutical products, raw material exploration, power plants, chemical goods and processing, and wool cotton and silk production. Even in supposedly encouraged sectors, the catalogue is full of conditions and clauses, and the full and detailed restrictions for each industry can only be found by referring to the specific laws and regulations for that industry.

It is in the interpretation of this regulatory confusion that many foreign actors think that the Chinese authorities are avoiding some of the commitments that they made to openness and liberalization in joining the WTO. Notably, these regulations seem to be deployed selectively when overall economic trends dictate a move back from openness—as appears to be the case in China's response to the global economic crisis in 2008. In this respect, it is not that state support is always there on a daily basis, but that it provides some form of safety net for producers if and when the going gets tough. In addition, exporters can negotiate tax deals to increase their profitability and to allow them to produce at margins that might not otherwise be commercially viable. When many of these breaks were removed in the summer of 2007, China's leaders faced a barrage of complaints from exporters in China's coastal provinces and collectively spent their summers visiting those areas. As a result of the problems that these overwhelmingly private sector enterprises were facing, there was a retreat from the original policy in the summer of 2008 (before the impact of the global crisis began to hit China) and a reinstitution of support. While such state support was replicated in many parts of the world in 2009, the extent of state support for exporters over a long period does perhaps mark the Chinese case out as being different from the 'norm'.

China's exchange rate controls have also been the source of considerable political debate and tension in recent times. Like Japan prior to the Plaza Accord, currency policy is a significant tool that the state uses to promote and protect domestic companies and focuses critical attention on rigged markets and unfair playing fields. Whilst an undervalued exchange rate has very different consequences for (net) importers and exporters, it does not entail choosing which companies get special help and which ones do not. In this respect, the state can be seen to be shaping the contours of the (domestic) market rather than privileging different actors *within* that market.

Private but Not Independent?

The negotiation of tax breaks brings us to the way in which market actors often retain dependent relations with state actors—particularly local state actors. In an early study of different ownership forms in China, Wank (1998) found that the official legal status of an enterprise was irrelevant— having a good relationship with local party state officials was much more important for doing business than the formal ownership classification of that enterprise. Enterprises that were formally classified as 'private' were often effectively dependent on local governments for financial help and on local SOEs for supplies (often at preferential rates). This hand-in-glove relationship often emerged as enterprises were privatized, or as new private enterprises sprung up alongside existing state enterprises, benefiting from an advantageous relationship with the SOE as either supplier, market, or both. This close relationship was helped by the way in which relatives of political officials were often the owners of new private entities (Dickson, 2003), with the long-term success of these new enterprises contingent on new owners' relationship with the local government (Cai, 2002; Walder, 2002; Li and Rozelle, 2003). In the process, it is fair to say that a number of officials used the opportunity to move state assets into private hands (Ding, 2000; Yang, 2004).

Times have moved on since these early studies, and the legal status of private enterprises and their theoretical right to access to finance and markets has been formalized. Nevertheless, and notwithstanding liberalization of most economic sectors and the dominance of 'market'-based levers of macroeconomic control, the state can (and indeed does) utilize a lack of transparency in market conditions and regulatory requirements, a flexible interpretation of fiscal responsibilities, and its authority over the financial system to support and protect favoured actors. Indeed, Chou (2006) goes as far as to suggest that the regulatory structure gives local authorities in particular the ability to control who is allowed to operate and who is not.

Access to finance is also an area where truly private companies fair less well than their state-owned or state-related counterparts. Quite simply, 'when the institutional environment is relatively underdeveloped and when law enforcement is capricious and weak' (Chen et al., 2009: 172) as it is in China, political connections matter: be that gaining access to domestic finance, the terms and conditions on which credit might be given, or being able to raise money through IPOs at home and abroad.[5]

In the literature debating whether TVEs were part of the state sector or not, three key features kept re-emerging to distinguish them from truly private enterprise: they had special and preferred access to credit, benefited from trading relations with SOEs, and received support and protection from local governments not afforded to individual or private enterprises (Che and Qian, 1998). If we take this basic idea and bring it forward to the contemporary era, we can argue that this remains the case for a number of enterprises that are nominally in the private sector. They might not be formally part of the state sector, but neither are they wholly independent from the state, and benefit from its protection and support. To be sure, China is far from the only place where the state looks after domestic actors, but as Gabriele (2009: 17) argues, in the Chinese case it is 'qualitatively different and deeper than that of their counterparts in capitalist countries' (Gabriele, 2009: 17).

The State, the Local State, and Economic Control

So the state is still central to the functioning of the Chinese economy. But this does not necessarily mean that the *central* state is central. Local governments have considerable leeway to pursue their own development strategies with two important consequences for this study. First, there is considerable regional disparity in the dominant types of economic activity and forms of ownership. For example, Huang Yasheng (2008) points to local government support for the private sector and a hands-off policy in Zhejiang, while neighbouring Jiangsu and Shanghai are much more 'statist'. As such, trying to generalize the situation in China as a whole can at best only result in broad indications of the nature of state–industry relations that will not match reality in large parts of the country.

Second, we should not think of state–industry relations in China as a national project organized in Beijing and implemented across the country.

---

[5] For empirical examples, see Li et al. (2008); Hung et al. (2008); and Francis et al. (2009).

On the contrary, a considerable amount of the central government's time and effort is taken up by trying to coordinate the national economy and prevent local governments from developing their own sometimes competing and overlapping strategies. This relative lack of national level coordination and the extent of decentralized control marks China out as a rather different developmental state from others of the genus.[6]

The lack of central control was particularly acute in the 1980s and early 1990s when a number of administrative and economic reforms combined to give some provinces close to financial autonomy from the centre. Fiscal reforms in the 1990s and the abolition of the myriad ad hoc fees that local governments used to levy went a long way in reducing the financial autonomy of local governments by the turn of the millennium. But the local state remains a key determinant of the functioning of the Chinese economy and in some respects fiscal reform has actually reinforced local governments' relations with local enterprises as they need to ensure that local companies make profits and provide them with tax revenues. As noted in a recent report, local governments' 'reliance on value-added tax (VAT) and business tax means they tend to encourage investments that maximize their fiscal incomes regardless of the overall market situation' (Berger, 2010: 11).

The local state also retains strong control over land. Since 1988, land has been commodified—it has a price and land usage can be transferred from one entity to another—but it has not been privatized. Through what Hsing calls 'the urbanization of the local state' (Hsing, 2010: 6), local governments have increasingly come to rely on selling land use rights (国有土地使用权出让收 *guoyou tudi shiyongquan rang shou*) as a major source of local government income. Provincial level governments get just under half of their income through transfers from the central government—44 per cent in 2010. Having increased by over 40 per cent in 2009 (Naughton, 2010: 32), fees from land use rights sales further increased by 100 per cent in 2010 to account for 72 per cent of locally collected revenues. In the process, the total revenue controlled by local governments doubled in a single year (Ministry of Finance, 2011).

Responding to Crisis

This tendency to lever financial institutions to loan money to favoured enterprises gains significance when the central government loosens credit controls—as it did in response to the global crisis in 2008–9. With the global crisis resulting in a collapse in demand for Chinese exports, the government responded in two ways. First, on 9 November 2008, it announced a RMB 4

---

[6] I am grateful to Tat Yan Kong for making this observation.

trillion stimulus package. On closer inspection, it turned out that some of the fund had already been pledged as part of the Sichuan earthquake recovery strategy and that the central government was only committed to funding around a quarter of the total (Dyer, 2008). With the remainder to come from local sources, the centre took the shackles off local government spending, loosened credit controls, and urged banks to expand liquidity. By the end of 2009, new bank loans in China reached RMB 9.6 trillion—much of it used by the 10,000 investment companies that local governments use as ways of getting round restrictions on them borrowing directly from the banks (PBOC, 2011: 6). About 80 per cent of the funding for these local investment companies in 2009 came from the banks, and they collectively spent 62 per cent of their money on infrastructure projects (and a further 11 per cent on land purchases) (NAO, 2011). Putting all the figures together, about half of the new loans disbursed in 2009 indirectly ended up funding local government infrastructure projects (Wang, 2010).

As these debts started to become due for repayment in 2011, the extent of the resulting debt in local governments began to become evident—though not wholly clear as different people came up with conflicting figures. The official National Audit Office (NAO) investigation put the combined debt of all levels of local governments and their investment companies in 2010 at RMB 10.71 trillion (NAO, 2011). Victor Shih (2011) combined a number of top-end estimates to get to what he admits is a highest end estimate of RMB 20.1 trillion. Notably, the debt of local governments as a share of local revenues in Western and Central China is much larger than on the coast, suggesting that, once again, viewing China as a single economic entity is fraught with problems.

China is in a strong position to deal with debts which probably (when added to the debts of central organizations) equalled something like 60 per cent of GDP in 2010. But even if the long-term consequences of this response to the crisis are less worrying than some seem to think, the events of 2008–9 are important here for three reasons. First, it shows the state's ability to mobilize the key levers of the financial system in support of political objectives when required. To be sure, many states responded with fiscal stimulus packages, but few if any were able to use the banks as such a massive source of finance as was the case in China (not least because the fragility of the banks was a key source of the crisis in the first place in much of the West). Second, it highlights the key role that the local state plays, and the significance of local level government–enterprise relations. Finally, the response to the crisis seems to have been largely (and disproportionally) based on the state sector. This is partly because of the expansion of infrastructure spending, where SOEs are pretty much the only game in town. But it also seems that non-state SMEs (small and medium-sized enterprises) found it difficult to get access to money to tide them through the decline in export markets even during this period of expansive bank lending. In the second half of 2009, the idea of guojin mintui 国进民退 or 'the expansion of the state, and the retreat of the private' began to gain increased attention in China.

This was partly because of the above-mentioned disparity in access to bank loans, which strengthened the state sector whilst leaving some private SMEs with nowhere to go other than bankruptcy (Bao, 2010). But it was also because of an increase in acquisitions of private companies by state enterprises—including the acquisition of some of those that were finding it difficult to get other forms of funding to survive. The official position was that this was simply a result of the strong taking over the weak, combined with changes to rules that allow, for example, greater state ownership in mining sectors where private mines also have terrible safety records (Xie, 2010), and that private investment was still very much welcome. Whatever happens in the future, the response to the crisis suggests that the space that market actors have to operate in is contingent on this private space being deemed to benefit the national project; if it is not, that space can change and even shrink.

Conclusion

At a micro level, China looks and feels very much like a market capitalist system. On a daily basis, the vast majority of what happens in the Chinese economy happens in firms that are not part of the state sector, with the market dictating the price and distribution of what is produced. Market forces, rather than the state, determined the price of 96 per cent of retail commodities, 97 per cent of agro- and sideline products, and 87 per cent of capital goods by the middle of the last decade (*People's Daily*, 2005). In export industries in some coastal provinces, China looks and feels like one of the most liberal economies in the world, with private and foreign-owned factories importing and exporting with only limited bureaucratic obstacles in the way.

But this market is not a full and free one. The small percentage of commodities and goods where prices are still set by the state are in sectors that feed into virtually every other sphere of economic activity. The state is also prepared to restore price controls if other measures are not working—as it did in 2011 in an attempt to bring down inflation. Despite the growth of the private sector, large SOEs still maintain monopolies in key sectors, while smaller locally owned state enterprises are linchpins of local economic activity. While the state primarily uses macroeconomic regulation through interest rate and money supply management to influence the pace of development, it uses more direct measures to support state enterprises. This is a contingent market system—one that is contingent on it continuing to serve the state's objectives. It is also an economy where firms with strong relations with the state (either through complex ownership systems or through less formal mechanisms and relationships) play important roles within this quasi-market. And there is evidence to suggest that a retreat back to the state and away from the market was already underway even before the onset of the global crisis led to a rethink of the long-term viability of China's growth mode (Huang, 2011; Yu, 2011).

If capitalism is defined as an economic system where the market distributes surplus to the class that owns and/or controls the means of production, then China has a sort of capitalist system. As with other developmental states before it, it is difficult to make a clear separation between the bourgeoisie as market actor and those state actors that regulate the market, participate in the market, and who are also often the beneficiaries of the distribution of surplus. As Sun (2008: 107) argues, because privatization and the rise of the market occurred under conditions of regime continuity, 'the formation of elites in China during its market transition has not been a process of replacing different types of elites with new elites', but more a generational transition of power within the existing broadly defined elite.

Perhaps this understanding that China is in some ways capitalist needs qualifying in two ways. First, there is a case for thinking of China not as a single economic system, but as a number of 'local' systems operating within a national framework. Zheng Yongnian's classification (2007) of China as being 'de facto' federalist sounds like a contradiction in terms; federalism is a legal (de jure) concept, not an informal one. But this apparent contradiction is actually an apt summary of the gap between the way that China is meant to be administered and governed, and how it actually is in reality.

Second, just as the market is contingent, so too is capitalism. To be sure, China is not unique here; neo-liberalism proved to be highly contingent when it generated crises in Europe and the United States, resulting in increased state intervention and nationalization. Nevertheless, there is a key difference in that in the West, it is intervention that needs to be justified, whereas in China, intervention is much more legitimate and it is the market—and particularly the perceived negative consequences of marketization such as corruption, inequality, and unemployment—that needs to be justified and legitimated. In previous eras, the capitalist developmental state was underpinned by the idea that resources needed to be mobilized behind a national effort to ensure national renewal (in the case of Japan) and even to ensure the survival of the state (in South Korea and Taiwan). In a similar vein, that policy changes and indeed radical systemic transformations are justified in terms of the national interest underlines the national(ist) basis not just of the Chinese economy but also of the contemporary Chinese body politic.

3

Not of a Piece: Developmental States, Industrial Policy, and Evolving Patterns of Capitalism in Japan, Korea, and Taiwan

Karl J. Fields

Revealing his penchant for both determinism and parsimony, Karl Marx opens his three-volume treatise on capitalism with the sweeping prediction that the 'country that is more developed industrially only shows, to the less developed, the image of its own future'. In the intervening 150 years, both events and scholarship have called into question this claim of convergence with 'iron necessity towards inevitable results' (Marx, 1867: Preface). Striking a keynote, Alexander Gerschenkron warned that this 'half-truth' neglected the historical reality that temporal delay—'backwardness'—creates both the opportunity and necessity for 'substitution' and therefore variation in the institutional domains of national political economies (Gerschenkron, 1962).

Perhaps no region of the world offers a better venue for testing Marx and Gerschenkron's hypotheses than the East Asian 'developmental states' (DS) of Japan, South Korea (henceforth Korea), and Taiwan, which were 'born out of crisis...and are by their very nature manifestations of the imperative to respond to external and internal pressures for change' (Thurbon, 2001: 261). This chapter describes the evolution of the institutional domains of capitalism in these three East Asian national economies over the past two decades and seeks to explain these trajectories. Because state formation preceded industrialization and modern capitalist development in all three, understanding the origin, nature, and evolution of their respective varieties of capitalism (VoC) requires attention to the 'co-evolution' of the institutional domains of both government and business (Carney et al., 2009). Industrial policy broadly defined provides the seminal conduit of the interdependent relationship between these two domains and serves as the primary focus of this chapter.

Decades of high-speed growth in Japan (1953–73), Taiwan (1960–85), and Korea (1965–89) led a generation of scholars to herald the emergence of an East Asian DS marked by internally coherent and cross-nationally comparable political economic institutions and strategic policy packages. During their high-growth eras, each of these three national economies could claim a highly capable and relatively autonomous state apparatus pursuing developmental goals through discretionary, interventionist industrial policies. Likewise, diversified business groups with dense institutional linkages to the state dominated each of these economies. Not surprisingly, however, in a region experiencing such rapid change, key actors, core institutions, and prevailing ideologies have evolved over the past two decades. Forces of globalization, periodic waves of financial crisis, shifting national priorities, growing corporate autonomy, and international and domestic pressures for both economic and political liberalization have prompted institutional changes. These evolutionary changes have in turn challenged the political viability, relative isomorphism, and certainly the intellectual consensus regarding this model of developmental capitalism.

Acknowledging this evolution, scholarly attention has turned more recently to the drifting of these three national political economies away from their common *dirigiste* heritage, the apparent demise of their DS, and the seeming convergence of these three political economies towards a neo-liberal Anglo-American model of capitalism.[1] This chapter takes issue with each of these conclusions. First, although not a primary focus of this chapter, scholars clearly overstated early claims of an isomorphic East Asian DS model (Johnson, 1987). More recent contentions of institutional divergence away from the DS among the three are truer in form than substance and pronouncements of the end of the East Asian DS are premature. Finally, neither the path-dependent persistence of functional or dysfunctional institutions nor the piecemeal evolution of these government–business arrangements warrants the conclusion of convergence upon a neo-liberal order of capitalism. In short, Cheng's 1990 claim of an East Asian model, but one 'not of a piece' (1990: 139), remains true on both counts twenty years hence.

In support of these claims, this chapter proceeds in three parts. The following section briefly clarifies the institutional domains of the East Asian DS and their business systems at the outset of this period of examination and offers industrial policy as a useful means of comparing the co-evolution of these two domains. The next section outlines the trajectories of government–business relations by examining the evolution of industrial policies in Japan, Korea, and Taiwan since 1990. In keeping with the theoretical framework of this volume, the third section seeks to identify the *causes* of institutional change (and stasis) over these two decades. In brief, this chapter concludes that at the

---

[1] See, for example, Minns (2001) and Pirie (2006).

time of the collapse of its asset bubbles in the early 1990s, Japan possessed a 'networked' capitalist economy with dense connections within and among firms and persistent ties between the corporate sector and the state. Over the course of the next two decades of persistent economic malaise, even as bureaucrats and capitalists have 'remodelled' industrial policies and refashioned corporate strategies (Vogel, 2006), the state's developmental orientation and substantive intervention and private capital's continued reliance on its corporate and bureaucratic networks have persisted. During this same period, Taiwan began the 1990s with a 'state-led' model of capitalism characterized by a tripartite economy of upstream state- and party-owned enterprises, midstream family-owned diversified business groups, and downstream private small- and medium-sized firms and extensive government financial control. Since that time, Taiwan has developed a 'co-governed' mode of capitalism marked by the growing economic clout and political influence of private business groups and close collaboration between an 'adaptive' state (Wong, 2004a) and private capital (both large and small) in fostering innovation in high-technology sectors and integrating Taiwan's firms into sophisticated regional and global value chains. Finally, Korea has experienced the most extensive evolution of the three during this period as the DS in this 'co-governed' capitalist system has receded substantially. The waning capacity of the Korean state has been matched by the growing political influence, financial independence, and continued economic dominance of the *chaebol* or private conglomerates.

In accounting for the evolutions and variations between and within these three national economies, the final section argues that emerging change coalitions, declining state autonomy and capacity, and a policy discourse of neo-liberalism have attenuated the DS in all three cases. But in each instance, 'sticky' institutional arrangements constituting the respective DS have proven difficult to dislodge, even in the face of unprecedented economic crises, recessions, long-term structural changes, and prevailing global norms. Thus, the institutional *forms* of state intervention, industrial policy, and corporate organization as well as the relative balance of power within the respective arrangements of this 'governed interdependence' (Weiss, 2000) have changed much more than their substance. While this continuity is more prominent in Taiwan than in Japan or Korea, we may still speak of East Asian VoC with developmental orientations and interventionist institutions.

Developmental States, Business Groups, and Industrial Policies

Drawing developmental comparisons across the three advanced East Asian national economies at different stages of development poses real challenges. However, comparing similar but staggered developmental experiences highlights how evolving institutional arrangements have mediated the respective national responses to the shared opportunities and vagaries of globalization and permits us to consider the 'specific transitional challenges for nations at different levels of development within an evolutionary and systematic framework' (Dodgson, 2009: 606). This chapter contends that the institutional differences in the respective business systems across these three national political economies are in large part the conscious result of industrial policies carried out by each DS. To gauge the nature and degree of political and economic change and account for it, we must begin by understanding the organizational structure of the national bureaucratic apparatuses, predominant business systems, and the institutional networks that tie them together.

By 1990, the vaunted corporatist arrangements of Japan's post-war developmental state had begun to show their age (Pempel, 1998; Overholt, 2002). Although the collapse of Japan's asset bubbles in the early 1990s dealt a substantial blow to the legitimacy of this DS system, the unfolding of the next two decades would demonstrate that increasing institutional dysfunction does not necessarily yield dismantling. Path dependency, institutional inertia, vested interests, and no small degree of rational retention have kept Japan's DS relatively coherent in spite of increasing calls for change and significant remodelling. Likewise, successful development trajectories in Korea and Taiwan had by 1990 strengthened the hand of private capital and civil society, which in turn led to substantial measures of economic and financial liberalization and dramatic democratic transitions, calling into question the utility and legitimacy of their elitist developmental models (Carney et al., 2009). Even so, both parties continued to benefit from their collaborative ties and the institutional networks binding them together.

By the early 1990s, private enterprise groups dominated the economies of Japan (the horizontal inter-market *kigyo shudan* and vertical or lineage *keiretsu*), Korea (the *chaebol*), and, to a lesser degree, Taiwan (*guanxiqiye*).[2] Although diversified business groups were central to each of these political economies, Taiwan's 'state-led' system differed from Japan's 'networked' and Korea's 'co-governed' VoC. These institutional differences in the respective business systems are in large part the conscious result of industrial policies (Fields, 1995). Business groups in each political economy are 'creatures of market imperfections, government intervention, and socio-cultural environments', and recurrent state intervention and persistent sociocultural norms guarantee the continued significance of these networks of firms (Chang, 2006). In turn, these institutional arrangements influenced the relative

---

[2] Taiwan's 'tripartite market structure' includes a division of labour among upstream SOEs, intermediate stream private business groups, and downstream SME exporters (Fields, 1997; Wu, 2007).

competitiveness of each economy, structured the ways in which global production networks have accommodated and been shaped by these different
business systems, and influenced the manner in which these political economies have coped with external crises and internal pressures for change.

In particular, Japan's diversified groups and Korea's conglomerate organizational structure have emphasized scope and scale over Taiwan's niche market
strategy. As Taiwan and Korea have joined Japan at the forefront of innovation
in technology sectors, Taiwan has relied upon small-scale original equipment
manufacturing (OEM) featuring a 'virtually integrated production structure
with vertical division of labour primarily through agglomeration externalities'
(Tung, 2001: 283–4). Whereas Korea has generally opted for an intra-firm and
intra-group production strategy, Japan and Taiwan have relied more extensively on inter-firm subcontracting networks (Kim, 2008). Japan's networks
tend to be tight and vertical, whereas Taiwan has developed horizontal and
loose networks in industries lending themselves to clustering and fragmentation. This industrial strategy has drawn Taiwan most closely into East Asian
regional production networks, increasing its dependence on intra-industry
trade and investment with China.

Although controversy persists regarding the effect of the DS and its industrial policies on overall growth,[3] few question the state's significant impact in
shaping East Asia's business systems or the growing influence of private capital
in reconfiguring these DS. In fact, this 'synergy' between government and
business constitutes 'the key logic of these developmental states' (Onis, 1991).
Analysing government industrial policies and the policy networks linking the
state and business offers the most effective means of tracing the influence of
the state on the VoC in East Asia and gauging the formal and informal
interaction between these states and the business sector. In one sense, the
diversified business groups, state industrial policies, and the policy networks
that bind them are all institutional responses to market failures. The centrality
of these policies and policy networks to the developmental experiences of
Japan, Korea, and Taiwan provide a useful means of charting and explaining
the evolution of government–business relations over the past two decades.

Tracing the Trajectory of Government–Business Relations

In spite of explicit modelling by policymakers in all three political economies,
the particular packages of industrial policies adopted in each case remain
firmly 'anchored in the local context' (Haque, 2007: 4). These local contexts

---

[3] See Haque (2007); Wang (2007); Wu (2007); and Beeson (2009).

gave rise to comparable but nonetheless distinct strategies and institutions that emerged and matured during their respective high-growth eras.

By the 1970s in Japan and the late 1980s in Korea and Taiwan, high-speed, catch-up imitative growth gave way to more mature industrialization and the need for innovative capacity. The differences in pre-existing institutional arrangements and regime orientations in each of these DS yielded distinct competitive advantages and structural weaknesses that government policy-makers in all three political economies sought to exploit and address. At the same time, sticky institutional domains restricted policy options even as these states faced new pressures to sell state assets, lessen intervention, loosen trade and investment controls, and show more deference to the marketplace (Minns, 2001). But in all three cases, even as policymakers stepped away from explicit sectoral and firm-level targeting, they continued to promote horizontal and functional industrial policies and invest heavily in the technologies, infrastructures, and skills that would permit national industry to move up the product cycle and technological food chain (Hernandez, 2004). In short, in Japan, we see an evolutionary process of institutional change in which formal and informal policies and practices have been 'remodelled' (Vogel, 2006) through a dynamic process of institutional retention, conversion, and displacement. Korea, by contrast, has experienced a relatively abrupt *retreat* from the developmental state through conscious and explicit institutional reforms and a refining (rather than rejection) of the state's interventionist tendencies. Unlike Korea, Taiwan has *retained* much of the institutional capacity of its developmental state and adjusted and adapted formal institutions to cope with new circumstances.

Japan: Remodelling the Developmental State

The Japan that faced the devastating collapse of its asset bubbles in 1991 was no stranger to neo-liberal economic reform. Since the 1970s, the Japanese state took significant steps to liberalize its economy, but over the course of the 1990s forces converged pressuring policymakers to further open Japan's economy and retire the state's industrial policy tools. In response, successive Japanese governments obliged, seeking to resuscitate Japan's depressed economy and respond to neo-liberal demands of trade partners through deregulation and privatization. These policies sought to reduce the scope of intervention in the market and establish more transparent relations between government and business (Yoshimatsu, 2003). Measures included reducing, eliminating, or simplifying a wide-ranging array of regulations on business activities, including banking and financial services, competition policy, and information technology (Nezu, 2007). Most heralded among these were the 1997–2001 'Big Bang' financial reforms intended to bring foreign competition to the domestic financial sector and create, in Prime Minister Hashimoto's words, 'free, fair, and global' markets (Takahashi, this volume). Among other consequences, the reforms were to apply transformative pressure on local firms to weaken or even eliminate key pillars of the Japanese DS model, including the *keiretsu* organization of firms and labour practices such as life-time employment and the seniority wage system (Weiss, 2000; Elder, 2003; Yoshimatsu, 2003; Sako and Kokosaka, this volume).

Dramatic reform efforts continued in the 2000s. These included in 2001 a large-scale reorganization of the economic bureaucracy that among other things renamed Ministry of Trade and Industry (MITI) and expanded its ministerial jurisdiction to include the entire economy beyond just trade and industry (METI). This reorganized METI championed deregulation measures, working closely with the Koizumi government that came to office that year to implement substantial reforms. During its five-year tenure to 2006, the Koizumi government removed some 1,500 regulations, producing measurable results (Nezu, 2007). These steps included Koizumi's dramatic (and initially successful) efforts to weaken the bureaucracy's policy clout by privatizing Japan Post. This state-owned enterprise (SOE) not only operated Japan's postal services but also controlled savings and insurance policy assets worth some US$3 trillion and for decades provided targeted industrial policy loans through the bureaucracy's 'second budget' Fiscal Investment and Loan Program (Amyx et al., 2005). In another effort to weaken collusive government–business ties, the Koizumi government's Free Trade Commission became much more vigorous in combating bid-rigging (*dango*) in public procurement projects in the construction sector (Nezu, 2007).

However, not all of these reform measures have succeeded as intended, nor have they occurred in a vacuum. While Japan's financial reforms unquestion-ably weakened ties between the financial and industrial sectors and under-mined bureaucratic policy tools, the 'reform process has been anything but a "big bang"' (Beeson, 2009: 19). Moreover, even as policymakers implemented neo-liberal reforms, they simultaneously 'displaced' old policy instruments with new measures designed to strengthen Japanese firms and 'converted' existing policies to new purposes in revitalizing Japanese industry (Streeck and Thelen, 2005). In fact, with the onset of national crisis, state intervention in many areas actually increased. In 1997, MITI launched a new programme fostering the development and commercialization of new technologies in growth industries by coordinating funding and supporting collaboration (Weiss, 2000). In 1999, the government implemented an 'Industrial Revitali-zation Law' offering tax breaks and low-interest loans to 'sunset' industries such as steel and chemicals to reduce capacity and provided subsidies and regulatory exemptions to encourage investment in high technology and other growth sectors. This measure 'effectively resurrected industrial policy with a new purpose: to facilitate corporate restructuring and shift the economy into new growth sectors' (Vogel, 2006: 86).

And even as the reconstituted METI has supported selective neo-liberal reforms, the ministry's flagship policy bureau has been strengthened, its sphere of influence expanded, and 'efforts to promote specific industries have not stopped' (Elder, 2003: 179). METI has often replaced old policies with new measures promoting the more diffuse upgrading of technological capacities rather than targeting specific sectors, supporting bottom-up strategic alliances rather than top-down cartels, and spurring innovation by encouraging private investment rather than guiding its path. Although these measures have seen only modest results, their scope has been ambitious. They include the 2001 Regional Cluster Plan designed to promote collaboration among government, private business, and universities; steps in 2002 to eliminate minimal capital requirement funds for new companies; and 2003 revisions to the Industrial Revitalization Law that provide incentives to companies to pursue joint ventures in reducing capacity and fostering innovation (Vogel, 2006). METI also drew up a 'New Economic Growth Strategy' in 2006 targeting seven strategic industrial sectors with high growth potential (Nezu, 2007). In 2010, the government announced a comprehensive plan to create a new 'Japan, Inc.' by deepening linkages between business and government and promoting key technologies in strategic sunrise industries (*Economist*, 2010).

In short, while the Japanese DS of the 2000s differs significantly from its 1960s' high-growth predecessor, the Japanese state retains its commitment to promoting national competitiveness and much of its confidence in state-guided development (Elder, 2003; Yoshimatsu, 2003). In key policy areas, bureaucrats retain significant formal and informal influence and industrial policy activism persists (Pekkanen, 2004: 382). In part, policy networks persist because of sticky path dependencies. Scholars point to the limited impact of both neo-liberal financial reforms (Walter, 2006; Beeson, 2009) and industrial policy reforms (Elder, 2003; Vogel, 2006). In the latter area, liberalization measures 'did not fundamentally overturn the existing policy regime' (Vogel, 2006: 112). Instead, modest institutional change has come to Japan's variant of capitalism through a combination of gradual, routine adjustments and conscious policy innovations. But at the same time, the state faces an evolving corporate sector that has become more discriminating in its choice of network partnerships; less isomorphic in its organization and practices; and more open to embracing institutional innovations from foreign managers, investors, and partners. Japan's current model of capitalism is not a stable equilibrium, but rather a complex matrix of institutions undergoing continuous evolution and redefinition (Chapter 1; Vogel, 2006: 224).

Korea: Retreating from the Developmental State

Korea's financial crisis arrived at the end of the 1990s, not the beginning, but like Japan the Korean political economy had already experienced substantial economic and political liberalization prior to the 1990s. In response to an earlier recession, debt crisis, and political emergency (1979–82), the unpopular Chun Doo-hwan government sought to enhance political legitimacy by employing measured financial liberalization as a means to establish some distance between the state and the *chaebol*. The Chun government phased out the 1970s' Heavy and Chemical Industrialization drive and ended preferential subsidies to those industries. Strict price controls had already ended in 1973 and foreign exchange controls were relaxed beginning in 1987. The partially privatized banks expanded equity financing through the stock market and trimmed policy loans in an effort to gradually wean the conglomerates from state credit (and in so doing simultaneously weakened the state's capacity to control the *chaebol*). This liberalization push might have been temporary if not for the simultaneous ascendance of American-trained neo-liberal economic bureaucrats who 'spearheaded a battle to dismantle the Korean model that became conjoined with the aims of financial liberalisation' (Weiss, 2000: 34). A dramatic democratic transition in 1987 ushered in the Roh Tae-woo government (1988–93), which continued this gradual liberalization process and shifted the state's policy orientation from targeted and sectoral industrial policies to a more functional approach in support of high technology and other strategic industries.

But with the ascendance of the Kim Young-sam government (1993–8), neo-liberal policymakers 'explicitly sought to end government "guidance" of the private sector' through a series of conscious measures designed to bring the Korean economy in line with the liberal markets of the advanced industrialized economies (Thurbon, 2001: 249). In 1994, the government abolished five-year plans—a practice guiding the economy since 1960—and announced the termination of all policy loans by 1997. In 1995, it ended the 'industry specialization' policy that had unsuccessfully sought to curtail the expansion of the *chaebol* outside of their areas of core competency. The most telling measure, however, was the dismantling of the Economic Planning Board (EPB), the vaunted 'pilot agency' of the Korean DS. Its powers were transferred to the Ministry of Finance and Economy (MOFE), which in turn gradually lost influence as its monetary policy authority was ceded in 1997 to a newly autonomous Bank of Korea (long subservient to the finance ministry). These measures struck a telling blow to indicative planning in Korea (Chang et al., 1998).

With these and other measures, the Korean state relinquished much of its control over the financial sector as it deregulated interest rates, authorized the establishment of private banks and nonbank financial institutions, and opened the capital account. These steps dramatically increased corporate access to independent financing, which not only permitted the *chaebol* to rapidly expand their borrowing both domestically and overseas but also saddled the conglomerates and the Korean economy with overexpansion, overcapacity, and heavy debt (Chang, 1998; Wade, 1998). These liberalization measures also severely limited the capacity of the Korean state to rationalize overcapacity and reign in corporate borrowing as it had done previously in the early 1970s and again in the 1980s. At the same time, the Kim government supported questionable expansionary investments by *chaebol* with close ties to the government in steel (Hanbo) and automobiles (Samsung) that ended disastrously. These ventures said much about the decline of state autonomy and developmental administrative guidance and the rise of particularistic political exchanges (Chang et al., 1998; Thurbon, 2001).

The Asian financial crisis (AFC) revealed that neither state intervention nor market discipline was providing effective oversight of private capital in Korea. Ironically, it also compelled the newly elected Kim Dae-jung government (1998–2003), despite its decidedly anti-statist inclinations, to increase state intervention after the crisis in the name of neo-liberalism to carry out reforms and address the Korean economy's structural weaknesses (Ha and Lee, 2007). Policymakers used the crisis to establish 'a new unambiguously neo-liberal regulatory regime...; something they had desired to do for some time but had previously found impossible' (Pirie, 2006: 49). Bolstered by like-minded lenders at the International Monetary Fund (IMF), policymakers continued the liberalization efforts of the previous government, including additional measures of trade and financial liberalization, asset privatization, corporate governance reform, and labour-market deregulation (Wang, 2007; Kalinowski, 2008).

In so doing, the Kim Dae-jung government reduced the role of the state and stood up to the powerful, but now chastened, *chaebol* in ways the previous two governments had been unable to do. In the wake of the crisis, policymakers permitted fully one-fourth of the *chaebol* to collapse (including Daewoo and sixteen other groups in 1999 alone).[4] The government pressured the *chaebol* to restructure and sought, not for the first time, to force the groups to focus on core businesses. Economic nationalism gave way to economic globalism, as portfolio and direct foreign investment opened Korea's corporate sector widely to foreign investors. Efforts at *chaebol* reform continued under the Roh Moo-hyun government (2003–8), including the Korean Fair Trade Commission's implementation of a comprehensive corporate regulatory system.

---

[4] See Minns (2001); and Chu (2002). At the same time, the government rescued politically and strategically important *chaebol*—most notably Hyundai, which was spearheading the government's ill-fated North Korean 'sunshine policy'—by compelling banks to keep them afloat (see Walter, 2008; Zhang, in this volume).

But while these reforms indicate a substantial departure from Korea's past *dirigiste* system and considerable neo-liberalism in areas such as corporate governance and financial deregulation (Ha and Lee, 2007), significant practices and institutional legacies of the DS model persist. Even as the state's capacity to strategically intervene has weakened, this interventionist tendency has been refined, not rejected. Moreover, this reinvention has been motivated not just by neo-liberal ideas and inclinations but also by the state's efforts to promote the transition to innovation-driven industrialization. As in Japan, the Korean state has replaced targeted industrial policies with a more diffuse functional approach in support of high technology and other strategic industries and supplanted micro-level industrial and export promotion with measures designed to internationalize the *chaebol*, liberalize capital markets, and enhance Korea's national competitiveness (Weiss, 2000; Wong, 2004*b*). Direct government subsidies and guarantees have replaced policy loans as the means for state financing of development (Kalinowski, 2008). But even in the realm of financial policy, arguably the area of greatest liberalization, 'a still considerable element of political intervention' persists and 'Korean practice remains very far from the Western ideal type' (Walter, 2008: 178).

Taiwan: Adapting the Developmental State

Like Korea, Taiwan has experienced substantial economic and political liberalization over the past two decades, with significant consequence for government–business relations. Decades of authoritarian rule gave way in the late 1980s to the ending of martial law and a democratic breakthrough. But whereas successive elected governments in Korea sought popular support by employing neo-liberal policies to scale back an interventionist state and weaken ties with private conglomerates, the evolution of Taiwan's political and corporate structures yielded different results. During the high-growth era, the émigré KMT (Kuomintang) party-state restricted the growth of private, local capital and fostered the development of upstream capital-intensive SOEs and a labour-intensive, petit-bourgeois, downstream private sector in the hands of local Taiwanese (Fields, 1995). But the 'Taiwanization' of the KMT and democratization of the regime fostered a growing alliance between the state and the island's diversified family business groups and strengthened the economic and political influence of these private conglomerates (Wu, 2007). While neither the expanding influence of private capital and democratic forces nor the pressures of neo-liberalism managed to dismantle Taiwan's developmental state, the balance of power in Taiwan's industrial policy regime has evolved substantially.

Even during the period of high-speed growth, Taiwan's DS intervened less directly and less systematically in promoting sectoral growth than its counterparts in Japan and Korea. However, industrial policy provided a key component of Taiwan's rapid development. Working within the guidelines of the 1960 Statute for the Encouragement of Investment (SEI), policymakers employed low-interest loans, tax breaks, tariff barriers, and other incentives to foster and guide Taiwan's ascent of the product cycle from consumer goods (1960s) to capital investments (1970s) to the promotion of high-technology sectors (1980s) (Hernandez, 2004). Throughout this period, policymakers employed a variety of sectoral policies, including the 1984 targeting of key strategic industries and the 1987 revision and expansion of this list (Kondoh, 2002).

By the early 1990s, policymakers realized Taiwan could no longer rely upon upstream SOEs to pursue the 'dynamics and complexity of technology intensive industries' and that it had become essential for the state to 'reinvigorate its steering capacity' (Chu, 2002: 40). In 1990, the government replaced the 1960 SEI with the Statute for Upgrading Industries (SUI), with the stated objectives to transform the structure of the manufacturing sector, hasten technological upgrading, and enhance competitiveness (Weiss, 2000). Unlike its predecessor, this statute resulted from extensive discussions between bureaucrats and private sector business leaders (Kondoh, 2002). This shift required reliance on private capital (both large and small) as engines of high-technology innovation and growth and agents of industrial upgrading. The SUI established functional industrial policies designed to incubate a new generation of high-technology firms capable of participating in global value chains as highly flexible OEM suppliers. This conscious institutional transformation of the DS required substantially reforming the education, banking, and legal systems; restructuring the capital market and trade regime; upgrading the state's analytical and planning capacity; and overhauling the bureaucratic apparatus for promoting high-technology industries. It involved 'close collaboration between the state and industry in identifying and defining the trajectories of technological change' (Kondoh, 2002: 40). The six-year plan that emerged from the SUI identified ten strategic industries, targeted twenty-five products for future development, and authorized significant measures to promote R&D and technical innovation and to alleviate the collective action problems plaguing Taiwan's diffuse private SME (small and medium-sized enterprise) sector (Fields, 1997; Weiss, 2000).

Taiwan's dramatic success in promoting its semiconductor industry provides a useful window for examining the nature of its reinvigorated industrial policy during this period. The government's 'catalytic' role in overcoming market failures and establishing key institutions deserves much of the credit (Tung, 2001). Given the high entry barriers, the state initially provided the lion's share of research and development, infrastructure, and human capital investment. But over the course of the 1990s, the ventures grew increasingly collaborative as state-owned research institutes brought private firms into

R&D projects and spun off the technology, equipment, and skilled personnel to private sector alliances. In many cases, the state still provided substantial funding, but this too declined over time as private firms saw more opportunity for profit and as the state promoted stock market financing for established firms. More recently, the state has begun to offer direct grants and subsidies to fund private R&D efforts and has promoted venture capital funds (Hernandez, 2004). These policies facilitated a reverse brain drain, fostered an entrepreneurial culture, and promoted industrial clusters. Without state support, Taiwan's particular industrial structure would probably not have been able to overcome the substantial entry barriers or to generate the public goods the private sector was unwilling and unable to provide (Tung, 2001; Chu, 2002).

Taiwan has not, however, been spared the pressures of economic liberalization. From the mid-1980s and over the course of the next decade, the government began to gradually reduce state intervention and increase the role of the market. Policymakers permitted currency appreciation, reduced tariff protections, authorized the establishment of private banks, loosened controls on interest rates, and liberalized outward FDI (Tsai, 2001). From the mid-1990s, the government also authorized the gradual privatization of state-owned banks and began promoting Taiwan as a regional financial hub. But in contrast to Korea, these neo-liberal steps were taken cautiously and accompanied by 're-regulation and the formulation of new policy instruments aimed at promoting financial stability and industrial development' (Thurbon, 2001: 251).

The limited scope and cautious pace of Taiwan's liberalization shielded the island's economy from the strongest gales of the AFC.[5] Although Taiwan faced its own financial difficulties by the end of the 1990s, the robust policy networks that developed in the previous decade limited the deleterious impact of the crisis by facilitating monitoring and fostering swift countermeasures such as stimulating domestic demand and targeting rescue packages (Kondoh, 2002). Unlike Korea, Taiwan maintained its developmental pilot agency and adjusted its coordinating institutions as needed to cope with new circumstances (Thurbon, 2001: 256). At least through the early 2000s, Taiwan managed better than Japan or Korea to cope with the vicissitudes of globalization and development in part because the state retained its main developmental attributes (Kondoh, 2002: 53).

Developmental capitalism in Taiwan has also faced its own challenges. As in Korea, opposition politics first introduced new popular welfare and environmental demands and then ushered in opposition governments that promoted neo-liberalism as a means to weaken existing authoritarian structures. In Taiwan, successive Democratic Progressive Party (DPP) governments

---

[5] See Wade (1998); Weiss (2000); and Thurbon (2001).

(2000–8) presided over declining state autonomy and growing collusive alliances with private conglomerates that challenged state capacity and threatened economic development (Wu, 2007). Social policy and identity politics, not strategic industrial policy, became the coin of this new democratic realm and close ties with corporate interests filled campaign coffers. In 2006, the government cracked down on China-bound investment and fined Taiwan's United Microelectronics Corporation (UMC), the world's second largest supplier of made-to-order microchips, sending a shock wave through Taiwan's corporate sector (Chu, 2007). State technocrats found it increasingly difficult to promote 'comprehensive developmentalism' and looked instead to the privatization of SOEs as an alternative means to promote development (Tsai, 2001). But this privatization too became politicized.[6] In short, democratization challenged developmentalism, as industrial policy took back seat to the interests of a political machine (Wu, 2007).

But declining economic growth fostered a degree of developmental nostalgia and brought a conservative KMT government back into power in 2008, elected on a slogan of 'It's the economy, stupid', with a highly respected former economic bureaucrat as vice president (Gold, 2010). The government wasted no time working with bureaucrats and businesses in implementing a Statute for Industrial Innovation to replace the decade-old SUI, designating six core sectors for innovation and providing a policy package of incentives and other industrial policies (*Economic News*, 2010). Taiwan's recent rediscovery of the virtues of industrial policy has also been prompted by the island's increasingly dense and intricate economic engagement with China. This relationship offers both risks and opportunities as Taiwanese manufacturers find themselves drawn ever more tightly into emerging regional production networks involving China. Although Taiwan and China enjoy significant complementarities in this regional division of labour, the real political and economic dangers posed by this complex interdependence have compelled the state to attempt to retain substantial control over the development of these ties.

Explaining Change in the Institutional Domains of State–Business Relations

In recent decades, these three East Asian national political economies have faced largely comparable exogenous forces, including structural economic trends such as the emergence of a new knowledge-based global economy,

---

[6] A 2006 criminal investigation implicated DPP President Chen Shuibian's wife in collusive privatization deals placing the shares of former SOEs in the hands of private business tycoons (Chu, 2007: 45). In 2009, President Chen and his wife were both sentenced to life imprisonment, and their son, daughter, and their spouses, as well as former officials and business associates, were all convicted of corruption, money laundering, and embezzlement (Gold, 2010: 73).

the globalization of financial markets and value chains, the rise of China as a low-cost manufacturer moving rapidly up the product cycle and periodic financial crises (Chu, 2002). External political forces have included the winding down of the Cold War and with it the decline in US military aid and support for domestic authoritarian and security regimes. Ideational factors have also been important, most significantly the hegemonic influence of economic neo-liberalism and the formidable pressure it has exerted through a host of international organizations, trade agreements, as well as in education and political discourse (Haque, 2007; Beeson, 2009).

Given these comparable technological, structural, and ideational influences, the VoC literature provides important purchase on explaining why the past two decades have produced different cross-national institutional outcomes in government–business relations and industrial policies. This volume begins with the theoretical claim that economic forces, indeed all structural forces, are 'crucially intermediated by social and political institutions and by policy discourses' and identifies change coalitions, state action and capacity, and policy discourses as causal agents of change. Industrial policymaking thus becomes 'not simply a response to economic development but...a highly political process conditioned by the interaction between evolving ideas about the economy and the shifting political pressures that government faces' (Hall, 1994: 149). Adopting these three categories as organizing principles, this section briefly examines the ways in which social and political forces and policy discourses have both facilitated and stifled institutional change.

In all three cases, path dependencies have prolonged the life of the DS. Predictably, this resistance to change has proven most successful in 'arthritic' Japan (Lincoln, 2001), which boasts the oldest and most fully entrenched DS. In Japan, long-term structural forces and neo-liberal pressures combined with prolonged recession to activate domestic and foreign agents of change that have weakened bureaucratic capacity, narrowed the scope of bureaucratic policy space, loosened firm networks, and attenuated government–business ties. But these pressures have been insufficient to overcome longstanding institutions, fundamentally transform government–business relations, or unwind policy networks. In Korea, an elective affinity of interests emerged among political leaders, bureaucrats, and the *chaebol* to pursue neo-liberal reforms that coalesced with progressive forces in civil society to substantially dismantle key institutions of the DS. These measures unleashed the *chaebol* and left the economy vulnerable to the AFC, which in turn enhanced the capacity of social democratic governments to pursue additional liberalization bolstered by the IMF, foreign investors, and prevailing global norms of neo-liberalism. But despite these significant reforms, popular economic nationalism and technological imperatives have justified periodic state intervention and limited the scope and pace of institutional transformation. Facing a similar external environment, Taiwan's DS has in many ways remained sufficiently capable and flexible to adapt its industrial strategies, policies, and networks even as it shifted from a state-led to a co-governed capitalist model. These adaptations permitted Taiwan to adjust its industrial structure, accommodate its evolving political environment, exploit international opportunities, and retain a legitimate if transformed role for its DS.

Change (and Stasis) Coalitions

Even before the onset of the 1991 financial crisis, Japan's shrinking population, its arrival at the threshold of innovation technologies, the hollowing out of its highly competitive manufacturing sector, and the persistence of a protected and unproductive service sector brought pressure upon businesses and bureaucrats alike to adjust the policy and institutional framework of Japanese industry (Nezu, 2007; Beeson, 2009). The winding down of single-party dominance also eroded the solidarity of this 'well-oiled conservative regime' (Pempel, 1998), prompted substantive administrative reform, gave politicians inroads into areas of previous bureaucratic autonomy and expertise, and fostered the 'growth of multiple principals' as potential partners in coalitions pursuing policy change (Ehrhardt, 2009: 625). Factional disputes within the ruling LDP led to a short-lived opposition coalition government in 1993, open conflict within the ruling party during the 2000s, and then decisive electoral defeat once again at the hands of a much strengthened opposition in 2009. This political activism has been both cause and consequence of the emergence of more vocal, numerous, and independent Japanese civil society groups, which are forging new relationships with political parties, particularly the governing Democratic Party (Pekkanen, 2004). Foreign investors and agents of the US government and international organizations have also pressed Japan to lift bureaucratic regulations and further open markets.

At the same time, the 'persistent, symbiotic relationship between government and business' has nurtured a loyal constituency in the corporate sector that has successfully resisted institutional change across the board (Walter, 2006: 407; see also Sako and Kotosaka, this volume). Keidanren, Japan's peak business association, has sought in many ways to block METI's retreat from the old industrial policy regime that favoured large established companies towards new policies designed to assist entrepreneurs (Nezu, 2007). Japan's protected service and agricultural sectors have been, if anything, even more resistant to change (Pempel, 2010; Steinmo, 2010). And unlike distributional coalitions in other countries that may range across the political spectrum and push policy in many directions, Japan's vested interests are all conservative and comprise a stasis coalition that has quite effectively blocked change (Schaede, 2004; Beeson, 2009). A significant portion of the general population also retains a stake in the old regime and therefore has little incentive to push for reform (Lincoln, 2001).

Korea's political struggle for economic liberalization pitted a beleaguered and increasingly illegitimate DS against an array of social forces, including massive labour unrest, broad social demands for democracy, and the powerful *chaebol*. Labour and democratic forces sought to sever collusive ties between the *chaebol* and an interventionist state, while the conglomerates, for their part, pushed for the liberalization of financial and other regulatory controls hindering their expansion. Korea's Fordist development strategy demanded huge financial and technological inputs, which galvanized the interests of the Federation for Korean Industry—mouthpiece of the *chaebol*—and leading politicians, who argued that Korean corporate competitiveness required access to global capital and technological alliances. Aspirations for OECD membership further aligned public and private interests and spurred additional deregulation and the opening of Korea's capital account (Ha and Lee, 2007). With the onset of the AFC, others joined politicians and policymakers, including local NGOs representing shareholders, the public at large, and the IMF. Although the IMF did not instigate the reform process, its influence shifted the balance of power within the 'Korean state-capital complex', creating the political space to fundamentally alter Korea's political economy (Pirie, 2006: 58).

But as in Japan, the degree of Korean liberalization since the AFC has varied widely across sectors because of both *chaebol* tactics intended to subvert or reverse liberalization policies and a strong popular nationalist backlash against foreign financial speculation and threats to national sovereignty. Reforms in 2007 intended to restructure underdeveloped financial institutions, inflexible labour markets, and indebted *chaebol* failed because *chaebol* interests were able to bribe and persuade politicians to bail out highly indebted firms (Ha and Lee, 2007). And because Korea has drifted further from its DS heritage than Japan or Taiwan, prospects for greater neo-liberal convergence beyond its current hybrid form of co-governed capitalism hinge significantly on social factors, including the economic and political clout of the corporate sector, Korean nationalist sentiment, and informal networks that may impede institutional change. Other factors include the increased influence and activism of foreign investors and local minority shareholders (Chang, 2006; Kalinowski, 2008). Foreign-owned shares accounted for more than 50 per cent of the ten largest *chaebol* in 2004 and foreign investors have used this leverage to press both *chaebol* firms and policymakers to pursue corporate reforms (Zhang, 2010).

Although Taiwan began the 1990s as a state-led capitalist economy, forces of globalization and democratization fostered over the course of that decade the formation of an unlikely domestic reform coalition. Economic policymakers recognized the island's dual industrial structure of capital-intensive upstream SOEs and labour-intensive downstream SMEs left Taiwan at a competitive disadvantage. In response, the bureaucracy strengthened policy networks with the private sector and adopted a new industrial strategy that privatized the SOEs, liberalized Taiwan's financial markets, enhanced public–private cooperation, and expanded the scope and scale of the private sector in a programme of industrial upgrading (Kondoh, 2002). These measures increased the political influence of private business groups, which supported SOE privatization and other liberalization measures as means to increase profits and enhance accumulation. Their interests converged with those of both the ruling KMT and opposition DPP in a 'surprising consensus' to promote neo-liberal reforms (Tsai, 2001: 372). The opposition hoped liberalization would sever ties between the ruling KMT and the state-owned corporate sector, and the KMT saw privatization as a means to sanitize and secure its huge stable of party-owned enterprises, arguably Taiwan's largest 'private' business group.

At the same time, this democratic transition created and empowered new interests and social movements that voiced competing welfare, environmental, labour, consumer, and national identity demands. But even as civil society expanded, the state managed through the 1990s to maintain 'pragmatic flexibility' and its guiding role in promoting development (Hernandez, 2004). The PRC's potential military threat also ruled out a full retreat by Taiwan's DS (Weiss, 2000). Domestically, none of the interest groups that emerged during this period, including big business, was sufficiently strong to 'make the state apparatus directly serve their class interests' (Tsai, 2001: 370). At the same time, Taiwan's diplomatic pariah status and exclusion from the purview and membership of international lending institutions and other transnational organizations shielded its political economy from the kind of leveraged influence both Japan and Korea have experienced (Wu, 2007). By the 2000s, like their Japanese and Korean counterparts, Taiwan's private business groups had grown more powerful and self-reliant, pressing for greater independence from state control and greater influence on public policy. The distributive pressures from these new coalitions also fragmented the ruling elite, reduced their ideological cohesion, and weakened state capacity (Tsai, 2001).

State Action and Capacity

The Japanese state's capacity to act as an agent of institutional change was substantially weakened by reforms, giving Japanese companies the ability to secure their own financing, and by foreign competition, compelling these firms to secure much of their technology through in-house production (Pekkanen, 2004). This growing corporate financial and technological independence combined with the declining prestige of the once-vaunted bureaucracy limited policymakers' capacity to promote change and increased private (local and foreign) capital's ability to exert and extort political influence. But perhaps not surprisingly, this 'grandfather' of the East Asian DS has also been the most path dependent, with many vested interests both motivated and highly capable of resisting change. Chief among these are the bureaucrats, who have remained especially vigilant and protective. In negotiating reforms, the bureaucracy as a whole and each relevant ministry in particular has pursued its own agenda, maintained its own view of the national interest, sought to preserve its own power, and brokered the various interests of its constituent industries. Consistently, bureaucrats 'have resisted the devolution of authority to independent regulatory agencies, have guarded their discretion in implementing policy, and have designed reforms to maintain some leverage over industry' (Vogel, 2006: 63). Even when bureaucrats have championed reforms, they have often sought to manage the very reforms originally designed to curb their influence (Schaede, 2004).

The extra-legal status of administrative guidance and many other informal policy networks have made these institutions particularly sticky even under conditions of deregulation (Pekkanen, 2004). Factional and interparty infighting among politicians has also given this weakened bureaucracy the means to divide and conquer potential agents of change. While administrative reform did increase political control over bureaucrats, 'actual reform policies often constrained political power, something that would not have happened prior to the emergence of multiple principals' (Ehrhardt, 2009: 644). Although Japan's financial sector bureaucracies have implemented neo-liberal regulatory standards, a coalition of private sector and political interests has blocked 'substantive compliance' (Walter, 2006: 409). In both the financial and manufacturing sectors, key political and bureaucratic actors have facilitated non-compliance with neo-liberal reforms, in large part because of fears that extensive corporate restructuring would harm the SME sector responsible for much of Japan's employment (Walter, 2006; Steinmo, 2010).

Like Japan, as *chaebol* financial independence and political strength increased over the 1990s, the Korean DS's capacity as a change agent declined. The success of the Kim Young-sam government in implementing neo-liberal reforms 'institutionalized procedures and formalised and depersonalised political leadership, limiting presidential discretion and narrowing ... room for economic intervention' (Kondoh, 2002: 236). The establishment of private banks and nonbank financial institutions proved particularly telling in this regard, enhancing not only the political autonomy of the *chaebol* but also the economy's broader vulnerability to financial shocks. Ironically, the onset of Korea's financial crisis also provided a mandate and reinvigorated the capacity of the Kim Dae-jung government (1998–2003) to harness the policy instruments of the state in imposing a new round of neo-liberal reforms. This social democratic government was neither ideologically nor politically beholden to a corporate sector the public had branded as perpetrators of the crisis. The Kim government utilized this autonomy and the support of a neo-liberal change coalition to retrench the role of the state and effectively block the *chaebol*'s ability to veto post-crisis restructuring (Pirie, 2006).

Unlike its Japanese and Korean counterparts, through the 1990s, Taiwan's DS in important ways managed to preserve its institutional capacity and autonomy (Tsai, 2001: 370). In part, this reflects the island's dual economic structure of upstream SOEs and decentralized private corporate sector. Policy-makers also proceeded much more cautiously than Korea in opening Taiwan's capital account before the AFC and, in its wake, successfully coordinated a strategy of reregulation that was independent of the IFIs (Weiss, 2000: 30; Wu, 2007). But the growing self-reliance and political clout of Taiwan's private business groups have led them in the past decade to press for greater independence from state control and greater influence on public policy. Likewise, increasingly democratic elections led to divided government, which weakened developmentalism (Wu, 2007: 978). Chen Shuibian's DPP presidency was marked by increased corporate influence and political conflict over economic policies (Wu, 2004). Under these conditions, the absence of either dramatic developmental policy measures or significant steps towards neo-liberal reform should not be surprising.

Policy Discourses

In all three political economies, the efforts of neo-liberal change coalitions and like-minded government officials have been bolstered by the ideational 'diffusion of international norms of best practices' (Vogel, 2006: 112). While this ideational diffusion has been important for political entrepreneurs in all three countries who have tapped these ideas in promoting reform narratives, they have carried particular weight and leverage first in Japan, and more recently in Korea as these two political economies have deepened their embeddedness in neo-liberal international organizations. Taiwan's exclusion from most of these institutions has lessened this impact; however, trade dependency; aspirations of inclusion in international organizations; and the fostering of relatively dense, informal international ties have certainly informed reform narratives in Taiwan as well (Wu, 2007).

This influence has been most pronounced in Korea since the AFC, where neither the nationalist right nor the radical socialist left was able to offer a coherent or convincing alternative narrative to the policy discourse promoting neo-liberal reforms (Pirie, 2006: 58–9). Sharp disagreement persisted, however, between bureaucratic policymakers and *chaebol*-sponsored think-tank economists over the speed and sequence of reform measures including significant financial liberalization, corporate restructuring, labour market flex-ibility, and privatization. As negotiations continued the IMF intervened, authorizing the government to pursue temporary Keynesian stimulus mea-sures and increase welfare spending to resuscitate the economy, a process facilitated by a corporatist tripartite committee representing government, business, and labour. This pact eventually broke down as the state ultimately sided against labour in the face of IMF pressure and the 'prevailing logic of globalization' (Ha and Lee, 2007: 912). Neo-liberal norms have continued to influence domestic Korean policy because they have been consistent with domestic policy discourses promoted by reform-minded politicians, bureau-crats, and civil society proponents, and because closed DS policy networks have gradually loosened (Zhang, 2010).

Taiwan too has faced pressures to open its economy. But unlike its East Asian neighbours whose liberalization projects in large part reflected weaken-ing state autonomy vis-à-vis domestic interests, Taiwan's reform programme has been, in the first instance, a result of external concerns regarding its diplomatic status and economic vulnerability. In this environment, political entrepreneurs in an increasingly pluralist Taiwan have offered competing narratives in the name of both development and neo-liberal reform (Wong, 2004a). Policymakers have promoted strategic industrial policies through 'deepening' (information technology), 'conglomeration' (finance), and 'up-grading' (biotechnology) even as they continue to liberalize capital controls (Wu, 2007).

Finally, in Japan, counter-narratives warning of the risks of institutional change remain influential. The ongoing recession combined with a long-standing 'growth-centred' social contract binding Japan's vested interests has made questioning these institutional arrangements difficult when the public believes growth is precisely what is needed. Conservative policies promising to protect jobs resonate with existing social norms and this growth-centred pact, strengthening the position of vested interests (Schaede, 2004: 278).

Conclusion

Over the past twenty years, institutions of developmental capitalism have been adapted in Taiwan, remodelled in Japan, and receded in Korea. Coali-tions of social and political actors in each political economy have exploited crises and drawn on contending neo-liberal and *dirigiste* ideas to construct narratives in support of either institutional reform or retrenchment. Even after two decades of economic malaise, Japan continues to revise rather than reject its networked variant of East Asian developmental capitalism. Although

Taiwan has witnessed significant transformation during this same period from state-led to co-governed capitalism, it has remained truer to its developmental heritage. Korea has retreated from but not yet fully rejected its co-governed model of capitalism, even as government–business ties have weakened, policy networks have opened, and the balance of economic power continues to shift from the state to the *chaebol*. In all three cases, two decades of globalization, liberalization, and democratization have brought not so much convergence with an Anglo-American neo-liberal model but rather varying degrees of adjustment and adaptation of the DS. Instead of fully abandoning state control or clinging exclusively to traditional policy instruments, each has maintained and modified existing industrial policies as it has pursued liberalization in an effort to appease vested interests, appeal to new stakeholders, and retain or regain economic competitiveness.

What do Japan's remodelled, Korea's receded, and Taiwan's adaptive DS tell us about the evolution of the institutional domains of capitalism in East Asia? First, contrary to Marx's sweeping conclusion, although institutional reform and evolution are inevitable, convergence is not. Second, the DS, as both model and institutional domain, remains viable, particularly in light of the most recent crisis of global capitalism and the rise of China, which has chosen explicitly to emulate the industrial policy regimes of the East Asian DS (Breslin, this volume). Third, the imperatives of global competition, the logic of global production networks, and the lure of neo-liberal norms will retain significant, but not necessarily determinative, influence on these three political economies. And finally, the establishment of consolidated democracy and the persistence of developmental capitalism in these three remarkably successful political economies confirm that these two objectives remain compatible, if not permissive sets of institutional arrangements.

4

State–Business Linkages in Southeast Asia: The Developmental State, Neo-liberalism, and Enterprise Development

Edmund Terence Gomez

Forms of enterprise development within Asia and within countries in this continent vary far more considerably than suggested in the various capitalism literature (Hall and Soskice, 2001; Amable, 2003). Japan's *keiretsu* system involves extensive interlocking ownership ties between companies and banks. South Korea's highly diversified *chaebols* are predominantly family firms, while Taiwan's driver of growth is small and medium-scale enterprises (SMEs). Southeast Asian economies, where the conglomerate pattern of enterprise development is popular, depend heavily on foreign direct investments (FDI) to generate growth.

A defining characteristic of industrialized Asia's developmental state model involving considerable state intervention in the economy is public–private cooperation, with the government a key player in steering resources to companies in order to attain its economic and social goals. In this model, a pact between the state, capital, and labour fosters stability in policy planning and implementation. However, the developmental state model employed in Japan, characterized by this state–capital–labour compact, has not been replicated in South Korea, Taiwan, Singapore, Malaysia, Thailand, and Indonesia, countries that reputedly adopted a similar mode of development.

This chapter argues that better informed insights into the benefits and repercussions of the forms of economic and enterprise development adopted by these Asian countries can be obtained when the theoretical perspectives from two different bodies of literature are employed collectively. If concepts from the developmental state literature are used in combination with those from the school of business history, based on the work of Alfred Chandler, Jr., the forms of capital development in Asia can be better understood. A case study of enterprise and economic development in Malaysia will help substantiate this argument.

The Developmental State and Business History

The developmental state literature elucidates well economic progress in East Asia (see Johnson, 1982; Deyo, 1987; Amsden, 1989; Wade, 1990; Evans, 1995), but it insufficiently explains the dynamism of private firms actively promoted by governments or the reasons for the stalling of growth or demise of others that possessed entrepreneurial capacity. To garner deeper insights into forms of enterprise development in East Asia, it is necessary to incorporate a business history approach, specifically the concepts employed in the work of Chandler.[1]

The developmental state's core concern is the nature of state–business ties, involving the steering of government-generated rents to private firms to advance industrialization. There are, however, fundamental differences in the manner in which these East Asian governments have intervened in their economies. The unique features of the East Asian developmental state economies include an autonomous political–bureaucratic elite, public–private cooperation for a common goal determined by an influential state planning agency, and a strong emphasis on investing in education to nurture the requisite human capital (Johnson, 1982). The pattern and extent of state intervention in these economies have been crucial in determining the type of capital—big, small, or state-owned—that has secured a prominent presence in these East Asian countries.

While the analytical focus of the developmental state school is principally on economic sectors and the state, Chandler's methods entail an exhaustive assessment of the development of a firm, as well as its organizational and managerial structure, from its moment of incorporation. Chandler's primary concern (1990) was when and how change occurred within a firm, including in response to policies and incentives introduced by a government. The concept of 'organizational capabilities' was used to explain why cumulative learning within a firm had or had not taken place. Chandler (1977) attributed the decline of big business to its failure to invest sufficiently in three key areas: manufacturing, management, and marketing. The concept of 'administrative coordination' was used to indicate the growing professionalization of a company's management to avoid institutional failure, a crucial factor that explains

---

[1] See Chandler (1962, 1977, 1990) and Chandler et al. (1997). See also Penrose (1980).

the dynamism of firms. He noted how as managerial hierarchies got more embedded into an enterprise, professional control structures became separate from ownership.

Chandler's (1977) review of the evolution of managerial form, from a family-owned enterprise to a professionally managed firm, revealed that the growth of modern industry was not primarily due to the quality of a company's management and its access to capital, but to its capacity to upgrade its technology for mass production and to enhance its ability to distribute its products widely. To achieve both objectives, managers inevitably had to look internally, at a firm's organizational structure, to rectify or introduce new mechanisms to augment innovation and increase market share of its products. Chandler noted that firms and markets evolve together, though arguing that business organization can shape markets in the industrial sector.

However, employing Chandler's work in isolation would not be helpful in analysing economic and enterprise development in East Asia. His mode of analysis fundamentally differs from the organizing ideas within the developmental state literature in one notable manner. Chandler's assessment of the conduct of business does not offer an appraisal of the politics of a government or the role of the state in encouraging enterprise development. The literature on the political economy of East Asia is replete with studies revealing that rents distributed by the state have often been determined by factors such as political expediency (Deyo, 1987; Pempel, 1999a). Moreover, the historical relationship between the state and capital in East Asia is one that has been fraught with friction (Gomez, 2002). This hostility between state and capital was, in part, rooted in the fact that political and economic power was held by different groups (Yoshihara, 1988). The pattern of power distribution and the consequence of power shifts, due to political struggles, have appreciably reconfigured ownership and control patterns of East Asian firms.

Importantly too, although most economies are reputed to have depended on a particular type of development model, governments consider, adopt, and apply a number of policy options which have an impact on the mode of enterprise development. Asian economies have been subjected to a mix of policies based on the developmental state and neo-liberal models of development. Interestingly, since the espoused economic doctrines of neo-liberalism include limiting state intervention in the economy and the endorsement of privatization, liberalization, and deregulation, this model of development is fundamentally different from the developmental state; neo-liberals actively advocate 'small government' and the virtues of allowing the private sector to drive economic growth (Harvey, 2005).

Singapore, for example, widely seen as a 'pragmatic state', has had such a mix of developmental state and neo-liberal-type strategies. Singapore, however, practised selective privatization, with key sectors kept under state control, such as the airline industry. Malaysia partially privatized key enterprises such as those involved in power distribution and telecommunications. By subscribing to the main tenets of neo-liberalism, a number of states in Southeast Asia actively encouraged the aggressive participation of foreign firms in their economies. FDI was to become a key driver of industrial growth in Southeast Asia.

What is therefore required, as noted in Chapter 1 of this volume, is an analysis of the political and economic contexts in which the firm functions, to offer insights into the conditions that it has to operate in and adapt to in order to continue to accumulate and ascend the corporate sector. To explain the outcomes of the range of policies adopted by Asian states to promote economic and enterprise development, this study will assess the history of Malaysia's corporate sector since the 1980s.

Enterprise Development in Developing Malaysia

Malaysia's subscription to developmental state-type policies began during the premiership of Mahathir Mohamad (1981–2003), in an attempt by him to replicate post-war Japan's form of economic growth. Since Mahathir's core concern was to nurture the rise of huge conglomerates, he was strongly influenced by East Asian corporate models, specifically the Japanese *zaibatsu* and South Korean *chaebol*, with their emphasis on the close links between the financial and industrial sectors to advance industrialization.[2]

Mahathir's vision of economic and enterprise development for Malaysia was, however, just as inspired by neo-liberalism, including its active promotion of privatization. Mahathir appeared above all enamoured with the stock market, an instrument which he felt had been effectively fostered by businesspeople in the United States to rapidly create huge firms (Gomez, 2009). Mahathir was probably aware that Japan, unlike the United States, had not been a stock market-centred economy. The active deployment of privatization and the stock market, pivotal features of a neo-liberal state, to cultivate big business had an immense impact on the pattern of development of publicly listed firms in Malaysia (see Gomez and Jomo, 1999; Searle, 1999; Sloane, 1999).

One common feature in both development models was the close nexus between state and capital, ostensibly to promote domestic enterprise, even though neo-liberalism involved reducing government intervention in the

---

[2] Mahathir appeared more enthusiastic about the family-controlled *zaibatsu* system than the interlocking stock ownership *keiretsu* pattern of corporate development, where corporate equity was very widely disbursed. The *zaibatsu* system would evolve into the *keiretsu* mode of corporate holding after World War II (Morck and Nakamura, 2003).

economy. This common feature offers insights into the conduct of political power in the development of corporate Malaysia. The government was comfortable with neo-liberal ideas because policies under this model allowed the state to distribute rents to the well connected, including firms controlled by the United Malays' National Organisation (UMNO), the hegemonic partner in the ruling *Barisan Nasional* (National Front) coalition. Although it appeared that the state was removing itself from the economy through privatization, UMNO leaders retained much control over the corporate sector by selectively distributing rents.

The simultaneous implementation of the developmental state and neo-liberal models was profoundly influenced by another major policy introduced by the government in 1970, the New Economic Policy (NEP). One aspect of the NEP, involving affirmative action, was the need to target a group within the business community as recipients of state-created rents to promote the rise of Malay-owned conglomerates. The NEP entailed greater state intervention, and during the first decade of its implementation, this was characterized by the active participation of state-owned enterprises, later called government-linked companies (GLCs), in the economy on behalf of the Bumiputera[3] community to ensure more equitable distribution of corporate equity between ethnic groups. The NEP also stipulated that 30 per cent of the equity of all quoted firms be transferred to Bumiputeras.

In 1970, although Chinese capital was well embedded throughout the economy, the community's ownership of corporate equity was small relative to foreign capital. That year, Chinese ownership of companies amounted to 27.2 per cent, while foreign enterprises accounted for nearly 64 per cent of total equity. Bumiputera ownership of corporate equity was a meagre 2.4 per cent (see Table 4.1). By 1990, when the targeted implementation of the twenty-year NEP came to an end, corporate wealth attributable to Bumiputera individuals and trust agencies had risen to 19.2 per cent. The most significant change in corporate ownership patterns since 1970 has been the appreciable decline in foreign ownership of Malaysian corporate equity—from 63.4 per cent in 1970 to 30.1 per cent in 2006, though this figure rose substantially to nearly 38 per cent in 2008 as the Malaysian economy fell into a recession following a global economic crisis. However, government figures on corporate ownership patterns along ethnic lines have been questioned.[4] And, even though official statistics indicate that the Chinese held nearly twice the volume of equity owned by Bumiputeras in 2008, there has been no review

---

[3] Bumiputera, which means 'sons of the soil', is the term used in reference to ethnic Malays and other indigenous peoples.

[4] See the report entitled 'Overview of the 9th Malaysia Plan' by the Center for Public Policy Studies at the website: http://www.cpps.org.my

Table 4.1. Ownership of share capital (at par value) of limited companies, 1969–2006 (in percentages)

	1969	1970	1975	1980	1985	1990	1995	1999	2004	2006	2008
Bumiputera individuals and trust agencies	1.5	2.4	9.2	12.5	19.1	19.2	20.6	19.1	18.9	19.4	21.9
Chinese	22.8	27.2	n.a.	n.a.	33.4	45.5	40.9	37.9	39.0	42.4	34.9
Indians	0.9	1.1	n.a.	n.a.	1.2	1.0	1.5	1.5	1.2	1.1	1.6
Others	–	–	–	–	–	–	–	0.9	0.4	0.4	0.1
Nominee companies	2.1	6.0	n.a.	n.a.	1.3	8.5	8.3	7.9	8.0	6.6	3.5
Locally controlled firms	10.1	–	–	–	7.2	0.3	1.0	–	–	–	–
Foreigners	62.1	63.4	53.3	42.9	26.0	25.4	27.7	32.7	32.5	30.1	37.9

Note: n.a.: not available.

Source: Seventh Malaysia Plan, Eighth Malaysia Plan, Mid-Term Review of the Ninth Malaysia Plan, Tenth Malaysia Plan.

as to why this was the case nearly four decades after equity redistribution initiatives had been instituted. Since Bumiputeras had still not obtained 30 per cent ownership of corporate equity by 1990, this reason was used by the government to persist with the policy of affirmative action.

Mahathir's grand vision when appointed Prime Minister was for Malaysia to achieve fully developed nation status by 2020, with industrialization driven by a new breed of internationally recognized Bumiputera-owned firms. While the government had used public enterprises to acquire equity on behalf of the Bumiputeras during the first decade of the NEP, Mahathir argued for the need to pick potential entrepreneurs and confer on them—without open tender—rents such as licences, contracts, and privatized projects, acquired with loans from government-owned banks. This tripartite link between the government, private capital, and financial institutions would aid the rapid rise of well-diversified conglomerates.

To achieve this vision, Mahathir moved to change the nature of Malaysia's interventionist state, reshaping it as a developmental state, encapsulated in his 'Look East' policy. His government would intervene in the market to alter the incentives available to businesses, targeting industries it considered imperative to achieve industrialized nation status. Within the bureaucracy, Mahathir stressed the importance of the Ministry of Trade and Industry (MITI), whose 'administrative guidance' would serve to determine the industrial sectors that private firms should venture into (Johnson, 1982). In spite of his overt focus on Japan, Mahathir was more influenced by the entrepreneurial form of the South Korean *chaebols* than by the innovative organizational capabilities of Japanese enterprises. Mahathir's government shared characteristics of the South Korean state that facilitated the promotion of the sorts of intervention he subscribed to: strong political authority, a clear national consensus for economic growth (though there was no consensus on the form of economic development), and a competent but increasingly subservient bureaucracy.

FDI was central to Malaysia's industrialization strategy, specifically its focus on heavy industries. This component of industrialization was implemented through state-owned Heavy Industries Corporation of Malaysia (HICOM), which collaborated with foreign, mainly Japanese companies, in industries ranging from steel and cement production to the manufacture of a national car, under the Proton model. The promotion of heavy industries through joint ventures involving GLCs and multinational companies (MNCs) was largely unsuccessful. Only the national car industry remains under domestic control, though the government is seeking out a foreign partner to salvage this enterprise. A restrictive vendor system appended to this GLC–MNC strategy to cultivate Bumiputera-owned SMEs in the industrial sector also proved unsuccessful. Claiming that private businesses would be reluctant to participate in heavy industries given the huge capital investments required and limited technological expertise, Mahathir bypassed the predominantly Chinese-controlled manufacturing sector. This 'ethnic bypass' policy was heavily criticized (Jomo, 1997: 250).

The stock market was actively employed to transfer wealth and quickly create large domestic enterprises. State rents were selectively distributed to private firms owned by an elite who used them through shares-for-assets swaps and reverse takeovers to capture control of quoted companies. These listed firms, in turn, were used for mergers, acquisitions, and takeovers to develop the size of their enterprise. As share prices escalated, their stock was used as security to obtain more loans from banks for further acquisitions. The injection of these rents into the stock market, Bursa Malaysia, helped these businessmen swiftly develop the value of their firms as well as the size of the local bourse.

Through privatization, state assets were sold to private individuals and GLCs that were listed on the stock exchange. There were a number of sizeable privatized public-listings including the gaming firm, Sports Toto, the national airline, Malaysia Airlines (MAS), and HICOM. By the mid-1980s, twenty-four state enterprises had been listed on the local stock exchange, and by 1995, privatized former state agencies accounted for 22 per cent of the local bourse's total market capitalization (Callen and Reynolds, 1997: 15). Between 1989 and 1993, equity market capitalization as a percentage of gross domestic product (GDP) increased from 105 to 342 per cent. By the mid-1990s, as the fourth largest bourse in Asia and the fifteenth largest in the world, Bursa Malaysia's market capitalization relative to GDP was the highest among Southeast Asian countries (Callen and Reynolds, 1997: 15).

Over a mere decade, a number of well-connected businesspeople would emerge as owners of huge publicly quoted firms. These business groups were controlled by Bumiputeras linked to one of the then three most powerful politicians—Prime Minister Mahathir, Deputy Prime Minister Anwar Ibrahim, and Finance Minister Daim Zainuddin (Gomez, 2004). A group of well-connected non-Malays also quickly developed huge enterprises with state patronage. All had been privy to major privatized rents.[5]

In 1997, when the Malaysian economy was adversely affected by the Asian currency crisis, Mahathir's plans to develop entrepreneurs quickly unravelled. In spite of Mahathir's oversight of these preferentially selected and treated firms, there had been little or no disciplining of them. The government bailed out several of these firms, sometimes at exorbitant prices, and renationalized major privatized projects. Well-connected firms had also fallen behind

---

[5] For an in-depth study of the rise of these well-connected Bumiputera and non-Bumiputera businessmen, see Gomez and Jomo (1999); Searle (1999); Sloane (1999); and Gomez (1999).

because of UMNO feuds. During a serious political fall-out between Mahathir and his deputy, Anwar, allegations of nepotism, cronyism, and corruption were hurled at each other. Anwar was removed from office in September 1998 and businessmen associated with him subsequently struggled to protect their corporate interests.[6]

While the unique nature of the government's policy preferences, specifically those associated with the developmental state, neo-liberalism, and affirmative action, has been introduced to industrialize the economy, these efforts have mostly failed. Mahathir gave an unexpectedly honest appraisal of his unsuccessful policies before stepping down as premier, arguing that long-term implementation of affirmative action had led to a 'crutch mentality' among Bumiputera businesspeople.[7] Such failures were a result of the state's pattern of selectively distributing rents, justified on the grounds that there was a need to expedite industrialization, to advance domestic capital to curb Malaysia's dependence on foreign firms to drive economic growth, and to ensure ethnic coexistence through fairly equitable distribution of the wealth generated. However, serious allegations of rent-seeking and corruption had emerged during the implementation of these policies.

Clearly, the tenets of the developmental state and of neo-liberalism were not applied in their full form, showing how selective the state had been when planning and implementing policies. While the government actively promoted privatization, there was no support for the creation of independent regulatory institutions with the retreat of the state; the labour market was not liberalized, with trade unions subjected to suppression, ostensibly to ensure investor-friendly market conditions; nor was there much support for social safety nets for the poor as privatization of health and education expanded.

Malaysia Reformed?

Abdullah Ahmad Badawi, while serving as Prime Minister between 2003 and 2009, persisted with a developmentalist agenda, though he intervened in different economic sectors. His administration emphasized commercializing agriculture to increase income in rural areas where poverty remains a serious issue, and actively nurtured SMEs which constitute approximately 99.2 per cent of business establishments in Malaysia. His promotion of SMEs was, however, still influenced by the government's attempts to cultivate Bumiputera businesses.

---

[6] For details on the takeover of assets controlled by Anwar allies, see Wain (2009).
[7] See Mahathir's speech entitled 'The New Malay Dilemma', delivered at the Harvard Club of Malaysia on 27 July 2002.

Abdullah's major institutional reform involved an attempt to utilize the GLCs more efficiently to generate growth. Reform of the GLCs was imperative as they had emerged as major publicly listed firms. In 2005, fifty-seven companies quoted on the Bursa Malaysia were GLCs, with a market capitalization of RM260 billion, constituting 36 per cent of the stock exchange's total capitalization. GLCs such as the Malaysian Biotech Corp (MBC), the Halal Industry Development Corp (HDC), and the Multimedia Development Corporation (MDeC) were created as part of a series of explicit governmental interventions to select, aid, and abet new industries. The promotion of information-base, high-technology industries by the mid-2000s, especially in biosciences and pharmaceuticals, was to be implemented through these GLCs.

Abdullah's primary focus was on supporting small firms financially, though scant Bumiputera presence in key sectors of the economy was not due to inadequate state funding. The major institution introduced to aid the expansion of Malay enterprise was Bank Bumiputra, incorporated in 1965. But mired repeatedly in financial scandals and subjected to numerous bailouts, Bank Bumiputra was subsequently merged with a private bank in 1999, and now functions as CIMB Bank, a top ten-listed enterprise in which the government has a majority interest. In 2005, the government merged two of its small finance-based development institutions, Bank Pembangunan and Bank Industri & Teknoloji, to create SME Bank, an attempt to channel financial aid more productively to small firms.

The government endeavoured to tie SMEs to GLCs and MNCs through its vendor system to help small firms gain greater access to local and foreign markets. Abdullah's use of the vendor system in the retailing sector was similar to the one employed by Proton, to create trade links between MNCs and SMEs. MNC hypermarkets, including Tesco, Nestle, and Carrefour, allot space for locally produced goods in both their domestic and foreign outlets. This was an important development as retailing, which is dominated by small outlets, had been losing customers to hypermarkets after the government began relaxing foreign ownership of the distributive trade sector from the mid-1980s.

Abdullah was, however, not able to foster entrepreneurial SMEs. The small number of SMEs that are dynamic, in terms of creating new technology, is due to flaws within public policies. Abdullah was wrong in assuming that he could simultaneously promote Bumiputera capital and SMEs without jeopardizing either endeavour.

A comparison of Malaysia's thriving second car project, Perusahaan Otomobil Kedua (Perodua), with Proton best reflects this misinformed assumption. By tying the growth of the automobile sector to a race-based vendor system, Mahathir had failed to achieve his dual objective of creating a new group of entrepreneurial Bumiputera firms and a viable export-driven car industry (Leutert and Sudhoff, 1999). Learning from the problems it had encountered from GLC–MNC linkages in the case of Proton, the state formulated a new joint-venture method for the second car project, Perodua, launched in 1993 to produce small-compact automobiles. Perodua has numerous shareholders: two GLCs, UMW, and PNB Equity Resource Corporation; Japanese enterprises Daihatsu and Mitsui; and a publicly listed Malaysian company, MBM Resources, a Chinese family firm, that is the lead domestic company in this joint venture. Toyota of Japan owns a 51.1 per cent stake in Daihatsu Japan and has an interest in UMW, giving the company a significant interest in the Perodua project (*Malaysian Business*, 1 February 2001). Perodua, unlike Proton, has emerged as a major enterprise with growing capacity to export its products.[8]

There is much evidence that non-race-based policies help nurture entrepreneurial firms. Malaysian firms that have ventured abroad and stand par with MNCs, even taking over major companies, have a common feature: they show sound engineering, management, and marketing skills, an indication of entrepreneurial capacity. Firms that have received rents from the government, learnt new technology, and invested in ventures abroad include Francis Yeoh's YTL Corp (power supply) and T. Ananda Krishnan's Maxis (telecommunications).

There is evidence of such entrepreneurial capacity among non-Bumiputera SMEs. Following a deep recession in the mid-1980s, the government amended legislation to encourage non-Bumiputera investments in manufacturing. Among the SMEs owned by ex-employees of MNCs that have created linkages with their former employers and have emerged as major enterprises in the electronics and electrical (E&E) sector include Unico Holdings, Eng Teknologi Holdings, and Globetronics Technology.

There are important lessons from the case of companies such as Globetronics and Eng Teknoloji. A historical assessment of these firms indicates that FDI–SME linkages that increase local R&D capabilities are particularly important to allow domestic enterprises to grow from their ties to a local foreign affiliate and emerge as broader global suppliers. Even the best SMEs can come to be 'stuck in the middle', that is, firms that are unable to evolve beyond the point where they are small-sized operations supplying lower value components to MNCs. Importantly too, Chinese firms thrive because they are aware that since the risks involved in investing are high, they have to be sure they have the capacity to turn a profit or secure adequate returns on their investments when they venture into business. Not all Chinese have survived in this environment, while entrepreneurial businesspeople have been reluctant to invest in R&D, preferring to remain small-sized firms operating merely as

---

[8] Interview with MBM Resources management, 3 July 2009.

subcontractors. Public policies were hindering entrepreneurial non-Bumiputera-owned SMEs from building on what they had learnt from their contact with MNCs.[9]

Abdullah probably had recognized the need to liberalize equity ownership patterns to forge productive MNC–SME links and nurture entrepreneurial domestic firms. He, however, lacked the political will to do so, given UMNO's limited support for such liberalization.

Crisis and a New Development Model

In the first half of 2009, as Malaysia slipped into a deep recession and FDI plummeted, Prime Minister Najib Razak argued that deregulation was imperative to halt the economic crisis. The government announced the liberalization of equity ownership regulation in key economic sectors, specifically services. Services had surpassed manufacturing as the leading contributor to GDP, with further expansion anticipated in key sub-sectors relating to Islamic financial products, outsourcing and shared services (OSS), information communication technology (ICT), along with projected growth in tourism, restaurants, and transportation.[10] The 30 per cent Bumiputera equity requirement was removed in twenty-seven sub-sectors within services, including health, tourism, computer services, and transport. The requirement that companies seeking a public listing offer 30 per cent of their equity to Bumiputeras was changed, with the quota cut to 12.5 per cent which could be further reduced if companies issued more shares. To encourage foreign firms to list on the Bursa Malaysia, the Bumiputera equity quota regulation would not apply, though Malaysia retained restrictions limiting foreign ownership to a minority interest in strategic industries such as telecommunications, finance, and energy.

In 2009, the government announced that the economy was caught in a 'high middle income country trap', an overt admission that domestic firms were unable to evolve beyond the point where they had the competence to develop and market new technology. This announcement was of major concern because one key requisite to achieve the status of a modern high-income economy is a productive domestic business sector with the capacity to upgrade or change technological and market conditions so that higher quality products and services become available.

---

[9] This point was made by representatives from the SME Association. Interview on 29 June 2009.
[10] See the *Ninth Malaysia Plan, 2006–2010*, for a discussion on the growing importance of the services sector to the economy.

One objective of this corporate equity deregulation exercise was to send a message to domestic firms that they could invest, without fear, in order to nurture productive and innovative enterprises. But, protests emerged from among Najib's own party members over this deregulation as Bumiputera equity ownership would decline appreciably among publicly listed firms. Crucially too, Bumiputera firms had a strong presence in the services sector.

When Najib released his *Government Transformation Plan* (GTP), the *New Economic Model for Malaysia* (NEM), and the *Tenth Malaysia Plan, 2011–2015*, between early 2010 and 2011, these documents acknowledged serious social and economic problems: the economy is 'stuck in the middle', the education system is in dire need of restoration, crime and corruption mount, hardcore poverty remains to be eliminated, public transportation is mired in a jam, and basic infrastructure in rural areas has to be created. To deal with these social and economic problems, the government recognized the need to create a more efficient and coordinated strategy involving the state and capital that would focus resources on prioritized goals. The government acknowledged the need to reduce overlap, red tape, and bureaucratic delays. A new unit, the Performance Management and Delivery Unit (PEMANDU), run by contracted professionals outside the civil service, was created to deliver policies. PEMANDU was situated in the Prime Minister's office to ensure 'end-to-end delivery' by working with the relevant ministries and bureaucrats to enforce delivery of public policies.

These government plans involve an attempt to reconstruct policies of the past, with little institutional reforms to reduce rent-seeking and corruption. There was no attempt by these new plans to incorporate trade unions into discussions about economic planning; nor was there any attempt to bring trade unions and capital into dialogue to ensure, among other things, an equitable wage system. In spite of the GLCs dominant presence in the economy, the private sector would drive growth, with continued persistence of neo-liberal ideas such as privatization. The government would persevere with affirmative action, though the policy would now be 'market-friendly'. To ensure proper implementation of affirmative action, 'rent-seeking' and 'patronage' are to be curbed.

But given the structure of Malaysia's political system, for these new economic plans to be seen as credible, there had to be one major reform—devolution of power to key institutions, providing them with the autonomy to act without favour. There is, however, no mention in the NEM, the GTP, or the *Tenth Malaysia Plan* of institutional reforms to curb corruption and rent-seeking. What is stressed, however, in spite of these problems within the reform package announced by Najib was the need for social dialogue and democracy, particularly through his '1Malaysia' slogan, one he introduced to indicate the inclusive nature of his government.

Inevitably, these government documents are fraught with the idea of a state confronting a serious conundrum. For example, in the GTP, on one hand the government contends that since the proportion of corporate stock owned by Bumiputeras has 'remained stagnant', a new state-led private equity institution is required to increase this community's participation in the economy. On the other hand, the GTP admits that one outcome of policies such as affirmative action is 'rising discontent', as well as a huge brain drain and widening inequality, including growing intra-Bumiputera wealth and income disparity. There is an obvious reason for this conundrum. If a government plan does not explicitly mention that Bumiputera economic interests will be promoted, UMNO fears that this may jeopardize its support from the Malay electorate, particularly from those in rural areas. Najib's dilemma is how to promote the idea of inclusive and supportive economic plans while promulgating policies or introducing institutions that have an ethnic slant. A review of ownership and control of the corporate sector would indicate the need for Najib to move away from targeted-based policies in his economic and enterprise development plans.

Assessing Policy Outcomes

In stark contrast to corporate ownership patterns in the 1960s (Puthucheary, 1960; Lim, 1981), at the end of 2009, there was no evidence of interlocking stock ownership involving business groups suggesting little concentration of control over the economy among the top 100 quoted firms (Gomez, 2009). No business group under the control of one family or individual dominates the top twenty. The state, through the GLCs, is a major owner of publicly listed equity. There is a high level of ownership concentration by an individual or a family only within a business group, primarily through intricate interlocking shareholdings, or pyramiding. Since there is no concentration of industry, capital remains extremely subservient to the state, while business associations play no prominent role in protecting their members' interests. The dominant presence of GLCs in the corporate sector indicates that the state, particularly the Prime Minister given his hegemonic position in government, has the capacity to dictate the pattern of enterprise development.

There is further evidence to corroborate the wide dispersal of equity ownership which further strengthens the state's capacity to dictate affairs in the corporate sector. Six of the top ten publicly listed companies in 2009 were GLCs. Only three of the top ten firms are Chinese owned. In spite of phenomenal state support for the development of Malay capital, not one of the top ten companies is owned by a Bumiputera. None of the top ten is owned by a foreign enterprise. Crucially too, no company in the top fifty is involved in new economic sectors such as information technology, biotechnology, agro-industries, pharmaceuticals, and medical services, in spite of the government's active efforts to promote these sectors (Gomez, 2009; Yusuf and Nabeshima, 2009).

That no company in the top ten is involved in industrial sector is an indication of the state's failure to develop huge enterprises with an active participation in manufacturing. Not one of the top 100 firms in the late 1960s has retained its position as a leading manufacturer. This suggests manufacturing firms of old have fallen behind in terms of investing in new plant and equipment, introducing novel products or pursuing new markets. This further suggests that large firms have hardly been in the forefront of promoting R&D, enhancing productivity, and encouraging innovation, a reason too for little evidence of industrial concentration.

Old capital in manufacturing has fallen behind because public policies have bypassed them or have undermined their activities. This factor contributed to businesspeople investing abroad, seen cogently in the case of Robert Kuok who remains Malaysia's richest business figure.[11] The diminishing presence of entrepreneurial old capital is serious as the state has failed to nurture a new cluster of industrial capitalists. Most Bumiputeras are in finance, construction, and property development, confirming that those who benefited from state patronage in the manufacturing and heavy industry sectors, including through the vendor system, have not managed to cultivate an industrial base.

The key reason why there is no evidence of concentration of corporate power is that well-connected firms that had emerged by mid-1990s, such as HICOM, Renong/UEM, and MAS, were taken over by the government or other well-connected firms because of disputes involving their political patrons or their own fall-out with state elites. This nexus of politics and business based on patronage and political loyalty had, inevitably, served to severely undermine the development of Bumiputera entrepreneurship.

Non-Bumiputeras have also had to tie up with influential politicians given the presence of a strong state. Chinese firms in the top twenty include the YTL Corp, Genting, Hong Leong, and Berjaya groups, enterprises that have been privy to state patronage. Three firms in the top twenty—Public Bank, PPB Group, and Kuala Lumpur-Kepong (KLK)—belong to corporate groups that have some semblance of political independence, but they are led by people or families with proven entrepreneurial skills. In all cases, these firms have formulated ties with politicians alone, not collectively, a key reason why big businesses have not had the capacity to stand up to the state.

A key feature of the top business groups is that they are family firms or are still founder led. Family firms constitute about 40 per cent of all publicly listed

---

[11] For an in-depth case study of Robert Kuok, see Gomez (1999). For a list of the richest businesspeople in Malaysia, see *Malaysian Business*, 16 February 2010.

companies. However, the extent to which the management of these firms has been professionalized, a core factor to help them escape the high middle income trap, specifically by investing in R&D, has not been addressed. In Taiwan, the professionalization of the management was a key factor in its industrialization process (Momoko, 2007). Given the highly diversified nature of these business groups, such as the Genting, Kuok Brothers, Usaha Tegas, Hong Leong, Berjaya, YTL Corp, MMC Corp, and Lion Group, there is an obvious need to incorporate professional managers to efficiently run the operations.

A crucial distinction is required here between an entrepreneurial firm and a managerial firm. The owners of some business groups make this demarcation clear, through the use of a holding company for entrepreneurial activities, while competent professionals manage their companies. These groups include Kuok Brothers, Hong Leong, and Usaha Tegas. Some leading family firms, such as KLK and YTL, are led by a professionally trained second generation.

What is obvious about these major groups is the heterogeneous nature through which they develop their enterprises, bringing into question the idea of a homogenous business system among ethnic Chinese or Asian businesspeople (see Whitley, 1992). The Hong Leong group is an example of growth through diversification, in manufacturing, property development, banking, and insurance. The group has created industrial–financial links, though the Hong Leong Bank does not have a direct stake in Hong Leong Industries. That the group has an 'in-house bank', akin to large groups in Japan (Johnson, 1982; Agnblad et al., 2001), suggests that this has helped it expand its international presence. This group has a managerial hierarchy, a pyramidal framework of managers with a top-down structure in which strategic decisions were made by top levels of management. This separation of ownership from management is important as seldom do managers reveal entrepreneurial capacity. In this pyramid shareholding system, however, there is no separation of ownership from control or full managerial discretion, as the owners still dictate key decisions such as investment or divestment of a firm or entry or exit from a key sector.

This suggests that separating ownership from management is crucial. There is, however, little indication of new organizational and technological gains among most enterprises, including the GLCs and family-owned firms. This is also no evidence of brand products being produced among the top fifty firms, with the possible exception of AirAsia.[12] This suggests that while product

---

[12] Brand products are emerging among smaller-sized firms, for example, Secret Recipe, Marry Brown, Bonia, and Royal Selangor. Brand products nurtured by foreign companies that have been acquired by Malaysian firms include Crabtree & Evelyn (KLK), Laura Ashley (MUI Group), and the South China Morning Post (Robert Kuok) (*Malaysian Business*, 1 December 2009).

innovation is important, organizational innovation is an issue that requires much consideration.

Malaysia in Comparative Perspective

The Malaysian state's attempt to selectively cultivate firms to drive industrialization and promote domestic enterprise is not unique. In the United States, the government accepted Alexander Hamilton's argument that during the economy's catching-up phase, it had to nurture and protect infant industries. In Germany, the government adopted Friedrich List's contention of its need to create and nurture a strong domestic business sector through systematic, but temporary, protection of infant industries. A similar pattern of state–business cooperation occurred in late nineteenth century Japan where the government built its own factories in key industries in an attempt to catch up with the West. These factories were subsequently sold by the state to favoured private businesses at low rates, with Mitsui and Mitsubishi developed through such state patronage. This system of patronage was again promoted after 1945 to rebuild the economy (Johnson, 1982). Similar state–capital linkages involving a focus on priority sectors to drive industrialization, promote domestic capital, and bring about structural change, including reducing poverty, have occurred in South Korea and Taiwan (Amsden, 1989; Wade, 1990; Evans, 1995).

While the US, German, and East Asian economies now have thriving industrial bases, in Malaysia, the state's developmentalism with neo-liberal policies has had serious economic repercussions, while its attempt to create *Bumiputera* entrepreneurial firms through affirmative action, especially in the industrial sector, has failed. Selective patronage was not exercised in a transparent manner with the primary criteria being the need to 'pick winners' in a particular sector. The state's stress on targeting firms for selective patronage along ethnic lines tempered its choice of the 'winners'. According preferential treatment to one ethnic community, at least during the early years when the state began its pursuit of heavy industrialization, undermined the development of domestic firms.

And, unlike Japan, South Korea, and Taiwan, but similar to other more developed Southeast Asian economies, Malaysia heavily cultivated foreign capital to drive industrialization. In Malaysia's case, this was to ensure that Chinese capital did not secure ascendancy in the economy as well as to provide the state with time to cultivate Malay entrepreneurs. Malaysia's form of governance, specifically executive hegemony in government as well as UMNO's dominance over coalition partners in the Barisan Nasional, led to unproductive political–business ties, while also contributing to the state's failure to develop large, Malay-owned firms.

A number of well-connected and preferentially treated Malaysian firms developed business strategies that were heavily influenced by their easy access to funds, from banks as well as the stock market; this factor eventually worked to their detriment. In Japan, firms created with banks an interlocking owner-ship relationship that aided the implementation of long-term business strategies (Dore, 2000). Japan's pattern of industrial growth was not replicated in Malaysia—or in Southeast Asia—though a large proportion of loans came from state-owned banks. Moreover, the state did not monitor these loans, nor was there sufficient regulation to ensure that banks disbursed loans in a fashion that conformed to the dictates of government policies.

While the state–business links created in South Korea and Japan to develop entrepreneurial firms facilitated the rise of internationally recognized companies, such ties have not been as successful in Malaysia. Some companies with state patronage have emerged as enterprises with foreign business ventures, including the gaming firm, Genting; financial services provider, Public Bank; as well as the business groups owned by Kuok, Ananda Krishnan, Francis Yeoh, Quek Leng Chan, and William Cheng. The failure of local enterprises supported by the Malaysian state to internationalize can be attributed to lax supervision of the financial sector and an unsustainable form of corporate growth through debt, as well as cronyism, corruption, and nepotism (see Yoshihara, 1988; Searle, 1999; Gomez, 2002).

That the leading Bumiputera firms are GLCs, in spite of privatization and affirmative action, is an indication of the poor state of privately owned Malay capital. These GLCs have not shown the ability to deal with the MNCs with whom joint ventures in heavy industries were created. In these joint ventures, the GLCs appeared concerned only with advancing industrialization, not developing entrepreneurial capacity. An attempt to promote managerial capitalism, in the Chandlerian tradition, would enhance the capacity of the GLCs to function far more productively in the economy (Chandler, 1977). After all, GLCs in South Korea, such as POSCO, have similarly driven industrialization, while Taiwan's early endeavours in this area during the 1950s were led by state enterprises. In spite of active privatization, by 1990, six of Taiwan's top ten companies, in terms of assets, were GLCs. The leading domestic enterprises in Singapore and China are GLCs.

In Malaysia, a factor contributing to the limited number of large industrial firms is the pattern of growth of these enterprises, involving conglomerate-style acquisitions and an overdependence on loans to expand. The emergence of a diversified pattern of growth through loans can be attributed to state policies, specifically those dealing with the control and use of the financial sector to promote corporate expansion. This pattern became a popular strategy among large firms due to the desire of businesspeople to venture into any field that promised quick profits or had potentially strong consumer demand. A problem with firms adopting this pattern of growth was the considerable overdiversification of their corporate base, funded primarily by short-term loans and foreign portfolio investments. The core businesses of a number of businesspeople who adopted this growth model were severely impaired by the 1997 crisis, an experience that helped them cope better with the 2008 financial meltdown. This suggests the business style of many of these firms and the manner of their growth—whether a vertical, horizontal, or diversified pattern was employed— are factors determining their capacity to deal with economic crises.

Since policies to cultivate entrepreneurial firms have long been tempered with the need to promote Bumiputera capital, a crucial goal of affirmative action, this has impacted negatively on non-Malay businesses, curbing their willingness to invest further in their enterprise. Non-Bumiputeras are reluctant to spend on R&D and learn new technology for fear that ethnic-based policies would work against them as they develop their ventures. This inadequate investment in R&D is the reason for the presence of only a handful of large entrepreneurial firms with a long corporate history and for the demise of firms owned by some of Malaysia's leading businesspeople. Trust in the government's willingness to protect property rights is missing, inhibiting risk taking and thus curbing entrepreneurial ventures.

However, this mix of policies to fashion the development of domestic firms may not have been detrimental to the economy had public institutions been allowed to ensure transparency and accountability in the award of rents, and if race had not figured as a criterion in the award of these rents. An attempt was made to connect these businesses in the industrial sector with financial capital. This was crucial as leading enterprises in East Asia, specifically in Japan and South Korea, have shown how a strong link between industrial and financial capital was crucial in nurturing a dynamic domestic entrepreneurial base. And, some non-Malay firms that had obtained state rents went on to acquire an international presence. However, even these Malaysian firms do not have the technological base of large MNCs that have emerged in East Asia, specifically in Japan and South Korea. This is a major concern as these large East Asian enterprises have been responsible for accelerating technological upgrading as well as promoting innovation (Yusuf and Nabeshima, 2009: 139).

The ownership structure employed by these firms also provides insights into the small number of innovative enterprises. This assessment of Malaysian firms suggests that their organizational structure, investment strategies, and productive capabilities are conditioned by the context in which they operate (Lazonick, 2003: 33). Firms with more R&D intensity face potentially greater losses from public policies though they are aware that such investment is crucial to further the process of innovation.

The need to support R&D is imperative because even large firms have not invested sufficiently in this area. The need to concentrate on R&D to allow for domestic enterprises to grow is crucial if local firms are to emerge as key global suppliers. Malaysia's R&D spending as a share of GDP was 0.95 per cent, a growth compared to 0.4 per cent in the late 1990s, though still very much behind other East Asian countries such as Japan (3.4 per cent), Singapore (2.39 per cent), and South Korea (3.23 per cent) (Yusuf and Nabeshima, 2009: 160). But to encourage progressive R&D, there has to be little fear among domestic investors of expropriation due to affirmative action. The pyramiding holding structure utilized by owners of family- and privately owned firms is one outcome of the need to employ mechanisms to protect their corporate interest with a limited amount of capital while leveraging control of these enterprises.

The history of East Asia further indicates that political reforms, when they happened, had positive outcomes in the corporate sector. The Kuomintang (KMT), for example, has relinquished its vast ownership over key sectors of the economy following its electoral defeat. Such outcomes in Taiwan indicate the need for institutional reforms, specifically devolution of power to autonomous agencies to check corruption; this point is evident in other East Asian countries such as South Korea. This indicates that political institutions and their functioning are key factors which shape investment patterns and the outcomes of policies that serve to nurture domestic enterprise.

The economic downturn in Malaysia and elsewhere in East Asia has shown the need to get public policies right to ensure sustainable and equitable growth, though it appears that in cases where neo-liberal policies have been employed, the outcomes have been particularly dire. In Malaysia, the added problem that Prime Minister Najib faces is finding a way to introduce meaningful institutional reforms to ensure checks and balances in the economy, as he does not have the support of his party, UMNO, on this matter. Meanwhile, Najib has to infuse confidence among investors that their ownership of an enterprise will be protected. However, no meaningful institutional reforms are even being considered, an indication of the authoritarian nature of Malaysia's political system.

Najib has to resolve this problem because the key lesson here is the importance of policies, specifically as its mix, including affirmative action to foster domestic enterprise, have hindered the emergence of entrepreneurial firms. Najib has numerous factors in his favour that would facilitate conducive and swift structural change: no concentration of corporate wealth in an elite; well-capitalized, government-controlled banks as well as the strong presence of GLCs in key economic sectors, though a merit-based professional management is required to help the state direct growth effectively; and well-placed bureaucratic institutions equipped to aid entrepreneurial SMEs, a core factor to encourage innovation and entrepreneurship from the bottom. To get these factors to work in tandem, the economic and business history of East Asia indicates that the following are imperative: respect of property rights through legislation that protects business ownership; institutional reforms that ensure checks and balances; and a compact comprising state, capital, and labour that encourages dialogue. Failing this, the investor confidence that is vital to nurture forms of innovative entrepreneurship that can get Malaysia out of the high middle income trap is unlikely to occur.

Part Three
Labour Markets and Industrial Relations

5

Reform and Institutional Change in East Asian Labour Markets[1]

Frederic C. Deyo

This chapter examines trajectories of labour market changes in East Asia since the 1980s. It compares four countries that present widely varied developmental contexts within which reform has been implemented: China, a case of post-Socialist market reform in a low-income country; Korea, a high-income country transitioning from export manufacturing into information and service-based industries; the Philippines, an economically more stagnant country whose early and more sustained market reform has been driven in larger measure by the conditions of external debt and economic vulnerability; and Thailand, a capitalist, lower-middle-income developing country now seeking to transition into high-value niches of world markets. My focus is on the industrial sectors in these four countries, a choice dictated by the critical role manufacturing has played, and continues to play, in the development 'miracles' of the region.[2]

In the context of these four countries, and returning to the characterization of pre-1980s Asian economic regimes in Chapter 1 of this volume, I first ask how market-oriented reform has both reflected and altered the labour market regimes associated with state-domination in China, state–business co-governance in Korea, and personalism/clientelism in the Philippines and Thailand. I then seek to explain the divergent trajectories of labour market regimes in these countries by reference to economic pressures, elite economic interests, and political pressures, arguing in this regard that even in this

---

[1] This chapter draws on 'The Deregulatory Face of Labor Reform.' In *Reforming Asian Labor Systems: Economic Tensions and Worker Dissent* by Frederic C. Deyo. Copyright © 2012 by Cornell University. Used by permission of the publisher, Cornell University Press.

[2] As a per cent of world manufacturing, value-added, Asian manufacturing continues to grow: rising from 11.2 per cent in 1995 to 20.1 per cent in 2008.

'labour-weak' region, labour politics have played an important if varied role in pushing reform trajectories towards greater social protections and accommodation, particularly following the late 1990s regional financial/economic crisis.

Divergent Patterns of Labour Market Changes

China

Until the early 1980s, Chinese labour 'markets' hardly existed at all. Strict residency rules (the *houkou* system) largely confined workers to local residence both by denying them protection and social services outside their home districts and by discouraging their employment in other places. Urban jobs were generally allocated by local offices of the Ministry of Labor. State-owned enterprises (SOEs), wherein workers were generally guaranteed lifetime jobs, employed over three-quarters of the urban workforce (NBSC, 1996). Work units (*danwei*) were given little latitude in the selection of employees, workers generally stayed with the same work unit for many years, and job mobility was low.

Post-1978 reform brought dramatic and continuing changes to this state-led system. Under the household responsibility system, implemented in 1984, rural families were able to diversify income sources and establish non-agricultural enterprises, thus encouraging an employment shift from agriculture into rural services and industry. As well, the greater economic freedom now enjoyed by rural families encouraged increased rural–urban migration, although lack of secure title to land alongside lack of legal access to urban services continued to encourage migratory workers to return home on a seasonal basis.

Rural reform was paralleled by labour-market deregulation within the SOE sector itself. As described in Chapter 1 of this volume, workers in the still dominant state enterprise sector enjoyed long-term employment and extensive, if shallow, rights to housing, health protection, pensions, and training opportunities, but within a context of tightly controlled unions and lack of voice in the organization of work. But this system began to disintegrate under mid-decade SOE reforms. Under the 1986 legislation, newly hired SOE workers joined workers in foreign-invested and foreign-owned enterprises in China's special economic zones in working under fixed-duration employment contracts (Chen, 2003: 112; World Bank, 2006: 123), a departure from earlier practice, and one that fostered increased labour flexibility while at the same time retaining some job security for older workers. In cases of outright enterprise sale to private investors, even workers with many years of service found themselves working on a temporary basis or under one-year contracts. In this regard, Chen and Hou (2008) estimate that temporary workers comprise a larger proportion (roughly

50 per cent) of workers in private firms than in either foreign-invested firms or state enterprises, thus suggesting that the substantial reduction in SOE employment has increased the ranks of temporary employment. In a separate survey, they report that only 23.2 per cent of formal sector workers had the status of 'regular' workers. Further, it is estimated that by 1990, 18 per cent of SOE workers were fixed-term contract workers (Naughton, 1995), a percentage that continued to rise thereafter under 1994 legislative change that mandated extension of fixed-term labour contracts to all workers other than SOE workers with over ten years' seniority (Chen and Hou, 2008). From 1992, SOE managers were given further discretionary rights in setting prices and wages, and in hiring and firing. Under these and other legislative changes, earlier mandated worker benefits including schooling, housing, and medical assistance were to be phased out in order to enhance the operational competitiveness and employment flexibility of firms. Finally, under the terms of entry into the WTO, local governments were urged to relax private sector labour codes in order to enhance operating flexibility (ADB, 2005: 62).

A final indication that Chinese labour markets have undergone continuing deregulation is data showing a marked decline, stretching over nearly two decades, in the per cent of manufacturing workers in 'paid' employment (vs. own-account work and unpaid family labour), from 60 per cent in the early 1990s to less than 30 per cent in the mid-2000s, when self-employed workers accounted for nearly 70 per cent of all manufacturing workers (Deyo, forthcoming). This decline in paid employment, while an uncertain proxy for informalization, suggests at a minimum a shrinking pool of workers for whom formal protections are a real possibility. In this regard, Chen and Hou (2008; see also Solinger, 1999) note a gradual increase in Chinese informal sector work, estimating that between 1996 and 2001 the ratio of informal to formal sector workers increased from 1:4 to 1:2 in response to growing numbers of rural migrant workers and other workers laid off by state enterprises. This indirect indication of growing informalization is also supported by the ADB's (Asian Development Bank) more systematic research suggesting that the retrenchment of SOE (formal sector) workers combined with an easing of restrictions on rural–urban migration has increased the extent of China's informal sector employment (ADB, 2005).

Finally, one should note the devolution of regulatory controls to municipal and local levels, and to the governing boards of expanding export-processing zones, as part of China's integration into international markets. This devolution of responsibility, part of a larger policy of local reform experimentation, eventuates in substantial local autonomy in managing labour markets. This devolution has sometimes disadvantaged workers, who now increasingly confront local and municipal officials whose interests are often closely aligned with those of local and foreign employers.

But before concluding that labour market reform has had the effect of fundamentally 'deregulating' Chinese labour markets, several cautionary observations are in order. First, labour market deregulation has in fact been only partial. Rural workers may now legally travel to urban industrial areas for work, eventuating in the presence by 2006 of 150 million migrant workers (roughly 11.5 per cent of the total population) in cities. Nonetheless, such migration remains tightly controlled, inasmuch as workers must obtain government-issued temporary residence permits to live and work in urban zones, and return to their home districts upon loss of employment. Until very recently, migration has been further restricted by rules denying migrants access to a variety of social services and benefits enjoyed by permanent local residents; harassment by local police in cases of labour disturbances; and a variety of management abuses, discussed below, encouraged by these same restrictions.

Second, it was noted that SOE labour market reform has, in conformity with a more general policy of 'gradualism', been incrementally introduced. The labour contract system does not change terms of employment for workers hired before 1992, and numerous other legal provisions have softened the bite of the market for laid-off workers, including continuance of pay without work, the seconding of released workers to other firms, and other social safety net policies to be discussed below. In this regard, Chen and Hou (2008) note that of the 28 million SOE workers laid off between 1998 and 2005, 19 million received re-employment through a variety of forms of public assistance.

Third, Chinese labour legislation continues to offer a broad range of formal labour protections, including, inter alia, employment contracts; the option for workers with at least ten years' seniority to shift to non-fixed-term, regular contracts; restriction of probationary employment status to six months; restrictions on dismissal including severance payments and prior notice; minimum wage requirements; limitations on working hours; and occupational and safety rules.[3] But while these legislative protections are in principle quite progressive, their substantive impact is reduced by a growing body of legal exemptions available to firms and local officials relating to economic contingencies, competitive pressures, and the like. This is in addition to widespread gaps in local enforcement. Thus, while formal legislative protections remain substantial, de facto protections have become ever weaker, thus enhancing the flexibility of actual employment even among formal sector workers.

Fourth, of course, is the important observation so often neglected in state-centric accounts of labour market deregulation, that state agencies and

---

[3] For a useful review, see World Bank. *Doing Business 2007: How to Reform*. New York: World Bank, 2006. Also Gaelle Pierre and Stefano Scarpetta (2004), 'How labor market policy can combine workers' protection and job creation'. Background Paper for the WDR, 2005: partially reproduced in World Bank, *World Development Report*, 2005, pp. 145 and 147. Also see a formal codification of these protections in China's new Labor Contract Law that took effect 1 January 2008.

regulatory regimes comprise but one element in functioning regulatory orders. As important are a host of societal organizations, networks, and regulatory structures that continue to function even under the most dirigiste governmental regimes. Chen and Hou (2008; see also Lee, 1998) cite the findings of a recent worker survey showing the continued, if diminished, importance of worker networks of friendship, kinship, and home locality in organizing job search and mutual assistance even amidst otherwise disorderly labour markets.

Fifth, and finally, in response to growing numbers of worker disputes and protests, and to broader patterns of social instability, governing elites, particularly at national levels, have sought to provide new or expanded social safety nets for the increasing numbers of workers either displaced from the shrinking state enterprise sector or subject to the insecurities and hardships of casualized and temporary work in expanding industrial zones. In this context, the central government is now launching a new social insurance fund to cover unemployment, pension, sickness, worker compensation, and maternity. The fund is to this point limited to a very small percentage of the working population, fails to cover the large number of migrant urban workers flooding into urban export zones, and has been compromised by entrenched corruption (Chen, 2003). It nonetheless signals a new awareness of and institutional response to emergent social tensions which are widely perceived as threatening a situation of 'ungovernability'.

Korea

During the 1980s, and as discussed in Chapter 1 of this volume, South Korean labour markets functioned within a context of authoritarian state guidance; concentrated corporate ownership; and coercively controlled, state-regulated unionism. At the same time, however, a range of important protections among formal sector workers in large firms served to stabilize labour relations. Among those workers, job security was promoted through restrictions embodied in the Labor Standards Act on the rights of companies with more than five employees to fire workers without establishing just cause, thus legally buttressing a long-standing tradition of lifetime employment in large firms (World Bank, 2006). In addition, the Korean government, in part to compensate politically restive workers for the privations of repressive industrial relations policies (Yang and Moon, 2005), instituted labour regulations to protect wages and working conditions. While in practice, largely confined to the ranks of regular workers in large firms, these various provisions placed Korea among the top OECD countries in terms of the strictness of employment protection (Kim et al., 2000; Yang and Moon, 2005). Given this historical background, it is not surprising that efforts in the late 1990s to deregulate Korean labour markets would become so politically charged.

At the same time, under repressive military-based rule from the early 1970s to the late 1980s, Korea's 'productivist' labour regimes sought to bolster exports and economic growth in part through strict controls over workers and unions. Such restrictions, while directed primarily at the labour process, had the indirect effect of containing labour costs and thus distorting labour markets in support of export promotion. Under labour market deregulation, such direct state intervention in the labour process was later to give way to fuller reliance on the less visible but equally effective discipline of the market.

In December 1996, the Kim Young Sam government passed legislation easing lay-off requirements for regular employers and making it easier to replace union with non-union workers.[4] The new legislation, contained in an amendment to the Labor Standards Act of 1997, weakened a long-standing tradition of job security among formal sector workers in larger firms by permitting employers to dismiss workers for 'economic' reasons, such as the need to reduce costs and enhance competitiveness (Kang et al., 2001).[5] In addition, the new legislation permitted more flexible work hours and freer use of temporary workers, while also legalizing the 'leasing out' of employees to other firms. Beginning in 1998, further legislation contained in the Dispatched Workers Act opened the way for a proliferation of manpower placement firms to hire out temporary workers for periods of up to two years in twenty-six occupations requiring special skills and experience (Yang and Moon, 2005). That same year, restrictions were eased on employment under fixed-term contracts, while firms were granted increased power to engage in collective dismissals for 'managerial reasons', although such dismissals continued to require government approval. Subsequent Supreme Court rulings reduced employment protections in cases of mergers and acquisitions. In this regard, Yang and Moon (2005) document a decline in the ranks of regular workers, both overall and in manufacturing specifically, alongside increased reliance on temporary and daily workers between 1996 and 2000, following which the percentage of non-regular workers remained relatively stable. In the context of high levels of open unemployment during the financial crisis, these various deregulatory measures were defended as increasing employment by reducing impediments to labour mobility (Kang et al., 2001: 106). In part too, increased labour market flexibility was linked to official efforts to shift Korea's economy more decisively towards 'knowledge-based' industries and to attract increased direct foreign investment.

---

[4] In the face of protracted labour opposition, this legislation only came into effect in 2003.

[5] These labour market changes are often attributed to IMF pressures during the late 1990s economic crisis. In fact, earlier enabling legislation began in 1989, and the new lay-off rules were introduced in 1996, before the crisis.

In actuality, the new legislation did not entirely deregulate labour markets. A range of other provisions continued to protect regular, formal-sector workers, including requirements that lay-offs and dismissals could only be taken for 'justifiable reason', a sixty-day required notice of termination, limits on the duration of fixed-term employment contracts, provision of severance pay, and the like (ADB, 2005). But since many of these protections were restricted to regular, long-term workers and did not extend to irregular and part-time workers or to workers in very small firms,[6] they tended to encourage many firms to replace regular with non-regular workers, thus effectively undercutting the bargaining power of regular workers. In the context of increasing reliance on skilled and technical labour in Korea's advanced industries, the choice was less often to casualize labour than to find new ways to combine flexibility with high levels of worker skill, commitment, and initiative. In part, this was accomplished in traditional ways, by offering skilled, core-function workers good pay, job security, and advancement opportunities within internal labour markets, thus effectively re-regulating labour markets by partially embedding them within organizational and career hierarchies. Here, labour flexibility was to be achieved less by 'numerical' flexibility in external labour markets than by 'functional' flexibilities deriving from continuous, multi-skill training and adaptable work organization and technology. But if this high-road labour strategy comprised one means of combining flexibility with high-value labour, another increasingly common strategy is to hire technical labour under generous but fixed-duration individual contracts. This second, increasingly common approach extends employment contingency to the growing ranks of skilled and technical labour.

A final, though important, note relates to growing numbers of low-skill immigrant workers among whom casual labour is more often the rule. Most such workers find work in small-enterprise-based manufacturing, construction, and fishing enterprises that are unable to meet the growing costs of employing Korean workers. These immigrant workers, estimated at one-third million in the early 2000s, cannot legally be hired as regular employees. Rather they must remain 'trainees' on three-year contracts, and are largely precluded from the protections and benefits accruing either to regular workers or to skilled contract workers (US Department of Labour, 2003).

Of the four countries included in this study, only South Korea has moved aggressively to institute a comprehensive social insurance program, largely in response to strong union pressure. Under Korea's Employment Insurance System (EIS), laid-off workers receive modest pay for a designated period of time, conditional upon their availability for retraining and job placement.

---

[6] Of less than five workers, thus excluding roughly one-third of all Korean workers. See Lim, Kim, and Kim (2003).

Even using the relatively stringent criterion of coverage under injury compensation insurance,[7] over two-thirds of Korean manufacturing workers were insured from the 1980s on (64 per cent in 1988, 68 per cent in 2004), with approximately 40 per cent of the *total* workforce covered during those years (34 per cent in 1988, 46 per cent in 2004). Similarly, unemployment insurance covered 40 per cent of manufacturing workers in 1995, and 64 per cent in 2004 (KNSO).

Korea, of course, stands out as one of the 'miracle' economies of the region. What of the other economies where economic upgrading has only recently become a possibility and where irregular, casual, and short-term contractual labour has played a noticeably greater role?

The Philippines

This country shares with Thailand a very large informal sector of small, family-based firms within which hiring and worker discipline are based on personal and family relationships. In larger, formal-sector firms, workers in principle enjoy a broader range of legal protections and benefits, but these are largely at the discretion of employers (see Chapter 1 in this volume), given serious problems of lack of enforcement of existing labour legislation and a fragmented, ineffectual trade unionism largely unable to protect the interests of workers. A portrayal of labour market reform in such a context must therefore take into account the important regulatory role of personalized relations and networks (vs. state law) in the actual functioning of labour markets.[8]

To the somewhat circumscribed extent that national labour legislation did regulate private sector labour markets among formal sector workers in larger firms, it was modelled after US labour legislation. Until the 1972 declaration of martial law by President Marcos, Philippine legislation was both progressive and protective. And even under martial law, the 1974 Labor Code provided strong employment protections for workers, regulating employment contracts, minimum wage, limitations on temporary employment, advance notice of termination, statutory protections from arbitrary dismissal, etc. While the Labor Code also provided guidelines for collective bargaining and tripartite deliberations, those guidelines were largely ignored until passage of a new post-martial law constitution in 1987 (ADB, 2005).

The recent experience of labour deregulation in the Philippines must be understood in the somewhat unique political context of early labour

---

[7] This includes medical care, sick leave, disability insurance, survivors' benefits, and funeral benefits.

[8] This statement applies more fully to the private sector than to state enterprises, where the regulatory role of the state is more substantial.

mobilization, followed by autocratic repression and then a new politicization associated with the popular mid-1980s revolt against the Marcos regime. In this politically charged context, recent labour 'deregulation' has only in part taken the form of the de jure, legislative rescinding of earlier protections. Under 1989 revisions to the 1974 Labor Code, restrictions on subcontracting were eased, and job security was compromised under new rules that permit lay-offs in cases of technological displacement, economic redundancy, retrenchment to permit losses, and plant closings, but with the important safeguard that those lay-offs require official approval.[9] Reflective of these changes are data reported by the ADB showing increases in the percentage of 'non-regular' Philippine workers from approximately 20 per cent of the total workforce in 1991 to 28 per cent in 1997, 30.6 per cent in 1998, and 32 per cent in 2004 (ADB, 2005). Similarly, Sibal and Amente (2008) find a continuing trend towards contract labour beginning in the 1990s (doubling between 1991 and 1997) and continuing into the early 2000s. These changes were accompanied by continuing declines in inflation-adjusted, real minimum wage rates, and selective but widespread non-enforcement (versus rescinding) of earlier, protective labour legislation (McKay, 2006: 15–16), thus both permitting and encouraging very high rates of non-compliance by firms (ADB, 2005).[10] Further de facto deregulation was achieved through the covert reclassification and misclassification of large numbers of workers as non-regular, contractual, and temporary, thus permitting employers to evade existing worker protections that apply only to regular workers by shifting reclassified workers into labour systems less encumbered by protective legislation (Quintos, 2003). These practices contribute to a larger problem of selective non-enforcement rooted in part in the corrupt networks of personalism that characterize relations between firms and official agencies, as discussed in Chapter 1 of this volume.

If these changes have eventuated in de facto 'deregulation' at the level of national legislation and enforcement, they have thus also been associated with a new regulatory augmentation at local levels. Most important were a devolution (as in China) of economic and labour regulation to local levels of government, and a quasi-privatization of labour regulation to new governing bodies in export-processing zones and strategic industrial centres in both cases justified as enhancing the adaptability of firms and at making labour markets more flexible and responsive to local circumstances. Several legislative changes highlight this regulatory/scalar shift. In 1990, minimum wage determination was shifted from the National Wages Council to regional tripartite

---

[9] Both collective and individual dismissals still require government approval. See ADB (2005: 56).
[10] The ADB estimates that roughly one-half of all firms were in non-compliance with major provisions of labour law during the 1990s.

wage and productivity boards, even as the government tends not to enforce existing minimum wages.[11] Export-processing zones in particular were progressively freed from direct central controls, and were increasingly privatized and governed by semi-autonomous regulatory boards, especially the Philippine Economic Zone Authority (PEZA). PEZA has assumed a particularly prominent role in matters of labour recruitment, worker housing, management of labour relations, and labour control in communities (McKay, 2006: 60). The devolution and privatization of labour regimes, a core element of reform, has the primary effect less of deregulating than of rescaling social regulation in ways that enhance flexibility, empower local governmental elites and firms, and establish a more indirect government role in creating regulatory regimes within which local elites assume the primary role in managing the workforce.

Finally, what of the implications of the Philippines' labour export strategy? Hutchison notes that in 2003, 3.85 million Filipinos (roughly 10 per cent of total employment) were working temporarily on fixed-term contracts overseas. A substantial portion of other overseas workers, whose inclusion brings the grand total to 25 per cent of total employment, work on an irregular basis, in many cases in informal sectors in construction, entertainment, domestic service, and manufacturing sweat shops. In some instances, as in the entertainment industry, these workers may participate in illegal, bonded labour systems. Data presented by Hutchison, based on Philippine Overseas Employment Agency (POEA) figures for 2003 (Hutchison, 2006), suggest the presence of large numbers of temporary workers in the Middle East, and East and Southeast Asia, and of 'irregular' workers heavily concentrated in Asia and the United States. This implies that labour export policies, part of a larger export-development strategy, may have the indirect, structural deregulatory outcome of enlarging informal employment sectors that do not appear in official Philippine data. Conversely, of course, it must be recalled that substantial numbers of expatriate Filipinos are employed in professional or semi-professional positions in information technology, health care, law, and other fields. The major difference between these 'contingent' workers and more casualized Filipino workers is that they are typically employed under more generous, secure contracts.

Thailand

The regulation of Thai labour markets takes a variety of forms, of which three are most relevant here. First, public sector employment in the civil services and in SOEs is on the one hand formally regulated by rules governing pay grades,

---

[11] Hutchison (2006: 52) estimates that lax government minimum wage enforcement results in below minimum wages for some 60 per cent of the workforce.

employment security, health and retirement programs, and other protective measures, and on the other, more informally by vertical networks of personal loyalty and clientelism, as made clear in Chapter 1 of this volume, through which career advancement is often secured. Second, and in the wake of widening student and worker militancy during the early 1970s, new legislation established a tripartite Central Wage Committee to set minimum wages, a worker compensation program, and the beginnings of a national social insurance program that was to be expanded in later years. More recently, the Labour Protection Act of 1998 requires that all firms offer twenty-five-day severance pay; injury compensation[12] for permanent workers; and a range of additional benefits including holiday pay, overtime pay, sick leave, pregnancy/maternity pay, and payment priority in case of bankruptcy (Brown, 2003: 258–9). Of particular importance here, reliance on mandatory severance pay, while reducing labour market flexibility by imposing costs on firms that dismiss regular workers (ADB, 2005; Caraway, 2007), is justified as reducing public pressure for unemployment relief, a rationale often voiced in the Philippines as well.

While in principle these protections have defined a fairly comprehensive social safety net, they are restricted to non-agricultural (Brown, 2003: 259) formal sector workers, thus failing to cover major segments of the workforce including a huge informal sector of small firms, agricultural labourers, home-based workers, etc. Further, increased competitive pressures have pushed Thai employers to hire larger numbers of contingent workers in order to enhance flexibility, reduce costs, and forestall unionization (Lawler and Suttawet, 2000).

As important, very weak and inadequate enforcement of existing legislation has imparted more flexibility to this system than one might conclude from formal statistics and legislative provisions.[13] Pay flexibility has always been substantial, given union weaknesses in collective bargaining on the one hand, and very low (and thus often substantively irrelevant) minimum wage rates on the other. That private sector labour markets have in fact been quite 'wage-flexible' in recent years is suggested by substantial private sector pay reductions (alongside layoffs) averaging 20–40 per cent during Thailand's late 1990s financial crisis (Birdsall and Haggard, 2002; Athukorala et al., 2000: 44). Further, wage flexibility was further enhanced under the 1998 legislation decentralizing tripartite wage setting to provincial and local bodies. And

---

[12] A Workers' Compensation Fund, with mandatory company contributions, was established in 1970s The Asian Development Bank (ADB, 2005) notes Thailand's relative high mandated severance awards.

[13] The author spent a day with a government labour inspections officer visiting factories in Khonkaen, a city in Thailand's Northeast, during 1994. Virtually all the factories were in violation of some health, safety, pay, or worker benefits provisions of labour legislation in effect that year. None of these violations, however, resulted in immediate further government action. While filing the day's reports at her office later that day, the labour inspector explained that to take action against these firms would have compromised their profitability.

finally, as in China, legislative coverage is quite limited. Not only are workers in the huge informal sector excluded but the Labour Protection Act of 1998 also specifically excludes the huge category of agricultural workers.

To the limited extent Thai workers are in fact covered by employment protections, this legislation has had the predictable consequence of encouraging private sector employers to restrict the number of workers legally qualifying as eligible permanent staff, and to rotate many other workers through extended periods of temporary, casual, and probationary employment, thus effectively bypassing existing regulatory requirements while also further enlarging the unprotected informal sector itself. Such efforts to avoid expensive legislative mandates eventuates in marked labour market dualism, reflected in substantial differences in the terms of employment and job security of permanent large-firm employees on the one hand, and other workers (including those in small and family-based firms) on the other. Of course, this dualism might have been even more pronounced had existing labour legislation been more vigorously enforced during this period.

The Thai reform experience up to very recent times might best be described as one of expanding formal protections for a small segment of the workforce, especially public sector workers, while engendering huge gaps in effective private sector coverage even among workers nominally covered by social insurance and other protective labour legislation. In this context, labour market 'deregulation' resides less in legislative reform than in non-enforcement and in the informal practices of employers (especially in small and medium-sized firms) as they confront growing market pressures under economic deregulation, trade liberalization, and intensified competition.

Social Insurance and Its Recent Expansion

It has been noted that social insurance programs have played an important role in East Asian social policy over recent years, particularly following the late 1990s financial crisis. This augmentation in worker social protections, best seen in China and Korea, may be understood by reference to two critical drivers of labour market policy: the first relating to economic agendas and requirements, and the second to political pressures from workers. This section addresses the changing influence of each of these drivers of workers protections.

Changing Economic Agendas

Social insurance programs, while in principle directed at livelihood security and the socialization of market risk, are in fact consonant with market reform insofar as they institutionalize worker protections in (legally enforceable) private employment contracts, funded by employers and workers rather than by the state. In part for this reason, these programs have been encouraged by the International Labour Organization (ILO) and International Financial Institutions (IFIs) as fostering labour market flexibility, providing short-term support as workers seek alternate training and employment, and replacing a direct government fiscal role with a more indirect regulatory role. In these senses, these as yet largely underdeveloped programs of social protection may be viewed as institutional complementarities to market-oriented reform, rather than as compensations for market failures, and as enhancing, rather than reducing labour market flexibility itself.

This conclusion relates closely to a broader issue traditionally highlighted in the literature on East Asian social policy: that of welfare 'productivism'. A productivist depiction of Asian social policy is rooted in a broader model of developmentalism within which states employ economic and social policy largely in pursuit of economic goals (see Holliday and Wilding, 2003; Kwon, 2005b). For this reason, productivist social policy centres on human capital formation (e.g. education and training), productivity, and the management or suppression of labour conflict. But here, the imprint of market reform suggests an important distinction between two substantive orientations of regulatory regimes: developmentalism and market augmentation. The tendential 1990s shift from developmentalism in some East Asian countries (e.g. Korea) to a greater emphasis on market augmentation and market-led global integration suggests that social security, basic livelihood protections, and even human capital investments are increasingly driven by efforts to encourage a deepened incorporation of the workforce into more flexible labour markets, rather than mainly by the needs of developmental upgrading. This shift, perhaps best illustrated by Korea's EIS program, fundamentally redefines the focus of the third substantive orientation of social policy: livelihood protections. Such protections are now less focused on compensating workers for market risk or loss of employment than by efforts to flexibilize markets by maintaining, retraining, and moving mobile and now more contingent workers from one job to another on a regular basis (Jayasuriya, 2006).

The Impact of Labour Politics

But if new social programs and protections have been implemented and function in part to enhance the institutional flexibility of labour markets, they have responded to political pressures as well, pressures that have influenced the ways in which the problematic social outcomes of reform have been addressed. The deregulatory aspects of labour market reform, alongside other structural reforms, have frequently brought employment insecurity and contingency, increased work intensification to meet heightened competitive pressures, growing economic inequality, a commodification of social services and protections such as to exclude large numbers of low-paid workers, and a more general transfer of market risk from states to working-class families themselves. In this context, it is to be expected that enhanced social policy has in part been driven by demands on the part of politically mobilized workers and popular sector groups.[14]

It will be recalled that the social insurance programs discussed to this point are largely confined to formal sector, 'regular' workers. In part, this problem, and the growing political pressures which have given it increased prominence in public policy, has been addressed through a broadening of protections beyond the ranks of formal sector workers, and in part through creation of new forms of livelihood support. In this regard, China has begun to expand the existing enterprise-based social security net to include greater numbers of workers, including self-employed workers on a voluntary basis. As important, beginning in 1997, a new Minimum Livelihood Guarantee scheme has been implemented for the disabled and poor, initially in response to growing protests among laid-off SOE workers. This program has been accompanied by other initiatives, including reduced school and medical fees and taxes in rural areas and increased rights on the part of urban migrant workers to housing, education, and medical care. These varied programs have been publically supported and justified by reference to growing problems of social instability.

In South Korea, the increasing numbers of irregular (part-time, temporary, casual) workers, alongside their now-legal representation by trade unions under democratic reforms, has been met by an extension of EIS and other social insurance benefits to unemployed and non-regular workers. And for those still ineligible for those benefits, Korean's Livelihood Protection Program, initially established in 1961, was expanded in 1998 to cover 2.5 per cent of the population, and subsequently further enlarged to provide assistance and loans to persons not yet covered by the EIS.

While workers in the Philippines and Thailand, many of whom work in small and family-based firms, lack the political or union-based influence of their Korean counterparts, they too have played an important role in pushing for an extension of social protections to the great majority of workers employed in the informal sectors of these two countries. Here, workers have turned to organizational alliances with broader social groups and movements, particularly in rural areas, or, alternatively, have sought non-union influence through labour-oriented NGOs that have been able to skirt both formal and informal constraints on union activism. This observation leads directly to the question of labour's political efficacy, to which I now turn.

---

[14] See, for example, Wong (2004a) on the impact of democratic reforms on health policy in Taiwan and South Korea.

The Question of Labour Efficacy

A dominant political trajectory in this region has been one of worker disempowerment, reduced union membership, lack of enforcement of existing labour law, and growth of employment contingency. The primary sources of this more negative trend is largely to be found in the economic structural changes associated with economic reform: privatization, external trade liberalization, devolution of economic authority to local levels, and the increased mobility of global capital. But despite these disempowering outcomes of reform for organized labour, workers have in fact been able to influence social policy trajectories in important ways.

In China, labour disputes have risen substantially during the first decade of the twenty-first century, escalating to an extent that has alarmed national and local governments. But even as public and enterprise-level labour disturbances have become something of an everyday event in many industrial areas, their impact on employment practices and state policy remains elusive and indirect at best. Lacking political latitude to organize independent unions, worker militancy tends to be localized, disorganized, and focused on very narrow and immediate issues such a wage arrears, unsafe work conditions, excessive overtime, etc., thus permitting employers to respond to disturbances in a limited and piecemeal fashion as they occur. While the aggregate policy effect of social disorder and disorganized protest may be substantial, its specific impact on labour market reform is substantially compromised by lack of coherence and organization.

But having said this, one must recognize as well the obvious concern on the part particularly of national leaders to escalating public disturbances and protests both in cities and rural areas, and the increased attention to social policy in addressing social instability and political disorder (*WSJ* 2011: A1). In thus stepping back from a narrow focus on 'labour militancy' to a broader appreciation of the growing risk of ungovernability, the influence of workers and the working population becomes clear.

If organized labour plays only a marginal and state-subordinated policy role in China, South Korea presents a striking contrast. There, starting from the union organizing drives of the late 1980s and in the context of democratic reforms rooted in the political upheaval of those same years, trade unions have assumed a critical role in influencing the course of economic liberalization and labour market reform. This role became most apparent in the late 1990s, when the two major national labour federations, the Korean Confederation of Trade Unions (KCTU) and the Federation of Korean Trade Unions (FKTU), represented workers in tripartite national bargaining over the terms of labour market reforms. Those negotiations produced a settlement under which labour was able to extract several important institutional concessions, including the extension of unionization rights to previously excluded groups (teachers, civil servants, unemployed workers, etc.) while agreeing to new legislation easing employer restrictions on hiring and firing and granting increased latitude in hiring temporary and part-time workers. Given continuing declines in Korean union membership, it is somewhat surprising that the union federations were thus able to influence the new reform legislation. But recognition of the path dependencies created by earlier-won legal recognition, particularly of the more independent and militant KCTU, and of industrial tripartism, makes clearer the institutional, rather than numerical, basis of union influence in this country.

Thailand offers a third, somewhat different, scenario in which workers, broadly construed to include rural and urban workers along with the poor and unemployed, have achieved at least modest policy influence but only in the context of political mobilization around the populist agenda of a new political party (the Thai Rak Thai) that came to power in 2001. While this national party played a critical role in building a populist political base, it could only do this by mobilizing and incorporating a variety of NGO-led social movements based most importantly in impoverished rural areas of the Northeast and North. Those movements, in turn, provided the opportunity for trade unions, particularly those representing state enterprise workers, to form alliances and support coalitions though which to push for a broadening of the social protections and health services that so distinguish Thai social policy from that of the other countries and that appear to have survived a more recent countermove on the part of urban elites and the military. As in China, the policy outcomes of this populist politics largely bypass narrowly defined worker agendas, attending more predominantly to a broadly defined politics of collective consumption. Nonetheless, labour interests have been able to find a degree of policy leverage through this engagement with these dynamic national social movements.

The Philippines is in some ways the outlier in this account of the multiple ways in which workers have been able to influence national social policy. Even more so than in Thailand, trade unionism has played a marginal political role in reform policy. This role is further diminished by the lack of political influence projected by state enterprise unions, long debilitated by aggressive earlier programs of economic reform. Here, social movements and NGOs play the major advocacy role for workers, but have not enjoyed the political leverage afforded by elite populist mobilization, as in Thailand. It is this organizational and political weakness of labour that partly explains the relative success of post-1987 Philippine governments in introducing labour market reforms without substantial labour opposition.

To the uneven extent that labour politics has thus influenced social policy in the last decade or so, an important final consideration relates to the relationship between institutional economic influences as mediated by elite economic strategies on the one hand, and political pressures from below on the other. Whereas this relationship was largely conflictual during earlier years, especially under authoritarian early export-led developmentalism, the relationship has incrementally transitioned to one of somewhat greater mutuality. This shift reflects not only the industrial transition to higher value activities requiring greater worker skills and technical competence and increased shop floor involvement in quality improvement but as well the institutional requirements of flexible, reformed, labour markets themselves. This transition creates new synergies between social policy and industrial restructuring that augment the power of labour politics in critical areas of social regulation. In this way, labour market reform may bring with it a partial realignment of market requirements with political pressures in shaping social policy.

Conclusion

A few final observations help to place the discussion of this chapter in broader perspective. First, it was noted that economic structural reforms and change have played as important a role in influencing labour market institutions as labour and social reform itself. One such structural reform not yet mentioned, that of external financial deregulation, has been particularly important in this regard. It is widely acknowledged that the liberalization of transnational flows of capital has substantially destabilized national economies, and thus augmented both market risk and the fluidity of employment for workers. The resulting employment instability may be seen as a key driver of enterprise and national policies of labour market flexibility. While these risks and the larger economic instabilities with which they are associated has in part been met by new efforts to stabilize financial systems, both national and global, they have also driven corresponding efforts, especially social security initiatives, to address livelihood risks among workers. In this sense, it may be seen that financial and labour market reforms have followed parallel trajectories, not only because of their shared origins in a broader neo-liberal project but also because of their functional interrelations.

While the labour reform trajectories of these four countries have been quite different, they do generally suggest a deregulatory shift to more flexible labour markets in which managerial strategies have increasingly displaced the regulatory constraints of social arrangements and state requirements. This deregulation, however, and the informalization it sometimes engenders, has in turn taken quite different forms. De jure labour market deregulation applies with greatest force to state enterprises (especially in China) and to larger firms (e.g. in Korea) wherein reform has sought to loosen the rigidities of labour protections and union contracts. In many cases, regulatory regimes have gained in coverage what they have lost in depth. Even as labour regulatory requirements have been relaxed in Korea, the scope of remaining require-ments has grown to embrace ever smaller firms and increasing numbers of workers. In other cases, as in the Philippines and Thailand, deregulation has more often been de facto, given a lack of effective enforcement in those countries. This less visible form of deregulation has the great advantage of reducing the likelihood of political challenge.

These differences in market reform trajectories in part reflect path depen-dencies rooted in earlier patterns of labour market institutions. Following the typology suggested in Chapter 1 of this volume, China's state-led system has augmented the role of markets in the allocation of industrial labour by reduc-ing employment in existing state enterprises in favour of private and informal, family enterprise within a web of authoritarian political institutions that have precluded the political mobilization of workers while pushing labour dissent into even more disruptive patterns of street politics and disorganized protest. Korea's co-governed structure of concentrated private–corporate ownership and state guidance, and the structured, if adversarial, labour relations system with which it was associated, has been reformed largely through labour mar-ket reforms negotiated at national levels through tripartite bargaining among employers, government, and national trade union federations. In the more personalized, informalized, and decentralized institutional settings of the Philippines and Thailand, labour markets have retained a de facto flexibility rooted in localized discretionary practice on the one hand and lack of enforce-ment of labour protections on the other.

In this regard, if differences between formal and informal sectors on the one hand and state and private sectors on the other had previously demarcated politically defined boundaries of disparate labour markets and labour systems, enterprise labour strategies now became more determinative in regulating labour. The greater employment discretion of enterprise management in the organization of work has the further important consequence of more sharply segmenting labour not only across firms but within firms as well. The survey of Chinese firms reported by Chen and Hou (2008), for example, notes the way in which SOE labour contracts reinforce employment segmentation through the link between type of work and length of contract: ranging from fifteen to sixteen months for migrant and temporary workers to twenty-nine months for technical workers and thirty-two months for professionals. In the Philip-pines, similarly, the expansion of contingent work has been paralleled by *increased* protection of regular primary workers in the higher skilled core activities of some firms, thus further increasing within-firm labour segmenta-tion (Sibal and Amente, 2008). The resulting increase in the diversity of labour regimes and conditions of employment is further enhanced by the devolution of regulatory control from national to local levels.

These different pathways to labour market reform have in turn been associated with quite different forms of labour politics in these four countries. It has been argued that while political, institutional, and structural factors have differentially influenced the ways in which workers have organized or sought to influence policy, labour politics has been consequential in all four countries in pushing for expanded social protections. This observation, which runs contrary to a common assumption that Asian labour generally lacks political influence, is in turn related to the further argument that economic and political forces are less in contradiction with one another than during earlier years of political repression and export-led development. In this regard, it is suggested that further research must address the ways in which social policies relating to social reproduction and protection respond on the one hand to the institutional requirements of labour market reform and on the other to social instabilities and political demands reflecting increased livelihood insecurities and instabilities engendered by that reform. The resolution of both economic and sociopolitical tensions of reform provides an important starting point for understanding recent trajectories of social policy change and for very sustainability of market reform itself.

6

Durable Subordination: Chinese Labour Regime through a South Korean Lens

Ching Kwan Lee

Two historical processes have fundamentally transformed the worlds of Chinese employment in the past three decades: commoditization and casualization. Adhering to a model of economic development dependent on high rates of exploitation, the Chinese leadership has sponsored a historic overhaul of the socialist employment system since the 1980s, disempowering the working class at the point of production while ordaining a panoply of worker 'rights' in the legal and administrative systems. Laws and edicts legitimize and regulate commodification and casualization, undermining workers' class power in the name of giving them legal rights. If Chinese labour under Mao was a state-controlled and organized class, as hinted in Chapter 1 of this volume, in the reform period, a formidable alliance of interest between the Chinese state and capital, both global and domestic, has rendered it disorganized and individualized. It is capable of occasional sparkles of rebellion but lacks sustainable collective power. But all of this is, sadly, hardly unique—labour in the rest of Asia and indeed worldwide has been subjected to the assault of commodification and casualization perpetuated by a pervasive state and capital collusion in the neo-liberal era (Gamble et al., 2007; Benson and Zhu, 2011; Deyo, this volume). What might be specifically Chinese, as a brief comparison with South Korea's working-class history shows, are two mechanisms responsible for the durable subordination of Chinese labour—the *hukou* system that treats migrant workers as second-class citizens and the weak capability of Chinese civil society that deprives workers of more general, cross-class mobilization support. Behind both mechanisms stands the Communist state, which sees a zero-sum relation between, on the one hand, its unequivocal imperative in accumulation and political control, and on the other, Chinese workers' power and welfare.

Commodification of Labour

Around the world, examples abound about the erosion of the 'social' contract, multiple forms of 'flexible' employment, and dispossession of worker entitlements, all legalized in national labour laws. Yet, the enormity of the Chinese workforce—the world's largest at more than 800 million—and the centrality of China in the global economy give particular poignancy and importance to the condition of Chinese labour.

The commodification of labour has been the constitutive process of China's turn to capitalism. Like other kinds of commodities, the human capacity to transform nature can now be alienated from one person and sold to others. This process has been tumultuous and painful for Chinese workers, not the least because the Chinese employment system put in place under the state socialist period, from the 1950s to the late 1980s, was a de-commodified one. Vividly captured by the famous Chinese expression the 'iron rice bowl', it was a system in which urban workers were administratively allocated to a de facto job tenure system in urban work units which formed a hierarchy of their own, with state-owned enterprises (SOEs) at the apex, followed by collective enterprises run by various levels of the government. Workers formed a sociopolitical status group whose lifestyle and life chances (i.e. cradle-to-grave welfare, entitlements to pensions, housing, medical care, and educational opportunity) were guaranteed and enforced by the state, to whom workers would pledge political loyalty and compliance. Hence, the notion of the 'socialist social contract'. During this period, there were a minority of casual workers recruited from the countryside into SOEs during production campaigns. But by and large, the Chinese workplace was characterized by lifetime employment with minimal mobility, while also serving as the most basic unit of political control organized by the Chinese Communist Party (CCP) (Walder, 1986).

The socialist system of employment was overhauled along with the restructuring of the Chinese economy away from central planning and state ownership, towards one driven by market competition and multiple ownership forms. With the rise of the private and foreign economic sectors not bounded or burdened by the iron rice bowl employment system, state enterprises were compelled to break the iron rice bowl policy to stay competitive. Over a protracted period of about twenty years, the Chinese government attempted to institutionalize a labour rule of law, or to regulate employment relations through a series of labour legislations, all founded on the notion of the market-oriented, voluntaristic, and individualistic 'labour contract'. Not only did workers lose their right to employment but reform of the pension, housing, and medical systems throughout the 1980s and 1990s have also drastically curtailed workers' rights to welfare entitlements. Most of these benefits are now delivered on the basis of employer and employee contributions to insurance plans, responsibilities that by law should be stipulated in the labour contract (Lee, 2007: ch. 1).

The shift from socialist social contract to legal labour contract has proven a Herculean task, because enforcement of the National Labour Law, the touchstone of the new employment system in the reform period, has come up against different kinds of resistance. The National Labour Law took effect in 1995, and formally requires that all employees in all types of enterprises sign labour contracts with their employers. However, from the beginning, compliance has been spotty, especially so in the private and foreign sectors which have outgrown the state sector in terms of employment and account for just above 50 per cent of all urban employment today (Figure 6.1). In a 2007 report to the National People's Congress, China's legislative body, an official responsible for labour legislation stated that only about 50 per cent of all enterprises have signed contracts with their employees, and the rate among non-state firms was only 20 per cent. Among the labour contracts that were signed,

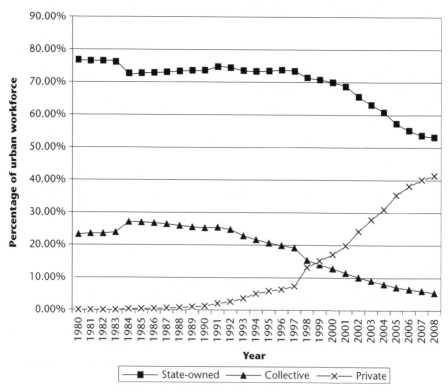

Figure 6.1. Urban employment by ownership type
Source: China Statistical Yearbook, 2009 (Beijing: zhongguo tongji chubanshe).

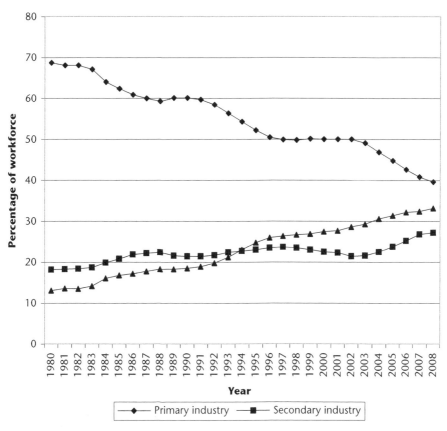

Figure 6.2. Type of employment, 1980–2008

Source: China Statistical Yearbook, 1991, 1994, 2009 (Beijing: *zhongguo tongji chubanshe*).

60–70 per cent were short-term contracts of under one year (Eastern Centre for Legal Culture, 2008: 5). The State Council's 2006 *Research Report on China's Migrant Workers* provides an authoritative portrait of precarious labour in which labour rule of law is conspicuously absent. According to a forty-city survey conducted by the Labour and Social Security Ministry in 2004, among the 120 million strong migrant labour force from the countryside, a paltry 12.5 per cent has signed a labour contract, while only 15 per cent participates in social security schemes, and 10 per cent has medical insurance (State Council Research Office Team, 2006: 13). Less than half (48 per cent) of the migrant workforce get paid regularly while 52 per cent reported regular or occasional wage non-payment (ibid.: 116). Sixty-eight per cent of migrant workers work without any weekly day of rest, 54 per cent of migrant workers have never been paid overtime wages as required by law, and 76 per cent do not receive the legal holiday overtime wages (ibid.: 214). These are only some of the most egregious violations of the National Labour Law, a decade after its promulgation.

Casualization of Employment

Running in tandem with the general trend of privatization in the state-owned sector and an evisceration of the social contract, employment in China has become greatly informalized across nearly all sectors. Two economists have mined various sources of statistics and found 'an unprecedented rise in informal employment in urban China since the mid-1990s. By 2005, 10 per cent of urban workers were registered as self-employed and another 36 per cent were undocumented, neither reported by employers or self-registered' (Park and Cai, 2007). The increasingly informal nature of employment can be seen through an analysis of two dominant trends within China: (*a*) the reorganization of employment away from manufacturing and (*b*) the increasing prevalence of temporary and 'dispatch' workers in all sectors of the economy, including the state-owned manufacturing sector and in heavy industry.

As argued by Evans and Staveteig (2009), China's model of development is markedly distinct from the classic English one in the sense that a relatively small percentage of the country has been employed in the manufacturing sector. The percentage of Chinese workers employed in manufacturing peaked in the mid-late 1990s and began to gradually decline. Although it picked up again after WTO entry in 2001, it has been obviously outpaced by growth in tertiary industries (Figure 6.2). In addition, the contribution of tertiary industries to economic growth has been increasing quite rapidly, with its share of GDP rising to 47.4 per cent in the first half of 2009 (*People's Daily Online*, 27 July 2009).

As China begins to move up the value chain and increasingly focuses on capital-, rather than labour-, intensive industries, it is unlikely that surplus agricultural labour will continue to be absorbed by manufacturing. The collapse of the export economy in late 2008 has compounded the problem. With the percentage of workers employed in tertiary industries increasing from 19.8 per cent in 1992 to 33.2 per cent in 2008 (*zhongguo tongji zhaiyao*, 2009: 44), most of the recent gains in employment have come in the service sector. Without a doubt, a significant portion of these jobs are white-collar office jobs, which tend to come with at least somewhat higher pay, better benefits, and closer adherence to relevant labour laws. But the bulk of new service sector employment is in industries such as food and beverage, hotels, entertainment, cleaning, health care, etc. Workers in such industries are highly subject to the vagaries of the market as well as personal recriminations from employers. Although union presence is not necessarily an indicator of greater stability in employment, unions subordinate to the All China Federation of Trade Unions (ACFTU) have, until quite recently, overlooked the service sector. In general, legal enforcement and state supervision is weak to non-existent, and a huge number of workers are still employed without a contract, thereby leaving them more subject to summary wage deductions, firings, etc. Without a collective or institutional mechanism for enforcing labour laws, employment in the service sector has been, and continues to be, highly informal. Since more and more Chinese workers are employed in this sector, the implication is that more and more jobs are informal ones.

But even in the comparatively formalized manufacturing sector, the unmistakable trend has been towards increased flexibilization of employment relations (see also Deyo, this volume). Referred to in China as 'dispatch workers', these individuals are employed by hiring companies which then 'dispatch' them to manufacturers in need of a highly flexible, and highly exploitable, workforce. Estimated to number about 270 million in 2008 (Qiao, 2009: 322), dispatch workers are only supposed to be employed at temporary, auxiliary, or substitute positions, and they are to be remunerated according to the principle of 'equal pay for equal work', according to the 2008 Labour Contract Law (Y. Liu, 2009). Although the emergence of dispatch workers is a relatively recent occurrence, there have already been many indications that managers (who are not the employers) use their ambiguous formal position vis-à-vis workers in order to routinely violate existing labour laws (Coke Concerned Student Group, 2009), something which the government has so far done little to correct (Sun, 2009). By obfuscating the relationship between manager, worker, and employer, the dispatch labour system leaves workers in an incredibly precarious position in which they enjoy almost no job security whatsoever.

This method of employment has not been relegated to small enterprises in labour-intensive industries as one might expect, but rather has penetrated even highly rationalized, highly mechanized, capital-intensive industries in which workers used to enjoy a high level of security and relative material prosperity. In SOEs, previously the domain of the iron rice bowl, flexible, tiered employment systems have become increasingly popular among managers (Gallagher, 2004, 2005; O. Zhang, 2009), with dispatch workers appearing even in key industries such as petrochemicals, railways, and telecommunications (Li, 2005). Among centrally controlled SOEs, about 10 per cent of employees are dispatch workers (Qiao, 2009: 322). Sectors such as the auto industry (L. Zhang, 2008) and elevator manufacturers, both of which require a relatively skilled workforce, employ regular contract workers alongside dispatch, temporary, or 'intern' workers who necessarily receive markedly lower wages, benefits, and job security. The effect of such a tiered employment system is that, in addition to subjecting the informal workers to poor treatment, solidarity and cohesion among the workforce is broken (L. Zhang, 2008). Thus, such an arrangement is problematic not just from the perspective of the informal workers but also from the regular workers who will find it increasingly difficult to make collective demands on their employers.

Labour Conditions and Rights Violations

Commodified and casualized labour in a market economy do not come about as pure economic and market phenomenon. As Polanyi (1944) has long ago observed, self-regulating market is a myth, and laissez-faire is planned. In China, as elsewhere, there are government regulation and laws supporting and enforcing commodification and casualization. Unfolding concomitantly with economic reform in the past thirty years, Chinese legal reform entails a remarkable and momentous increase in law-making activities by the central authority and the professionalization of the judiciary and the legal workforce. 'Ruling the country by law' was written into the Constitution in 1999 and has become part of the lexicon widely adopted in government, legislature, and Party reports, often mentioned as a means of maintaining social stability. Among the more than 400 laws enacted by the National People's Congress since 1979 are major labour legislations, including the National Labour Law (1994), the revised Trade Union Law (1992 and 2002), the Labour Contract Law (2007), the Employment Promotion Law (2007), and the Labour Dispute Mediation and Arbitration Law (2007). In addition, a large number of State Council edicts and ministry regulations (with various shades of formal legality) stipulate everything from minimum wage levels, workplace injury compensation, to medical coverage and pension rules. The problem has always been one of enforcement.

Notwithstanding the huge variation in working conditions based on sector, type of ownership, region, and workforce composition, several common labour violations have plagued the Chinese workplace. While the government's occasional efforts to address such problems are welcome, labour rights violations are still endemic. This is in large part due to the fact that local governments—supposedly responsible for the implementation of national labour laws—are frequently much more concerned with capital accumulation than with law enforcement, a state of affairs that is tolerated by the central government. With the Chinese judiciary dependent on local governments for financing and personnel appointment, and with local officials prioritizing accumulation and economic development, the courts are under enormous pressure to respond to political contingency in meting out decisions. Herein lies the systemic sources of abysmal labour standards, a fundamental feature of the model of development that the Chinese state has pursued over the past thirty years.

The most common problems faced by Chinese workers include long hours, low pay, employer failure to pay overtime and social insurance, wage arrears, lack of proper health and safety precautions, discrimination (ethnic, gender, etc.), illegal firings, and severe fines for common workplace errors (A. Chan, 2001). Among these, the following specific types of rights violations have received quite a lot of attention from researchers, the media, and the government:

1. *Non-payment of wages and wage arrears.* As one small indication of the severity of the problem, the ACFTU discovered in a partial survey of enterprises that have established a union that RMB 41.7 billion (USD 6.1 billion) in wages were in arrears in 2003 (*zhong xin wang*, 7 November 2004). This is surely but a small portion of the total sum. While this phenomenon is widespread in many industries in both the industrial and service sectors, it has been particularly pronounced in construction. This is in large part because of the convoluted nature of the systems of financing and employment within the industry.

2. *Unpaid overtime wages.* While regulations for payment of overtime have been widely publicized in recent years, employers frequently employ non-transparent methods of wage calculations, resulting in massive theft of overtime wages.

3. *Deaths in the coal industry.* China's transition to a market economy and the increased importance of non-state-owned mines in coal production have lead to an increase in accidents (Wright, 2004). As a result, around 6000 miners a year were killed annually in the first several years of the decade (Liu et al., 2005: 510).

4. *Long/uneven hours.* Particularly prominent in the highly seasonal consumer goods industries, it is not at all unusual for employers to demand that employees work for twelve or more hours a day, often times without enjoying even a single day off per month.[1]

---

[1] These problems have not gone unnoticed by certain agents of the state, namely the trade union and the labour department have taken steps to try to resolve the most egregious violations. Perhaps of greatest note is the 2008 Labour Contract Law (discussed in greater detail below), which has been an attempt to assert greater adherence to the law in labour relations. This law greatly increased possible fines on employers for refusing to sign contracts with employees, and there have been numerous reports that this has been relatively effective. More specifically, the government has recently undertaken an ambitious restructuring of the coal industry, in part to try to reduce the huge volume of deaths each year. According to official figures, there have been significant reductions in mining deaths as 2,632 workers were killed in 2009, an 18 per cent year-on-year reduction (*Guardian*, 20 January 2010). Additionally, unions and labour departments in large cities have made efforts to deal with the problem of non-payment of wages. According to the national Ministry of Human Resources and Social Security, labour departments around the country recovered RMB 8.33 billion in back wages in 2008.

Contested Terrains

Legal Mobilization

As a consequence of the government's promotion of 'rule by law', the promulgation of labour legislations, and the reform of the labour dispute resolution system, there has been a massive increase in formally processed labour disputes (Table 6.1). Filing for labour dispute arbitration is the pre-requisite for filing civil lawsuits.

Beneath this aggregate rise in the volume of arbitrated disputes, certain patterns can be discerned, illustrating the focus and distribution of labour conflicts. Firstly, the most contentious provinces in the 1990s have been Guangdong, Chongqing, Shanghai, Fujian and Jiangsu, regions which experienced the most rapid economic growth. Shenzhen, with its huge contingent of migrant workers numbering more than 6 million by 2000, alone accounted for one-tenth of the national total of arbitrated labour disputes by 1999. On the other hand, in terms of increase in arbitration, Sichuan, Inner Mongolia, Tianjin, Gansu, Shanxi, and Xinjiang all registered triple digit rates in 1995, reflecting perhaps the rapid deterioration in employment conditions among workers in the state-owned sector. Secondly, in terms of ownership type, and taking the year 1996 as an example, SOEs account for 34 per cent of arbitrated disputes, while foreign-invested, collective, and private enterprises, respectively, account for 21, 26, and 10 per cent of the total of 48,121 cases, involving 189,120 employees. Thirdly, most disputes are economic in nature, with wages, welfare, and social insurance payment being the most common (50 per cent) causes of conflicts, and another 30 per cent or so about contract

Table 6.1. National total of arbitrated labour disputes, 1994–2007

Year	Arbitrated labour dispute (cases)	Arbitrated collective dispute (cases)	Employees involved
1994	19,098	1,482	77,794
1995	33,030	2,588	122,512
1996	47,951	3,150	189,120
1997	71,524	4,109	221,115
1998	93,649	6,767	358,531
1999	120,191	9,043	473,957
2000	135,206	8,247	422,617
2001	154,621	9,847	467,150
2002	184,116	11,024	608,396
2003	226,391	10,823	801,042
2005	314,000	19,000	740,000
2006	447,000	14,000	680,000
2007	500,000	13,000	650,000

Source: Labour and Social Security Statistical Yearbooks, various years (2005–6 are from summary statistics released by the Ministry of Labour and Social Security). The first column indicates the total for both individual and collective disputes. Collective disputes are cases involving five or more workers.

termination and dismissal. Wage arrears are particularly pronounced in private and foreign-invested firms (those that are owned or partially owned by foreign capital).[2]

Most of these dispute cases originated in petitions by employees rather than employers. They succeeded in redressing grievances in 50–80 per cent of cases depending on the locality. However, the protection of workers' rights is still wanting, as implementing arbitral awards is not always guaranteed, and the labour dispute arbitration committees easily yield to pressure by local government and employers. Notwithstanding these shortcomings, both the government and the working public have taken this institution seriously and a new Labour Mediation and Arbitration Law was passed in 2007 to streamline the process of arbitration, eliminate arbitration fees, and extend the time limit for aggrieved workers to file for dispute arbitration. In the first three quarters of 2008, China's labour dispute arbitration committees accepted 520,000 new cases, a 50 per cent increase over the same period in 2007. The figure is expected to increase sharply in the following years, reflecting the rise in the number of factory closures and mass lay-offs in the southeast coastal region.[3] Also, the boundary between institutional and non-institutional, legal and extra-legal activism can be elusive. When workers are encouraged to seek legal and bureaucratic redress, only to find that the local state often colludes with employers, they are emboldened to resort to collective action to draw the attention of superior levels of government to right local wrongs.

Worker Protests

Though labour unrest was certainly not unheard of during the Maoist period (Lee, 2010), the acceleration of privatization, restructuring, and redundancies in the state-owned sector triggered levels of insurgency unknown in the history of the People's Republic. While protests occurred throughout the country, they were particularly severe in the country's industrial heartland of the Northeast (Hurst, 2009). Suddenly subject to lay-offs, increased precariousness, reduced wages and benefits, and 'subsistence crises' (Chen, 2000), workers in the state-owned sector began actively and explicitly drawing on the concepts and ideology of Maoism in defence of their suddenly impinged-upon livelihoods (Lee, 2000, 2002). The volume of such protest expanded through the late 1990s and early 2000s, and was symbolically capped by the spectacular protests in Liaoyang in the spring of 2002. While worker protest may have

---

[2] *Laodong Zhengyi Chuli Yu Yanjiu* (*Labour Disputes: Handling and Research*) 1995, 1996, 1997, various articles; see also *Chinese Labour and Social Security Yearbook* from 1995 to 2001 (Beijing: Zhongguo Laodong he Shehuibaozhang Chubanshi).

[3] *China Labour Bulletin*, 12 January 2009, http://www.clb.org.hk/en/node/100366 (accessed 10 April 2009).

had the effect of slowing down the process of privatization and convincing the state to hold on to a significant number of large enterprises (Cai, 2002), none of these episodes have been effective in arresting the processes of commodification and casualization.

Far removed socially, and often time spatially, from the protests in the state sector is the resistance among China's 'new' working class of migrants from the countryside. Although these workers are younger, less educated, and more frequently female than their counterparts in the state-owned sector, over the past ten years they have defied stereotypes of docility and passivity and have been engaging in all manner of resistance (Pun, 2005; Chan, 2006), both covert and incredibly overt. While in general accepting of the hegemonic discourse of 'rule by law', migrant workers in China's industrial heartland have become increasingly willing to take radical direct action if/when official channels fail to resolve their grievances. Non-payment of wages, working and living conditions, managerial abuse, workplace injuries, and low pay are the most common problems which can all incite outbursts of insurgency. Typically, migrants will attempt some sort of legal resolution to their grievances first, and if they manage to endure the exceedingly long process of mediation, arbitration, and possibility litigation, they have a good chance of winning compensation. But many times cases are deemed unfit for official intervention or workers cannot wait a year or more for resolution, and they will resort to direct action. Some frequent tactics include strikes, road blockages, sit-ins, and threatening suicide. In recent years, there have been reports of more radical actions including factory occupations, riots, and murder (of bosses). Although there are exceptions, the state generally avoids harsh repression of migrant protest, and some concessions are often granted.[4]

While worker protest in China has yet to present a serious threat to the stability of the regime, the number of officially reported 'mass incidents' grew rapidly throughout the early 2000s, eventually hitting 87,000 in 2005. While this was the final year that the government released such numbers, there were widespread reports that the number had jumped to a record 120,000 in 2008 (*International Herald Tribune*, 9 February 2009). The percentage of these mass incidents that are worker related is unclear, but it surely accounts for a very significant share. As has been discussed, worker legal mobilization has been growing for more than fifteen years, and it only accelerated with the passage of the Labour Contract Law and the outbreak of the financial crisis in 2008. Nationally, labour disputes increased by 98 per cent in 2008, and the increase

---

[4] Several exceptions to the general cellularized and localized protest pattern have been widely reported. Both the Yantian Port strike and the protests in several steel mills involved copycat action by workers in the same industry. The local government reacted quickly and made concessions to workers.

continued into the first six months of 2009 with the three key provinces of Guangdong, Jiangsu, and Zhejiang reporting increases of 41, 50, and an unbelievable 160 per cent, respectively (*Caijing*, 13 July 2009).

'Organized' Labour: Official Unions and NGOs

One persistent measure of the Chinese government towards labour has been its staunch resistance to granting workers the right to organize their own unions. While the ACFTU has been quite effective in securing pro-labour legislation at the national, and sometimes provincial and municipal levels, enterprise-level unions remain incredibly weak and generally incapable of enforcing laws and contracts (Lau, 2001; Ding et al., 2002; F. Chen, 2009). The ACFTU claims a membership of 213 million, which would make it the largest national union federation in the world by a very large margin. As is well known, it is formally subordinate to the CCP, and all independent unionism is certain to be met by heavy-handed repression. Units at every level of the union hierarchy are subject to dual political control: firstly, by the structurally horizontal Party organization, and secondly, by the immediately superior trade union organization. Chinese unions think of themselves as, and behave like, government agencies (Lau, 2003). When unions do engage in representation, it is important to note where agency is located in the representative relationship: it is a top-down process of 'we represent you' (whether you like it or not), not a bottom-up 'we (workers) delegate authority to you'. Once this misunderstanding is clarified, much of the activity of the ACFTU and its subordinate unions is more easily interpretable.

Thus, the trade union's response to increasing worker insurgency has not been to try to direct this disorganized social movement towards a reorganization of power relations in society. Rather, it has been precisely what one would expect from an agency of the state: legislate and administrate. The Labour Law of 1995, Trade Union Law of 2001, and more recently the Labour Contract Law and Labour Mediation and Arbitration Law passed in 2007 have expanded legal protections for workers and increased the formal powers of the trade union. Although the ACFTU played a key role in advocating for these laws, nowhere was its presence more important than in the passage of the Labour Contract Law (the details of this law are discussed in more detail below). These legal reforms were in response to increased worker protest, and may not have been possible without the advocacy of the ACFTU.

However, as forcefully argued by Feng Chen (2007), this increase in individual legal protections for workers is undermined by the lack of *collective* rights, namely freedom of association, for Chinese workers. As has been demonstrated in many cases were workers have unsuccessfully tried to establish their own organizations, the ACFTU retains a complete monopoly on trade unionism. In the few instances in which grassroots union chairs have tried to be more assertive in fighting for their membership's interests, they often face unchecked retaliation from employers. Higher levels of the trade union rarely intervene effectively to stop such anti-worker activities. The most blatant such case was in early 2009 when an activist union chair was fired from a hotel that was owned by the Guangdong Federation of Trade Unions (*Nanfang ribao*, 23 April 2009). While the irony of a union activist being fired from a union-owned hotel incited significant public outcry, the basic pattern has appeared countless times throughout the country. With the union so fully subordinate to management at the point of production, there remain serious questions about the possibility of the individual rights enshrined in the law being enforced at all. Until workers have their own autonomous base of power, such a state of affairs is likely to continue.

Outside the ACFTU, starting in the mid-1990s, a number of labour-focused non-governmental organizations (NGOs) began to appear in Guangdong province's Pearl River Delta. This region of the country had been ground zero for the emergence of capitalist-style labour relations in the 1980s, and by the 1990s was populated by tens of millions of heavily exploited migrant workers. In part due to consumer movements in the Global North for 'sweat-free' products, and in part to the committed action of labour activists on the ground, several Chinese NGOs emerged which aimed to help workers defend their rights. Two salient points about the activities of these NGOs are relevant to this discussion: (*a*) They have, by and large, been active participants in the state's project of 'rule by law', and have sought to shepherd individual worker grievances into the systems of arbitration and the courts. (*b*) They have been subject to constant harassment and surveillance by the state, and as a result the scope of their activities remains quite limited.

Both the international and domestic political and institutional contexts are imprinted on the form and content of Chinese labour NGOs. What is particularly worth noting, however, is how successful the state has been in channelling international support for NGOs towards the goals of individualization and bureaucratization of labour conflicts. As has been the case in many other developing countries, foundations and international organizations have had a profound influence on the development of the NGO sector (Luong and Weinthal, 1999; Bartley, 2007), one result of which has been that grievances as defined by Chinese workers themselves are often overlooked (Friedman, 2009). In part because of the restrictive political environment in China, many foreign foundations (most of which hope to maintain good ties with the government) are committed to programmes that promote 'rule of law'. Banned from membership-based funding, the result has been that most of the labour NGOs in China have adjusted to these requirements.

With both foreign funders and the Chinese state backing legalistic approaches to labour rights activism, most organizations are primarily engaged in legal advising and legal training (Yue, 2007; Yin and Yang, 2009; Lee and Shen, forthcoming). It is true that some NGOs have been somewhat more daring and attempted dormitory organizing or establishing worker committees (J. W.-l. Chan, 2006), and there have been instances where they have provided workers with guidance, if not leadership, in more confrontational struggles with management. Most labour NGOs' attention is, however, focused on providing workers with advice on how to attempt to resolve grievances through the officially administered processes of mediation, arbitration, and litigation. While many activists are aware that legalistic approaches can be quite limiting, the political sensitivity of labour issues for the state, combined with foundation support for law-oriented programmes, means that they are often left with little choice.

Even though most labour NGOs in China have been quite conservative and generally not engaged in any direct political activities, they have faced frequent harassment and repression from the state. A leaked internal report written by the Guangdong Communist Party Committee's Law and Politics Committee in January 2009 is proof of deep paranoia on the part of the local state with regards to the development of labour NGOs. The report focuses on 'citizen's agents' and NGOs, many of which are specifically named, and argues that they present 'a real impact and a potential threat to social stability in Guangdong province'. These groups are said to 'intensify conflicts', 'damage labour relations', 'cause disorder in public management', and, most seriously, 'harm state security'.[5] That the report implies a direct connection between labour rights work and 'anti-Chinese' sentiment reveals something fundamental about the character of the post-Mao state. But the more relevant point is that, despite any credible evidence of anti-state activity among NGOs, these organizations have very little space within which to operate, and therefore face incredible challenges in their day-to-day operations.

To recapitulate, the transformation of China's labour system in the past thirty years pivots around by the twin processes of commodification and casualization, codified and legalized by a range of labour regulations and laws, backed by an authoritarian state. Labour rights are routinely violated due to the pro-capital interests of the government, especially among local governments wielding political and financial power over local judiciary and labour administrators.

---

[5] 1 January 2009. 'guanyu guangdongsheng "zhiye gongmin dailiren" wenti de diaocha baogao'. [Research report on the problem of 'professional citizen's agents' in Guangdong Province.] *Zhonggong Guangdong shengwei zhengfa weiyuanhui.*

While Chinese labour standards may be glaringly low by world standards, these master processes and features underlying labour's predicaments are certainly not unique to China. South Korea, for instance, has pursued a similar strategy of labour intensive, export-oriented industrialization in the 1960s and 1970s, sponsored by a highly repressive regime against labour. Yet, a combative and daring labour movement has emerged since the 1960s, further empowered by the democratization movement in the 1980s (Koo, 2001). State authoritarianism cannot be the answer to this puzzle: why South Korea, and not China, witnessed a strong labour movement even as both countries pursued a similar strategy of development. Also, as in China, employment casualization has proliferated, and erosion of social contract exacerbated by the neo-liberal policies after the 1997 Asian financial crisis. Yet, in South Korea but not in China, marginalized workers in a number of low-wage service industries have pulled off highly visible collective action garnering tremendous social sympathy and winning battles for higher wages and benefits (Chung, 2009).

Accounting for Chinese Anomalies

What factors may explain the palpable differences in workers' organizational and political capacity in these two Asian countries? Seen through the lens of South Korea, there are two root causes for Chinese workers' durable subordination: an unequal citizenship regime buttressed by the household registration system and the lack of social movement support for workers in Chinese civil society.

Chinese Anomaly I: Rural–Urban Hierarchical Citizenship

The peculiar nature of the Chinese migration system is fundamental to the supply of low-wage migrant labour as well as in preventing labour unrest from radicalization and scale escalation. According to a national survey conducted by the ACFTU in 2007, the migrant workforce is estimated to be 120 million strong (the media has more commonly put the estimate at 200 million), and accounts for 64.4 per cent of all workers in industrial employment and 33 per cent of employees in the service sector (Qiao, 2009: 315). The vast majority of these young migrant workers (with an average age of 32 and an average 10.4 years of education) holds a rural *hukou* or household registration status. That means they have to apply for special permits to be in the cities and many local pension regulations, medical policies, and employment practices discriminate against them because they are residents without local *hukou*. This two-tier citizenship hierarchy, enforced since the late 1950s, has functioned as a means of state control over the physical and social mobility of the population and has guaranteed the transfer of rural surplus to urban industrialization. The system has been gradually loosened up since the 1980s to provide an enormous labour pool for domestic and foreign capital and has made possible China's export-oriented, labour-intensive industrialization strategy. The cornerstone of this Chinese system of migrant labour is the collective land ownership arrangement in the villages where these workers originate. By law, every rural resident is entitled to a plot of land in her native village, owned and allocated by the village collective to which she is a member by birth. To date, despite the increase in land seizure in rural areas close to urban development centres, migrant workers maintain long-term social and economic ties to the family farmland, especially in times of unemployment, marriage, and childbirth.

As long as the migration regime and household registration system keep migrants' entitlement to education and medical care in the city inferior or inadequate, and the rural economy largely impoverished, Chinese migrant workers are locked in the position of being *permanent* migrants. Without the legal right to become urban citizens, migrants are reliant on jobs in the city to support family livelihood and social reproduction in the countryside. Shifting the cost of social reproduction from employers and urban governments to the rural self-provisioning is one of the enduring institutional conditions for China's supply of *cheap* labour. Last but not the least, their second-class citizenship status have insidious and pernicious psychological and cultural effects on migrant workers and urban residents. There is widespread discrimination and stigmatization against migrants (Pun, 2005), so much so that their self-esteem and political efficacy are also low (Lee, 2007).

This situation stands in sharp contrast to South Korea. Hagen Koo's important work on Korean labour illustrates a process of rapid 'proletarianization'. Between the early 1960s and the mid-1980s, there was a four-fold increase in wage earners. 'A nation of small cultivators became a nation of urban wage earners' (Koo, 2001: 34). It is not so much the speed of change that sets Korea apart from China but the pattern of 'proletarianization'. Korean factory workers represented a fully committed industrial workforce. 'Few of them may be characterized as "semi-proletariat" or "part-time proletariat", ... referring to those only partially committed to factory employment, maintaining close ties with their rural households' (ibid.: 42). Moving into large-scale industries which were geographically concentrated in industrial parks promoted by the Korean developmental state, the Korean working class is highly homogeneous. '(I)n South Korea geographical origin of margin workers did not produce significant internal division within the urban proletariat. Unlike in China, for example, native-place identity or the politics of "place" was largely insignificant in Korean labour activism' (ibid.: 42).

Without the safety valve of returning to and relying on rural subsistence in their native villages, South Korean workers have only their labour to exchange for wage and livelihood—a classic route of proletarianization as experienced by the English working class analysed in Karl Marx's *Capital* Vol. 1. While this factor cannot be isolated as if in a controlled experiment, my ethnographic study on the processes of labour agitation in Guangdong has found that the lack of permanent membership in the cities made it difficult for aggrieved workers to sustain a labour strife or legal battle. In times of unemployment or labour conflict, workers tend to dissipate to their respective home villages or to other cities in search of jobs, before their collective action bears fruit. Therefore, their weak associational (no independent union) and workplace (mostly doing low-skilled jobs) leverage is further stymied by the lack of sustained collective mobilization.

Chinese Anomaly II: Weakness of Civil Society

Chinese workers have mobilized to fight exploitation and degradation. But their level of militancy and their collective vision pale in comparison with South Korean workers. From the women workers in the textile and garment industries to male workers in automobile and chemical, South Korean labour politics has always involved larger scale, more collective, confrontational and radical resistance and had a clear goal of forming grassroots unions. Besides the unequal citizenship regime, another important reason for this difference between China and South Korea is the absence of grassroots political alliance for Chinese labour activism. In South Korea, churches and student-activists were workers' crucial allies, providing organizational, moral, and intellectual support. As Koo (2001) points out, the organizational capacity of the church derives from its international networks, internal organizational structure, and ideological legitimacy. In the 1980s, when the military regime turned increasingly repressive towards all kinds of democratic forces, the student movement and oppositional political parties began seeing workers as their potential allies in their battle against the authoritarian state. Korean intellectuals and students also instigated counter-hegemonic cultural movements (e.g. *minjung* movement), producing a cross-class articulation of a national identity. Male semi-skilled workers in large auto and chemical plants and white-collar workers then formed the backbone of the unionization movement that lasted from the late 1980s to the mid-1990s.

Chinese labour struggles in the reform period have largely been confined to localized, cellularized agitations by workers in the same factory, without support from intellectuals or other social movements. The only brief exception to this pattern was during the 1989 Pro-democracy Movement when workers in major cities joined students in Beijing's Tiananmen Square, demanding a freedom of news and 'democracy', protesting against corruption and inflation. Workers seized the initial euphoric moments of mass uprising and elite cleavage to form independent unions in sixteen cities in May 1989. Within a month, the movement was suppressed and worker leaders arrested and imprisoned. Since the bloody crackdown in 1989, China took a decisive turn to economic liberalization and the economic growth that ensued and was sustained for two decades have benefited the urban middle class, especially the highly educated and the professionals. The government has successfully channelled their ambition from mass politics and social movements to accumulation of individual wealth in the globalizing market economy. Notwithstanding the vibrant growth of NGOs, in areas ranging from environmentalism, consumer right, migrant service to education and HIV/AIDS, the Chinese state has kept a tight grip on their independent development through stringent regulations on their finance and registration, co-optation, harassment, and crackdown. Thanks to government concern with any kind of organized dissent, these NGOs do not and cannot form broad alliances, much less cross-class movement. Many of them are struggling to secure their organization's survival in the hostile political and economic environment in China and are too weak to offer support for workers' agitation.

The China–South Korea labour difference continues to shape the divergent response of workers to the challenge of flexible accumulation and casualization of employment. In a new and important book, Jennifer Chun depicts marginalized workers' deployment of 'symbolic politics' to contest the noncontractual elements of labour contract when neo-liberal labour law refuses to classify contingent workers as 'workers', and therefore not within the purview of the law. 'When existing institutional channels for adjudicating workers' grievances are blocked or constrained . . . workers and their collective organizations have escalated narrow labour disputes into oppositional classification struggles and public drama to pressure employers and the state to redress their disputes through alternative means' (Chun, 2009: 174). Symbolic leverage is founded on public dramas and morally charged struggles against the injustice of their living and working conditions. For it to be effective, society's recognition of workers' rights and social empathy with workers' plight are critical. In South Korea, at least among the cases she documented—janitors, golf caddies, home care workers—the legacy of cross-class alliance in earlier mobilization has built the foundation for workers to turn to symbolic politics as well as for civil society's recognition and moral support for workers' cause in the current period of informalization.

In stark contrast, the challenge of casualization elicits a very different response in China. It is the Chinese government that took the initiative to deal with the challenge of informalization which it fears would generate even more social discontent and raise the spectre of instability. Their response is to strengthen the force of contract through yet another labour legislation—the

127

Labour Contract Law. Like other labour legislations, this law empowers workers with *individualized* legal rights without giving them the collective right to organize and bargain with employers. The intention of the government is once again to bureaucratize the process of labour conflict resolution without redressing the fundamental imbalance of power at the point of production. While it is too early to assess the effectiveness of this law in protecting workers from aggravated casualization, a discussion on the circumstance of its passage and immediate effects provides a glimpse into the latest developments in Chinese labour conditions.

Conclusion: Crisis and Law

The Labour Contract Law, which we have already touched on, was widely viewed as the most important change to China's labour relations legal framework since the 1995 Labour Law. This new law had aroused more public debate than perhaps any piece of legislation in the history of the PRC. After posting a draft version of the law in 2006, the government received in excess of 190,000 public comments, many of them from regular workers. While the official trade unions and workers (in individual comments) tended to be supportive of the law, foreign and domestic capital publicly mobilized against it in a way which had not been done previously in China. Although the law was significantly watered down before enactment, it was widely hailed as a victory for workers. While we do not debate that the law may have positive material consequences for certain segments of workers, the promulgation of the law is yet another strong indication of the state's attempt to 'rule by law' and to cellularize labour conflict. Given this set of political circumstances, there is little reason to believe that the new law will adequately address the deep power asymmetry at the point of production.

At the most general level, the Labour Contract Law was viewed by the authorities as a means by which to formalize labour relations as part of a broader attempt to reduce social conflict and address growing economic inequality. One of the most important features of the new law are the provisions relating to 'non-fixed term' contracts, which make it more difficult to dismiss employees (J. W.-l. Chan, 2009; Wang et al., 2009). According to the law, workers are entitled to demand a non-fixed term contract after signing two successive fixed-term contracts or after being employed for ten years by the same employer. The law also includes an expanded role for the trade union in negotiating collective contracts, the determination of workplace rules, and lay-offs. Finally, the law requires enhanced severance payments in the event of lay-offs, something which is particularly important in a country with a very weak system of unemployment insurance (Cooney et al., 2007).

It is still too early to render a final analysis of the effects of the Labour Contract Law on labour relations in China. It does appear that the intense public debate around the law caused more workers to take notice, one result of which has been many more workers filing complaints with the labour bureau. In particular, there appear to be many cases of workers filing against employers for failing to provide them with a contract, something which is heavily punishable under the new law. The huge increase in official labour disputes in 2008 can be attributed as much to the implementation of the Labour Contract Law as to the financial crisis, as disputes were on the rise even in the first half of the year. There are also signs that the law has been more useful to employees with other cultural or social resources at their disposal (Cooney et al., 2007), and who occupy a relatively strong position in the labour market. Successful pushback by white-collar employees at Wal-Mart and tech giant Huawei are clear examples of such a phenomenon. While it is not clear that the laws are being enforced more strictly than before, it does appear that more workers now have written contracts, and in this sense a first step towards formalization has been achieved.

It is precisely when we come to this issue of providing workers with contracts we can see that the Labour Contract Law is at base a further attempt to guide individual worker grievances into the official system of labour mediation. True, there are provisions in the law for collective bargaining and a marginally enhanced role for the union in determining work rules and consulting around lay-offs. But in the absence of a union that can constitute its membership as a collective force (or that has any substantive connections to workers whatsoever), such provisions are rendered insignificant. Why then is this law a further manifestation of the state's attempts to 'rule by law' and to cellularize labour conflict? Because the strongest censure in the law is reserved for employers who do not provide their workers with contracts (and because this feature has been highly publicized), more and more workers now have access to such contracts. This is absolutely crucial for the state, because without a written contract the labour bureau cannot process a grievance. The provision of contracts to workers is thus necessary in order for the state to be able to absorb conflict and (attempt) to keep it out of the workplace and the streets. And yet, the severely overburdened labour bureaus are frequently unable to efficiently and fairly resolve such conflicts, the consequence of which is that workers still must resort to direct action.

Such problems became painfully apparent when the global financial crisis hit in late 2008. In mid-December, an official from the Guangdong government revealed that 15,661 small and medium enterprises had closed or gone bankrupt during the year, but awkwardly maintained that 'there has not been a "wave of closings"' (*Yangcheng wanbao*, 17 December 2008). In the manufacturing town of Dongguan, the government reported that 117 bosses skipped town without paying workers their owed wages. For the factories that did not shut down, their orders were dramatically reduced, which resulted in massive lay-offs. While millions of workers simply went home for Chinese New Year, many of them without receiving their due wages, there were thousands of disputes, official complaints, strikes, and riots. As has already been mentioned, disputes grew particularly rapidly in the export-oriented provinces of Jiangsu, Zhejiang, and Guangdong. There were reports of militant direct action with 1,000 workers at a Shanghai electronics plant staging a massive sit-in to protest six months of unpaid overtime wages and benefits (*AFP*, 9 December 2009), and an occupation of a textile mill by 6,000 workers in the Northern city of Linfen (*The Sunday Times*, 1 February 2009). The unrest was not restricted to the manufacturing sector as taxi drivers staged a nearly unprecedented nation-wide wave of strikes, with drivers walking off the job in Chongqing, Guangzhou, Shantou, Foshan, Sanya, Xiamen, Jingzhou, Suizhou, Zhouzhi, Nanyang, Anling, Dali, and Yongdeng. In Dongguan, hundreds of workers from a toy factory rampaged through their workplace, eventually battling police, smashing and overturning a police vehicle (*Guangzhou ribao*, 26 November 2008). Finally, in at least a few cases, legal violations pertaining to lay-offs and severance pay resulted in workers murdering their managers (*Nanfang dushi bao*, 31 March 2009).

On the whole, though, the crisis revealed the extent to which the state has accepted the interests of capital as hegemonic. The central government announced that it would allow localities to freeze increases in the minimum wage, and that they could reduce employer contributions to their employees' social insurance (*Wall Street Journal*, 16 January 2009), something many municipalities took advantage of. Of even greater concern were widespread reports that government officials were overlooking legal violations by employers in the hopes of keeping investors happy. In Shandong, there was a report of a government official telling a foreign investor not to 'worry so much' about the Labour Contract Law (*China Law Blog*, January 2009), and in Guangdong legal enforcers were told that investigations against managers suspected of breaking the law could be postponed (*Guangzhou ribao*, 1 January 2009). The Guangdong government argued that 'this method is to ensure the normal functioning of the enterprise, and certainly is not to provide suspects with protection' (*Xin kuai bao*, 1 January 2009).

Once again, the working class's inability to exercise coordinated collective power meant that worker interests were overlooked and violated. With resolution of labour arbitration cases frequently taking one or even two years, the legal system proved incapable of delivering justice to workers when they needed it most. Additionally, in the absence of a strong lobby from organized labour, the response of the state was, by and large, directed towards assisting employers. Deprived of organized political power, working-class insurgency

130

erupted throughout the country, in an attempt (frequently in vain) to redress deep grievances. The basic pattern of legal violations by capital, failure to resolve conflicts through legal mediation, followed by worker direct action has been developing throughout the period of marketization; the economic crisis merely increased the frequency and intensity of such a dynamic.

It is clear from the above that crucial institutional changes have taken place in the Chinese labour market regime over the past three decades, the changes that have primarily been manifest in the process of commodification and informalization. As made clear in the foregoing analysis, the global ideological crusade against unionized labour, the development imperatives of the Chinese government, and the marketizing forces unleashed by sustained economic reforms have combined to reshape industrial relations in China. While market and systemic factors are causally important, their impact has been mediated through the dominant developmental coalition that has centred around CCP elites and corporate capitalists, both state and private. This coalitional structure has also underpinned the continuation of the *hukou* system and a weak civil society that has in turn kept labour poorly organized and politically impotent—with important consequences for both China's economy and that of the world. The impact of coalitional dynamics is revealed even more forcefully in the brief yet illuminating comparison of the cross-country variation in the organization and power of labour forces in China and South Korea.

7

Continuity and Change in the Japanese Economy: Evidence of Institutional Interactions between Financial and Labour Markets

Mari Sako and Masahiro Kotosaka

Two decades have gone by since the heyday of Japan's economic success. What has changed since, and what has stayed the same, in the institutional under-pinnings of the Japanese form of capitalism? A time span of two decades enables us to address this question by investigating incremental institutional changes that might remain undetected if we were to take a shorter period for analysis.

The political economy of Japan has been characterized by tightly knit institutions of relational coordination, specifically the main bank system, lifetime employment, trust-based inter-firm relations, and neo-corporatist business–labour–government relations. These institutions tended to enforce homogeneity in practices and high-level performance. By the late 1990s, however, diverse patterns of organizing have become evident (Aoki et al., 2007).

This chapter aims to shed light on the nature of institutional change and continuity in the Japanese economy. When, why, and how has institutional change occurred in the Japanese capital and labour markets? And how do institutions within and between capital and labour markets interact to bring about changes? This chapter addresses these questions by focusing on the institutional environment for entrepreneurial start-ups, whilst giving regard to the context of the Japanese economic system as a whole.

The chapter begins by developing a framework for analysing institutional continuity and change in the first section. The second section examines the nature of institutional changes in capital markets, and the third section the nature of institutional transformation in labour markets. The fourth section turns to the analysis of institutional interactions in these capital and labour markets from the perspective of entrepreneurial start-ups.

The key contributions of this study are as follows. First, we advance a model of institutional change in a specific direction, namely towards liberalization. This direction of change involves the dismantling of collective action, and is marked by a diverse pace of change (due to non-collective defection and adoption) and increased organizational diversity within the system. The model also identifies agents for change, their capacity for action, and ambiguity in institutions as affecting the pace and extent of institutional change. Second, the empirical analysis demonstrates that institutional change has gone much further in labour markets than in capital markets, and finds reasons for the difference in the stronger political power of agents for change and the greater ambiguity of institutions in the former than the latter. Third, this study examines institutional interactions in financial and labour markets taken together, rather than treating each market arena separately. This level of analysis is essential to tackle the question of whether incremental institutional change (IIC) amounts to systemic change at the national level. We argue that unlike the functionalist perspective that leads us to look for a high degree of institutional interaction between capital and labour markets, we observe much looser and decoupled arrangements. The case of Rakuten provides insights into the extent to which agents entering the system depend on, or remain relatively independent of, specific institutions. Thus, entrepreneurs may use, avoid, or recombine specific institutions to suit their purpose.

Institutional Continuity and Change

Comparative institutional analysis has proven to be a useful framework for identifying differences and similarities in economic and political institutions that underpin capitalist development (Morgan et al., 2010). This intellectual tradition may be traced back to Max Weber's ideal-type approach, and more recently to Andrew Shonfield who traced the role of institutions surrounding market and mixed economies in the process of modernization (Shonfield, 1965). In the 1980s, social scientists resumed this pursuit (e.g. Hollingsworth and Boyer, 1997; Whitley, 1999). In attempts to articulate how institutions fit together in a national system, these frameworks came to emphasize stability. Moreover, by identifying more than one ideal type, the notion of convergence gave way to the idea of persistent divergence as national systems fended off common pressures of globalization in different ways.

The relative demise of the United States, Germany, and Japan compared to emerging markets (including the so-called BRICs) provides good empirical grounds for reconsidering this dominant theoretical lens of comparative statics. Considerable progress has been made recently in moving away from dichotomous typologies (Amable, 2003; Crouch, 2005), and in explicitly recognizing that slow and incremental change may bring about transformation in the nature of institutions (Streeck and Thelen, 2005). This section builds on these insights to create a dynamic analytical framework of use for empirical work on Japan. We argue that Japan is a coordinated market economy (CME) moving in the direction of a liberal market economy (LME) (Hall and Soskice, 2001), and a welfare capitalist system moving towards stock market capitalism (Dore, 2000). In terms of the four-way typology adopted in Chapter 1 of this book, Japan remains a 'networked' system, albeit with power shifting away from labour towards capital.[1]

Two Contrasting Perspectives on Institutional Change

In order to make explicit some of the implicit assumptions behind notions of institutional stability and change, let us first summarize the essence of two contrasting approaches. One approach, varieties of capitalism (VoC), sees change as rare, with long periods of institutional stability disturbed by a radical breakdown. The other approach, incremental institutional change (IIC), focuses on a slow pace of continual deinstitutionalization and reinstitutionalization.

The highly stylized VoC framework identifies institutions in four subsystems, namely in corporate governance, inter-firm relations, labour markets, and education and training (Hall and Soskice, 2001). A national system consists of these elements that are mutually reinforcing, or 'institutionally complementary'. Two institutions are complementary if the presence of one increases the returns from the other. Thus, institutional complementarity is an aspect of cohesion or synergy between institutions that is predicated solely on performance outcomes. By implication, any piecemeal institutional change brings about suboptimal performance outcomes. Consequently, institutional change is either an adaptive adjustment to preserve the existing self-equilibrating system or a radical disruption that occurs rarely due typically to exogenous shocks such as wars and crises.

The contrasting IIC approach of Streeck and Thelen (2005) regards institutions as 'regimes' in which rule-makers and rule-takers interact to enact the rules in question. They identify five mechanisms via which transformative institutional change may occur even if the change is gradual. *Displacement* happens when new models emerge and diffuse, and agents defect from existing, previously taken-for-granted institutional arrangements. *Layering* occurs

---

[1] This power shift should not be confused with a move towards a 'personalized' system, as stronger capital has not made ownership structures, corporate governance, and labour–management relations in Japan more personalized than before.

when a new institution is placed alongside an old institution. Whilst the two may coexist for some time, faster growth of the new siphons off support for the old. *Drift* results from neglect of existing institutions when rules may remain unchanged in the face of evolving external conditions. *Conversion* refers to the redeployment of old institutions to new purposes and goals. *Exhaustion* involves the gradual breakdown of institutions as they are over-extended in use and encounter diminishing returns.

The two approaches are contrasting in a number of important respects. First, the VoC approach is overly functionalist in linking system coherence and stability to the notion of institutional complementarity. By contrast, the IIC approach posits a much looser interconnectedness amongst institutions, which are often ambiguous. Second, this difference in attributing tight or loose system coherence results from a difference in what stability signifies. VoC theorists adopt an economist's notion of stability as an equilibrium in which all agents' incentives are aligned with each other at every point. By contrast, IIC theorists regard institutional stability as a political compromise reached by actors with conflicting interests. Third, institutions are, therefore, resources to be used by actors in the IIC framework, whereas they are constraints that define actors' preferences in the VoC framework. Fourth, changes are brought about primarily through exogenous factors in the VoC framework, whereas the IIC approach places endogenous change on centre stage.

To summarize, if extreme versions of the two approaches were taken at face value, we would make a mockery of the distinction between institutional continuity and change. The VoC approach places such faith in the ability of institutions to self-equilibrate that it sees long waves of continuity rarely broken by radical changes. By contrast, the IIC approach views the institutions of advanced economies as being in a constant state of flux, with various actors—the state, employers, and labour—vying with each other to redefine those institutions to their own advantage. Thus, nearly all periods of stability contain seeds of IIC.

Causes and Mechanisms of Incremental Institutional Change

In order to go beyond this disagreement—seeing stability or change in the same empirical phenomenon—we need to focus our attention on causes of IIC as a way of gauging the sustainability of such change. It is difficult to judge whether transformational institutional change has reached a tipping point, or a point of irreversibility, just by examining the extent of change. This is because the mode of IIC affects the extent of change in a system, with some modes—such as layering or exhaustion—leading to a prolonged period of high organizational diversity within the system (Sako, 2005). We need to identify not just the outcome but also the underlying causes of such

Mode of Institutional Change		
	Layering	Conversion
Financial	New stock exchanges (e.g. Mothers, Hercules)	Venture capital
Labour	Atypical employment (e.g. temporary, agency labour)	Shunto wage bargaining

(Markets)

Figure 7.1. Typology of institutional change

within-system diversity. Therefore, the analysis requires identifying economy-wide conditions for deinstitutionalization, collective agents of change, and their capacity for action.

Adapting Oliver's approach (1992), an important cause of institutional change is deinstitutionalization, an opportunity to shift the basis of legitimacy of an established and taken-for-granted institution. It may occur because of a decline in the instrumental value of the institution, a change in political power distribution, or normative fragmentation. When the legitimacy of an institution is at stake, institutional ambiguity—with different actors attaching different meanings to a specific institution—is likely to be greater, creating scope for contestation (Jackson, 2005). Institutions are regulative, cognitive, or normative (Scott, 2001), and ambiguity may arise from changes in cognition, norms, or regulation.

Next, the analysis must identify collective agents of change and their 'capacity for action' depending on the resources—economic, social, and political—that they can command to bring about change (Greenwood and Hinings, 1996). These agents may be new entrants or incumbents, and incumbents may, or may not, be resisting institutional change. A typology similar to the one proposed by Mahoney and Thelen (2010) emerges. As a proposition, the more ambiguous institutions are, and the greater the capacity for action of agents for change, the more widely diffused and sustainable the institutional change in question is likely to be.

The rest of this chapter updates the empirical evidence in Sako (2007), which chose to study the 'layering' of new stock exchanges and the 'conversion' of venture capital in the financial market, and the 'conversion' of Shunto and the 'layering' of atypical forms of employment in the labour market (Figure 7.1). The evidence in the next two sections indicates that institutional change has been more extensive and sustained in the labour market than in the financial market.

Changes in Financial Market Institutions for Start-ups

In this section, we examine the creation of new stock exchanges for start-ups from 1999—a case of layering—and the gradual conversion in the nature of venture capital funding from loans to investment. We then analyse how these two institutions, new exchanges and venture capital, interact to provide financing for start-ups. By focusing on financing for start-ups, rather than financing for established corporations, we are able to focus on agents for change, their power (or lack thereof) to influence and bring about institutional change, and the impact of existing financial institutions on the emergence of new institutions.

The Thin Layering of New Stock Exchanges during 1999–2009

In the late 1990s, NASDAQ US's effort to enter the Japanese market faced elusive opposition from within. However, Nasal US eventually managed to identify a willing partner in Softbank Corporation which became a joint venture partner to create Nasal Japan. The Tokyo Stock Exchange (TSE) then responded by creating a Market for High Growth and Emerging Stocks (Mothers). Both exchanges sought to attract new and recent start-up companies particularly in high-tech sectors. Cumulatively, by 2009–10, seven new stock markets have attracted more than 1000 initial public offerings (IPOs) (see Table 7.1).[2]

The first decade, from 1999 to 2009, was challenging for the new stock exchanges in Japan. Soon after their opening, these new markets suffered a general decline in the volume of trading in stocks and shares due to the end of the dot-com bubble. In the United States, NASDAQ peaked at 5048 points on 10 March 2000, sharply collapsing thereafter until the market touched the lowest point in mid-2002. The performance of the two new markets in Japan reflected this US trend (Figure 7.2). The number of IPOs reached bottom in 2001 for Mothers and in 2003 for NASDAQ Japan.

Further, both markets suffered an image problem early on as a result of a number of major bankruptcies and suspicion of involvement by the Japanese mafia in companies planning to list on TSE Mothers. With a sluggish growth prospect, NASDAQ US pulled out of NASDAQ Japan only after a couple of years, and the Osaka Stock Exchange came to the rescue to host the exchange as Hercules from December 2002.

---

[2] However, of those, 867 are in JASDAQ, which was established as long time ago as 1963, and attract both established and new businesses.

Table 7.1. New stock exchanges in Japan

		Date of establishment	No. of listed companies	Total market capitalization (billion US$*1)	Average market capitalization (billion US$)	Source
New stock exchanges	JASDAC	2/1963	867	103.9	0.120	*2
	TSE Mothers	11/1999	186	19.0	0.102	*2
	Hercules total (growth + standard)	5/2000	147	9.8	0.067	*2
	Centrex (Nagoya)	10/1999	28	0.5	0.019	*3
	Ambitious (Sapporo)	4/2000	10	0.1	0.013	*4
	Q Board (Fukuoka)	5/2000	10	0.1	0.005	*5
	NEO	8/2007	6	0.04	0.007	*6
Established stock exchanges	Tokyo Stock Exchange First Section	5/1878	1676	3589.5	2.142	*2
	Tokyo Stock Exchange Second Section	10/1961	441	40.5	0.092	*2
	NYSE		1503	11012.1	7.327	*7
	NASDAQ	7/1971	2222	3151.0	1.418	*7

Sources:

*1 Oanda (2010) OANDA Historical Exchange Rates (2009 average) [online]. http://www.oanda.com/currency/historical-rates/ [accessed date 01/04/2010].

*2 Quick (2010) Nikkei Quicktrader [online]. Quick Corporation. Available from: http://corporate.quick.co.jp/service/product/quick_trader.html [accessed date 27/04/2010].

*3 Centrex (2010) NSE Monthly Statistics [online]. Nagoya Stock Exchange. Available from: http://www.nse.or.jp/j/toukei/j-gepo2010.html [accessed date 31/03/2010].

*4 Ambitious (2010) SSE Statistics data [online]. Sapporo Securities Exchange. Available from: http://www.sse.or.jp/statistics/distribute.html [accessed date 31/03/2010].

*5 Q-Board (2010) Fukuoka Stock Exchange Statistics [online]. Fukuoka Stock Exchange. Available from: http://www.fse.or.jp/statistics/index.php [accessed date 31/03/2010].

*6 Neo (2010) Osaka Securities Exchange Market Information [online]. Osaka Securities Exchange. Available from: http://www.ose.or.jp/market/55 [accessed date 28/02/2010].

*7 Capital IQ (2010) Capital IQ Markets [online]. Capital IQ. Available from: https://www.capitaliq.com [accessed date 31/03/2010].

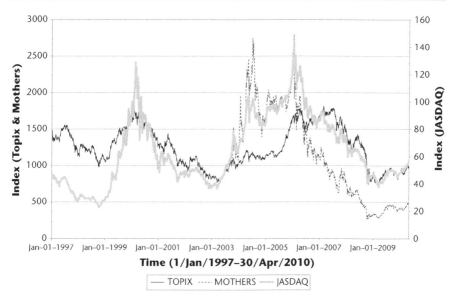

Figure 7.2. Stock price indices in Japan, 1997–2010
Source: Capital IQ (2010).

The markets picked up somewhat since then, so that by the end of 2005, there were 150 listed companies in TSE Mothers, and 127 listed companies in Hercules. TSE Mothers touched the highest mark at 2800 points on 16 January 2006, and Hercules reached 4200 points on the same day. However, the Livedoor scandal, in which the founder, Takafumi Horie, and four other executives of the company were found guilty of securities fraud, destroyed the two markets. Both markets again suffered an image problem, turning away potential investors and companies wishing to go public. Consequently, the TSE Mothers index bottomed out at 269.41 points, which was one-tenth of the peak reached before the Livedoor scandal. At the end of 2009, the TSE Mothers index was still 416.22 and the Heracles index was 558.70.

Thus, the layering of new stock exchanges onto the existing stock exchanges has not taken off and remains thin. The market clapitalization of these exchanges is also tiny; for example, TSE Mothers at $19 billion accounts for less than 1 per cent of the market capitalization of TSE as a whole (see Table 7.1). At the same time, the new stock exchanges rely on domestic individuals for three-quarters of their market value, which is in great contrast to the ability of TSE First Section to attract investors from overseas (Table 7.2).

Partial Conversion of Venture Capital during 1999–2009

Venture capital, originating in the United States, provides early-stage funding for high-risk, high-return entrepreneurial start-ups. In Japan, by contrast, the

Table 7.2. Composition of market participants at Japanese stock exchanges (%, value base, 2007)

	TSE First Section	TSE Second Section	TES Mothers	JASDAQ	Hercules
Financial institutions	7.9	3.7	1.4	3.1	1.3
Mutual funds	2.6	2.3	0.7	1.9	0.8
Business entities	2.1	3.4	2.2	2.2	1.7
Other entities	0.4	0.9	0.2	0.5	0.2
Securities companies	0.7	4	4.4	0.8	4.9
Individuals	27.6	64	76.3	79	78.5
Investment from overseas	58.7	21.7	14.8	12.5	12.6

Source: METI, 2008.

origin and growth of venture capital followed a very different trajectory, resulting in different sources of funds and investment patterns as detailed below. Consequently, venture capital arms of Japanese financial institutions advanced loans and made low-risk, low-return investment decisions. Since the late 1990s, however, Japanese venture capital has undergone a slow process of conversion, moving away from being embedded firmly in a bank-based system towards gaining some (but not all) characteristics of an equity-based financial system.

The 1970s and 1980s saw banks, securities firms, trading companies, regional banks, and insurance companies establish their venture capital subsidiaries. Until the early 1990s, major venture capital subsidiaries had extended more loans than equity finance, a legacy dating from the 1970s recession in which they survived by engaging in straight lending. Gradual conversion took place since the late 1990s, preceding the Limited Partnership Act for Venture Capital Investment in 1998, which defined the legal basis for the limited liability of non-general partners in venture capital funds. This piece of legislation came about following some Japanese venture capitalists adopting US-style venture funds in the form of a 'voluntary partnership'. The regulatory body realized that the absence of legal protection was undermining investors' incentive to take a stake in venture capital investment.

Whereas in 1990, 65 per cent of venture capital came from loans, by 2008, less than 0.1 per cent did (Figure 7.3). It is unlikely that the recessionary pressures in the late 2000s would reverse this trend towards the elimination of loans advanced by venture capitalists. During the same period, the proportion of investment committed through syndicated venture capital funds rather than through own accounts (i.e. without syndication) increased from 9 to 73 per cent.

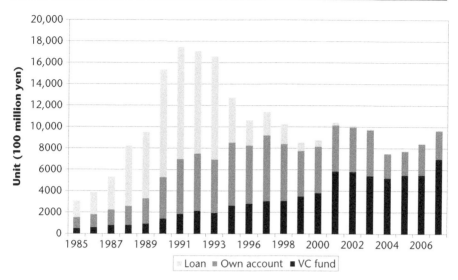

Figure 7.3. Venture capital investment and loans outstanding in Japan
Sources: VEC, various years.

Institutional Interaction between Venture Capital and New Stock Exchanges

Why has change in capital market institutions for start-ups been limited and slow in Japan? Answers can be found in the way institutions interact in capital markets. A comparison of Japan with the United States in the three phases of the 'venture capital cycle' (Gompers and Lerner, 1999) highlights such institutional interaction.

FUNDRAISING

In the United States, venture capitalists raise money from individuals and institutions to invest in early stage start-ups. Pension funds, financial institutions, and institutional investors dominate as sources of funds (Figure 7.4). In Japan, the distribution of sources of funds is quite different. Financial institutions such as banks and insurance companies accounted for 31 per cent of the newly formed venture capital funds in 2006, whilst business corporations accounted for 19 per cent. Pension funds and endowments accounted for less than 5 per cent. A large majority of the investors are domestic players, and foreign investors provided only 1 per cent of funds.

These sources of funds for venture capital in Japan militate against high-risk, high-return investment. In fact, the average return to Japanese venture capital investment was below 3 per cent, compared to 10–20 per cent in the United States and Europe (EVCA, 2007; NVCA, 2007; VEC, 2007). A small number of 'real' venture capital funds in Japan may achieve high returns from taking high risk. But generally, Japanese venture capital today functions as a lower return investment vehicle. This creates a vicious circle in which only those

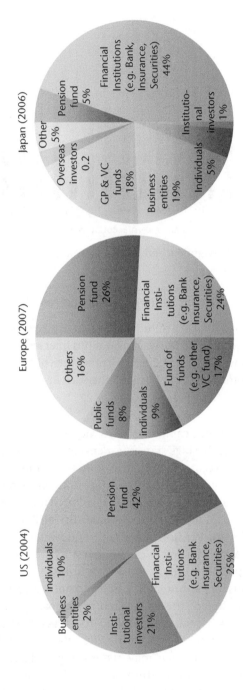

Figure 7.4. Composition of venture capital investors (%, value base)

Sources: VEC, 2007; METI, 2008; and OANDA, 2010.

investors who accept the status quo—domestic rather than foreign investors—provide funds.

INVESTING

In the United States, venture capitalists invest in only a handful of entrepreneurial ventures selected from hundreds of proposals. Once an investment decision is made, a principal investor fulfils most of their financial needs, if necessary by syndicating further investments. Venture capitalists are actively involved in the running of portfolio companies, often demanding a seat on the board of directors. They tend to accumulate requisite skills to monitor and advise portfolio companies by specializing in a particular industry or a specific stage of development.

In Japan, these characteristics are often absent. Excepting a small number of private venture capitalists who have the same investment approach as their US counterparts, venture capital funds take a more 'hands-off' approach. Three factors underpin this practice. First, Japanese venture capital firms have a wide portfolio of thinly spread small investment projects. Indeed, the average size of investment in Japan, at $0.5 million, is one-eighth of the average in the United States (see Table 7.3). With a wide portfolio, there is insufficient time to monitor each project. Second, venture capital firms that are subsidiaries of banks and insurance companies may use the same sort of criteria for investment decision as for advancing loans with collateral. Third, there is a lack of specialization amongst Japanese venture capital firms, as most continue to provide funds for all stages of financing. In 2009, only 8 per cent of venture capital investment was made to support the establishment of new ventures (i.e. start-ups less than one year old), while 49 per cent of investment was committed to ventures with a track record of five years or longer (VEC, 2009).

Exiting

Venture capitalists turn illiquid stakes in private portfolio companies into realized returns. They can do so by 'exiting' an investment in a number of ways, including mergers and acquisitions (M&A) and IPOs. The risk-adverse characteristics of Japanese venture financing is also evident when exiting. During 2004 and 2008, nearly 80 per cent of Japanese start-ups were said to 'exit' venture capital finance via either IPO (42 per cent) or M&A (37 per cent); only 19 per cent resulted in bankruptcy or liquidation (Figure 7.5). By contrast, in the United States, only 47 per cent of exits were via IPO or M&A.

Until ten years ago, it was virtually unthinkable for young ventures to go public in Japan because of strict listing requirements. As a result, venture capital firms in Japan have realized gains mainly from interest payments on loans and normal returns on investment until around early 1990s. The opening of TSE

Table 7.3. Venture capital investment by stage

		No. of deals	Total (million US$)	Average size (million US$)
Japan[a]				
Stage	Start-up/seeds	300	173.2	0.6
	2–4 years	269	144.7	0.5
	4–7 years	246	125.7	0.5
	More than 7 years	496	267.8	0.5
The United States[b]				
Stage	Start-up/seeds	429	1548.7	3.6
	Early stage	1009	5245.7	5.2
	Expansion	1101	9050.0	8.2
	Later stage	1065	9526.3	8.9

[a]Japan data (2008) from a survey of sixty-three Japanese venture capitals, exchange rate is 1 US$ = 93.616 yen (2009 average).
[b]US data is based on a survey of all NVCA members and, is an average of year 2007, 2008, and 2009.
Sources: NVCA, 2010; VEC, 2009; OANDA, 2010.

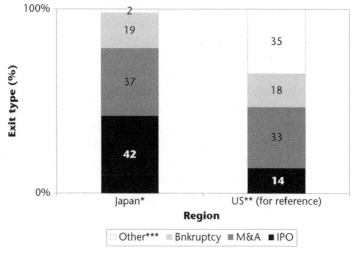

Figure 7.5. Venture capital investment by type of exit
* Japan data from April 2004 until March 2008
** US data from FY1991 to FY 2000
*** 'Other' includes exits when the investment is deemed unsuccessful.
Sources: VEC, 2009; NVCA, 2010.

Mothers and NASDAQ Japan produced a step change in this situation. Further, the government has been the agent of institutional change, legislating for the 1995 revision of the anti-trust law that permits venture capital investors to take board seats at portfolio companies, the 1997 legalization of stock options for all companies, and the 1998 Limited Partnership Act for Venture Investment. However, soon after their opening, these new markets' image problems led the government and other stakeholders to tighten the listing requirements for IPO. These raised the cost of listing for entrepreneurs, deterring some from IPO.

To summarize, since the late 1990s, the demonstration effect of the US dot-com boom and the private action by NASDAQ US and Softbank, followed by state actions, led to a step change in the rules for new companies in Japan, providing an option to go public. However, the layering of new stock exchanges onto a bank-based system remains thin, due in part not only to the mafia and scandals but also to the slow conversion of Japanese venture capital. It took over thirty years for Silicon Valley to develop an effective venture financing model. It is therefore too early to reach conclusions about the ultimate effects of new stock exchanges and venture capital in Japan. However, we observe for now a case of IIC in which the process of layering and conversion is here to stay for some time, putting a brake on each other rather than fuelling the speed of change. Moreover, in a sea of internationalizing financial markets, the Japanese financial institutions for start-ups remain remarkably domestic in their sources of funds, because of the absence of attractive high-return investment opportunities in Japan.

Changes in Labour Market Institutions

In labour markets, we examine two institutions. First, we present a case of conversion in Shunto, the annual pay bargaining round which went through a process of redirecting its goals, from being a 'spring offensive' for wage hikes into a discussion forum on the macroeconomy to accommodate wage restraint and pay dispersion. Second, we analyse the layering of atypical forms of employment onto the lifetime employment norm, triggered in part by labour law reforms implemented through a public policymaking process that came to exclude labour. We end this section by analysing the impact of these two institutional changes on lifetime employment.

Shunto Wage Bargaining as a Case of Conversion

Shunto—the Spring Offensive—is a highly coordinated annual wage-bargaining round, which began in 1955 when radical union leaders sought greater solidarity in bargaining to overcome the shortcomings of enterprise unions (see Sako, 1997 for details). Nevertheless, formal negotiations and settlements over pay and bonuses take place at the decentralized level of the enterprise, leading some writers such as Calmfors and Driffil (1988) to classify the Japanese bargaining structure as one of the most decentralized in the world.

Such characterization, however, misses the key mechanisms of information sharing and coordination that ensured that Shunto settlements were compatible with good macroeconomic performance and superior international competitiveness. First, at the national level, the two peak organizations, Rengo (Japanese Trade Union Confederation) and Nippon Keidanren (Japan Federation of Economic Organizations), issued 'guidelines' for non-inflationary wage demands and offers that Japan could afford. Second, unions and leading companies in export-oriented manufacturing sectors became pattern setters with powerful sanctions to stick to an agreed settlement that was uniformly applied to all bargaining units. Third, pay settlements were highly synchronized on a particular date in the spring, thus eliminating the possibility of wage leapfrogging. Fourth, wage settlement norms diffused in an orderly fashion from the private sector to the public sector, from leading pattern-setting sectors to follower sectors, from large to small firms, and from corporate headquarters to subsidiaries and affiliates.

Shunto thus acted as the functional equivalent of an encompassing organization (in Olson's sense (Olson, 1982)). Encompassing organizations police free riders and provide members with incentives to internalize externalities (here in the form of wage-push inflation). The Olsonian logic of collective action worked along three channels: first, through the organized business interests at the national and industry levels; second, through organized labour articulated from national, industry, down to enterprise levels; and third, through the institutional nexus between labour and product markets in bargaining within the corporate group. Union coordination via *roren* federations mirrored employer coordination within corporate groups (Sako, 2006).

A breakdown in this sort of collective action is evident in government statistics (Ministry of Health and Labour (MHL), annual). A survey of large firms demonstrates that over time, 'company performance' (i.e. the ability to pay) has grown in importance as a determinant in Shunto wage settlements, relative to the 'social norm', that is, setting wages according to the going rate that is seen to be socially acceptable (Figure 7.6). The same MHL survey shows that the dispersion of Shunto wage settlements, with spikes due to economic shocks, is on a secular upward trend (Figure 7.7). Moreover, with union density declining from over 30 per cent in the 1970s to 18.7 per cent in 2008, the survey captures an ever-diminishing segment of the Japanese economy.

In short, the rise in wage dispersion has been caused by a conversion in the goals of Shunto. Shunto may well be an institution whose utility has passed its sell-by date in the prolonged period of low inflation and low growth.

Layering of Atypical Forms of Employment

Since the late 1990s, labour markets in Japan have become decisively more diverse and flexible, due in part to a number of changes in the law as well as in corporate strategy. Non-regular or atypical employees increased from 8.8 million

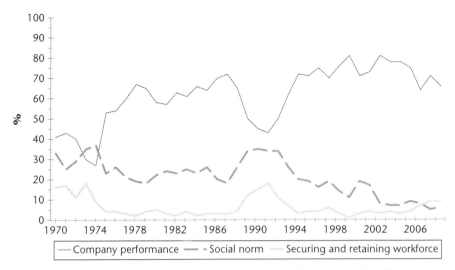

Figure 7.6. The most important factors (top three) in settling pay during Shunto negotiations
Source: MHLW, 2009b.

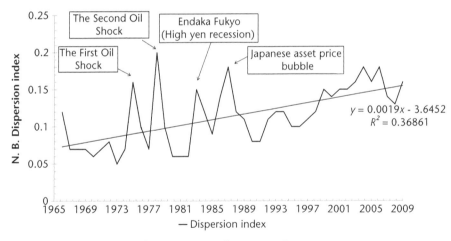

Figure 7.7. Dispersion in Shunto wage settlements in Japan
Note: Dispersion Index = (3rd quartile − 1st quartile)/(2 × average).
Source: MHLW, 2009a.

(20 per cent of the Japanese workforce) in 1999 to 17.6 million (34 per cent) by 2008 (JILPT, 2010: 36). In 2007, of 17.6 million atypical employees, the largest group remained part-time workers (22.5 per cent of total workers), followed by 'dispatched workers' (*haken rodosha*) provided by labour placement agencies (4.7 per cent of total workers). Although proportionately insignificant, the number of registered dispatched workers increased six-fold in just over a decade, from 437,000 in 1994 to around 3 million in 2007 (JILPT, 2010).

The labour market in post-war Japan has always been somewhat segmented. Thus, non-regular workers such as part-timers and seasonal workers were in use in the 1960s. But the period after the late 1990s has been marked by a greater use of different types of atypical workers. Whereas in the past these workers were hired as a buffer to cope with cyclical fluctuations in demand, the prolonged recession of the 1990s has encouraged firms to use them on a continuous basis to reduce personnel costs and to turn fixed costs into variable costs (Sanseiken, 2004). Competition from China has put extra pressure on Japanese firms to make greater efforts towards cost reduction. This also means that contingent labour has become more prevalent on the manufacturing shop floor. In manufacturing, there are as many workplaces where regular and non-regular workers are doing the same tasks as workplaces where the two are clearly separated (Sato et al., 2004: 81).

Legislative changes accelerated since the late 1990s, when employers' demand for deregulation found a more receptive government during and after the Hosokawa administration. Although the tripartite labour advisory council had been the main body for deliberating and formulating new bills, it came to be bypassed by the Deregulation Subcommittee that systematically gave greater voice to employers and the state at the exclusion of labour representatives (Nakamura, 2009). Labour, through its peak organization Rengo, changed tack by shifting its focus from advisory councils to the Diet, that is, from a relatively consensual bureaucratic policymaking process to a more contentious political forum involving lobbying and negotiations with political parties (Miura, 2003).

In this climate, it became possible to pass a large number of revisions in labour law. The 1985 Labour Dispatching Law (*haken ho*), legalizing temporary agency work for specific occupations, was revised in 1996 to increase the number of permitted occupations from sixteen to twenty-six. The 1999 revision then turned this positive list of permitted occupations into a 'negative list' of prohibited occupations, most importantly in manufacturing. The 2003 revision finally lifted the prohibition of the use of agency labour in manufacturing, and extended the maximum period of continuous employment of agency workers from one to three years.

Before the prohibition was lifted, on-site contractors (*kounai ukeoi*)—who must provide machinery and equipment as well as supervision of labour—came to occupy manufacturing areas where employers would have preferred to hire agency labour. They are concentrated in electronic components manufacturing, automobile assembly and parts manufacturing, and telecommunications equipment (Sato et al., 2004: 30). However, agency workers have come to replace on-site contractors in production areas where employers prefer direct supervision. On-site contractors are therefore being forced to rethink their business strategy, by diversifying into labour placement agency business or by focusing on more specialist high-skill tasks (Kimura et al., 2004).

Moreover, the 2003 revision of the Labour Standards Law extended the maximum length of fixed-term contracts of directly employed temporary workers from one year to three years, and this has increased their use. At Toyota, for example, the number of fixed-term employees increased from 3140 in 2000 to 9520 in 2004, constituting 25 per cent of the total shop floor workforce (Sanseiken, 2004: 50). At the forty-four supplier companies surveyed by Chubu Sanseiken, the proportion of non-standard workers to total workforce ranged from 9 to 80 per cent. At one extreme, six out of the forty-four suppliers had 50 per cent or more of their workforce on non-standard contracts (Sanseiken, 2004: 1). Similarly at Nissan Oppama Factory, 20 per cent of a total of 2560 shop floor workers were on fixed-term contracts in 2003.[3]

The 1998 revision to the Labour Standards Law introduced the notion of discretionary work for non-professional white collar. This enables more flexible working and no overtime payment for a wider range of white-collar workers in a variety of sectors of the economy.

A wider use of contingent labour in the name of greater numerical flexibility and labour cost reduction has adverse implications for industrial relations. Enterprise unions are 'hollowed out'; if management ignores or simply informs unions on hiring atypical workers, unions' bargaining power and voice will become weaker. Moreover, in the new national politics of labour, Rengo (the trade union confederation) must perform a delicate balancing act as it attempts to represent the unorganized without exposing disagreements among affiliated unions on this issue.

Impact of the New Layer on the Old Institution of Lifetime Employment

The layering of atypical forms of employment appears to be gaining traction, in the sense that these new elements are gradually destabilizing the old institution of lifetime employment. The fringe has grown and has been eating into the old core slowly but surely in a number of ways. It is worthwhile clarifying what 'typical' or 'standard' employment is before identifying what it is not (Ogura, 2005). In Japan, 'atypical' refer to workers who are not in full-time employment with an indefinite contract length. However, implicit in the notion of 'lifetime employment' is the absence of restrictions placed on job scope and workplace location (Sato et al., 2004: 44). In theory, therefore, 'typical' employees would have no restriction on either, whilst 'atypical' workers would have limited job

---

[3] Factory visit by the first author as part of the International Motor Vehicle Program (IMVP) plant tour, 10 September 2003.

scope and no expectation of relocation. In reality, however, regular contracts have come to impose restrictions on work location or job scope, thus blurring the boundary between a typical and an atypical employment contract. A loyal company man who is willing to work at any location to do any job for the firm is on the decline.

Other restrictions came to undermine the ideal notion of lifetime employment. Whereas in the past it meant a job guarantee within a single firm, lifetime employment came to be redefined as an income guarantee with career support within a corporate group, and then further redefined as job security but with no income level guarantee in the 1990s. The pervasive use of early retirement at an earlier and earlier age—from 55 to 50 to 45 years of age—was applied to some established firms such as NTT Group (Sako and Jackson, 2006). This would eventually put an end to the essence of lifetime employment, be it job security or as income guarantee. Over time, mid-career hires are increasing gradually, occupying managerial positions as well as specialist positions in corporate hierarchies, undermining the notion of internal promotion.

In summary, by the late 1990s, Shunto had converted its goal from coordinated pay bargaining to acquiescing in wage restraint, facilitating greater pay dispersion and diverse forms of employment. Japan has had a core-periphery dual labour market. But the layering of atypical forms of employment has become much more significant, seriously threatening the institution of lifetime employment and enterprise unionism. Employment in Japan has become more diverse with greater reliance on numerical rather than functional flexibility, all in the name of defending employment security for the core workforce. As the core employees with secure employment and pay diminish over time, there will be at some point a qualitative change in people's perception of lifetime employment as a social norm.

Compared with financial market institutions, incremental changes in labour markets appear to be closer to this tipping point. The key reason for this lies in the greater capacity for action by the agent of change in labour markets. Management in the mainstream large corporate sector has had the capacity to act at the firm-level via corporate restructuring, and at the national-level via lobbying for policy changes. Management's upper hand has resulted from weaker organized labour on the domestic front and the exit option of closing Japanese factories and relocating to cheaper Asian locations on the international front.

Institutional Interactions for Start-ups

We now turn to the corporate level in order to observe how agency at this level has had a hand in transforming institutions. This section focuses on the case of a business start-up, in order to investigate how it takes advantage of institutional interactions in capital and labour markets and copes with relatively unfavourable institutions by avoiding their use. We analyse the case of Rakuten, one of the most successful venture start-ups in Japan since the 1990s. Established in 1997, Rakuten group grew rapidly, reaching a consolidated sales turnover of 298.2 billion yen and 5810 employees in 2009. The company is listed on JASDAC with a market capitalization of 885.5 billion yen (US$9.4 billion as of 31 March 2010). Its core business, Rakuten Ichiba, is Japan's largest online shopping mall, which accommodates 31,831 online stores and generated gross merchandise sales of 1186.1 billion yen (US$12.6 billion) during FY2009.

Starting the Business by Avoiding Existing Institutions

In the initial stage, the founder of Rakuten, Hiroshi Mikitani, teamed up with a number of university students with deep knowledge of the Internet. His charismatic background with a Harvard MBA and work experience as an investment banker at a prestigious Japanese bank attracted young talent.

The online shopping mall business requires a relatively large initial investment to exploit economies of scale, with a small incremental cost for each new store. However, Rakuten did not seek any funding from venture capital and relied on internally generated funds. This was possible partly because the firm avoided spending amounts on system development by employing young yet skilled IT engineers. Moreover, it could generate an abundant cash flow by charging a monthly usage fee (initially 50,000 yen per month) to participating online stores regardless of their merchandise sales level. Thus, after completing the development of the system, the key to growth lay in attracting as many new stores as possible.

Consequently, Rakuten promoted its online business aggressively to small locally based shops across Japan. Partially due to the Internet boom in the late 1990s, many of these shops were considering starting an online business but did not know how. Rakuten reached out to them by recruiting relatively inexperienced workers and trained them to become sales representatives. Thus, Rakuten developed a business model of revenue generation that avoided reliance on external financial institutions and the normal channel of recruitment in the labour market.

Growth through Crafting its Own Ecosystem

The next stage of sustainable growth came with implementing an aggressive M&A strategy financed with internally generated cash, executive head hunting, and mass new-graduate hiring. Rakuten went public, listing on JASDAQ, on 19 April 2000, and started to seek M&A opportunities. In pursuing M&A successfully, Mikitani used his investment banking knowledge to its full and collaborated with other Japanese start-ups such as SoftBank and Culture Convenience Club. In the decade to 2010, Rakuten executed more than twenty acquisitions and investments, including a $425 million acquisition of Link-Share Corporation, $105 million for eBANK Corporation, and $109 million for Ctrip.com International. These large acquisitions were enabled by Rakuten's market capitalization, which grew from $5.4 billion to $10.1 billion during 2004–10, and the cash-rich nature of its core business. In 2010, Rakuten Group consisted of around fifty companies operating in seven different business segments (Table 7.4).

Especially after the IPO in 2000 and the establishment of a professional baseball team, Rakuten Golden Eagles, in 2004, Rakuten enhanced its visibility and reputation. Consequently, recruiting became easier than before. Rakuten Ichiba, the original core business of online shopping malls, grew from only 169 employees in 2000 to almost 6000 in 2010. This rapid expansion in employment required a two-pronged human resource policy to attract suitable talent.

Firstly, Rakuten found top talent through headhunting firms and via its acquisitions, and assigned such talent to the management of the portfolio companies. They often came from investment banks or consulting firms and engaged in corporate planning and/or deal execution. Acquisitions also worked as an important recruiting tool for Rakuten. It treated top management talent in the acquired firms with extreme care, providing attractive compensation packages. Internal promotion to top management at Rakuten companies is not impossible, but said to be unlikely without experience in M&A or strategy advice, the sort of capabilities that are difficult to acquire within the Rakuten firms.

Secondly, Rakuten also hires a large number of fresh graduates. Starting in 2001, new-graduate hire has been increasing. It planned to hire 400 new graduates in FY2009 and 600 in FY2010. New graduates typically become either programmers or sales representatives. Top performers are seldom promoted to management, however. Labour turnover is said to be relatively high. An ex-employee of Rakuten mentioned that extremely tough on-the-job training and sales targets could nurture excellent talent, but also trigger dropouts and departures.

The Ecosystem: Mobile Personnel and Liquid Funds

Once Rakuten became large, it became easier to access sufficient funds and talent. The challenges faced when the enterprise was young and small faded away as it developed a conglomerate governance model that functions as a start-up incubation system.[4]

---

[4] A similar strategy to Rakuten has been pursued by other Japanese start-ups including Cyber Agent (an online ad agency), dwango, GMO Internet, and Softbank (see Sako, 2003, for Softbank).

Table 7.4. Rakuten's group companies

Primary industry	Business	Company name	% Owned
Commerce	Online shopping mall	Rakuten, Inc. (JASDAQ:4755)	–
	Online shopping mall	Rakuten USA, Inc.	100
	Online shopping mall	Rakuten Thailand Co., LTD	100
	Online shopping mall	TARAD Dot Com Co., Ltd.	67
	Online shopping mall	Rakuten Taiwan	51
	Online supermarket	Net's Partners, Inc.	79
	Wine sales	Fine Wine	100
Net service	Betting ticket sales	Keiba Mall	100
	Donation agency	CauseLoyalty, LLC	100
	Online auction	Rakuten Auction Inc.	60
	Online portal	Infoseek Japan K.K.	100
	Photo printing	Rakuten Shashinkan, Inc.	67
	Second-hand sales	Bizseek, Inc.	83
	Q&A service	OKWave	19
Service	Dating service	O-net, Inc.	100
	Hospitality service	Signaturejapan Co., Ltd.	100
	Recruiting agency	Rakuten Sociobusiness	100
	Ticket agency	Rakuten Enterprises	100
Travel and logistics	Logistics	Kajiyama Warehouse Co., Ltd	100
	Logistics	Rakuten Bus Services Co., Ltd.	75
	Travel	Rakuten Travel Korea Inc.	100
	Travel	Rakuten Travel Guam Inc.	100
	Travel	Rakuten ANA Travel Online	50
	Travel	World Travel System	20
	Travel	Rakuten Travel Inc.	100
Media	Database marketing	Target, Inc.	100
	Loyalty programme	Freecause, Inc.	100
	Marketing agency	LinkShare Corporation	100
	Marketing agency	LinkSare International	100
	Marketing agency	Traffic Gate., Ltd	100
	Marketing research	Rakuten Research, Inc.	100
	TV broadcasting	ShowTime, Inc.	100
	Asset management	Rakuten Securities, Inc., Asset Management Arm	100
	Asset management	Rakuten Investment Management, Inc.	100
	Bank	eBANK Corporation	70
	Consumer finance	Rakuten Credit, Inc.	100
	Credit card	Rakuten KC Co., Ltd.	97
	Investment	RS Empowerment	100
	Real estate roan	Rakuten Mortgage Co., Ltd.	100
	Securities	Rakuten Securities, Inc.	100
	Securities	Dot Commodety Inc.	57
IT	Systems development	Ebank Systems Corporation	58
	Systems development	TechMatrix Corporation	32
	Systems development	Drecom Co., Ltd.	20
	Systems development	Synergy Marketing, Inc.	14
Sports	Baseball	Rakuten Baseball, Inc.	100
	Merchandising	Rakuten Sports Properties, Inc.	100
Telecommunication	Broadband	Fusion Communications Corp.	74
	Network service	Fusion Gol	100
Real estate	Real estate agency	Next Co. Ltd.	17
	Real estate management	Rakuten Realty management	100

Source: Capital IQ, 2010.

The core business, Rakuten Ichiba, provides corporate venture capital (CVC). It invests in or acquires new businesses and provides not only financial resources but also intangible resources such as networks, business know-how, a high-profile brand name, and human resources. Different from a typical CVC model, Rakuten only invests in their group (or acquired) companies. The core business endorses and attracts new customers and potential job applicants who perceive the small companies as an integral part of the core business. However, in many cases, these small start-ups are managed relatively independently of the core business, especially if the business area is different. This unique model may be considered a hybrid between a Japanese *keiretsu* system and a Silicon Valley business cluster. Internal financing and internal job rotation resemble the keiretsu system, but the way the independent companies operate and core business support of them is closer to the US start-up incubation model.

There are several reasons behind this development of a hybrid conglomerate incubator model at Rakuten. First, in order to avoid the inhospitable fundraising and recruitment climate in Japan, new ventures become subsidiaries in a corporate group to obtain capital and access to management talent. Second, the domestic focus of the parent company also contributes to building a conglomerate. Once the domestic market is saturated, the only way it can grow further is to start or acquire new businesses. The pressure for high growth due to the high valuation of the firm also pushes it to go for aggressive growth via acquisition. Third, relatively low liquidity and a small quantity of stock options allocated to employees weaken their incentive to monetize the stock options and start new businesses.

Despite a relatively difficult institutional environment, a small number of start-ups have achieved high growth. No dominant successful venture incubation model has emerged in Japan to cope with the Japanese business system. However, as illustrated by the Rakuten case, one response has been to build a financial and managerial employment ecosystem and to protect the business 'family' from a harsh external environment. With global financial market integration, corporate groups may have lost some of their rationale in established business, but a corporate group as a start-up incubator may retain its *raison d'etre* in Japan and other emerging economies.

Discussion and Conclusions

This chapter analysed how institutions within and between financial and labour markets interacted in Japan in the past two decades. It also addressed the impact of changes in business and labour relations with the state. We advanced a model of IIC elaborated by Streeck and Thelen (2005) with explicit regard to institutional ambiguity, collective agents for change, and their capacity for action as causes of institutional change.

In financial markets, venture capital in Japan experienced 'conversion'—shifting its goal and function from being part of the Japanese institution of relational banking towards being more part of an equity-based finance system, but the pace of change is slow. New stock exchanges were opened for start-ups, but remain layered without directly threatening the existing institutions of relational banking and stock exchanges for established public corporations. Thus, the layering and the conversion of these institutions are neither threatening nor undermining the pre-existing, bank-based institutions (see also Fields, this volume).

In labour markets, Shunto is portrayed as a case of 'conversion', with its function changing from coordinated pay bargaining to a mechanism for legitimizing pay restraint and dispersion. At the same time, atypical work was identified as a case of 'layering' onto the norm of lifetime employment. Although the Japanese economy had always had a dual labour market, legislative changes and firm-level practices that fuelled the use of agency labour and on-site contracting in manufacturing threaten the norm of lifetime employment more fundamentally than in earlier periods. Thus, unlike in financial markets, layering and conversion in labour market institutions are stronger and appear irreversible.

Why should institutional change appear more extensive and sustainable in labour markets than in financial markets? The answer resides in differential causes of change. In financial markets, organizational diversity has increased within the Japanese economy due to the continued layering of new stock exchanges and venture capital, two elements of an equity-based financial system. However, they do not seem to threaten the bank-based financial system at the heart of the Japanese economy. This add-on diversity, therefore, is not a sign of gradual breakdown of the system. The agents of change are foreign (e.g. NASDAQ), non-establishment (e.g. Softbank), and small and unorganized (e.g. start-up entrepreneurs). Their power base is weak and peripheral compared to the established political clout of the financial and corporate world of *Zaikai*. These powerful incumbents in the main financial system do not have a direct vested interest in the layered segment for start-ups, a sphere therefore defined more by indifference than contestation. We should note, however, that our study did not address the entire financial system in Japan (but see Takahashi, this volume), which itself has been changing gradually to incorporate new hybrid forms of corporate governance (Ahmadjian and Robinson, 2005; Jackson, 2009).

In labour markets, much more drastic and active changes have occurred in the last decade. The extent of conversion of Shunto seems so fundamental, resulting essentially from the shift in the shift of power from unions to employers. As argued above, the nature of layering of atypical forms of employment is also more threatening to labour, potentially leading to de facto displacement of the institution of lifetime employment. Institutional change is more extensive in the Japanese labour market because the agent of change here is management in the mainstream large corporate sector, who have the capacity to enact the desired institutional changes via managerial action at the firm-level, collective action in wage bargaining, and influencing policymaking at the national level. Japanese management benefited from fragmented organized labour and was able to strengthen their bargaining and political power. Moreover, whilst labour–management relations are always contested, employers have been able to exploit the ambiguity in the normative institution of lifetime employment to their advantage.

In order to examine the extent to which the impact of institutional changes in financial markets depends on institutional arrangements in labour markets, and vice versa, this chapter analysed the development of Rakuten, an online shopping mall. We found that Rakuten did not rely on external financial institutions at the outset, developing instead a hybrid labour policy of hiring mid-career managerial talent and new graduates for its sales force. As the company grew, Rakuten internalized its capital market, acting as CVC to finance as many as fifty new start-ups, keeping them as part of a corporate group rather than managing a cycle of investment and exit for each firm. This is just one in a variety of patterns that result from entrepreneurial efforts to start a new business within the Japanese system. But it is consistent with the coexistence of hybrid forms of corporate governance (Jackson, 2009). It also illustrates clearly that the institutional interaction between financial and labour markets can remain relatively loose.

It is difficult to predict whether or not 'layering' may eventually lead to displacement of the old by the new institution, and the extent to which 'conversion' may lead to the de facto disappearance of an institution. Nevertheless, the analysis contained in this chapter, by focusing on causes of institutional change, provides some grounds for why we might conclude that institutional change may be much more sustainable in labour markets than in financial markets. Generally in Japan, as elsewhere, the world is much 'flatter' in financial markets than in labour markets. However, this study demonstrates that far from the internationalization of financial markets putting pressure on Japanese firms to adopt more market-oriented labour practices, employers' interest in liberalizing labour markets is gaining more traction than their interest in deregulating financial markets.

Part Four

Financial Market Structures

8

Political Hierarchy and Finance: The Politics of China's Financial Development

Richard W. Carney

In comparison to other countries at similar levels of development, China relies far more heavily on banks, with state ownership of both financial and nonfinancial institutions predominating. At the same time, its stock markets have exhibited stunning, though volatile, growth since their launch in the early 1990s. Yet both banks and stock markets have had continuing problems with respect to the accumulation of nonperforming loans (NPLs) and the expropriation of minority shareholders, respectively. Recent efforts have sought to address these problems with seemingly contradictory approaches: by introducing international standards of best practice that strengthen market mechanisms while also placing the management of the largest banks and enterprises firmly under the central leadership's control. This chapter presents a political explanation for China's financial development since it initiated market reforms in 1978 and concludes that the introduction of best practices from abroad are unlikely to substantially reduce the state's role in its financial system, though the role and motivations of the state differ between the national and local levels.

To explain various attributes of China's financial arrangements, scholars have pointed to the overriding power of senior leaders in Beijing (Green, 2004), competition between political elites from different factions (Shih, 2008), leadership dynamics in combination with external conditions and crisis (Yang, 2004), and inter- and intra-bureaucratic bargaining and incrementalism (Lieberthal and Oksenberg, 1988; Lampton and Lieberthal, 1992). However, these arguments have difficulty accounting for dynamics at the local level because they focus primarily on regulatory battles at the national level. But in a large economy with decentralized power centres, the distinction between local and national can be especially important (Montinola et al.,

1995; Redding and Witt, 2007). Accordingly, the argument made in this chapter focuses on the implications that arise from party officials' incentive to meet specific economic growth targets for their jurisdiction (village, town, city, provincial, or national) in order to be promoted. The process resembles that of a rank-ordered tournament (Lazear and Rosen, 1981).

Because of fierce competition for promotion, political officials are likely to use the financial system to generate higher growth for their specific jurisdiction while diffusely spreading the costs onto the broader Chinese society (Olson, 1965). Baye et al. (2012) have developed a model that is particularly suitable to this situation since it explicitly incorporates the possibility for negative externalities into a rank-ordered tournament. As the jurisdiction of a Chinese Communist Party (CCP) leader increases from the local to the national level, the ease of achieving economic growth by passing costs off onto others diminishes. In other words, distributive welfare calculations give way to aggregate welfare calculations. Thus, when total costs generated by local political incentives reach crisis levels, national leaders must act before a genuine economic crisis ensues, creating the possibility for dramatic financial reforms.

The problems associated with accumulating externalities become greater as: (a) the number of local jurisdictions increases in relation to the total size of the state, and (b) the power wielded by local authorities grows. These two attributes distinguish China from other East Asian states where centralized control has been easier to achieve. In these smaller settings, coalitional conflicts and/ or personal and networked political logics prevail as discussed in Chapter 1 of this volume as well as in the Pepinsky and Zhang chapters.

This chapter is divided into the following sections: (a) the presentation of the political argument; (b) an analytic narrative of the changes that have occurred across three financial dimensions—banking, corporate governance, and equities markets—since 1978; (c) a discussion of the dysfunctionalities that persist in China's financial system; and (d) a concluding section on how China's financial system fits with respect to the country's labour relations and business systems as well as implications for other countries.

Political Hierarchy and Financial Implications

Among scholars of American politics, the re-election incentive is a central premise for numerous theories about the behaviour of politicians and political parties, the evolving structure of many political institutions, and a wide array of economic policies and outcomes (Mayhew, 1974; McCubbins and Sullivan, 1987; Persson and Tabellini, 2002; Jacobson, 2004). China's policymakers operate under very different incentives since they are not democratically elected. Yet, work on American politics demonstrates the importance of understanding political leaders' core incentives and the wide-ranging implications they can have on political and economic outcomes.

In China, political officials' core incentive is promotion (Li and Zhou, 2005). The mechanism by which CCP officials vie for promotion resembles that of a rank-ordered tournament in which participants are given a ranking relative to others rather than being assessed based on absolute performance criteria (Lazear and Rosen, 1981). The ranking primarily depends on the capacity of an official to meet (and preferably exceed) specific growth targets for their political jurisdiction (Chen et al., 2005).

There are five criteria that must be satisfied for the tournament model to work effectively. First, elite leaders must have the power to set measurement criteria and promotion. Second, the criteria must be clearly measurable. Third, individual performance must be clearly separable from others. Fourth, individuals must also be able to create better performance with more effort. And fifth, participants must not be able to form a conspiracy against elite leaders. China's promotion system effectively meets these criteria, and thus generates a highly competitive tournament among CCP officials.

However, competitive pressures are amplified in two ways. First, the incentive effect and aggregate growth consequences are magnified by the five levels of government that set growth targets: village, town, city, provincial, and central. The tournament occurs at each level, and to outperform their peers, officials at the lower levels of the political hierarchy commonly set higher growth targets than those proposed by the central government. Second, incentives are further enhanced by the difficulty of finding positions outside of the political system once officials enter into it; in other words, there is effectively no external job market and officials are locked into the system for life once they enter it (Li and Zhou, 2005). As a result, competition for promotion is fierce.

Although this system has helped China to achieve high levels of economic growth, there are also a variety of negative externalities as well as clear implications for the structure of the financial system. In the pursuit of economic growth, local leaders use every policy strategy, including all financial instruments available. Local officials have an incentive to encourage over-lending and over-borrowing for the benefit of their local jurisdiction while passing the costs off onto the broader Chinese society. Because state-owned enterprises (SOEs) and banks can be confident of being rescued, firms become uncompetitive and unprofitable over time, and banks accumulate NPLs. And even when firms are not state owned, local politicians have an incentive to help private firms by overspending on infrastructure or granting overly generous lending arrangements to foster local growth. In addition to excessive bank lending, selling equities to the public is another potential way to raise financing cheaply, but it is also open to abuse. With a weak judiciary, this option can easily turn into a predatory form of financing, with individual investors lacking any effective recourse from having their investments expropriated.

The weak legal system is particularly problematic to remedy since the promotion tournament creates incentives for local leaders to retain influence over it. Why, after all, would they want to allow legal decisions that could harm them or their efforts to promote economic growth or their career? Consider that in addition to the CCP's capacity to choose judges, whose terms of office are not secure and thus subject to political influence, the financial resources of the local people's courts are provided by their respective local governments. In order to sustain or to get more resources, the people's courts often take into consideration the effects of their judgements towards the administration (Peerenboom, 2002). This situation contributes to the prevalence and persistence of corruption. The financial system is particularly vulnerable since its effectiveness depends upon an effective legal system with strong protections for investors (in stock markets) as well as for lenders and borrowers (for banking).

These institutional arrangements create strong incentives for owners to retain concentrated ownership of their enterprise. The poor legal system also makes the emergence of pyramidal corporate structures more likely for two reasons. On the one hand, corporate groups are useful for internalizing factor markets when the costs of contracting outside the firm are high (Khanna and Palepu, 2000). At the same time, pyramidal structures enable owners to magnify the assets under their control and generate higher profits both through the ownership of larger corporate groups as well as via tunnelling (Johnson et al., 2000).

With CCP officials incentivized to maximize growth in their local political jurisdiction in order to win promotion, and with this competition occurring across numerous levels from the local village to the national level, negative externalities can quickly accumulate. Over time, the increase in NPLs and the expropriation of minority shareholders may lead to a political/economic crisis if left unaddressed. In such situations, national leaders must act on behalf of the nation's aggregate welfare.

How to react is an important political choice, and it forces us to consider what Chinese national leaders regard as their top political priorities. First, and foremost, is the survival of the CCP. This is mainly based on two things: (a) ensuring loyalty to the party and its hierarchy among CCP members and preventing challengers, and (b) sustaining a minimum level of economic growth in order to generate jobs and rising incomes. The first statement explains why CCP leaders are fearful of allowing large privately owned firms since this could enable the emergence of interests that do not depend on the CCP for their survival, and which could potentially rival the CCP for influence. The second statement reflects that CCP leaders have been most concerned about civil unrest from two key groups: workers and peasants (i.e. farmers).

With respect to the second point, consider that the leadership called rural unrest a 'life or death' issue for the party at the central party meeting in 2004 (Watts, 2005).[1] And in February 2007, Chinese Premier Wen Jiaobo emphasized that China was still poor, and that all the other objectives China seeks depend on economic development; hence, escaping from poverty is the essential pre-requisite, and development 'is the only hard truth' (Naughton, 2007a). But just to meet the growing demand for jobs (from graduates of college, vocational school, secondary school, ex-soldiers, rural–urban migrants, laid-off workers, and the urban unemployed), the Chinese economy must grow at least 7 per cent annually, according to the former vice president of the CCP Party School Zheng Bijian (Shirk, 2007).

Although workers and farmers lack political representation in China's government, they exercise unusual political influence because of Chinese leaders' fears of popular upheaval. Consequently, Chinese officials placate these groups while at the same time shifting the economy in a market-oriented direction, and integrating it into the global economy. Doing this necessarily means moving the economy away from agriculture towards industry, introducing more flexible employment, and allowing unsuccessful businesses to fail and for their workers to lose their jobs. But because of the large numbers of non-competitive SOEs, and the potentially huge job losses, Chinese leaders have good reasons to tread carefully to avoid a political backlash (see Figure 6.1 in Lee's chapter in this volume for the magnitude of urban employment among SOEs). Local politics reinforces this political pressure: 'branch managers sometimes face political pressure from local government leaders to continue to supply [state-owned enterprise] funding, because this keeps the largest employers in the area afloat, and it is in the interest of both the local government and the bank itself to protect local jobs' (Farrell et al., 2006).

How do national leaders concerned with aggregate welfare respond to the high costs generated by ambitious local officials? They transform the costs from spatially determined (i.e. geographically determined) to temporally determined (i.e. passed on to the future). The strategy is to reduce the size of current costs as a fraction of gross domestic product (GDP) by increasing the size of national GDP over time via rapid economic growth. At the same time, institutional changes are being implemented to reduce moral hazard

[1] 2010 also marked the seventh consecutive year that the government's annual No. 1 Document has emphasized rural issues. This document is jointly issued by the Central Committee of the CCP and the State Council to highlight significant economic concerns of the State. Consider that the rural population was estimated at 58 per cent of the total in 2007 according to the CIA World Factbook.

(i.e. imposing stricter lending criteria on banks), to improve protections for investors, as well as to shift responsibility for key areas particularly prone to local exploitation up to the national level.

To implement appropriate reforms, CCP leaders have looked for ideas from foreign market economies, and from individuals and companies with relevant experience. However, the ideas are implemented only if they do not weaken the CCP's power over the Chinese economy and political system, and if they do not threaten to generate social instability (Foot and Walter, 2011). Such reforms are most likely to occur when national leadership changes; the most transformational political decisions are likely to be implemented in response to a perceived imminent crisis (Yang, 2004). Thus, the promotion model is useful for explaining the evolution of the financial system since 1978, but it has evolved within broader constraints specified by national political leaders (i.e. the welfare of workers and farmers; Carney, 2009). Conflicts between agencies/bureaucracies at the national level occur once the basic priorities of loyalty to the CCP and economic growth/social stability are satisfied.

But there are two important problems that emerge from China's promotion-based political system. One is that it produces a fundamental contradiction in the behaviour of local officials. In their formal dealings with central party leaders, local officials want to demonstrate their unquestioning loyalty to the CCP to win promotion and to present the best possible image of themselves and their political jurisdiction. But when they return home, local officials face incentives to ignore regulations handed down from Beijing if they weaken the local official's power to decide how resources are allocated and to control/manipulate the reporting of information to CCP leaders so that s/he may win promotion. Control over the judiciary and the media exacerbate the problem by preventing third-party monitoring. Thus, the promotion model has the paradoxical effect of generating greater autonomy at the local level and concentrating powers in the hands of local officials while simultaneously seeking to bolster loyalty to the central leadership. With numerous local political jurisdictions and incentives to retain autonomy from the central leadership, externalities can quickly accumulate.

A second problem that emerges from the use of the promotion system is that its capacity to preserve loyalty to the CCP hierarchy may weaken as incomes rise. The problem is that people will value things other than rising incomes once they reach a minimally sufficient income level (e.g. environmental quality, education, social welfare). As a result, more non-measurable criteria may become important to preserving social stability, and promotion criteria may be difficult to specify clearly and to apply in a way that every participant regards as fair (Holmstrom and Milgrom, 1991; Naughton, 2009a). And even if loyalty to the CCP hierarchy is preserved, local leaders only face incentives to respond to the interests of leaders higher up in the hierarchy rather than local citizens. Citizens have no mechanism by which to hold their local leaders accountable from below, which becomes increasingly problematic as citizens' preferences become more multidimensional (i.e. economic growth is no longer their only or even their primary concern; see Mertha, 2010; Whyte, 2010). As these concerns grow, the increasing independence of the judiciary from political influence may provide a channel by which citizens can voice their grievances; this may lead to stronger protections for minority shareholders and lower levels of corruption with beneficial consequences for China's financial development. But such events are uncertain at present.

China's Financial Development

During the first thirty years of the CCP's rule, from 1949 to 1978, the command economy relied on a single monobank to allocate funds among state-owned and managed production units. To quell growing domestic unrest, China began marketizing its economy in 1978. As a result of the growing economy, households and unincorporated businesses began increasing their savings, which predominantly flowed into the banking system. The money measure M2, consisting of currency plus demand and savings deposits, increased steadily from 32 per cent of GDP in 1978 to 162 per cent in 2005, which is much higher than most other economies, and higher than East Asian economies, such as Japan. Household savings deposits increased from 6 to 77 per cent of GDP between 1978 and 2005 (Naughton, 2007b). The substantial increases in both of these ratios led to banks taking on a new important intermediation role.

To ensure savings continued to flow into the banking system, household term-saving deposits have been given supplemental interest at the rate of CPI increase during periods of high inflation, protecting their value. But with a banking system flush with cash, government officials have regularly tapped into bank surpluses to fund their clients, pet projects, and numerous loss-making SOEs. This led to an enormous stockpiling of NPLs and only at the end of the 1990s, after witnessing the dire consequences for other Asian countries during the 1997–8 financial crisis, did policymakers begin to grapple with the real costs of strengthening the banking system.

As NPLs accumulated, firms and government officials began looking to the stock market as an alternative financing vehicle. Since 1992, stock exchanges developed rapidly, becoming the second largest in Asia, after Japan, by some measures in 2000. They fell from 2000 to 2005, but have since rebounded due to efforts to improve corporate governance and protections for investors. At the same time, the largest banks went through substantial reforms and foreign partners were granted minority stakes. Table 8.1 depicts the broad changes

Table 8.1. China's financial development

	Banking	Corporate governance	Stock markets
Command economy, 1949–78	Monobank	State owned and managed	NA
Transition period, 1978–93	State owned; local decision-making power predominates	SOEs are dominated by local government influence	NA
Second phase of reform, 1993–present	Increasing centralized control to contain the proliferation of NPLs and 'agency costs' in the largest banks and SOEs		
1993–8, Li Peng	NPLs very high with initial efforts at reform	Limited market-enhancing reforms	Initiated, but highly corrupt
1998–2003, Zhu Rongji	Stronger NPLs reforms in wake of the Asian financial crisis	Limited foreign governance codes introduced	Limited reforms
2003–present, Wen Jiabao	NPLs moved off the largest banks' balance sheets; limited foreign ownership introduced but the state retains majority ownership via a centralized agency: Central Huijin Investment	Largest SOEs placed under the control of the SASAC to enhance management practices and to reduce 'agency costs'	Substantial reforms to protect individual investors due to growing public anger

that have occurred to China's banking system, corporate governance arrangements, and stock markets since 1949.

The basic pattern has been to move decision-making authority to the national level where aggregate welfare considerations trump the distributive welfare calculations and attendant costs generated by the highly competitive political system, and to introduce reforms from overseas within the political constraints of the CCP. Bold changes have usually occurred in response to heightened concerns about domestic unrest and with a change in leadership.

Command Economy, 1949–78

During the first thirty years of CCP control, the State was constituted and mandated by the Chinese people to own and manage all production. A 'governance system' in the Western sense did not exist (Tai and Wong, 2003). All power was provided to the public sector under a centrally planned system. Managers of SOEs were appointed and dismissed by government agencies in the same way as any other government official. Managers were not evaluated by the financial performance of the SOE, but instead by their ability to meet production quotas set by government agencies. Any excess financial surplus (profit) was remitted back to the State. Under this system, banks served as State financial distributors, providing the required financing to SOEs to carry out the production and distribution of goods and services according to State production targets (Tenev et al., 2002). But ongoing political and economic hardship, culminating in the Cultural Revolution, produced a legitimacy crisis for the post-Mao leadership. To retain its power, the CCP, led by Deng Xiaoping, shifted towards fostering continuous growth and raising people's living standards through economic liberalization and market-oriented reforms.

Transition Period, 1978–93

CCP leaders were concerned that introducing full-fledged market mechanisms could undermine the power of the party. To retain and bolster loyalty to the CCP while simultaneously fostering economic growth, dual-track reforms were introduced. Managers of SOEs were encouraged to expand production and focus on profits after fulfilling government production quotas. Changes to the financial system became necessary, including banking and corporate governance arrangements. Likewise, promotion of party officials within the CCP would be based on achieving economic growth targets, the overriding objective of the CCP for maintaining power.

In order to replace State budgetary grants and subsidies to SOEs, bank loans were gradually introduced from 1979. The People's Bank of China (PBOC) was formally established by the government in 1983 as the country's central bank, and its commercial banking activities were shifted to four newly created state-owned banks: the Agricultural Bank of China, the Bank of China, the China Construction Bank, and the Industrial and Commercial Bank of China, reflecting the State's perceived importance of these sectors to the overall economy (Naughton, 2007b). As state-owned financial institutions, however, the banks' loan policies ultimately remained under governmental control. As a result, the banking system was used to ensure that workers in inefficient firms did not lose their jobs due to increasing competition (Farrell et al., 2006). Many 'zombie firms' were kept alive by steady infusions of credit from the state banking system and a large buildup of NPLs inevitably occurred. At the same time, protections against inflation for savers led to banks often paying a relatively high price for the savings they controlled. For example, in 1995 the banks were paying 24 per cent annually for long-term deposits while charging 14 per cent annually for long-term loans. As bank profitability was impaired, their capital steadily eroded, thereby compounding the NPLs problem. By the mid-1990s, the banking system was in desperate shape (Lardy, 1998: 92–127).

As part of the effort to reform SOEs, the 'State-Owned Industrial Enterprises Law' (SOE Law) was introduced in 1988. Three specific features were established with respect to China's corporate governance arrangements (World Bank, 1997). First, the basic principle of separating ownership from management was introduced by granting managers of SOEs the power to act as legal representatives of the enterprise, including responsibility for the company's financial position. This feature thus initiated the separation of ownership and management in SOEs and incentivized managers to pursue profit-maximizing activities. Second, however, the SOE Law also ensured that local government would continue to oversee the implementation of the CCP's guiding principles and policies. Even though the separation of ownership and management was initiated, this provision ensured that the State would retain significant political influence over the management and operation of SOEs. Third, enterprises were permitted to introduce a more democratic management philosophy (e.g. through the employees' congress and trade unions). Unions were permitted to represent and protect the interests of employees, although the hierarchical structures of SOEs with a high concentration of power at the management level seldom provided employee organizations the possibility of playing a meaningful role (see World Bank, 1997; Lee, this volume). In summary, the law helped to introduce market incentives by granting managers greater autonomy over running the firm, but it simultaneously reinforced loyalty to the CCP and its hierarchical incentive structure.

Second Phase of Reform, 1993–Present

The second phase of reform reinvigorated the process of marketizing the economy. This was accomplished partly by reforming the banking system and its corporate governance arrangements with selective implementation of rules from abroad, as well as by dealing with the vast amount of NPLs. Corporate governance reforms to nonfinancial firms were also given new impetus, and stock markets were introduced as another avenue to raise financing with regulatory improvements being implemented over time. Despite all of these reform efforts, the political hierarchy that ensures CCP control and which creates incentives for abuse by officials seeking promotion has remained a central feature influencing the development of China's financial system.

Corresponding to initiatives to reform the financial system by national leaders worried about accumulating costs, particularly in response to potential social instability, the evolution of financial regulations can be seen as occurring in three phases: (a) 1993–8: Li Peng responds to fast accumulating NPLs and formally sanctions stock markets; (b) 1998–2003: Zhu Rongji responds to the Asian financial crisis (AFC) and China's future WTO membership with stronger efforts at dealing with banks' NPLs and implementing corporate governance reforms; (c) 2003–present: Wen Jiabao responds to growing public anger over the stock market with substantial reforms to protect minority shareholders, as well as placing the largest SOEs and banks under centralized administrative agencies—SASAC and Huijin—charged with improving their corporate governance and overall performance, and to this end allowing limited foreign ownership.

1993–8, Li Peng

BANKING

From 1994 through 1998, bank reforms were introduced to improve the commercial basis of the Big Four, and to separate commercial banking from state-directed lending. In 1993, three policy development banks were established to take over state-directed banking.[2] New laws were passed in 1995 to make bank management accountable for bank performance and to improve lending standards by making them more in line with international rules.[3] Additionally, loan officers were made individually responsible for new NPLs.[4] Although the state-owned banks were supposed to be responsible for dealing with NPLs incurred after 1996, their continuing accumulation was partly a reflection of underlying incentives to promote growth.

CORPORATE GOVERNANCE

As part of the broader effort to marketize the economy, the Company Law issued in December 1993 specified the maximization of owners' interests as the primary goal of corporate practice (Wang and Cui, 2006). The Company Law had a far-reaching impact on corporate governance and the economy as a whole by enabling many SOEs to corporatize and hence make initial public offerings in China's nascent stock exchanges (World Bank, 1997). Because managers typically owned non-tradable shares of these listed SOEs, managers had a much stronger incentive than before to produce authentic profits.

STOCK MARKETS

In the late 1980s, Shanghai and Shenzhen invested resources in building stock markets, but it was not until 1991 that the central government formally sanctioned them, with strong support from Zhu Rongji. Chinese stock

---

[2] The policy banks included the Agricultural Development Bank of China, the China Development Bank, and the Export–Import Bank of China.

[3] The new laws included the Commercial Banking Law and the Law of the People's Bank of China.

[4] To support the restructuring effort, the PBOC removed RMB 1.4 trillion (USD 170 billion) worth of pre-1996 NPLs and injected RMB 270 billion (USD 33 billion) (Li, 2009).

markets were permitted partly because of the role they could play in reforming the state enterprise sector as later stipulated by the 1993 Company Law (Naughton, 2007*b*). But the main reason they were approved is that they promised to create a new source of funding for SOEs. Revenue from the IPOs went to the listing firm or to its immediate parent which government officials accepted due to the financial position of SOEs; rarely would it go to the national treasury (Liu, 2006).

However, the new stock markets suffered from insider control and manipulation due to collusion among three types of agents: managers, securities companies, and regulators (Naughton, 2007*b*). The managers of state-owned firms had a strong interest in listing their company in order to gain access to cheap financing. Securities companies, which exercised a monopoly over trading and listing procedures, were 100 per cent state-owned companies until 2002 and typically owned by local governments. The China Securities Regulatory Commission (CSRC) held the ultimately scarce resource of permission to list, as well as regulatory approval of various transactions.

Resembling the initiation of bank reforms, local governments were major beneficiaries of the new arrangements through their ownership of securities companies and influence over SOEs (Bell and Feng, 2009). It was not uncommon for local governments to participate in making fraudulent corporate financial reports to deceive the public in order to get approval for a listing (Yu et al., 2005).

The secondary market also exhibited major problems since only one-third of the total shares were available to public investors and traded on the market.[5] The remaining two-thirds of the total shares of listed companies were held by government institutions (often local governments) and other SOEs and they could not be traded openly in the market; they could only be transferred privately or through occasional auctions. The highly restricted liquidity of the non-tradable shares resulted in their undervaluation, leading to a price discount against market prices of the tradable shares (Longstaff, 1995). Green (2003: 7) estimates that the state generally paid only a tenth of market prices for its equity holdings. Due to pervasive insider manipulation, Wu Jinglian, a prominent Chinese economist, saw the Chinese stock market as 'worse than a casino: at least in a casino there are rules' (Liu, 2006).

---

[5] Publicly tradable shares were further separated into A and B shares to limit the entrance of foreign investment. A shares were available only to domestic investors and purchasable in Renminbi, while B shares were those available to foreigners and Chinese investors purchasing in foreign currencies (US dollars in Shanghai and Hong Kong dollars in Shenzhen). However, A shares accounted for 95 per cent of the total tradable shares (Chen and Thomas, 2003). At the same time, a small number of Chinese companies were also listed in Hong Kong, with H shares.

1998–2003, Zhu Rongji

The beginning of Zhu Rongji's premiership coincided with the AFC of 1997–8, which demonstrated to Chinese leaders just how dangerous the fragility of the banking and broader financial system could be. As a result, several regulatory initiatives were launched and efforts made to place key parts more firmly under central government control where they would be less prone to abuse by local officials.

BANKING

In the wake of the AFC, Chinese policymakers began to recognize that rather than allowing the banking system to be looted, they needed to inject substantial resources into it in order to avert a potential crisis. Since 1998, strengthening the financial system has been perhaps the highest priority of Chinese policymakers (Naughton, 2007b). Shifting authority from the local to the national level was the answer.

One of the first initiatives was to restructure the PBOC by replacing its provincial-level branches with nine regional branches that would be less prone to local political influence. The central bank also began to actively conduct monetary policy, with a new monetary policy board established as a governance and advisory body. At the same time, state-run commercial banks soon faced more stringent budget constraints and stricter government oversight. In turn, they began to pass tougher standards on to their clients in SOEs.

To deal with the enormous problems of NPLs at the Big Four banks, which were estimated at 35 per cent of their total loan portfolio or 30 per cent of China's GDP (Liao and Liu, 2005), four asset management corporations were established in 1999 to take over most of them.[6] And in April 2003, a newly created China Bank Regulatory Commission (CBRC) acquired the PBOC's supervisory functions to bolster the financial supervision of banks and their lending practices. The goal was to improve banking supervision through the creation of a central administrative agency and to help the PBOC focus on the macroeconomy and currency policy.

CORPORATE GOVERNANCE

The 1998 Securities Law, also passed in response to the AFC, allowed investors to sue management and directors for releasing false or misleading company information, though these rights were rarely exercised to protect investors' interests (Kang et al., 2008). Nevertheless, the power of the CSRC was significantly strengthened and it took a more active role in monitoring and regulating publicly listed companies. For example, the CSRC published guidelines for

---

[6] The asset management corporations include Cinda, Huarong, China Orient, and Great Wall.

introducing independent directors to the Board of Directors in listed companies in August 2001, and it stipulated that at least one-third of trustee board members of all publicly listed companies should be independent directors. In January 2002, the CSRC and the State Economic and Trade Commission jointly issued the Code of Corporate Governance for Listed Companies, the first such code in China. It paid special attention to the protection of shareholders, especially small investors, and prohibited controlling shareholders from expropriating minority shareholders.

STOCK MARKETS

Corresponding to more assertive and centralized regulatory authority, a series of new regulations and harsh penalties from the CSRC were imposed on speculation beginning in 2000. As a result, the market index entered a prolonged decline and by 2005 more than half of all brokerages were effectively bankrupt (Naughton, 2007b). The market ceased to be a fundraising channel for domestic companies, and the huge numbers of bad loans in the banks that resulted from securities investments created the potential for extending risks in the stock market to the entire financial system.

While exploitation of the stock markets by local governments was reduced, the consequences of the market's fall became politically unaffordable for the regime. At least 25 million individual investors were affected, and more than 90 per cent of them faced losses, even though direct financing by the stock market constituted a small fraction of domestic lending in comparison to the banking sector (less than 10 per cent) (Green, 2003). Encouraged to invest in the stock market by deceptive policy and media campaigns, many felt betrayed by the government. According to one survey conducted in 2003, 62.5 per cent of investors would 'leave the market permanently' if they could have their principals back. In another national survey by the official Xinhua News Agency in 2005, the stock market was the issue of most concern to people, even surpassing the general issue of severe corruption (Bell and Feng, 2009). It was time for the central government to intervene more aggressively to rescue the stock market as it had recently begun to do with the banking system.

2003–Present, Wen Jiabao

The change in leadership reinvigorated efforts to reform the financial system. Public anger over the stock market led to reforms to protect individual shareholders and to related improvements to corporate governance with new, more assertive centralized control and regulations. Likewise, the ownership and management of the largest SOEs was placed under the control of a new state agency: the State Asset Supervision and Administration Commission (SASAC).

NPLs from the Big Four were shifted to the newly created asset management corporations and banks' governance mechanisms were enhanced partly not only through the sale of minority ownership stakes to foreign institutions but also by placing them under the administrative control of the Central Huijin Investment Corporation. Both SASAC and Huijin are directly controlled by the State Council, China's highest administrative authority.

A schism was clearly developing between Beijing and local governments. The stock markets, the largest SOEs, and the biggest banks were coming under greater centralized control, yet the incentives of local CCP officials had not changed. As a result, problems began to grow in other areas of the financial system not under Beijing's control such as local banks. Resistance to implementing reforms of national banks at the local level exacerbated the problems.

BANKING

In 2002, the State Council instructed the CBRC to implement banking reforms. Reforms to the largest banks came first. These reforms have been guided by international standards and best practices, including (a) the Core Principles for Effective Banking Supervision, (b) a combination of Basel I and Basel II capital accords, and (c) international practices in loan loss classification rules (CBRC, 2007). Efforts have also been made to bring in management practices from foreign banks through the sale of minority ownership stakes which appear to have improved bank performance (McGuinness and Keasey, 2009).

Although regulatory reforms of major banks were guided by international standards, their implementation exhibited numerous departures from the intention of the rules. For example, those standards that tended to concentrate key powers in the centre of banking and supervisory hierarchies were implemented rather vigorously, while principles that required independence of banks' boards and regulators were ignored in order to retain CCP control. Central Huijin Investment Ltd. clearly reflects this. It is a state-owned investment company established in December 2003 and controls major state-owned financial enterprises on behalf of the State. Its stated goal is to achieve the preservation and enhancement of the value of state-owned financial assets, beginning with the Big Four banks. Central Huijin's principal shareholder rights are exercised by the State Council. As a result, the incentives of bank managers are geared towards fulfilling objectives defined by the State Council and the Party even though these might be in contradiction with the long-term stability and profitability of the major banks.

The selective implementation of international standards has nevertheless helped to make the banking sector more transparent. But the lack of independence of supervisory bodies undermines the credibility of reported information. Such arrangements allow the continuation of soft-lending practices that result in heavy losses during surges in banking credit if the government deems it politically necessary. In short, the reforms did not reach the stage where the repetition of the vicious cycle of soft-lending followed by bail-out would be credibly prevented.

Further complications for meaningful banking reform have also been due to the weakness of a variety of supporting institutions, including accounting and auditing standards, a free financial press, and an independent judiciary. Reflecting the centre–periphery struggle, the legacy of large banks' branches functioning as semi-independent local banks with their regulators under local political control has proved very durable and has slowed the spread of new rules (Chiu and Lewis, 2006). Local government officials are reluctant to cede control over bank branches as it allows them to keep the benefits of reckless lending locally and to shift losses to the central government. These factors combined make banking operations based on international standards more difficult, even if these standards were fully implemented. Other characteristics of the Chinese economy such as 10 per cent growth, the 50 per cent saving rate, and liquidity generated by sterilization operations of the central bank have made it easier to postpone further reforms.

CORPORATE GOVERNANCE

National authorities have continued to implement corporate governance reforms that primarily target the largest firms. Although concentrated state ownership and a lack of independent board members remain common, the alignment of executive compensation with firms' performance has exhibited improvements and is consistent with the increased use of equity-based compensation (Conyon and He, 2008). Chinese authorities have also made important moves towards greater information disclosure and transparency with the 2007 'Regulations on Information Disclosure of Listed Companies'. While regulatory improvements have occurred, their effectiveness has been hampered by the lack of a strong legal system and a shortage of skilled accounting professionals (Lamper and Sullivan, 2008). As a result, capital markets remain inefficient, confidence in companies' financial statements remains weak, and minority shareholders lack effective legal protections.

This situation has contributed to the proliferation of pyramidal ownership in recent years (Liu, 2006). Pyramidal ownership, a common structure used in Korea, Singapore, Hong Kong, and other Asian economies, was not commonly observed in the earlier stage of China's stock market. But Fan et al. (2005) document that more than 70 per cent of government-controlled listed firms have two or more pyramidal layers, and almost all entrepreneur-controlled firms have more than two pyramidal layers.

Among entrepreneur-controlled firms, pyramiding is mainly driven by the lack of access to external funds. But among government-controlled firms, pyramiding often occurs in response to local government's incentives to enhance their rents by expropriating investors via 'tunnelling' (Tenev et al., 2002; Bai et al., 2004; Fan et al., 2005; Berkman et al., 2009).

To reduce these kinds of abuses, central government officials have begun centralizing and improving ownership and management of the largest SOEs, as was done with the largest banks. The management of the largest SOEs has been centralized and is now coordinated through a newly created agency, SASAC, which is under the direct control of the State Council. Its mandate is to 'own' these corporations and to manage them in the public interest (Naughton, 2007*b*).

STOCK MARKETS

The persistent market downturn from 2000 to 2005 and growing public anger forced leaders like Wen to reposition the function of the stock market away from predatory SOE financing to making it investor friendly (Naughton, 2003). Phrases such as 'protecting the interests of small and medium investors' were frequently recited in Wen's official and personal rhetoric (Naughton, 2007*a*).

An ambitious institutional reform, known as the Nine-Point Guide, was issued at a Cabinet meeting on 31 January 2004. It called for 'proactively and steadily resolving the issue of non-tradable state-owned shares' under the principles of 'respecting market rules, ensuring market stability and development, and protecting the interests of investors, especially public investors' (Bell and Feng, 2009).

It was clear that reforms had to be made that would privilege national welfare over local interests, but there was debate over what constituted the national welfare. Mandated to ensure the protection and promotion of state asset values, the SASAC favoured higher sales prices for its stock of securities. The CSRC by contrast is concerned with the stability of the market and regaining the regulator's credibility; it therefore tended to favour the interests of public investors.[7] Their opposing views held back reforms for almost two years, during 2003 and 2004 (Chen, 2004; Naughton, 2005). But the final programme of state share conversion (into public, tradable shares), announced in May 2005, was more in the CSRC's favour in terms of protecting individual shareholders' interests. Even Wu Jinglian, who was famous for his 'casino' comments, saw the new arrangement as more in favour of individual investors (Bell and Feng, 2009).

The share conversion scheme marked a credible commitment by the government to provide a level-playing field for state and non-state participants,

---

[7] However, the SASAC is the party that CSRC had to reach agreement with, not only because of the former's institutional stand but also because it controlled 168 listed companies, accounting for 33.8 per cent of domestic stock market value (Naughton, 2005).

including the rising presence of foreign institutional investors, thus paving the way for the internationalization of the market in the context of WTO-induced financial opening. The market subsequently witnessed a spectacular rise: the Shanghai Exchange shot up from a low of 1046 in July 2005 to 5589 in October 2007 with record-smashing volumes; as of May 2011 it was around 3000.

Dysfunctionalities

Since 1978, a schism between local and central control has emerged and intensified. While the centralization of control over the largest banks, SOEs, corporate governance codes, and stock markets has reduced local exploitation of these institutions, problems have grown in other areas not as firmly under the central leadership's control such as local control over branches of national banks and local/provincial banks. For example, NPLs ratios are considered to be much higher for banks that serve smaller towns and villages, and are known to be heavily influenced by local political considerations (Li, 2009).

At the same time, shifting authority over the largest financial institutions to the national level has generated new conflicts between national agencies and bureaucracies. This can augment distributional conflicts at the national level, potentially contribute to moral hazard problems, as well as create the potential for corruption as was observed among South Korea's *chaebols* in 1997. A contrasting model in which the state has (more) successfully governed the largest financial institutions and corporations is Singapore. However, an important difference between Singapore and Korea is their domestic dependence on inward foreign direct investment (FDI) and multinationals. Because Singapore relies so heavily on these, it is forced to cater to them by developing an effective judiciary for business, ensuring low levels of corruption, and fully complying with international rules and standards. For Korea, the IMF's intervention due to the financial crisis made such changes possible, but it still lags behind Singapore or even Taiwan (Zhang, this volume). Because China's domestic economy is so large, it faces less pressure to meet international standards and is thus more like Korea than Singapore, though with even less dependence on FDI than Korea. Thus, when domestic problems arise that could lead to social instability (e.g. the financial crisis of 2008), the Big Four banks and SOEs are likely to be called upon to make politically motivated, rather than commercially sound, business decisions; but because the size of the domestic economy is so large, the potential problems associated with making commercially unsound decisions are magnified. While China's centralization of the State's control over its largest banks and SOEs resembles Singapore's strategy, China lacks an effective judicial system, and has widespread corruption, further raising the potential for problems.

Another concern is that China may develop a dual economy like Japan's, with a competitive export sector and a non-competitive domestically oriented sector reliant on preferential treatment (e.g. subsidized lending) from local government officials. Although the decline in township–village enterprises corresponding to a rise in private enterprise at the local level suggests that more efficient market mechanisms are taking hold (Kung and Lin, 2007), strong political incentives to 'assist' them remain and Japan's dual economy illustrates that even without government ownership of local firms, private enterprise may nevertheless become dependent on government assistance. The desire for promotion creates incentives to facilitate over-lending and over-borrowing even for private firms, thereby exacerbating the problem of NPLs among local banks.

Conclusions

Despite the array of market-oriented reforms implemented since 1978, the state's power has remained a core and persistent feature. In fact, one could argue that the state's power has grown over time as it has claimed greater control over key domains of the financial system, including the largest banks, SOEs, and stock markets; or the 'commanding heights' of the economy as Breslin mentions (this volume). The main challenge to the state's dominance comes from the local level. The characterization of state control suggests a single monolithic authority, but China is perhaps better understood as having two types of state control: central and local. They both privilege banking and control over finance, but they have different motivations. Beijing seeks to maintain the CCP's control via economic growth and social stability. Local officials seek promotion and pursue local growth often at the expense of national welfare causing central CCP leaders to find ways to contain the costs.

This dichotomy offers a useful lens through which to view how changes to the financial system have co-evolved with the business and labour relations systems. For the largest firms and banks controlled by the State Council via Huijin and SASAC, state control is dominant and employment stability is relatively high. But among the smaller local firms, private ownership predominates. The importance of these firms to the national economy is substantial and growing, and employment in these firms is highly flexible as discussed in Ching Kwan Lee's chapter (Chapter 6).

The implications for other countries are most relevant for large nations where centre–periphery tensions are most likely to emerge. In fact, China's financial system reflects a problem not uncommon to other large states—costs generated by local governments being passed off to the central government. However, the specific mechanisms by which this occurs vary according to the structure of the country's political system. Brazil, for example, exhibited similar problems with respect to its fiscal situation in the early 1990s (Alfaro et al., 2001). But the difference is that Brazil was highly decentralized as stipulated by its constitution; the federal government was relatively weak. The lesson from China, therefore, is that even a strong central state does not necessarily prevent the accumulation of costs at the local level if the political incentives encourage it. Central leaders need to consider the incentives that drive political officials at both the national and local levels, and whether they produce complementary or conflicting outcomes.

9

The Political Economy of Financial Development in Southeast Asia

Thomas B. Pepinsky

Over the past half century, the emerging economies of Southeast Asia—Indonesia, Malaysia, the Philippines, and Thailand—have seen substantial growth and deepening of their financial systems. Today, Malaysia has one of the world's most dynamic equity markets, along with a large and deep banking sector that has grown rapidly since the 1960s. Thailand's financial system has also seen impressive growth since the 1960s, although it lags somewhat behind Malaysia. Indonesia and the Philippines remain relatively underdeveloped compared to their neighbours, but viewed in historical perspective, financial development in these countries has been nevertheless impressive.

In this chapter, I propose a political economy perspective on financial development in Southeast Asia that can explain differences across countries and changes over time. I focus on two issues: first, the origins of cross-national variation in financial development; and second, the institutional changes in national financial systems in Southeast Asia since the 1980s. Variation in financial development outcomes in Southeast Asia is the product of the political constraints and challenges facing regimes in the region. For various reasons that I outline in this chapter, financial development is potentially threatening to political regimes, especially fragile or newly consolidated regimes. But financial development also can promote economic development, something that political leaders throughout the region have been keen to harness for their own benefit. To manage this dilemma between the potential economic benefits and the potential political costs of financial development, political elites embedded financial orders within political orders as they jointly construct both. To explain the changing nature of financial development in Southeast Asia since the 1980s, this chapter focuses on the origins of political orders in the early postcolonial period and the strategies through which political regimes struggle to maintain them.

Variation in the political exigencies facing postcolonial regimes explains the variation in the financial systems that they constructed. This gives us leverage over the *origins of* financial systems. Malaysia's mobilizational regime, for instance, created the foundations for broad and deep financial development. In the Philippines, by contrast, a more personal style of rule was inimical to such a pattern of financial development. Facing a set of common external shocks in the 1980s, regimes in each country liberalized their financial sectors to a substantial degree, but they did so in different ways; the different regimes in turn responded to the subsequent 1997–8 financial crises in different ways as well. This explains *change and continuity* in financial systems across time.

This approach that I take in this chapter suggests that different constellations of economic and political power—which originate in the historical conditions of state formation and regime consolidation—are more important drivers of financial development than are institutional logics. What is striking, in terms of the typology of East Asian 'capitalisms' outlined in Chapter 1 of this volume, is in fact the broad similarity in the various financial architectures in each capitalism (see Table 9.1). Each variety of capitalism in East Asia features a pattern of corporate governance dominated by insider connections, each relies heavily on bank-based finance, and in each financial regulation is shaped by the state and private interests. These factors are indeed common to all four of the Southeast Asian financial systems surveyed in this chapter. The more interesting variation across these countries is in the depth and pace of financial development in Southeast Asia.

Putting that variation in financial development aside, there are of course other important differences among the varieties of East Asian capitalism: relative to state-led and personalized varieties, equity markets are more important in networked and co-governed varieties, while financial regulation features less private influence in the state-led variety than in the other three. These differences allow us to classify the four countries into different cells in the 1980s and 2000s, as shown in Table 9.1. Malaysia and Thailand, as I will discuss below, have deeper equity markets than do Indonesia and the Philippines. The state's role in directing finance regulation was larger in Indonesia prior to the 1990s than in any of the other three. But note that in contrast with the classifications developed in Chapter 1 of the volume, while Malaysia's broader economy could be described as state led in the 1980s, its financial architecture has more resembled that of a co-governed variety of capitalism throughout its independent history. Likewise, Thailand's financial architecture closely approximates a networked variety of capitalism than it does a personalized variety, even though the latter is perhaps more appropriate for studying the overall institutional contour of Thailand's political economy.

Table 9.1 Financial architectures in Southeast Asia, 1980s and 2000s

Variety	Co-governed	State led	Networked	Personalized
State	Strong	Strong	Weak	Weak
Society	Strong	Weak	Strong	Weak
Financial regulation	State-guided but with business influence	Heavily state controlled	State-influenced but significant business inputs and influences	State controlled but heavy private influence
Market structure	Largely bank based but better developed capital markets	Dominance of debt finance	Bank based but more important capital markets	Relation-oriented finance; poorly developed equity markets
Corporate governance	Insider model; insider practices in private firms	Highly bureaucratized in state-owned enterprises	Stakeholder/insider dominated	Insider model; dominated by owner–managers
National cases (1980s)	Malaysia	Indonesia	Thailand	The Philippines
National cases (2000s)	Malaysia		Thailand	Indonesia; The Philippines

Altogether, the argument in this chapter suggests that a political rather than an institutional logic best explains the origins and persistence of the cross-national variation in financial development in Southeast Asia.

Financial Development, 1960–2007

A proper accounting of financial development must take into account changes in both debt and equity markets, while also capturing the importance of the various functions of financial systems, from the mobilization of deposits to the assets of financial institutions to the provision of private credit to the domestic market. Financial development also implies an increase in capital market efficiency and a decrease in the cost of capital. Here, I draw on the most recent data available regarding key components of the financial systems of the four major Southeast Asian economies to provide an overview of financial development in Southeast Asia from 1960 until today.

Figure 9.1 begins with an overview of banking sectors from 1960 to 2007, drawing on data from the 2009 update of the Beck et al. (2000) database of financial structure and development (Beck and Al-Hussainy, 2010). Each panel captures a different indicator of development: the ratio of private financial sectors assets to public financial sector assets (Panel A), the assets of the banking sector relative to gross domestic product (GDP) (Panel B), the deposits

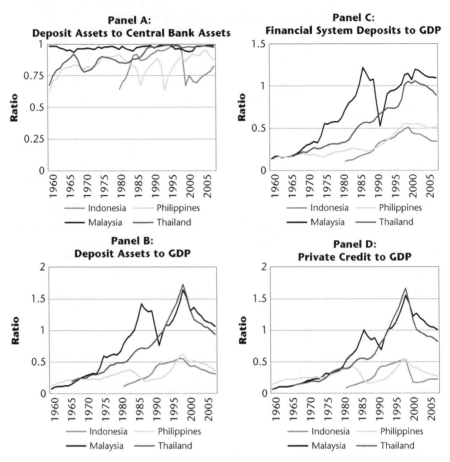

Figure 9.1. Banking sector development, 1960–2007
Source: Beck and Al-Hussainy, 2010.

in banks and other financial institutions relative to GDP (Panel C), and private sector domestic credit to GDP (Panel D). Most obvious in Figure 9.1 is that each of the four countries was significantly more financially developed in 2007 than it was in 1960 (or when data first became available). Also apparent is the dramatic setback in all indicators of financial development that corresponds to the 1997–8 Asian financial crisis (AFC). This downturn is so severe that most countries have yet to return to pre-crisis levels of financial development.

Despite these broad similarities, though, there are differences across countries in patterns of development over time. Today, Malaysia has the most developed banking system in the region (save Singapore). Note that while Malaysia's ratio of deposit money assets to central bank assets has always been higher than its neighbours, it reached independence with a banking system that by other measures was similar to the Philippines and

Thailand. By contrast, Indonesia and the Philippines score consistently lower in terms of banking system development than other countries today, even though they began at a similar point as did Malaysia.[1] Thailand lies between the two groups of countries. While in the 1960s its level of banking system development was roughly comparable to those in Indonesia and the Philippines, it has since developed in a way that brings it closer to Malaysia.

Figure 9.2 examines equity market development, using data from the same source and capturing stock market capitalization to GDP (Panel A), total share value to GDP (Panel B), share value relative to market capitalization (Panel C), and listed companies as a share of national population (Panel D). For each of these indicators, higher values correspond to higher levels of financial development. The patterns in each of the four panels reinforce the conclusions reached from Figure 9.1. All countries display substantial increases in equity market development between the mid-1970s (when data first became available) and today. As before, there is also clear evidence of a significant setback in three of the four indicators that corresponds to the AFC in the late 1990s (the exception is in the number of listed companies, which continues to increase steadily in each country).

As before, there are also cross-country differences in equity market development. The contrasts are less apparent in the stock market turnover ratio (Panel C) but the other three panels demonstrate them well. Malaysia has the most developed equity markets in terms of numbers of listed companies, stock market capitalization, and total share value; this was also true in the 1970s. Indonesia and the Philippines have always had significantly less developed equity markets. Thailand's equity markets remain relatively underdeveloped as well. They more closely parallel those in Indonesia and the Philippines, unlike its comparatively more developed banking sector. In all, then, these indicators of equity market development in Southeast Asia suggest patterns of cross-national variation that are roughly analogous to those observed in banking sector development.

Finally, because the indicators in Figures 9.1 and 9.2 are more properly indicators of financial depth than financial development, Figure 9.3 presents two measures of banking sector efficiency—average cost–income ratio (Panel A) and net interest margin (Panel B). For both of these measures, *lower* values should be considered indicators of greater efficiency (Demirgüç-Kunt and Huizinga, 1999), and hence *higher* development.[2] These data exhibit far more year-to-year variation than do the indicators in Figures 9.1 and 9.2, and the crises of the late 1990s yield large spikes that reflect unique market

---

[1] The figures from Indonesia are absent from prior to the 1980s, but extending these series backwards to 1960 would likely not change these conclusions.

[2] The logic is that higher cost–income ratios and net interest margins indicate that banks are able to realize super-ordinary profits from segmented, incomplete, or illiquid markets.

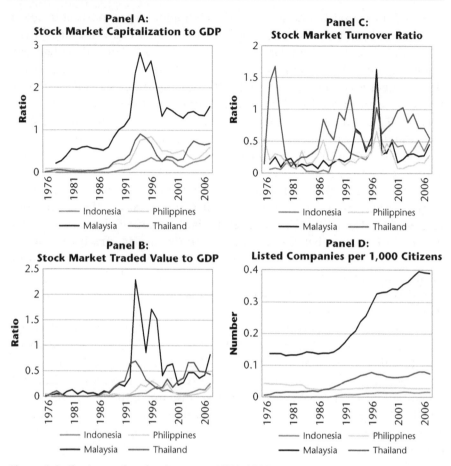

Figure 9.2. Equity market development, 1976–2007
Source: Beck and Al-Hussainy, 2010.

conditions more than fundamental system efficiency. But the trends indicate that, as before, Malaysia has on average a more efficient banking sector than do Indonesia, the Philippines, and Thailand.

Together, these data on financial development over the past fifty years illustrate important variation in financial development both across countries and across time. There is clear divide between relatively larger, deeper, and more efficient financial markets of Malaysia, and the relatively shallow and less efficient markets of Indonesia and the Philippines. Thailand is in some ways similar to Malaysia, and in others closer to Indonesia and the Philippines.

It is not obvious how to explain this variation. There is a relationship between the average level of financial development and general economic

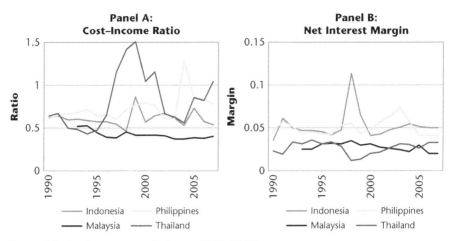

Figure 9.3. Banking sector efficiency, 1990–2007
Source: Beck and Al-Hussainy, 2010.

development across the four countries, but financial development may be a cause of economic development rather than a consequence of it (Levine, 1997). Moreover, economic development fares less well as an explanation of variation *within* countries over time in their level of financial development. Other common explanations for variation in financial development—colonial legacies, financial openness, property rights, and others—suffer from similar problems. Even if there is a relationship between one or more of these variables and financial development in a global sample, the experience of emerging Southeast Asia indicates that there is more variation within the region than can be explained by these factors alone.

As argued in Chapter 1 of this volume, political coalitions, policy discourses, and state action are expected to play important roles in shaping how economic institutions change and develop. These comprise the analytical building blocks upon which I build my account of change and continuity in the wake of external shocks such as decolonization and economic crises. But a focus on political coalitions or state action requires a principled account of why states and coalitions vary across countries. This is the task that the framework I outline below will address. Likewise, policy discourses on financial policy are alone incapable of explaining institutional change unless understood alongside the concrete political and economic events that give ideas currency and policy credibility. Policy discourses favouring financial liberalization, for example, only gained traction in the wake of the economic slump of the mid-1980s, and only survived until the 1997 financial crises. The following sections will make explicit the role of these events in shaping the changes in national financial systems since the 1980s.

Embedding Finance

The political approach to financial development that I propose here begins with the understanding that financial development is both politically valuable and politically dangerous. Developed financial markets are valuable because they are the foundations upon which economic growth occurs. Moreover, for leaders seeking to construct durable political orders, money is the 'sinews of power'. But developed financial markets are dangerous because they can never be subject to full political control. In the limit, a financial marketplace that efficiently channels funds to 'any entrepreneur or company with a sound project' and which 'can gauge, subdivide, and spread difficult risks, letting them rest where they can best be borne' (Rajan and Zingales, 2003a: 9) is one in which the holders of power can no longer use financial policy and preferential access to credit to reward politically favoured groups. Furthermore, financial development is potentially dangerous to incumbent politicians over the medium to long term because it may empower societal actors who will later turn against the incumbent regime. Rajan and Zingales' interest-group theory (2003) of financial development, for instance, holds that market actors who have prospered prior to financial development will block policies that increase the ability of their competitors to access finance, thereby hamstringing financial development. It is not hard to extend this logic to political competition: where existing political orders depend on the ability of political elites to direct credit to favoured constituents (demographic groups, business allies, or others), politicians will resist adopting policies that effectively undermine their ability to do so.

Moreover, in developed financial systems and underdeveloped ones alike, owners of capital retain important structural power through their ability to refuse to invest. They may withhold investment because they do not see opportunities for profit, or because they oppose the terms under which their investments take place. Politicians understand capital's structural power and this shapes their behaviour. This point is most frequently made with respect to international capital (see e.g. Winters, 1994), but the logic clearly applies to domestic capital as well.

Financial development is thus problematic. Financial development can foster economic development, and therefore it is potentially valuable. But financial development *by its very nature* opens the door to challenges to existing political systems. It might seem that the political dangers of financial development might outweigh whatever political benefits it may bring, suggesting that financial development must occur for reasons that are unrelated to regimes' strategies for consolidating and maintaining power. An examination of the historical record of financial development in Southeast

Asia that I will present in the following sections, though, indicates that regimes are not as cowed by the political challenges that financial development entails as might be expected. Rather than simply resisting the challenges of financial development, they have disciplined their financial systems. Of course, this has not gone unnoticed by political economists who have noted the interdependence of powerful political and economic actors across these countries, or by those who detail the resilience of economic elites to the challenges of modernization, economic change, and neo-liberalism, in the financial sphere as elsewhere (Rodan et al., 2005). Yet these broad observations have not been matched with closer attention to the differences in national experiences.

In sum, the choice facing politicians is not to promote financial development or not. The choice is how to develop a financial system that contains within it safeguards against the challenges that financial development will present to the existing political order. This suggests that it is critical to focus on what Polanyi (1944) called the 'embeddedness' of economic systems in broader social orders, for political intervention is the 'essential prerequisite for the formation of market relations' (Evans, 1995: 29). Quite naturally, different forms of political intervention in the financial sector will produce different financial development outcomes.

Close attention to the processes through which political orders are created will therefore shed light on the origins of financial development. This draws on insights from Chaudhry (1993) and Waldner (1999), both of whom saw interventionist economic policies as motivated (in broad terms) by the political exigencies that accompanied state building. Understanding changes over time, then, requires close attention to the ways in which rulers endeavour to reproduce their system of rule and the challenges that they face in doing so. Chief among these challenges in Southeast Asia are systemic pressures and international market conditions.

This sensitivity to the embeddedness of market relations in larger systems of power and influence comports well with the insight that 'state organization of economic activity in the region takes place within broad social contexts and is shaped and mediated by various societal institutions' (Walter and Zhang, Chapter 1, this volume). Where my approach differs is in its analytical focus: rather than 'the state' and 'society' conceived as forces that are either organized or not, I study the groups that construct political orders and the constituents that they mobilize or repress in doing so. This allows me to interrogate the interests and beliefs of the central political actors in each country, something that a state-and-society approach to comparative capitalism is ill-equipped to do.

The Origins of Financial Systems: The 1950s through 1980s

The origins of financial development in Southeast Asia are attributable to three different political configurations after colonialism. In Malaysia, a mobilizational regime sought to incorporate broad sections of its population into the new post-independence political order. The financial system became a site for state-directed dispensation of wealth that would tie the regime's constituents to the political status quo. In Indonesia and the Philippines, a more personalist style of rule (under Marcos in the Philippines and Soeharto in Indonesia) also relied on heavy political intervention in the allocation of credit, but rather than mobilizing popular wealth, regimes protected various particularistic economic interests among each regime's supporters. In Thailand, a relatively autonomous and conservative bureaucracy combined with rapid political turnover produced a political order that was relatively inattentive to the financial system as either a tool of high-level patronage or popular wealth mobilization.

The Dutch left Indonesia without even basic financial infrastructure, but the greater challenges facing Indonesia following independence were rampant corruption and incoherent policy planning, which produced, by the early 1960s, skyrocketing inflation and a near collapse of the economy. State institutions dominated both public and commercial financing throughout this period. Soeharto's New Order regime (1966–98) oversaw a shift in economic policymaking that allowed for significant deregulation of both the financial and real sectors. Foreign banks were permitted to enter the domestic market, and private domestic banks also saw their operational autonomy widened significantly. But this deregulation was halting and selective, and subservient to the broader goal of constructing a durable political regime. The New Order regime's political base relied in part on the support of a set of business cronies, many (though not all) of whom were members of the country's politically vulnerable ethnic Chinese minority. Preferential credit rules allowed the state to channel favouritism to the cronies in exchange for cooperative relations with the military's business interests (Pepinsky, 2009: 42–61). State banks, moreover, remained critically important non-competitive portions of the Indonesian financial market throughout this period. The consequence was a financial system that retained significant government controls over basic banking functions, and one that could not effectively mobilize deposits or channel credit to economically viable ventures (unless they happened to also be politically valuable).

The Philippines at independence faced the challenge of managing conflict between the entrenched landed elites and the poor and marginalized Filipinos in the subsistence and informal sectors. Policymaking remained fundamentally subservient to the interests of the oligarchs, who continually sought and achieved 'favorable access to state machinery' (de Dios and Hutchcroft, 2003: 48). After independence, the oligarchs ventured into the financial sector, founding commercial banks with direct links to their own corporate empires (Hutchcroft, 1993: 174–82). The result was a financial system marked by chronically weak and undercapitalized financial institutions whose primary purpose was to direct credit to related firms. Regulatory institutions were so eviscerated by the oligarchs that official oversight was almost non-existent. Unlike the New Order's hierarchical, top-down model of state intervention, economic policymaking remained subject to the particularistic demands of elites and their increasingly diversified conglomerates, and insulated from the interests of the majority of Filipinos. Ferdinand Marcos seized power in 1972 intending to restore political and economic order, but rather than rationalizing the country's disorganized, inefficient, and uncompetitive financial system, he simply centralized the system of patrimonial accumulation that had formerly been divided across many different families (Hutchcroft, 1998: 110–42).

Malaysia did inherit a relatively functional financial system at independence. This is due primarily to the British policy of emphasizing legal institutions in the Straits Settlements (Hamilton-Hart, 2002: 66–79), which allowed local banks aside from those controlled by the British to establish a commercial presence in the territory. The central political problem facing the newly independent government in Malaysia was the interethnic disparity in wealth between the relatively impoverished but numerically superior Malay majority and the relatively wealthy ethnic Chinese minority. Following a brief experiment with parliamentary democracy, the ruling United Malays National Organisation (UMNO, the main Malay party) took the lead in creating a more durable authoritarian coalition known as the National Front (Barisan Nasional, BN), founded in 1971. That coalition, which still rules today, espouses a pro-*bumiputera* economic agenda under the New Economic Policy (1971–90) and several successors policies. These policies shift wealth towards Malays, with the expectation that they would in turn come to see UMNO as their patron. The country's financial markets are instrumental for this task: the regime provides preferential credit facilities, maintains *bumiputera*-only unit trusts that provided affordable and easy-to-access access to the country's equity markets, and encourages Malay corporate ownership. Despite obvious problems of cronyism and inefficiency that these policies spawned (Gomez and Jomo, 1997: 117–65), the BN's mobilization of its Malay political base using the financial sector encouraged the development of a broad and deep financial system.

For Thailand, which avoided European colonization, the main challenge was managing the intense factionalism of Thai elite politics. The main sources of financial policy remained in the Thai bureaucracy, especially the relatively conservative and autonomous Bank of Thailand. The contrast with the Philippines is instructive: while the Philippines suffered from political instability much as did Thailand, and while both countries faced vexing problems of rural backwardness, Filipino economic governance was indistinguishable from the whims of oligarchs. In Thailand, perhaps due to the bureaucracy's institutional continuity from the mid-1800s, financial policymaking institutions were never so subordinated to particularistic interests (Doner and Unger, 1993). Moreover, under the conservative Sarit Thanarat and Thanom Kittikachorn regimes, abundant foreign aid from the United States made feasible a private sector-led, export-oriented development strategy that did not require the state to mobilize financial resources. Consequently, private financial institutions were relatively free of both state interference and state competition, and private banks' market presence grew substantially. Yet absent a political impetus to mobilize the wealth of the broader populace such as that found in Malaysia, Thai banks retained a bias towards urban consumers and commercial financing, leaving the system less developed than its southern neighbour.

By the early 1980s, then, the seeds of today's pattern of financial development had been sown. Descriptively, it is relatively straightforward to locate the four countries' financial systems in the typology of East Asian capitalisms developed in Chapter 1 of this volume (see Panel A in Table 9.2). Malaysia best approximated a co-governed economy in which the state and private business both played central roles in financial regulation, equity markets were relatively well developed, and insider practices prevailed in both private and public firms (the latter comprising a significant component of Malaysia's economy but never reaching the economy-wide penetration found in Indonesia). But Malaysia's co-governed type of capitalism was not the result of an organized state confronting an organized society, rather it was the natural consequence of post-independent elites' strategy to cement their claim on political power through economic populism. Indonesia, by contrast, was closest to the state-led model, due primarily to widespread state enterprise ownership. However, even this obscures certain features of Indonesia's political economy, for state domination of the economy under Soeharto still allowed domestic financiers wide latitude for investment and capital accumulation. The New Order state always cooperated with private financial interests, it never fully controlled or dominated them.

The Philippines matched the personalized variety of East Asian capitalism quite well. A disorganized society confronted a hollow state, meaning that the financial regulation was captured by private interests, banks dominated relationship-based financing, and insider connections plagued corporate governance. Thailand represents an interesting case that Walter and Zhang (Chapter 1, this volume) consider closer to a personalized system in the 1980s, but its financial architecture even at this time more closely resembled

Table 9.2. Financial architecture, 1980s and 2000s

	Indonesia	Malaysia	The Philippines	Thailand
Panel A: 1980s				
Financial regulation	State cooperation with private interests	State cooperation with private interests	State capture by private interests	Autonomous but ineffective state
Market structure	Bank based	Bank and equity-market based	Bank based	Bank based with important equity markets
Corporate governance	Insider model in private firms, widespread state ownership	Insider model in private firms, significant state ownership	Insider model in private firms, some state ownership	Insider model in private firms, some state ownership
Closest variety	State led	Co-governed	Personalized	Networked
Panel B: 2000s				
Financial regulation	State capture by private interests	State cooperation with private interests	State capture by private interests	Autonomous but ineffective state
Market structure	Bank based	Bank and equity-market based	Bank based	Bank based with important equity markets
Corporate governance	Insider model in private firms, some state ownership	Insider model in private firms, lower state ownership than in the 1980s	Insider model in private firms, some state ownership	Insider model in private firms, some state ownership
Closest variety	Personalized	Co-governed	Personalized	Networked

that of the networked variety. But as the only substantial difference between the financial architectures of these two types is in the relative importance of capital markets in networked varieties of capitalism, this distinction is perhaps inconsequential.

Crisis, Liberalization, Crisis, and Requilibration: From the 1980s to the 2000s

Since the 1980s, three events have shaped financial development in the region. The first is the global economic slowdown of the 1980s. The second is the resulting spate of financial deregulation. This, along with the economic boom that followed, contributed to further advances in banking sector development, and fed the growth of equity markets in Indonesia, the Philippines, and Thailand—the three countries where equity markets had previously been of only marginal significance. The third event, a consequence of the second, is the AFC, which affected all countries but again in different ways. Together, these have been the major trends shaping the past thirty years of financial development in Southeast Asia.

High global petroleum prices along with high interest rates in the early 1980s generated a global economic downturn that was felt particularly in emerging regions such as Southeast Asia. Between 1983 and 1987, all countries registered at least one year of negative economic growth (see Figure 9.4). This crisis would prove transformative for trajectories in financial development. In the Philippines, the global economic slowdown interacted with the increasingly brutal nature of the Marcos regime to produce mass pressure for regime change. The following years witnessed painful economic stagnation and the dissipation of the optimism that had accompanied the People Power movement that toppled the Marcos regime. Fidel Ramos was elected without a clear popular mandate, and consequently set about consolidating political support through skillful coalition building and economic policy reform. Notably, his government undertook a series of major administrative and macroeconomic reforms to restore fiscal discipline (Bautista and Lamberte, 1996: 18–20), and built upon previous liberalization efforts—initiated under Marcos, but which had stalled—to promote financial deregulation (Hutchison, 2005: 46–7). Liberalization and deregulation generated the first sustained improvements in financial development that the Philippines had witnessed in more than a decade, although on the whole the financial system retained its urban, middle-class bias (Hutchcroft, 1999: 168–72).

In Indonesia, the early 1980s were somewhat less painful, and did not lead to the breakdown of political order. But the regime's supporters in the business community, starved of credit and chafing under what were still fairly onerous

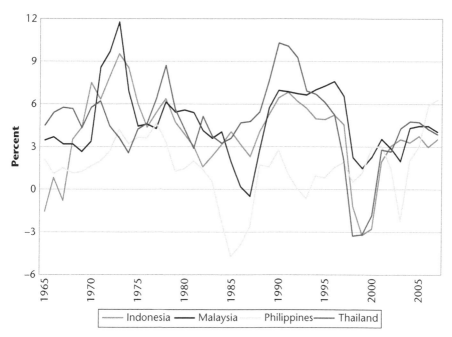

Figure 9.4. Growth in real GDP per capita, 1965–2007 (3-year moving averages)
Source: Heston et al., 2009.

restrictions on private sector finance, sought relief in the form of deregulation. This they obtained in two packages, one in 1983 and another in 1988, which removed most of the restrictions on the operations of domestic banks and greatly diminished Bank Indonesia's supervisory role in day-to-day operations. These liberalizing reforms did nothing to overturn the regime's system of regime maintenance, and indeed were pushed for by the very business interests that they most affected (Soesastro, 1989: 861–3). This illustrates the continued influence of the New Order's logic of political reproduction through capital accumulation within a relatively closed network of business conglomerates. The effect of the 1980s economic slowdown was simply to push the regime to find new tools through which to accomplish this task, for which privatization and financial deregulation proved useful. Far more so than in the Philippines, though, Indonesia's financial deregulation—which took place absent the types of political upheavals that marked Filipino politics during this period—led to the rapid growth of local financial institutions along with the blossoming of Indonesian equity markets.

In Thailand, following the collapse of several important financial institutions in the 1980s, a series of financial reforms were implemented that were designed to streamline and rationalize Thailand's financial markets. Thereafter, the Thai government also liberalized the financial sector, removing most controls on interest rates and capital flows, and licensing the growth of new banks and other financial institutions (Pasuk and Baker, 2002: 164–8). Consistent with the historically 'nondirigiste' approach of the Thai state to financial policymaking (Muscat, 1995: 113), financial liberalization was undertaken primarily at the behest of regulatory authorities in the Bank of Thailand and the Ministry of Finance. Liberalization occurred, moreover, during a period of some political instability, consistent with the earlier pattern in Thailand of frequent political turnover hampering the ability of particularistic interests to capture financial policymaking institutions (Doner and Unger, 1993: 116–22). Amidst the accompanying economic boom, equity markets flourished as well, providing powerful Thai business groups with new tools for mobilizing capital.

The early and mid-1980s were also a period of slow growth in Malaysia, and prompted the state to reverse its course from emphasizing state-led industrialization to privatization. Yet privatization was carried out in a way that rewarded those very same Malay business interests that state intervention had previously nurtured (Jomo and Gomez, 2000: 291–2). Unlike the other countries, there was no particular impetus for financial deregulation in Malaysia, for the sector was already fairly liberalized. Privatization, though, put the financial sector to work in a new way. Politically connected business groups found that they could use Malaysia's equity markets to expand their newly independent corporate empires, while the BN found still greater opportunities to use the country's booming equity markets to promote mass *bumiputera* participation in the country's growing economy. In this way, privatization of previously state-owned institutions employed the financial system to support the political order. The result, as elsewhere, was an expanding financial sector.

The mid- to late 1980s, in sum, was a period of financial deregulation and privatization throughout the region. Growth rates in stock market capitalization during 1988–96 far outpaced the average over the previous decade, making equity markets economically significant throughout the region, not just in Singapore and Kuala Lumpur. Banking systems continued to grow and deepen and credit flowed into the private sectors of all four economies. But liberalization and privatization was constrained by the political challenges facing each country in the wake of the mid-1980s economic slump. Tellingly, there was no appreciable change in banking sector efficiency in the years immediately following liberalization and deregulation (see Figure 9.3). Moreover, by all measures the rank order in levels of financial development across the region remained unchanged. Financial architectures therefore remained essentially unchanged despite the modest retreat of state finance in Indonesia and Malaysia and the emergence of new private financial firms in all countries. Throughout the region, insider practices remained prevalent, and political connections continued to shape lending patterns and equity investments alike. Financial systems changed in response to political and economic exigencies of the period, but never threatened broader political orders.

The broader consequence of these liberalization and privatization measures was a regional economic boom, one driven originally by strong export growth but eventually overwhelmed by financial overexpansion. The AFC exposed the worst excesses of this overexpansion. The details need not concern us here (see, among others, Pempel, 1999b; Haggard, 2000; Woo et al., 2000), but it is clear that the same political economy factors that contributed to the boom contributed to the eventual bust. The Philippines, which never enjoyed much of a boom due to its political and economic fragility, experienced the least of the bust, but growth ceased all the same. By all indicators of financial development, the four crisis economies experienced dramatic reversals. The follow-on economic contractions were severe as well (see Figure 9.4). And from the perspectives of individual governments, the politics costs were substantial, including the collapse of the New Order regime in Indonesia, new democratic governments in Thailand and the Philippines, and the most severe political crisis in Malaysia since 1969. The decade since the crisis has seen some important changes but also a good deal of continuity. Governments in each of the four countries intervened to put their financial houses back in order, but this re-regulation was in no case a permanent change away from the largely privatized financial systems to which they later reverted (Hamilton-Hart, 2008).

A more interesting question is whether there has been fundamental change in the nature of either financial politics or overall financial architectures as a result of the crisis. Nothing significant has changed in the Philippines, where financial institutions retain their urban and upper-class bias and remain subservient to the corporate empires of the country's oligarchs. This is due to the relatively shallow crisis that allowed existing patterns of financial politics (and existing weaknesses in the country's regulatory authorities) to persist (Hutchcroft, 1999: 167–72). Absent any lasting changes to the fractious and oligarchic Philippine political system in the wake of the crisis, the existing pathologies of financial development in the Philippines have continued.

For very different reasons, little has changed in Malaysia either. The crisis did put severe pressure on the country's financial sector, but the Mahathir government responded to the crisis with a firmly anti-IMF policy stance that gave authorities the policy space to recapitalize every fragile financial institution in the country. The unique configuration of political–economic interests in Malaysia—dependent on a thriving domestic financial market but unconcerned about the interests of international capital—enabled this policy response (Pepinsky, 2009). Successful resolution of the economic crisis allowed the regime to survive its most serious political crisis since 1969. Since 1999, while there have been some regulatory changes that are aimed at improving financial institutions' capital adequacy ratios, the basic contours of Malaysia's political economy have not changed. Policies still favour the country's Malay majority, and the financial sector still plays a central role in distributing the state's largesse as a strategy for maintaining the BN's hold on power.

Changes were more dramatic in Indonesia and Thailand, which unlike Malaysia received IMF bail-outs and experienced the painful restructuring that followed. In Indonesia, no less than the entire New Order regime collapsed as a result of the crisis. The Indonesian banking system was forced to undergo fundamental restructuring and recapitalization. New prudential regulations have been imposed. The crony-affiliated financial institutions which flourished under the New Order were mostly closed or nationalized, and foreign actors increased their stake in Indonesia's financial sector substantially (Sato, 2005: 102–8). But while prudential reforms have almost certainly helped to increase the stability of the Indonesian financial sector and eliminated the worst excesses of political interference in banking and equity markets, over ten years on, these reforms have not generated substantial improvements in Indonesia's level of financial development. Although the increased presence of foreign banks in Indonesia has helped, the cost of capital remains high. The economically powerful still continue to dominate Indonesia's political economy, but they do so in a decentralized political system that is no longer amenable to the same logic of accumulation as before. In such a system, especially in one still plagued by endemic corruption, there remain few incentives for politicians to adopt a mobilizational strategy that produced the type of broad and deep financial system as seen in Malaysia. There is certainly also no incentive for politicians to leave the financial sector alone—something which almost never happens anywhere in the world, let alone in post-crisis Indonesia. Responding to the new reality of a dramatically decentralized political system, state-led finance in Indonesia has been replaced by the grabbing hands of individual corporate empires and provincially based public banks. The result is continued financial underdevelopment, but now in a personalized rather than state-led system.

Thailand also suffered heavily from the crisis, and saw attendant political changes. Financial liberalization in the late 1980s had given new sources of capital to powerful domestic business groups, and the collapse of the financial sector generated momentum for political as well as financial reform. Also affected were those poor Thais, including the country's large rural population, who had never enjoyed much of the preceding economic boom but suffered from the bust anyway. Thailand's fractionalized political system contributed to a general view that its constitution impeded effective policymaking and policy implementation. The result was the rise of Thaksin Shinawatra and his Thai Rak Thai party, which Hewison (2005) argues embedded the interests of domestic capital within a political order that for the first time included a social contract that would generate tangible improvements in the livelihoods of the poor. This might have generated pressure for the creation of a more broad-based and inclusive financial sector, one similar to Malaysia's, but Thaksin's rule proved too short. Moreover, as Zhang (2007) argues, the inter-party factionalism that impeded financial development prior to Thaksin reappeared as intra-party factionalism under Thaksin. Since Thaksin's ouster, Thai financial politics has returned to its previous pattern. 'Pro-bank policies for particularistic interests by elected politicians' have led to 'systematic under-attention to the overall development of the capital market' (Zhang, 2007: 364), but regulatory authorities in the Bank of Thailand and Ministry of Finance remain relatively autonomous, thus avoiding the types of political interference that are the hallmark of the Philippines. If anything, this period has seen a setback in financial development as Thailand's endemic political instability continues to impede long-term policy planning.

Descriptively, the outcomes of these changes appear in the Panel B of Table 9.2, which characterizes the four countries at the end of the 2000s. Malaysia and the Philippines show no signs of change in their financial architectures from the 1980s aside from the decline in state ownership in Malaysia, and this is consistent with the absence of fundamental change in these countries broader political economies (aside from post-1980s privatization in Malaysia). Thailand's political economy has changed repeatedly since the 1980s, and might have completed a switch to a more co-governed variety of capitalism had Thaksin been able to consolidate power, but this did not occur. Only Indonesia has truly departed from the financial architecture of the 1980s with the nearly complete obliteration of state-led finance—a consequence of financial liberalization in the late 1980s and the collapse of the New Order in the late 1990s. While a strengthening of mass society might push Indonesia towards the networked or even co-governed variety of East Asian capitalism, as of the end of the 2000s, Indonesia's financial architecture most resembles a personalized variety.

Contemporary Financial Development and its Future

This chapter has taken a broad approach to financial development and proposed an analytical framework that focuses on the political logics underlying various trajectories of financial development across Southeast Asia. I conclude here by summarizing the central implications from this approach.

The central finding in this chapter is that different patterns of financial development are the products of different modalities of political intervention in the financial sector. The possible exception is Thailand's financial development from the 1950s until the 1970s, which was marked by political inattention rather than direct state intervention. This hands-off approach combined with a relatively autonomous central bank probably contributed to Thailand's relatively higher level of financial development as compared to Indonesia and the Philippines, but the absence of a direct state role in promoting domestic banking and equity markets kept Thailand's level of financial development below that of Malaysia. Of course, the Thai government's hands-off stance towards the Thai financial sector certainly did not prevent the build-up of significant financial vulnerabilities, either in the late 1970s or in the early 1990s. If Indonesia and the Philippines demonstrate the detrimental consequences of state interference in the allocation of credit, then Thailand illustrates how financial markets can develop systemic vulnerabilities on their own. Moreover, this inattention does not reflect the victory of some rational bureaucracy over particularistic interest groups, or of market principles over state interventionism, but rather a unique confluence of political factors (rapid leadership turnover, a conservative and relatively autonomous central bank, Sarit's political opposition to groups associated with state-protected industries, foreign support for the Sarit and Thanom governments, etc.) that rendered impossible any sustained or coherent plan for state intervention in the financial sector.

Taking a broader view of the lessons from these four countries, comparative political economists have suggested that differences across countries in the structure and function of capitalist economies can be attributable to different 'models' of capitalism. Chapter 1 of this volume identifies key differences in the varieties of capitalism found in East Asia based on the relative strength and organization of state and society. They emphasize variation across countries. By contrast, early examinations of capitalist Southeast Asia noted the importance of familial or other non-market relations in Asian economies (see e.g. Yoshihara, 1988), which to some suggested a particularly Asian mode of capitalism. Others noted the important differences between the successful developmentalist regimes in Northeast Asia and the more 'pilotless' ones in Southeast Asia (Weiss, 1998). The reaction of this literature to the AFC was profound, and questioned whether or not whatever model of capitalism the East and Southeast Asian economies were supposed to represent was fundamentally flawed.

The perspective adopted in this chapter is consistent with approaches to capitalism in East Asia that emphasize differences across countries rather than similarities among them. The Southeast Asian experience suggests that while 'models' of East Asian capitalism are handy tools for describing differences in financial architecture across countries, they do not offer much analytical traction over the more obvious variation across countries, which is not in corporate governance or financial regulation but rather in the level and pace of financial development. The features of the varieties of East Asian capitalism suggest why this is the case: insider practices in corporate governance, private influence on state regulation of finance, and bank-oriented financial systems are common features in each variety of East Asian capitalism. Malaysia and Thailand today illustrate the relatively more developed equity markets in co-governed and networked capitalisms, respectively, but the distinctions between the nature of private influence on state regulation of finance among networked, co-governed, personalized, and even (as Indonesia in the 1980s demonstrates) state-led capitalisms are imprecise even at a theoretical level.[3] The same is true for the prevalence or importance of insider connections in each of the four varieties.

Accordingly, it is possible to classify the four Southeast Asian countries into the different ideal–typical varieties of East Asian capitalism, but difficult to link these types to the actual variation that differentiates the financial systems among these countries. In Indonesia and in the Philippines, state-led and personalized varieties have both created underdeveloped financial systems, both as measured by banking sector depth/efficiency and by the relative importance of equity markets. Malaysia approximates the co-governed type and Thailand the networked type, but this does not explain why Malaysia rates consistently higher than Thailand in *all* indicators of financial development. To explain this, a focus on how elites create and maintain political order proves more useful.

I have only implicitly addressed the 'institutional complementarities' (Hall and Soskice, 2001) between national financial systems and other institutional spheres such as labour markets and business systems in this discussion. Financial systems naturally co-evolve with these other institutional spheres. In the Malaysian case, as Gomez (this volume) illustrates, the synergies between financial development and enterprise development are particularly clear, as capital markets are the tools through which the BN regime organizes political control over Malaysian enterprises and allocates patronage to its mass base. Under New Order Indonesia, too, the financial system developed in parallel with the *konglomerat* system; it is impossible to study one without the other. These two cases of strong state intervention suggest that institutional complementaries develop most easily when regimes have long-term visions for economic organization and the capacity to implement them. Still, in Thailand, the Philippines, and post-Soeharto Indonesia, financial markets and enterprise systems have co-evolved (in particular, firms' reliance on financing from banks within the same corporate empire), but these are cases of informal

---

[3] See the fine distinctions among state-'guided', 'controlled', and 'influenced' in Table 9.1.

and incidental co-evolution rather than planned, deliberate institutional engineering.

Institutional complementarities between financial and labour markets in contemporary Southeast Asia are more difficult to discern. Deyo (this volume) notes the weakening of labour's political efficacy in the Philippines, and that Thai labour's victories under Thaksin only came in concert with a broader populist agenda. In Malaysia, the same political order that mobilizes Malay financial resources has methodically disempowered all organized labour in Malaysia (Jomo and Todd, 1994). Setting differences in formal legal protections aside, the unifying characteristics of labour markets in contemporary Southeast Asia are labour's weak political voice, a profound urban bias in policymaking, and unorganized or selective provision of quality social insurance. These commonalities do not vary in ways that parallel cross-national differences in the institutional architectures of national financial systems.

A political approach to financial development in Southeast Asia has implications for any purported future convergence on a single model of capitalism, Anglo-American, Asian, or otherwise. There appears scant evidence that this is true in anything more than the superficial sense that the most of the staff of regulatory institutions believe that prudential oversight is a good thing and that the worst distortions in financial sectors should be eliminated. Beyond this, there is hardly any agreement on how to engineer financial development, or on what sort of political structure would best produce it. There even less optimism that even if there were such agreement, the very real political constraints in each country could be overcome anyway. This does not foreclose the possibility that some countries in the region will converge upon a common model of capitalism at some time in the future. But if they do, it will not be because of some inherent pull or superior logic of that model, but because politicians find it in their own political interests to do so.

10

The Japanese Financial Sector's Transition from High Growth to the 'Lost Decades'[1]

Wataru Takahashi

A key aspect of Japan's distinctive version of capitalism, its financial system was once closely associated with its highly successful economic development. More recently, it became seen as having played a crucial role in producing the bubble economy of the 1980s and its now longstanding low-growth aftermath. This chapter outlines the evolution of Japan's financial sector in recent decades, with attention paid to the growing role of market mechanisms and its influence on the rest of the Japanese economic system. It shows how this financial system needs to be seen in the broader context of the evolution of Japan's 'networked' political economy, which combined government intervention and mutual support amongst private agents (see Chapter 1 in this volume).

In such a system, implicit contracts between economic sectors including the government provide mutual support and risk sharing. During the high-growth era, this system experienced rapid evolution. The Japanese economy became more tolerant of risk taking due to rising income and the accumulation of financial assets. At the same time, the demand for risk sharing weakened as economic ties amongst actors weakened. Liberalizing reforms, including deregulation and privatization, contributed to rising labour mobility (Sako and Kotosaka, this volume). The development of capital markets also helped to weaken the relations of mutual dependence, as Japan moved

[1] This chapter was first presented at the London School of Economics (LSE) workshop on East Asian capitalism held on 3–4 June 2010. I would like to thank Kumiko Okazaki and Masazumi Hattori for their helpful discussion and Hiroyuki Oi for his excellent assistance. I also appreciate the comments of Jenny Corbett as a discussant and the workshop participants, in particular, Xiaoke Zhang and Andrew Walter, for their very thoughtful comments on the early draft of the chapter. Views expressed in this chapter are those of the author and do not necessarily reflect the official views of the Bank of Japan.

towards a less networked and more 'atomized' system.[2] These developments fostered the economic bubble, as well as the long-lasting financial problems in the wake of its implosion. In response, institutional reforms have been gradual but cumulatively significant (Fields, this volume; Amyx, 2004).

The first section briefly outlines the nature of Japan's model of networked capitalism and the role of the financial system within it. The second section then describes three main phases in the evolution of Japan's financial system, from the 1960s to the present day. Although this book focuses mainly on changes in Asian economies after the 1980s, for Japan it is appropriate to begin our discussion with the 1960s to better capture changes in the economic environment, given that financial liberalization in Japan began in the 1970s. The third section addresses the question of the uniqueness of the Japanese system by comparing it with China, which shares many important characteristics with the Japanese system in its early phase.

The Nature and Origins of Japanese Network Capitalism

Japan emerged as the first successful industrializing nation in East and South Asia, playing a key role as the region's leading capitalist economy following the Meiji Restoration in 1868. Thereafter, the Japanese government was a major force behind the nation's industrialization, particularly in its early stages of development. The government adopted a strategy of nurturing new industries by inviting foreign professionals in order to acquire modern production methods and management techniques of modern corporations. Many elements from the Western world such as legal and accounting systems were adopted. The establishment of state-owned corporations in important industries such as railways, textiles, and steel manufacturing enabled these firms to serve as engines of national industrialization. Large private businesses such as Mitsubishi and Mitsui expanded their scope by working hand in hand with the government. The rapid development that was achieved demonstrates the success of the government-led strategy in Japan during this period.

Although the Japanese economy suffered heavy damage during the Second World War and a new course became necessary, many characteristics of the government's pre-war development strategy were retained after 1945. Notably, despite significant political and economic reforms, the government continued to exercise leadership in developing the economy. Also, and in contrast to the more recent development strategies adopted by some of Japan's Asian neighbours, Japan promoted the development of national

[2] For an argument that little has changed in the Japanese political economy, see Mikuni and Murphy (2002).

industries rather than relying heavily on foreign capital. The resulting relative autonomy of the domestic Japanese system of government–business relations made it relatively unique, with Korea the closest comparator (Fields, this volume).

Japan's notable economic success during the high-growth period of the 1960s attracted much attention. By the 1970s, a growing number of Western scholars perceived a distinct Japanese 'developmental model' as a challenge to American and British versions of capitalism, laying the foundation for the literature on the developmental state (see e.g. Wade, 1990). Described by Johnson (1982) and Woo-Cumings (1999) as a product of 'catch-up nationalism', the Japanese developmental model was variously seen as characterized by the role of the Ministry of International Trade and Industry (MITI) as an economic 'pilot' agency (Johnson, 1982); by cooperative and non-hierarchical firm–labour relations (Dore, 1973) and a focus on continuous innovation and improvement (Womack et al., 1990); by cooperative relations between firms, suppliers, and banks (the *keiretsu* system); and by a long-term orientated, bank-based system of finance (Zysman, 1984). Nevertheless, its essential characteristic was government leadership within a system of networked, cooperative relations amongst key economic agents, who included the government and banks. The Ministry of Finance (MOF) was the dominant official actor in this system.

The Japanese scholarly literature has located the origins of the bank-based system in the late interwar period. After the 1868 Meiji Restoration, Japan adopted a national bank system modelled on US practice. With the consequent loosening of each bank's reserve requirements to issue banknotes, however, this decentralized banking system produced severe inflation. Accordingly, the Bank of Japan was established as the nation's central bank in 1882 to curb inflation, with currency issuance reserved to it alone. Between the Meiji Period (1868–1912) and the beginning of the wartime regime, the number of banks increased and many small banks expanded to a nationwide scale. Capital markets also developed rapidly during the interwar period and the economy moved towards a market orientation.

However, as the military increased its political power in the course of the 1930s, the government restructured and consolidated the economic system to prepare for the war. Under the National General Mobilisation Act in 1938, a planned economy was introduced and a wide range of government guidance was implemented for all industries. At the corporation level, the government promoted consolidation to enhance the efficiency of production. Crucially, the 'main bank' system was also formed during this time (Noguchi, 1995; see also Teranishi, 1994; Okazaki and Okuno-Fujiwara, 1999). This entailed substantial consolidation in the banking sector and government requirements on banks to provide funds to large-scale manufacturers; in particular, military industries were allocated 'main banks'. The banks in turn were closely controlled by the government, which provided them with protection under the 'convoy system'.[3]

As Noguchi (1995) explains, the essence of the pre-war economic system was preserved under the US occupation following the Second World War. Following the US model, the financial system was separated into banks, securities houses, and insurance companies.[4] This system functioned very effectively to promote Japan's dramatic economic success in the post-war period. It continued to be characterized by extensive government regulation and guidance, as well as government protection. On the one hand, bank returns and interest rates were set low in accordance with government policy. On the other hand, banks benefited from various government restrictions that limited competition. This 'financial repression' effectively recycled savings and taxed the household sector, whilst subsidizing manufacturing investment. Real interest rates on savings were often negative in Japan in the 1960s and 1970s, although interestingly not in the 1950s (Figure 10.1). Households nevertheless benefited from assured employment and rapid increases in income, which (combined with a high savings ratio) led to a rapid accumulation of household bank deposits.

Despite the separation of financial sector business in the post-war system, relations of mutual dependence were also preserved. Even between banks and life insurance companies, cross-holding of shares were extensive. Banking was specialized in the form of long-term and short-term credit banks. Despite the smaller number of branches permitted them, long-term credit banks were allowed to issue debentures. By holding these bank debentures, local banks supported the financing by which long-term credit banks received higher returns than deposit rates.

The Evolution of the Japanese Financial System

In describing the evolution of the Japanese financial system, we divide the post-war period into three segments: from the 1960s to 1974, from 1974 to 1989, and the 1990s and after. Interestingly, each of these three periods is characterized by strikingly different economic performance (Figure 10.2).

---

[3] In Japan, the number of banks varied dramatically before the Second World War. There were over 1,200 commercial banks in the late 1920s, but only half that number by the early 1930s. During the wartime period from 1941 to 1945, the number fell from 186 to 61. After the war, the number remained unchanged until the late 1980s.

[4] The banks were allowed to underwrite stocks and corporate bonds in the pre-war period. This was prohibited by the Securities and Exchange Act in 1948. Banks were partially allowed to undertake securities business by the new Banking Law and the new Securities and Exchange Act in 1981.

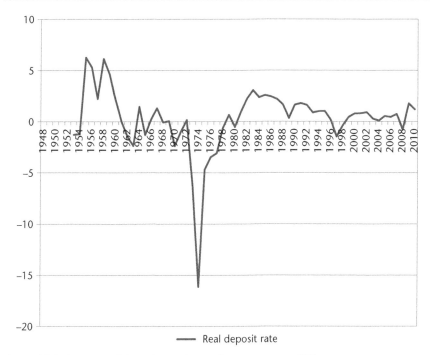

Figure 10.1. Japan: real deposit rate (annual interest rate—CPI)

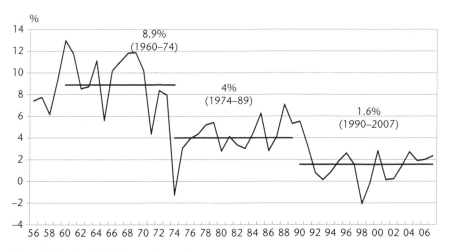

Figure 10.2. Real GDP growth rate, Japan

From the 1960s to 1974

A notable feature of the Japanese economy during this period is that it achieved high growth through a strong 'organizational' or 'relation-dependent' political and economic system that combined the government, the banking sector, and corporations. In addition to Japan's well-known main bank system, many long-term relationships amongst economic actors were observable in the economy. For instance, in the corporate sector, the system of mutual dependence based on established business ties (the *keiretsu* system)— for example, between large assembly makers and small parts makers and between wholesalers and retailers—had gradually been established. In labour relations, full-time employment had been established and labour unions became an important player in corporate management. Employment was guaranteed, but firms achieved wage flexibility by utilizing the bonus system. Employees acquired company-specific skills through on-the-job training, and labour relations were internalized within firms.

Many characteristic private sector practices came into being during this period, facilitated by government guidance. There is no firm conclusion as to when many of these elements such as the *keiretsu* system, lifetime employment, and company unions were established; some of them like the main bank system can be traced back to the pre-war period. But they became more firmly embedded during the high-growth period and were associated with rapid increases in productivity. In the financial sector, informal relationships were gradually institutionalized.

This system can be broadly characterized as a system of disciplined risk sharing. Various types of bargaining amongst economic actors took place inside firms and within *keiretsu*. Cross-holding of corporate stocks was a device to ensure that corporations would provide mutual support, particularly when they encountered economic difficulties. Networked relations of these kinds also provided discipline, as it was important for companies to maintain their reputation among peers. Disciplined risk sharing also characterized relations between banks and their corporate customers. It should be noted that strong ties were first achieved between large banks and relatively large corporations, which evolved into the main bank system. As for small and medium-sized enterprises (SMEs), their relations with banks remained rather less well defined; they became more institutionalized only after the 1980s, when banks began to lose large businesses as their dependent borrowers.

The system of income redistribution was also facilitated by another important aspect of Japan's economy during this period. In recent years, increasing income inequality has been observed in other Asian economies that are undergoing rapid development, such as China. Japan's development, by contrast, was characterized by more extensive management of the distribution of income, which helped to maintain the stability of the networked system (Teranishi,1997). Government policy in Japan was a major contributor through fiscal redistribution. By means of the local allocation tax system, a substantial portion of central government tax revenues was allocated to local governments. As explained later, as large banks (city banks) in Japanese urban areas were continuously borrowing funds from small banks (regional banks), a smaller part was played by the redistribution of income from large urban groups to small regional ones through the banking sector. During the high-growth period, industrialization took place mainly in the nation's central coastal area and the labour force shifted from regional localities to central hubs, thus reducing the potential for economic growth in rural areas. Income redistribution from urban to rural areas played an important role in softening the shocks engendered by the rapid changes during the high-growth period. Ironically, over time this redistributive mechanism would become an obstacle to reform and growth. Government policy also placed a high priority on the promotion and protection of savings; in the immediate post-war period, Japan was impoverished with a low level of financial assets. Most people could not afford to invest in securities, which were in any case deemed less safe than protected bank deposits. The one-year time deposit rate was fixed at around 5–6 per cent for nearly twenty years from 1951 to 1970.

In addition, banks' profits were virtually guaranteed by the government. Interest rates were regulated to generate 'rent' at banks via a sufficient margin between lending and deposit interest rates. Competition was also restricted: permission from the government was required to sell a new product or to open a new branch. The bank loan market was separated into long-term loans from long-term credit banks and short-term loans from the commercial banks (city banks and regional banks). In addition, by controlling the numbers of branches, the government essentially controlled the scope of operations of city banks and regional banks. These measures formed what was called the 'convoy system', in which the government protected the weakest banks and helped them avoid bankruptcy. Strict requirements were imposed on new bond issuance, and only a limited number of firms were allowed to issue bonds. These measures protected long-term credit banks, who as noted earlier were allowed to issue bank debentures.

Low-cost loans were allocated by banks as discretionary rationing. This encouraged capital expenditure and served as an engine of high economic growth.[5] Bank lending was the only effective route for corporate financing during this period, as the bond markets were underdeveloped and cross-shareholdings

---

[5] There is a counterargument that effective lending rates, which took into account the compensated deposit balance, were higher than advertised lending rates. Even so, banks could provide cheap funds by attracting low-cost deposits.

ensured that a substantial proportion of corporate equity was tied up in banks and life insurance companies. Since banks also underwrote and purchased corporate bonds, most of the credit in the economy was controlled by banks.

In this system, the banks took little account of lending risk. There was no market risk with regulated interest rates and no potential for maturity mismatches in the segmented loan market, so banks could seek to boost their size by increasing deposits with little consideration of risk. Bank size was also important, since the government's discretionary actions and 'voluntary' adjustments inside the banking sector were largely determined by reference to the size of banks' total assets and deposits. Due to the vigorous appetite for corporate investment, there was ample demand for bank credit. Banks could choose customers of good credit quality and control credit risk with little effort. Thus, in later years, when banks had to operate in an economic environment of financial liberalization, they lacked the necessary experience with risk management, especially where small corporations were concerned.

The main bank system gradually prevailed across the spectrum from large businesses to SMEs. The scope of business of banks in this period was broad. In addition to conventional activities such as monitoring and screening, banks conducted investment banking activities such as provision of advice and organization of customers' businesses as part of their standard services. They sometimes played a dominant role in running the businesses of clients in difficulty, sending staff to a customer corporation to serve as high-ranking managers.

The flow of finance in this system was thus fairly simple (Figure 10.3). Households held savings in the form of bank deposits,[6] small regional banks lent to major city banks, and the latter provided funds to growing industries such as large manufacturing firms based in urban areas. Through this activity, a portion of the profits of large corporations was effectively transferred to the small regional banks.

The banking sector was also one of the primary routes through which monetary policy was implemented. Tightening via the Bank of Japan's monetary operations tended to produce a relatively small increase in the official discount rate (ODR), to which lending and deposit rates were linked, and a relatively large rise in money market rates. Since city banks were borrowers and regional banks were lenders in the money market, profits were shifted from the city banks to the regional banks during periods of monetary stringency.

---

[6] During this period, a massive portion of household savings went into bank deposits. This occurred because the capital market was underdeveloped and overseas investment was restricted. However, even after liberalization, households still keep a significant part of their savings in the form of bank deposits.

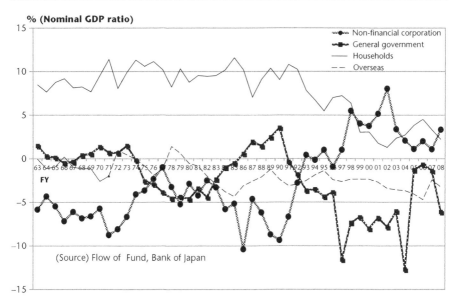

Figure 10.3. Flow of funds, Japan

Another key characteristic of the heavily regulated Japanese financial system during this period was its separation from international financial markets. Capital controls were imposed, although they were only selective and later they were relaxed. Inward foreign direct investment (FDI) was also restricted through controls on foreign ownership, cross-holdings of corporate shares, and the general underdevelopment of capital markets (Table 10.1). Foreign exchange transactions for trade-related transactions were permitted and were concentrated at 'forex' banks. This market was also heavily controlled by official position guidance (the forex position, the sum of the spot and forward rates, had to be squared by each bank every day).

From 1974 to 1989

Japan's high-growth period came to an end around the time of the first oil shock in 1973–4. The Japanese economy weathered both this oil shock, despite a subsequent hike in inflation, and the second one that followed in 1979. Indeed, compared to the performance of other advanced economies during this period, Japan's economic performance after 1973 remained exceptional. Nevertheless, as the Japanese economic system was implicitly designed assuming continuous high growth across many fronts, in facing decelerating growth it was approaching a turning point. One example of this was in labour relations. As the economy grew more slowly, it became costly to maintain the lifetime and seniority system. In addition, as foreign investors began to pay

Table 10.1. History of capital account liberalization in Japan

Year	Month	Changes in regulations
1964	April	Japan accepts IMF Article VIII obligations
		Japan becomes an OECD member
1968	February	Yen conversion controls introduced to restrict conversion of foreign currencies into yen and domestic investment in yen
1971	July	Upper limit on foreign securities purchased by investment trusts and insurance companies abolished
	August	The United States suspends dollar conversion to gold (the so-called 'Nixon Shock')
	December	IMF parity changed to 308/US$1 (Smithsonian rate) and band widened by +/− 2.5%
1972	February	Purchase of foreign securities by trust banks liberalized
	March	Purchase of foreign securities by commercial banks liberalized
	June	Outward foreign direct investment liberalized
1973	February	Floating exchange rate regime introduced
	May	Inward direct investment liberalized with exception of five categories of business
	December	Yen conversion controls on banks partially eased (non-residents permitted to hold yen accounts [except inter-office accounts])
1974	January	'Voluntary restraint' to balance net foreign securities investments by banks, securities companies, investment trusts, and insurance companies introduced
1976	November	Conditions attaching to outward long-term bank loans are eased
1977	March	'Voluntary restraint' on foreign securities investments by banks abolished
	June	Acquisition of foreign equities and bonds by residents belonging to foreign companies permitted
		Regulations on net open positions of residents abolished
1979	January	Regulations on acquisition of yen-denominated bonds excluding those with remaining maturity of more than one year by non-residents relaxed
	May	Repo transactions by non-residents liberalized (*gensaki* market)
		Certificate of deposit (CD) issuance commenced
	June	Short-term impact loans introduced and regulations on long-term impact loans lifted
1980	December	New Foreign Exchange and Foreign Trade Control Law implemented; in-and-out transactions free in principle
1984	April	Regulations based on the principle of real demand related to forward foreign exchange transactions abolished
	June	Regulations regarding the conversion of foreign currency-denominated funds into yen abolished
		Yen-denominated loans to residents contracted in overseas markets liberalized
1985	October	Interest rates on large time deposits liberalized
1986	December	Japan Offshore Market (JOM) established
1993	June	Interest rates on time deposit fully liberalized
1994	October	Interest rates on demand deposits (excluding current accounts) liberalized
1995	June	Restriction on the number of new branches a bank can establish removed
	August	Recycling restrictions on yen-denominated bonds issued by non-residents in overseas markets abolished
1996	November	'Big Bang' reform of capital market announced
1997	December	Ban on financial holding companies lifted
1998	April	Revised Foreign Exchange and Foreign Trade Law enforced

Source: Takahashi and Kobayakawa, 2003.

greater attention to Japanese firms, there was increasing pressure on the firms to boost profitability ratios such as return on equity (ROE). Thus, even as the well-known *Japan as Number One* was being published (Vogel, 1979), Japan's political economy was encountering difficulty.

Financial liberalization began in the 1970s but accelerated in the 1980s. During this period, controls on interest rates were relaxed and banks were allowed to enter the securities business. Although its pace accelerated further in the late 1980s, liberalization remained gradual: fifteen years were required for the liberalization of interest rates and thirty-four years for capital controls to be lifted (Tables 10.1 and 10.2; Takahashi and Kobayakawa, 2003). The main reason for the delay was the difficulty in coordinating the interests of players in the differing financial industries—it was already becoming clear that Japan's system of networked capitalism was inherently gradualist. Banks, securities houses, and life insurance companies were segmented by government regulations, and vested interests in each segment worked to prevent the coordination of reform. The balkanization of financial supervision, described as 'bureau-pluralism' by Aoki (2001), also fostered conflicts of interest amongst government authorities and contributed to further delay: banks, securities houses, and life insurance companies were supervised by separate bureaus inside the MOF; agricultural financial institutions, meanwhile, were supervised by the

Table 10.2. History of interest rate liberalization in Japan

Year	Month	Changes in regulations
1947	December	Temporary Interest Rates Adjustment Law enforced
1949	December	Foreign Exchange and Foreign Trade Control Law enforced
1979	April	Call rate liberalized
	May	Negotiable CDs introduced
	October	Trade bill rate liberalized
1980	January	Medium-term government bond funds introduced
	December	Foreign Exchange and Foreign Trade Control Law amended
1982	April	New Banking Law enforced
1984	April	Sales of foreign CDs and CP permitted
	December	Interest rates on short-term euro–yen CDs liberalized
1985	March	Money market certificates introduced
	July	Interest rates on medium- and long-term euro–yen CDs liberalized
	August	Large-lot open-end bond investment trusts introduced
	October	Interest rates on large time deposits over ¥1 billion liberalized
1986	March	Long-term government bond funds introduced
1989	June	Small-lot money market certificates over ¥3 million introduced
1991	November	Interest rates on time deposit over ¥3 million liberalized
1992	March	Money management funds introduced
1993	June	Interest rate on time deposits fully liberalized
1994	October	Interest rates on demand deposits (excluding current accounts) liberalized
1998	June	CD issue terms fully liberalized

Source: Takahashi and Kobayakawa, 2003.

Ministry of Agriculture. Some non-bank corporations such as credit card companies and finance lease companies were supervised by the MITI.

Financial sector liberalization during this period had multiple causes (Calder, 1997). First, a structural change in the flow of funds in the economy produced important changes in financial markets (Figure 10.3). In terms of the investment-saving (IS) balance, as economic growth slowed, capital spending decreased and corporate profits accumulated as corporate saving. The counterpart of the emergence of the corporate sector as a net saver was the emergence of the government as a net debtor. Households remained net savers, although the personal saving rate gradually declined. Overall, the current account increased, which meant that the foreign sector was as much of a net debtor as ever. As corporations had less need to borrow from banks, the latter began to lose customers to which to lend. This in turn spurred the banks to lobby for financial deregulation so as to develop new business lines.

Second, and related to the above, the development of bond markets was spurred by increasing public sector borrowing. Corporations also began raising large amounts of finance from the bond markets, further disintermediating the banks. Large Japanese corporations also started to issue corporate bonds in the flourishing offshore euro–yen market and Japanese institutional investors (e.g. life insurance companies) began to purchase them in the 1970s. In the 1980s, this market boomed, not least because euro-bond issuance was simpler than for the domestic bond market and because such bonds offered investors a higher yield than did bonds from the same Japanese corporations in the Japanese market. This produced a hollowing out of the domestic corporate bond market and a demand for the further relaxation of regulations in the domestic bond market and the liberalization of interest rates to attract investors to banks.[7]

Third, as household sector assets accumulated, there was demand by households for a greater variety of financial products that would permit an increase in risk taking. Often, this demand was voiced by the financial institutions in which household savings had accumulated and who were seeking to develop their retail financial businesses.

Fourth, in the wake of the breakdown of the Bretton Woods system of pegged exchange rates and the floating of the yen, opportunities opened up for investors in the foreign exchange markets. Non-financial corporations such as trading houses (sogo shosha) as well as financial corporations became active investors in the market and demanders of further liberalization.

Fifth, as Japan's export surplus continued to grow and as its manufacturing firms made further inroads in foreign markets, the US government intensified

---

[7] Bond issuance was fully liberalized in 1996, but because of the stagnant economy the primary markets have not been very active.

pressure on Japan to open Japanese markets to foreign financial firms and to purchase more US government bonds. The Yen-Dollar Committee was set up in 1983 and was followed by the broader Structural Impediments Initiative (SII) in 1989, which triggered larger scale deregulation in the 1990s (Osugi, 1990). Although Japan adopted a passive approach to the issue, the United States and Europe also brought pressure to bear on Japan in various multilateral negotiations.

An asset price bubble developed in Japan in the late 1980s, focussed on real estate and stocks. Financial liberalization was a permissive cause of this development, but it was also due to the easier monetary conditions following the Plaza Agreement in 1985, overconfidence about the outlook for the Japanese economy, poor credit risk management by banks, and weak prudential regulation. The latter two factors had their origins in the system that had been established in the early post-war period. The Japanese government's commitment to achieve domestic demand-led growth to reduce the trade surplus also played a role in the formation of optimistic expectations, since it was believed that the government would maintain its stimulus policies as long as Japan maintained its current account surplus (Hattori et al., 2009).

The bubble helped to accelerate changes already underway. As mentioned above, banks lost their long-standing, reliable customers as large manufacturers lost their appetite for loan-based funding and instead sought cheap bond and equity financing. Each bank sought to enhance its reputation as a financial partner for large corporations to boost the prospects for future business. Competition amongst banks grew intense; at the margin, a negative spread between deposit and lending rates appeared (Hattori et al., 2009; see also Figure 10.4). In retrospect, given the structural change in money flow, it is clear that the Japanese banking sector grew too large and should have been slimmed down. However, banks continued to seek to expand out of a belief that the expansion of the customer base was crucially important for future business. The legacy of the convoy system also provided a safety net. Even at this time, bank evaluation and guidance by the authorities still depended on a bank's loan volume.

Another legacy of the post-war system was the continuing lack of attention to credit risk. Banks played a key role in the creation of the real estate bubble. They extended credit to the real estate sector and/or corporations investing in real estate-related business, which banks regarded as a new base of high-quality borrowers. Although the banks' relationships with these new customers were not deep, they extended loans relying on real estate collateral, which spurred the vicious cycle behind the asset price bubble. Real estate was believed to be the most reliable form of collateral, since Japan had never experienced a prolonged decline in real estate prices during its period of rapid

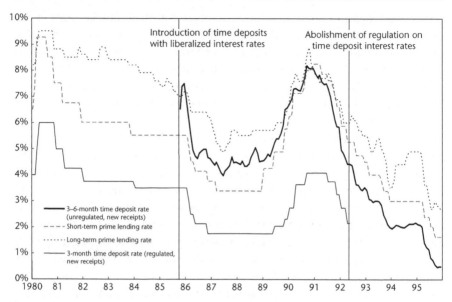

Figure 10.4. Time deposit rates and prime lending rates, Japan

Note: The '3–6-month time deposit rate (unregulated, new receipts)' is the average interest rate on newly received time deposits with unregulated interest rates of terms between 3 and 6 months. '3-month time deposit rate (regulated, new receipts)' is the interest rate set by the regulation on newly received 3-month time deposits.

Source: Hattori et al., 2009.

growth (and would not do so until the early 1990s). Prior to financial liberalization, the use of real estate as collateral had not always been very popular; it became so after large banks started to expand their loans to new customers such as SMEs and the real estate sector.

Thus, the asset price bubble can be regarded as a symptom of the friction caused by changing relationships in a dynamic system. Although Japanese finance was moving towards an atomized system characterized by securitization, banks sought to preserve the traditional system of relationship banking, this time based on real estate collateral. Aoki (2001) makes the additional point that the loosening of government control in the process of financial liberalization weakened discipline within banks, who failed to put in place adequate systems of corporate governance. Weak internal governance was also visible in the manufacturing sector during this period, helping to fuel banking sector indiscipline. Large manufacturing firms acted as a kind of shadow banking sector to Japanese banks, conducting active financial investment (dubbed *zaitech*) in ways that resemble the activities of the shadow banking sector in the recent US sub-prime crisis (Hattori et al., 2009).

The 1990s and After

The full consequences of the credit boom and associated asset price bubble of the 1980s only became clear over the course of the subsequent decade. In the 1990s, Japan's financial sector accumulated a massive amount of nonperforming loans (NPLs), which took banks much time to resolve. Financial sector activity weakened both in terms of volume and innovation. Although Japanese banks conducted investment banking activities prior to the 1990s, they did not enjoy great success in businesses such as mergers and acquisitions (M&A), in contrast to their American and European counterparts. In addition, Japanese banks were reluctant to expand their international activities; many that had previously established foreign operations withdrew from international activities over the course of the 1990s. This reflected their eroding capital position, which affected their ability to take risks, and the significantly lower regulatory capital requirement on domestic as opposed to internationally active banks. Although Japanese banks succeeded in avoiding major losses in connection with the recent sub-prime-related securities, they have lagged European and American financial institutions in the field of securitization. Until recently, low profitability plagued the banking and other financial sectors (Bank of Japan, 2010).

Financial and corporate sector deleveraging undoubtedly depressed economic growth, although other reasons have been cited for Japan's economic slump since the early 1990s. Hayashi and Prescott (2002), for example, attributed the slump to a decline in productivity due to shortened working hours and other non-financial reasons. From a broader viewpoint, however, it could be said that Japan's economic system faced difficulty in adjusting to its new environment. This process can be understood in several ways.

First, as the economy matured, consumer preferences diversified, and product differentiation accelerated. As a result, the nation's established system of mass production became obsolete. Small-scale production processes compatible with product differentiation were better suited to respond to changes in consumer preferences. The shift towards this new system of production in Japan was only gradual. This response was facilitated by the application of new information and communications technology (ICT). Although other advanced economies succeeded in adopting the new technology comparatively quickly, the threat that this posed to a significant proportion of the human skills embedded in long-term employment contracts delayed adjustment in the Japanese system. Thus, an important aspect of Japan's labour market institutions constrained its ability to adapt its system of production to changing patterns of demand.

Second, a mismatch emerged in Japan's financial sector as the underlying organizational structure of the economy changed. Previously, the economic system had been based on mutually dependent relations amongst networked agents in the system, but gradually it was transformed into an atomized system in which agents lacked close, long-standing ties. This reduced the effectiveness of the risk-sharing mechanism under the previous system, and the dual structure of the economy, consisting of large and small corporations—which had emerged in the high-growth period—became more apparent. From the 1970s, large business enterprises grew more independent of the banking sector and found it possible to finance their activities in the capital markets. By contrast, small corporations that found it difficult to access these markets had to rely on bank credit. For their part, banks expanded credit to SMEs as their business with large corporations shrank. As banking rents shrank with the deregulation of interest rates, banks could not afford to take as much credit risk as before, and so could not act like traditional main banks in providing cheap funds and rescuing troubled customers. The government responded by encouraging small and local banks to pursue 'relationship banking' with SMEs, including through enforcement by means of a special law.

However, in aggregate, the policy trend towards deregulation and reduced government intervention continued through the 1990s and into the 2000s. The advent of the administration of Prime Minister Junichiro Koizumi (2001–6), which drew partly on the economic philosophy of the Nakasone administration (1982–7), added fresh momentum to the process of institutional reform. Japan's economic performance, however, had not improved significantly prior to the global financial crisis of 2008–9.

In the field of finance, the comprehensive package of financial liberalization dubbed the 'Big Bang' was proposed by the government in 1996 (Table 10.3). In 2007, a new law governing financial services, the Financial Instruments and Exchange Act, was enacted. A new NASDAQ-type stock market was launched in 2000 (Sako and Kotosaka, this volume). In addition, a bankruptcy law for banks was introduced in 2000, formalizing the rules for bank bail-outs.[8]

Outside Japan's financial sector, a new corporate law characterized as more market orientated was enacted in 2005, a response to continued economic underperformance. Japan had fallen into last place amongst the world's developed countries in terms of replacing uncompetitive businesses, and to promote innovations in the economy the government believed it was necessary to simplify the processes for starting new businesses and increasing replacement through measures such as M&A. Japan also signalled in 2009 its willingness to adopt International Financial Reporting Standards (IFRS), with mandatory reporting by Japanese companies possible by 2015. The reform

---

[8] Following the Lehman crisis, it became evident that an equivalent legal framework had yet to be established in the United States and Europe.

Table 10.3. Japan's financial 'Big Bang'

1. Diversification of investment and financial choices

1998	April	Cross-border capital transaction liberalized
	September	Securitization of loan assets permitted
	December	Securities derivatives fully liberalized
		Sale of investment trusts by banks permitted
		Definition of 'securities' expanded and enhanced
2001	April	Over-the-counter sale of insurance products by banks partly permitted

2. Improvement of intermediary agent service quality and fostering competition

1998	March	Establishment of financial holding companies permitted
	December	Licensing of securities activities shifted to register system
1999	May	Range of fundraising for financial companies diversified
	October	Scope of business widened for subsidiaries of financial institutions
		Equity brokerage commissions fully liberalized

3. Development of user-friendly financial market

1997	July	Sale of unlisted and unregistered equities by securities companies permitted
1998	December	Stock exchange features improved, and off-exchange equities transactions permitted
		Over-the-counter market for equities improved (introduction of market maker and new register system)
		Features of financial futures contract improved

4. Development of credible, fair, and transparent business system

1998	December	Disclosure practices enhanced
1999	April	Prompt corrective action introduced
2001	April	Law on Sales of Financial Products enacted

of corporate accounting system has also required complementary reforms in auditing and general corporate governance.

Despite these continuing reforms of a neo-liberal kind, some partial reversals can be observed. Although corporations recognized that banks could no longer carry out the traditional role of a main bank in rescuing troubled customers, large business enterprises gradually increased their dependence on bank finance during the subdued economic expansion from the early 1990s. This may have reflected the continuing poor performance of Japanese equity markets. As Sako and Kotosaka (this volume) discuss, the liberalization of temporary workers' employment contracts has been significant in the recent phase. Following the Lehman crisis, however, because of massive redundancies amongst temporary workers, the government decided to support their employment by thoroughly reviewing the relevant regulations. Although this measure was aimed at fostering social stability, it could also decrease the mobility and speed of reallocation of the economy's resources.

To sum up, the experience in Japan shows that transformation of the economic system is a difficult task. Personalized or atomized capitalist systems are relatively flexible and efficient in adapting to structural economic change, particularly in the domains of corporate and employment restructuring. By comparison, a relationship-intensive networked system such as Japan's tends to adjust more slowly and less efficiently. The recent global crisis, however, suggests that a greater emphasis on risk sharing is called for, even if it might be less efficient. Although Japan's political economy has moved away from a networked system towards a more personalized one, this transition has been only partial and the desire for risk sharing remains significant.

A Comparison with Present-Day China

The contemporary Chinese banking system has a number of similarities with the post-war Japanese system before liberalization. In China, the banking sector plays a pre-eminent role in promoting economic growth through the provision of low-cost funds for fixed investment, as it did in Japan in the post-war period. Both are also characterized by a high degree of regulation, including the regulation of interest rates, the restriction of competition, and substantial control over foreign exchange transactions and cross-border capital investment. China's current position also resembles that of Japan in the early 1970s in that, as happened in Japan, the liberalization of China's foreign exchange market is likely to trigger a more extensive financial liberalization process.

However, there are also important differences between the two cases (see also Breslin, this volume). The Chinese banking sector's relationship with corporations differs in important respects from the earlier situation in Japan. First, the state's ownership role was always less important in Japan than in China. Although the Japanese government intervened through a wide range of instruments and direct intervention by the government played an important economic role—for example, in the form of the Fiscal Investment and Loan Programme as well as ordinary public expenditure—the government always encouraged the development of private firms. As a result, the size of the state was kept relatively small. Second, related to this, even though Chinese banks (in most cases state owned or controlled) have close financial ties with state-owned enterprises (SOEs), their ties with private enterprises are much weaker. This implies that risk sharing is weak in China compared to post-war Japan. Third, China lacks a Japanese-style system of redistribution between urban and local areas acting through the banking sector, despite much higher levels of income inequality. In China, when the central bank tightens the money supply, it resorts to window guidance to reduce bank lending or raises the regulated lending rates of commercial banks. The authorities ensure that the accompanying increase in money market interest rates is kept small, to avoid a profit squeeze at large state-owned banks—deposit rates are also, of course, controlled. This places substantial limits on the efficacy of the money market as a tool for monetary policy. Thus, in China, the role

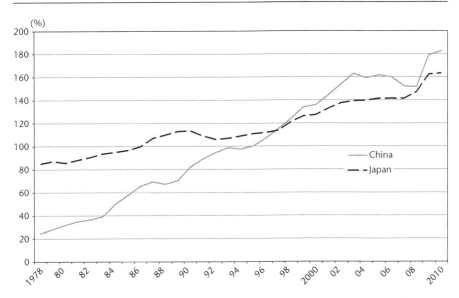

Figure 10.5. Comparison between Japan and China: ratios of money supply (M2 base) to GDP

Note: The M2 data of China are amounts outstanding at the year-end, while those of Japan are average amounts outstanding in December.

Sources: Cabinet Office of the Government of Japan; Bank of Japan; National Bureau of Statistics of China; People's Bank of China.

of market forces is much more limited than in Japan's earlier system and the degree of financial repression is probably larger (see also Lardy, 2008). With nominal growth of more than 10 per cent, lending rates in China have been kept significantly below those dictated by the rate of growth (Table 10.4). These distortions have naturally led to a rapid increase in bank lending and overinvestment in China (Figure 10.5).

These differences suggest that China's liberalization process will not necessarily follow the steps taken by Japan. In particular, unlike Japan before liberalization, China faces pressing issues of rising inequality in income and living standards between urban and rural areas even before full liberalization. This difference suggests that China's liberalization will be the more challenging. The Chinese government has devoted much effort to keeping massive numbers of workers employed at SOEs, a mission assigned to the state-owned banks who have continued to lend large amounts to state-owned firms. This system more closely resembles Japan's wartime regime. Thus, although this role of Chinese banks in supporting troubled SOEs and the associated NPL problem of the 1990s and early 2000s is sometimes compared to Japan in the 1990s, there is an important difference. Japan's bubble developed during financial liberalization, while China's bubble emerged prior to liberalization.

Table 10.4. Interest rates in Japan and China: a comparison

	Japan		China[1]	
	End of 1970	March-end, 2010	End of 1991	March-end, 2010
Long-term lending	8.50 (prime rate)	1.600[2] (prime rate)	9.00 (1–3 years, including three years)	5.40 (1–3 years, including 3 years)
Short-term lending (a)	6.25[3] (prime rate)	1.475[4] (prime rate)	8.10 (6 months or less)	4.86 (6 months or less)
Short-term deposits (3-month) (b)	4.00[5]	0.388[6]	3.24	1.71
(a)–(b)	2.25	1.087	4.86	3.15

Notes:
1. The legal interest rates (base rates) for renminbi lending and deposit set by the People's Bank of China.
2. The interest rate adopted and released by Mizuho Corporate Bank.
3. The rate surveyed under the Temporary Interest Rates Adjustment Law.
4. The lowest interest rate adopted by the 6 city banks. Since 23 January 1989, these banks have independently set the rate, taking into consideration funding costs and other factors.
5. The Bank of Japan guideline rate.
6. The average interest rate on 3-month time deposits of less than ¥3 million posted at financial institutions.

Source: Bank of Japan, People's Bank of China.

This implies that we cannot exclude the possibility that China will experience serious difficulties in the future as financial liberalization progresses. Although the process of reform in China is making headway and major banks have been listed on the stock market in Hong Kong, the economy has not yet undergone what could truly be called liberalization (Okazaki et al., 2011).

This has an implication for foreign exchange rate policy. To maintain regulated interest rates to support the banking sector in China, capital controls are necessary. Although Chinese banks have internationalized in recent years to some extent, it is uncertain how competitive they are against foreign rivals. State-owned banks will be expected to absorb losses stemming from further economic reforms such as the continuing urbanization of rural areas. This may be one reason why China remains cautious with regard to the liberalization of its regulated system and the foreign exchange market.

Conclusion

We have seen how Japan established a relationship-intensive networked economic system during the high-growth period. Government leadership and a complex system of long-term risk sharing were central characteristics of this system, although it produced a highly successful private sector that became increasingly independent of the state over time. As the economy developed, its dualistic structure—notably that obtained between large and small business sectors, and between the central and local economies—became increasingly evident. The risk-sharing system was exemplified by the substantial redistribution that occurred both through the central government budget and through the banking system itself, which functioned during the high-growth period as an important though less well appreciated redistributor of wealth. These mechanisms helped to ensure social stability amidst rapid economic growth, which was remarkable both by the standards of interwar Japan and compared to other advanced economies.

Despite its success, this networked system came under significant strain in later years. Although many Japanese industries did not require a high degree of protection as they prospered, the networked domestic political economy created a variety of barriers to entry for outsiders that eventually became politically problematic, particularly once Japan began accumulating large external surpluses and Japanese corporations started to obtain financing abroad. Foreign pressures for the resolution of increasing trade imbalances and escalating trade disputes accordingly played a significant role in promoting liberalization. As we have seen, the accumulation of financial assets during the high-growth period also produced a growing demand for liberalization within the domestic political economy. The shifting structure of the Japanese financial system also helped to produce the bubble of the 1980s. The inevitable bursting of this bubble and the long crisis that ensued played an important role in further sharpening the domestic and international pressures for renewed liberalization. The emergence of a regional division of labour in the East Asian region creates further challenges for Japan, as well as opportunities.

The long crisis since the 1990s also demonstrated that Japan's system of risk sharing functioned smoothly only when a limited magnitude of risk obtained. After the bubble burst, the significantly heightened level of risk led to increasingly deep strains in the networked system. Japan's networked political economy has undergone substantial changes and the financial system has moved in a more atomized direction. However, the process of convergence towards a more liberal market economy has been only partial, with remnants of the old system remaining. The gradual nature of Japan's liberalization process can be explained in part by the reluctance among various social actors to change generated by the very risk-sharing structure that produced such large benefits in the early decades of the post-war period.

11

Dominant Coalitions and Capital Market Changes in Northeast Asia

Xiaoke Zhang

For much of the post-war period, the financial system in both South Korea (henceforth Korea) and Taiwan was primarily bank based. Banks functioned as the central institutions not only for allocating financial resources but also for managing development policies. While the capital market had long been established, they remained small in size and languished in trading activity. The capital market, which played a marginal role in financial intermediation, remained on the periphery of the financial system. To be sure, the role of finance in the development process was different in that Korea instituted a far more activist industrial finance system than did Taiwan. But the overall defining features of the national financial architecture were noticeably comparable across the two economies.

The Korean and Taiwanese financial markets have experienced dramatic structural changes since the late 1980s. While these changes have manifested themselves in a sustained shift towards a more market-oriented financial architecture, salient cross-country variations have remained in key macrostructural dimensions. More specifically, the two economies have differed in the magnitude of equity market growth, as clearly demonstrated in Table 11.1. Over the past two decades, the size of the Taiwanese stock market, measured by stock market capitalization to gross domestic product (GDP), has been much larger than that of its Korean counterpart. The Taiwanese stock market has also been more active and liquid, as indicated in the higher ratio of stock market trading to GDP. In contrast, the Korean stock market remained virtually stagnant during much of the 1990s; it only came to life in the early 2000s. Despite the slower growth of its stock market, Korea has had a larger and more robust corporate bond market than Taiwan. How can these varied patterns of capital market development be explained?

Table 11.1. Stock market changes (in percentage, yearly average)

	1976–80	1981–5	1986–90	1991–5	1996–2000	2001–5	2006–8
Stock market capitalization/GDP							
Korea	9.04	5.88	31.86	34.84	37.04	52.18	102.77
Taiwan	13.40	12.92	67.06	69.91	95.54	110.56	181.87
Stock market trading value/GDP							
Korea	5.23	3.98	30.24	44.94	100.26	129.82	210.02
Taiwan	20.80	11.30	278.28	176.02	305.26	202.24	345.87
Private bond market capitalization/GDP							
Korea	–	–	28.23	34.39	45.99	58.88	59.02
Taiwan	–	–	13.63	14.71	24.75	25.99	24.45

Source: Author calculations based on data provided in Beck and Al-Hussainy (2010).

The central argument to be developed in this chapter posits that fundamental changes and variations in the financial market structure of Korea and Taiwan have been predicated on the emergence and configuration of the dominant coalitions. The coalitions have been forged by private market agents, economic policymakers, and political elites who have developed particular interests in financial market changes as a response to economic and political imperatives both at home and abroad. In Korea and Taiwan, the dominant coalitions that have born crucially on regulatory rules and market practices have differed in the policy preferences of key actors in the coalitions and the political strength of these actors. It is these differences that have exerted divergent shaping influences on capital market development.

Dominant Coalitions and Capital Market Changes

In Chapter 1 of this volume, exogenous forces, policy discourses, political coalitions, and state action are emphasized as the main explanations of institutional change. Exogenous forces and global market integration in particular have certainly been at play in the process of financial market changes in Korea and Taiwan and explained the simultaneity of their efforts to promote capital market growth in the 1980s and 1990s. In Korea and Taiwan, financial globalization has become a vehicle through which external market pressures have strongly impacted domestic institutional developments. But the systemic-centred explanation falls short of accounting for the varied patterns of financial market changes in Korea and Taiwan. Being both small and open economies, they have been operating in similar international milieus and are equally exposed to global market constraints. The systemic explanation thus confronts a puzzle of why the two economies have diverged so markedly in the trajectory of capital market development.

Systemic forces may work through the more subjective pressures of transnational norms. One of these norms has been the widespread belief in the marketization of finance and maximization of shareholder value as a new ideology for financial governance. In Korea and Taiwan, foreign investors and credit-rating agencies have incessantly promoted the virtues of the ideology over the past decades. Western governments and international financial institutions have often put their weight behind the export of the rhetoric and practice of financial liberalism. Prevailing global ideas have been introduced into domestic policy discourses and influenced regulatory reforms, as US-trained technocrats appear to have readily embraced these ideas (Zhang, 2009, 2010). While ideational forces have played a crucial role in shaping policy choices by transmitting policy-relevant knowledge, their influences over financial market development are indeterminate. The indeterminacy is born out in the fact that Korea and Taiwan that have both been subject to comparable subjective pressures of global ideas have differed in the patterns of capital market changes.

The argument of this chapter emphasizes the causal importance of political coalitions in shaping capital market development. An emerging body of scholarship (Gourevitch and Shinn, 2005; Carney, 2010) has focused on interest group alliances as a primary determinant of financial market structures. These works typically start by modelling the formation of alliances among societal actors who are a priori assumed to have different preferences vis- à-vis financial systems. Which alliances are able to defend or change existing market institutions is contingent upon their respective access to and relative power in policy processes that are in turn defined by broader political structures, such as electoral rules, patterns of inter-class conflicts, or party systems. While accepting the basic contention of this body of scholarship, this chapter makes two key claims that depart from the social alliance perspective.

The first claim is that societal actors do not work alone in the formation and change of financial market institutions and must operate through the state to achieve specific policy outcomes. Interest group alliances among farmers, workers, or capitalists do not by themselves produce regulatory rules and market changes. State institutions and action not only structure the articulation of societal interests but also shape the translation of these interests into policy processes. More crucially, state agencies make policy choices and formulate reform strategies in line with their own preferences. This point is particularly relevant in East Asia where the state has been traditionally identified as the crucial source of institutional changes in the political economy. However, this does not imply that the state singularly articulates collective policy preferences in the transformation of market institutions. Rather, it is the dominant coalitions that state elites deliberately forge with key societal actors that impinge crucially upon the process of institutional changes.

The second and more important claim is that the emphasis on dominant coalitions should not obscure the dynamics of realignments between state elites, economic policymakers, and societal actors. These dynamics are likely to be elided in the conventional assumption that the state and the coalitions that they form with sociopolitical groups are marked by organizational unity and stability. Just as societal groups are often internally divided, so are states 'fragmented into numerous quarrelling parts', in the words of Moran (1990). Divisions within societal groups and state agencies suggest that the lines of conflicts and compromises over regulatory and institutional reforms may be drawn not between the integrated state and the unified private sector but between political coalitions of different state agencies and actors and their constituent social allies. Pro-reform politicians and technocrats may be united in coalitions with societal actors with similar policy preferences against other coalitions made up in the same way that benefit from existing rules and institutions. Cross-country variations in financial market changes are thus an important function of the changing composition, policy preferences, and relative power of these coalitions.

Table 11.2 summarizes the changing dynamics of the dominant coalition in Korea and Taiwan over the past decades. In the 1980s and 1990s, the chaebol-state alliance that had underpinned the Korean political economy for much of the post-war period transmuted into a much broader coalition against the backdrop of democratization. While the chaebols remained essential and arguably dominant actors, new societal forces such as farmers and small and medium-sized enterprises (SMEs) were incorporated into the new coalition. This coalition had a strong pro-bank bias. The perennial desire of chaebol firms to maintain ownership controls and expand their size made them favour debt financing from banks and bond markets. Small industrialists and farmers who had limited access to the capital market relied primarily upon institutional credit (Laeven, 2002). Powerful bureaucrats from the Ministry of Finance (MOF)/the Ministry of Finance and Economy (MOFE, a merger between the MOF and the Economic Planning Board in 1995) saw the bank-based system as an effective instrument to orchestrate industrial development and maintain their regulatory power (Hundt, 2009: 75–880). Ruling politicians' preferences were tied in with these pro-bank policy interests, as they were keen to use banks to rein in the chaebols, promote the interests of SMEs and farmers, and seek campaign financing. While capital market reforms and pro-market policies were implemented, support for market-oriented changes was invariably subsumed under the converging preferences of key state and societal actors for debt over equity financing.

In the decade that followed the Asian crisis of the late 1990s, the coalition that dominated political and policy processes in Korea became increasingly reformist and progressive. While market pressures and neo-liberal reforms set

Table 11.2. Dominant coalitions and financial market structures

Changing dynamics of dominant coalitions	Preferences of key actors in dominant coalitions	Relative power of key actors in dominant coalitions	Policy changes and financial market outcomes
Korea Late 1980s–1997: from state-chaebol alliance to grand conservative coalition	Political leaders and MOE/MOFE officials: banks over capital markets; financial technocrats: balanced growth; chaebols: debt financing; SMEs/farmers: bank loans	Financial technocrats subordinate to politicians and MOE/MOFE officials; powerful chaebols; weak positions of SMEs/farmers/workers	Key role of banks in financial policy; rapid expansion and dominance of NBFIs; stronger growth of corporate bond market
Late 1990s–mid-2000s: from conservative coalition to more reformist and progressive alliance	Political leaders and MOFE officials: stronger preference for capital market but still focus on banks; chaebols: more inclined to seek equity funds but favour debt financing	Strengthened power of BOK/FSC technocrats; reduced influence of chaebols; increased power of SMEs and workers	More rapid growth of banks; reduced role of NBFIs, sustained capital market growth but more rapid development of bond market until mid-2000s
Taiwan Late 1980s–late 1999s: from more inclusive coalition to state-business alliance	CBC/MOF officials: balanced growth; KMT politicians: capital market; private firms: more inclined to go public; private financiers: stock market growth through banks	CBC/MOF more dominant than line ministries; increasing influence of private business and financial capitalists; positions of other social groups weak	Dominant role of banks but rapid stock market development; subdued growth of NBFIs and corporate bond market
Early and mid-2000s: consolidation of conservative alliance between state and big business	CBC/MOF officials: more emphasis on capital market growth; no change in preferences of other actors	Power of CBC/MOF reduced but that of politicians and big business increased; SMEs/farmers/workers largely excluded	Continued and rapid expansion of stock market; slower growth of NBFIs and bond market; more market-oriented financial structure

the stage for the more rapid growth of the stock market, the overall tendency of key actors in the coalition to favour bank-based institutions persisted. The position of SMEs and labour as crucial counter-chaebol forces significantly strengthened in the dominant coalition. The chaebols, while restructured and humbled, remained key development agents. Reformist technocrats in the Bank of Korea (BOK, the central bank) and newly established Financial Supervisory Commission (FSC) enjoyed moments of rising influence, but MOFE bureaucrats were often able to exercise veto authority over financial policy (*KH*, 23 June 2003: 19; Kim and Lee, 2006). Despite their reformist credentials, political leaders continued to favour the development of banks on which they depended for calling the chaebols to account and implementing loan-centred redistributive schemes.

In Taiwan, the ruling Kuomintang (KMT) party developed and cemented a narrow coalition with big business in the late 1980s and 1990s (Cheng and Chu, 2002). Many Taiwanese business groups developed their core operations in finance-related sectors, tied their assets in the securities industry, and saw the stock market as a vehicle for enhancing their performance (Chung and Mahmood, 2006). Likewise, major banks that traditionally maintained an arms-length relationship with industry found the stock market where quick returns on bank funds could be generated as an excellent outlet for lending large amounts of money profitably for short periods (Zhang, 2009). Equally important, powerful technocrats from the Central Bank of China (CBC) and the MOF saw pro-market institutional changes as the key to modernizing the financial sector and bolstering the profitability of private financiers (Kuo et al., 2000). The pro-market preferences of both private and public financiers dovetailed with the desire of ruling politicians to expand the KMT business empire through stock market growth (Cooper, 2007). Financial capitalists, public financiers, and KMT elites thus formed a dominant coalition to promote market-oriented policy and institutional changes, as summarized in Table 11.2.

The 2000 presidential election that ushered in the Democratic Progressive Party (DPP) realigned the dominant coalition but did not change its basic institutional parameters, composition, and policy preferences (Lee and Chu, 2008). Finance-centred business groups and influential private financiers again became the most sought-after allies in the new dominant coalition and enjoyed even greater political prominence in the DPP regime. They had an enhanced capacity to penetrate the state economic policymaking agencies and oriented capital market reforms even more closely with their interests. Despite the progressive bent of the DPP, workers, farmers, and small industrialists who pressed for credit support and pro-bank policies lacked political resources with which to contend with financial capitalists and remained on the fringes of the power structure in Taiwan (Cooper, 2009).

Different Coalitions and Varied Market Outcomes

This section examines the political process through which the Korean and Taiwanese capital markets have changed before and after the Asian crisis of 1997–8 on the basis of the argument developed in the previous section. The purpose is not to trace the evolution of their capital markets, which is well beyond the scope of this chapter, but to illustrate the causal links between the dynamics of the dominant coalitions and changes in the capital market structure of the two economies.

Korea

Having registered rapid growth on the back of a robust economic recovery and current account surpluses in the mid-1980s, the Korea Stock Exchange (KSE) got bogged down in the doldrums through 1993. While part of the overall financial liberalization programme, capital market reforms were invariably on the backburner. In the late 1980s and much of the 1990s, successive governments failed to enact any long-term policy and institutional changes to put capital market growth on a sustained footing. Instead, they resorted to highly ad hoc and dirigiste measures to control market conditions. The MOF/MOFE arm-twisted financial institutions to buy shares when the market tumbled and cajoled them to sell when prices shot up. These measures, often designed to achieve political objectives, such as boosting the electoral prospects of the incumbent president (*FEER*, 2 September 1993: 70; *KT*, 3 February 1994: 9), were inimical to capital market development.

In the late 1980s and 1990s, the government also moved to open the capital account. The United States exerted pressures for greater financial opening; these pressures accelerated against the backdrop of the Kim Young Sam government's effort to gain OECD membership. But external pressures did not dictate the patterns of capital account opening; rather, they reflected the preferences of the dominant coalition in the final analysis. Fearful of destabilizing portfolio movements but eager to tap overseas capital markets, the government restricted portfolio inflows and the entry of foreign securities firms but liberalized short-term trade credits. This uneven liberalization approach also reflected private interests. While the chaebols were keen to access overseas funds, they wanted to keep at bay foreign investors who were likely to weaken their managerial controls. By the same token, merchant banks mediated massive capital inflows at the behest of their chaebols owners (Lee et al., 2002), whereas stockbrokers and big industrialists allied against the deregulation of entry barriers to foreign firms and lobbied for restrictions on their operations (*FEER*, 2 August 1990: 44; *KT*, 20 November 1994: 9).

While the government liberalized capital inflows, it was keen to keep banks on a short leash. MOF/MOFE bureaucrats perceived equity funds as ancillary to debt financing and relied upon banks for implementing development policies and expanding their regulatory power (*FEER*, 13 June 1991: 64–5). More important, political leaders saw banks as a crucial instrument with which not only to rein in the chaebols but also to sustain the coalitional basis of their support. Through the banking sector, successive governments enacted various redistributive schemes targeted at small industrialists, farmers, and workers. For example, the Roh Tae-Woo regime launched a 2-million unit housing programme for these social groups that sucked in massive bank funds in the early 1990s (*ER*, July 1991: 32). Similarly, the governments of both Roh and Kim made concerted efforts to press banks to channel credit to the export-oriented, agricultural, and, most important, SME sectors that demanded policy loans (*KT*, 11 November 1990: 10, and 2 July 1992: 1; Hahm, 2003). As shown in Figure 11.1, bank loans to SMEs grew rapidly and took the lion's share of corporate loans. As in the past, the BOK was bombarded with the instructions to support policy-based lending and to relieve bad loans in banks.

Financial policies that prioritized the banking sector and capital account liberalization led to a systematic underattention to capital market reforms. The supply of tradable shares remained volatile and shallow; the number of listed firms virtually stagnated during the 1990s, as shown in Figure 11.2. These problems persisted despite the effort of the government to cajole more large firms to seek equity funds from the stock market. Chaebols that had enhanced access to overseas capital markets and continued to benefit from policy loans to the export-oriented sector were not inspired to go public or increase capital through rights offerings. To the extent that they needed to raise long-term and direct finance, they tended to favour corporate bonds. This was not only because bonds saved them the trouble of having to listen to outside shareholders but also because more than 80 per cent of bonds were guaranteed by banks and non-bank financial institutions (NBFIs) (*FEER*, 13 June 1991: 76–8, and 9 July 1992: 50–1; Park, 1999: 209).

To deepen the supply of shares and diversify the trading of shares that clustered around a handful of listed chaebol firms, the government resorted to the divestment of state assets. In the mid- and late 1980s, the privatization of a few large SOEs did increase the market capitalization of the KSE. During much of the 1990s, however, the divestment programme proceeded by fits

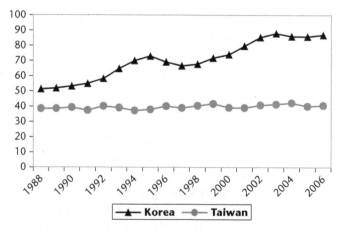

Figure 11.1. Bank loans to SMEs as a percentage of total corporate loans

Source: The FSC (Bank Management Statistics, various issues) and the CBC (Loans by Domestic Banks to SMEs).

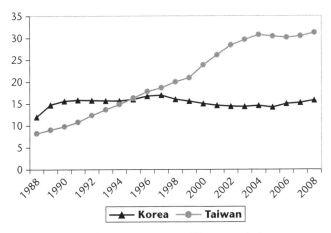

Figure 11.2. Number of listed companies per million population

Source: The BOK (Economics Statistics Yearbook, various issues) and the CBC (Financial Statistics Monthly, various issues).

and starts for several reasons. First, the MOF/MOFE and line ministries that heavily depended upon SOEs for managing national assets, maintaining regulatory power, and securing career advancement had little incentive to push for rapid privatization (Park, 2009). Second, labour unions that were increasingly engaged by Roh Tae-Woo and Kim Young Sam in their grand conservative coalition and upon which they relied for ensuring industrial peace were opposed to the divestment programme. And third, the Roh and Kim governments that sought to curb the power of big business were deeply worried that the cash-rich chaebols would gobble up privatized enterprises. They thus had no choice but to exercise extreme caution with privatization, particularly in the telecom and energy sectors that the chaebols had long craved to control (*EIUCR-Korea*, 4th Quarter 1997: 24–5; Jin, 2006).

The same logic of Korea's dominant coalition also undermined the cultivation of a stable and broad demand for shares. In Korea, as in many other emerging markets, individual investors typically owned more than 70 per cent of tradable shares in the stock market while institutional investors, mainly bank trust accounts, securities houses, investment trust companies, and insurance firms, owned about 15 per cent. This narrow and homogenous investor base rendered market liquidity low and share trading volatile, as poorly informed individuals were often subject to panics and jitters. With banks pressed to provide policy loans and NBFIs directed to support the excessive investment of their chaebol owners, institutional investors had a weak ability to foster a strong demand for shares. In 1990, the government mobilized 5 trillion won from institutional investors to buttress the sagging stock market. This paled to insignificance beside massive loans worth 51 trillion won

---

supplied to the manufacturing sector by NBFIs alone in that year (*BK*, June 1990: 63). Securities houses, the main providers of margin loans, and the Korea Securities Finance Corporation, the only institution permitted to specialize in securities financing in the early and mid-1990s, faced a chronic shortage of funds and played a limited role in the financing of share purchases (Hogan and Abiko, 1996).

The shallow and erratic demand for tradable shares also reflected the prevalence of high transaction costs in the capital market. The securities industry remained concentrated in a relatively small number of securities firms; extensive ownership controls of large firms by the chaebols further contributed to the oligopolistic structure of the industry. Financial liberalization in the 1990s failed to lower entry barriers significantly and increase competitiveness in the market. This generated high explicit costs of trading—inelastic commission rates and high settlement fees, as illustrated in Table 11.3. Extensive government intervention and weak market-oriented governance rules impeded information disclosure and resulted in the high implicit costs of share trading. These transaction costs deterred potential investors from entering the market and prevented existing investors from becoming active traders of equities. In late 1995, the government decided to levy higher tax rates on interest income

Table 11.3. Trading costs in equity markets

	Korea	Taiwan	Malaysia	Singapore	Thailand
4th Quarter 1997					
Explicit costs	60.77	52.55	71.36	55.32	66.79
Implicit costs	158.81	21.15	16.36	16.64	20.66
Total costs	219.58	73.70	87.72	71.96	87.45
4th Quarter 1999					
Explicit costs	20.47	25.62	53.66	31.17	35.00
Implicit costs	75.41	22.24	67.77	44.81	26.21
Total costs	95.88	47.86	121.43	75.98	61.21
4th Quarter 2001					
Explicit costs	48.51	44.00	52.07	31.47	54.35
Implicit costs	22.80	14.40	18.11	8.49	2.87
Total costs	71.31	58.40	70.18	39.96	57.22
2003					
Explicit costs	42.68	38.07	41.23	28.17	46.90
Implicit costs	18.35	12.02	16.88	10.14	10.99
Total costs	61.03	50.09	58.11	38.31	57.89
2005					
Explicit costs	40.85	37.47	37.06	27.33	40.30
Implicit costs	13.00	10.39	16.38	13.48	18.80
Total costs	53.85	47.86	53.44	40.81	59.10

Source: International Finance Corporation (*Emerging Stock Markets Factbook*, various issues) and Standard and Poor's (*Global Stock Markets Factbook*, various issues).

earned on debt instruments with a view to encouraging investors to shift funds to the stock market and stimulating share trading, but this had little effect (*BK*, October 1995: 23). As a result, the incidence of share ownership amongst the population was small by international standards and hovered around 6 per cent over 1995–7 (ASX, 2005: 2).

The Asian financial crisis of 1997–8 wrought dreadful havoc with banks, NBFIs, and the capital market in Korea. The Kim Dae-jung and Roh Moo-hyun governments emphasized bank rescues and restructuring as the key to restoring financial system stability. Massive public funds were mobilized from the state budget and from the asset management and deposit insurance corporations to purchase bad loans from banks and strengthen their capital bases. The recapitalization of banks, which had cost the Korean government more than 168 trillion won by mid-2006, was widely dubbed as one of the most expensive in recent history. Banks were privileged partly because a sound banking system gave the government a powerful instrument in restructuring the chaebols, a central plank in the post-crisis reform programme (Park, 2003). Moreover, policymakers were eager to put banks on a healthy footing so that they could be sold, particularly to foreigners, and the proceeds could buttress the increasingly fragile state coffers. However, the driving forces behind the bank-centred restructuring strategy were deeper than these policy considerations and reflected the changing dynamics of coalitional building in Korea.

In the first place, the strategy was a function of the enhanced position of SMEs in the dominant coalition. Both Kim Dae-jung and Roh Moo-hyun came to office with a longstanding belief that small industrialists had long been slighted by government policy. Elected on the platform of tackling distributive injustices and imbalanced industrial structures, they saw the promotion of SMEs through state-directed bank financing as an important way to fulfil their electoral mandates. The SME-promoting approach bore a discernible resemblance to the dirigiste and activist industrial finance system of the 1970s. In the wake of the crisis, the government pressed banks to repeatedly roll over SME debts; it then instituted a variety of funding schemes to provide SMEs with stable, preferential, and long-term financing (*KH*, 11 July 1998: 1; 11 November 2002: 11; 3 February 2004: 19; and 19 October 2006: 5). The chaebols promptly endorsed the SME policy, hoping to cement mutually supportive alliance with SMEs across a range of industrial sectors (*KH*, 17 April 1998: 12). As a result, bank loans to the SME sector witnessed a rapid growth in the post-crisis period, as illustrated in Figure 11.1.

Furthermore, workers and farmers who had benefitted from the housing-loan programmes of the Roh Tae-Woo and Kim Young Sam governments pressed hard for the expansion of the programmes in the late 1990s and 2000s. Many workers and farmers saw their disposable incomes decline sharply following the crisis and had to increasingly resort to bank borrowings

(Chung, 2009: 87–90). Kim Dae-jung and particularly Roh Moo-hyun who saw farmers and workers as key counteracting forces against the chaebols were strongly inclined to encourage banks to assist them. While foreign-owned banks were reluctant to make policy-directed lending, state-controlled and specialized institutions deferred (Hahm, 2007). The extension of bank loans to these social groups reinforced the growing dominance of household debts in the asset structure of banks and complicated monetary policymaking and prudential regulation. BOK and FSC technocrats urged the introduction of new regulatory constraints, but MOFE bureaucrats and their political masters had refused to budge until surging household debts threatened financial system stability (Kim and Lee, 2006).

While the development of banks was privileged, capital market reforms were relegated down the priority list. To be sure, many post-crisis financial reforms boded well for market-oriented institutional changes. Further capital decontrols removed most restrictions on foreign portfolio investments in the stock market and considerably lowered entry barriers to international securities firms, for instance; foreign-owned banks that had more operational autonomy shifted their asset portfolios away from the manufacturing sector and towards more liquid and securities-based transactions; corporate governance reforms along neo-liberal lines held the prospects of strengthening capital market rules and reducing transaction costs (Zhang, 2010). However, the government failed to show a well-planned and long-term effort to broaden and deepen equity financing and sustain the trajectory of stock market growth.

Despite the noticeable increase in stock market capitalization in the early and mid-2000s, the supply of tradable shares was far from stable and sturdy. The increased market value derived not so much from the main board of the KSE where the number of listed firms stagnated and even declined (Figure 11.2) as from the more vibrant KOSDAQ that attracted export-oriented and high-tech firms. This in large part reflected the ambivalent preference of the chaebols vis-à-vis equity financing. In the post-crisis period, large firms were more inclined to seek equity funds, partly because they had to issue more shares to meet the stringent requirement for reducing debt–equity ratios and partly because the lending capacity of banks and NBFIs was severely constrained by their fragile asset positions. However, chaebol firms still preferred debt financing through corporate bonds in order to retain managerial and control rights (*KH*, 25 January 2000: 8). Official efforts to structure capital market reforms around the development of the bond market also fostered this preference. The collapse of Daewoo Group in late 1999 and the accounting scandal in SK Group in early 2003 wrecked the corporate bond market and landed many large firms in liquidity crises. The government initiated a variety of funding schemes that provided partial guarantees on bond issues and restored liquidity to the market (*KH*, 17 January 2001: 10; Kim, 2004).

The reluctance of chaebol firms to resort to equity financing was also encouraged by the prospects of their securing privileged access to bank and NBFI credits. Despite its aggressive chaebol reform efforts, the government was not ready to allow systemically important business groups to fail. Nowhere was this more manifest than in the bail-out of three Hyundai flagship companies through debt rollovers and fresh bank loans in early 2001 (*KH*, 12 March 2001: 8). Whenever investments sagged and exports declined, policymakers were apt to provide chaebol firms with financial support in the hope that they would lead the national economy out of the slump (FSC interview, February 2007). Furthermore, the chaebols tightened their grip on NBFIs and relied even more heavily on them for debt financing. While many insolvent NBFIs were closed down and the sector shrank following the financial crisis, they still controlled a sizable share in the loan and deposit markets and continued to channel credits to the chaebol-dominated manufacturing sector (*KH*, 30 June 1999: 7, and 24 March 2001: 12).

With large chaebol firms clinging to debt financing, the government turned to the privatization of SOEs as an alternative strategy to boost the supply of tradable shares. In the late 1990s and early 2000s when external pressures were acute, the chaebols kept a relatively low political profile and workers were more willing to cooperate through the newly established Tripartite Commission, and Korea witnessed the hitherto most forceful privatization drive under Kim Dae-jung (Lim, 2003: 39–61). The divestment of some of the largest SOEs played a key role in increasing the market capitalization of the KSE. However, plans to privatize big SOEs in the utilities and infrastructural sectors were postponed or suspended under Roh Moo-hyun in the mid-2000s when the worst of the crisis waned, labour became more militant, and the chaebols flexed their muscle again (*EIUCR-Korea*, August 2004: 21–2; Park, 2009).

The government also had a mixed record in diversifying the investor base. The financial crisis enervated the ability of institutional investors to actively trade securities and contribute to the liquidity of equity markets. Instead of financing share trading, many chaebol-owned investment trust companies and securities firms helped listed chaebol firms to buy back their shares in order to fend off hostile takeover bids, particularly from foreign investors (*KH*, 3 January 2006: 6). In the circumstances, financial authorities moved to expand the securities investments of the country's public pension funds in 2005. Reflecting the desire of the government to prioritize the bond market, however, more than 80 per cent of these funds' assets were invested in bonds while merely 11 per cent were invested in shares in 2005 (*KH*, 12 December 2005: 5). At the same time, market regulators loosened restrictions on the establishment and operation of private equity funds to promote them as important institutional investors and, more important, to counter the extensive presence of foreign investors in the capital market (*ER*, January 2004:

38–9; *KH*, 25 August 2006: 6). But the penchant of the Kim and Roh governments for fostering the public pension funds as welfare-enhancing and redistributive instruments squeezed the growth of private equity funds. By the early 2000s, private pension assets had only accounted for 13 per cent of Korea's GDP, well below the average level for many OECD and emerging market countries (Gourevitch and Shinn, 2005: 217).

The growth of the equity market was also impeded by high transaction costs. With the entry of more international firms, the securities sector became more competitive in the 2000s. However, as the crisis reduced the number of securities firms and as top firms were affiliated to the chaebols, the concentrated structure of the market remained virtually intact. While stockbroking commissions and settlement fees were deregulated and declined significantly in the post-crisis period, they remained higher than those in Taiwan (Table 11.3). More crucially, the resistance of listed firms to comply with international corporate governance standards (Walter, 2008) and the inability of FSC officials to isolate themselves from political pressures left market transactions opaque and information disclosure poor. The Korean legal framework governing securities markets was more limited in scope and weaker in enforcement than not only Taiwan but also many other East Asian economies, as shown in Table 11.4. The oligopolistic structure and weak market regulation combined to keep the explicit and implicit costs of share trading high and deterred individual and institutional investors from actively purchasing and trading shares. The result is that the incidence of share ownership in the population averaged 8 per cent over 1998–2007 (ASX, 2005: 2; 2009: 34), only a slight increase from the mid-1990s.

Table 11.4. Securities market regulation

	2001	2002	2003	2004	2005	2007	2010	All years
Securities market rules[a]								
Korea	5.0	6.0	7.0	6.1	5.1	4.5	4.3	5.4
Taiwan	7.0	7.0	7.0	6.3	5.3	4.9	5.0	6.1
Group mean[b]	6.1	6.5	6.9	6.2	5.3	4.8	4.8	5.8
Enforcement of securities market rules								
Korea	3.0	3.0	3.5	5.0	4.0	3.9	2.8	3.6
Taiwan	4.0	5.0	5.0	4.6	4.9	4.7	4.7	4.7
Group mean	3.0	3.2	3.8	4.4	4.1	3.5	3.7	3.7

Source: CLSA Asia-Pacific Markets (*CG Watch*, various issues).

Notes: [a] The rules cover financial reporting standards, government efforts to improve securities laws, information disclosure, compliance with international best practices, independent board committees, and minority shareholder protection. The score ranges from 1 to 10, with 10 indicating the best. The score trended downwards across all the countries from 2005, primarily as a result of CLSA adopting a more rigorous ranking methodology. [b] This is the average score for eight East Asian economies—China, Indonesia, South Korea, Malaysia, the Philippines, Singapore, Taiwan, and Thailand.

Taiwan

The Taipei Stock Exchange (TSE), which had remained lacklustre for many years, sprang to life in the late 1980s, thanks to propitious economic conditions and, more importantly, regulatory reforms. Financial technocrats undertook reform measures to promote the growth of the TSE as an important way to channel swelling funds caused by Taiwan's large trade surpluses into industrial investment and achieve money supply control more efficiently (Woo and Liu, 1994; Shea, 1995). Curb market crises that were associated with the underdeveloped state of securities markets also opened a window of opportunity for private bankers to push for the liberalization of the securities industry (*FEER*, 21 January 1988: 48–9, and 19 May 1988: 85–6). For two years until 1990, financial authorities promulgated numerous amendments to the Securities and Exchange Law (SEL) and implemented a wide range of liberalizing measures that removed the regulatory barriers that segmented the securities industry and restricted the entry of new firms and allowed securities firms and banks to lend on margin. These regulatory reforms resulted in the Taiwanese bourse experiencing the hitherto strongest boom over 1988–90.

Like the KSE, the TSE was traditionally plagued by the dominance of small, poorly informed investors and by an associated narrow investor base. To foster the stable growth of the stock market, central bankers and finance ministry officials made joint efforts to promote institutional investment by liberalizing the rules governing the operations of institutional investors and removing entry barriers into the asset-management industry in the early and mid-1990s (Semkow, 1994: 166–9; Liu, 1997: 830–2). Official efforts also reflected the interests of private actors. Banks and securities firms, having gained the license to engage in margin financing, craved to expand into the asset-management segment of the market by running their own investment and mutual funds. Their policy demands were reinforced by many business groups that came to dominate the financial sector in the 1990s (*FEER*, 12 December 1991: 62–3; *WSJ*, 4 May 1992: A7A).

Public and private interests in market-oriented reforms pushed through amendments to the SEL that permitted the licensing and establishment of many new equity investment funds. For instance, the number of securities investment trust companies rocketed from 18 in 1990 to 200 in 1998. The ownership of TSE-listed companies by institutional investors, comprising government-run pension and trust funds, financial institutions, and securities investment companies, increased from no more than 6 per cent of market capitalization in 1990 to nearly 25 per cent in 1998 (TSE, 1999: 21). Unlike their Korean counterparts, Taiwanese securities firms and finance companies that were affiliated with cash-rich private banks, finance-centred business groups, or the ruling KMT were better positioned to provide ample liquidity to the financing of share purchases (Tashiro and Osman, 1996). Institutional investors played an important part in stabilizing and broadening the demand for shares. This was demonstrated in their role in pulling the TSE out of the doldrums in early 1993 and cushioning the market against massive sell-off in mid-1995 when China–Taiwan relations deteriorated sharply.

To encourage and sustain the interest of individual and institutional investors, financial authorities streamlined and reduced taxes on investment activities and earnings in the early and mid-1990s. Apart from the desire of public financiers to promote capital market growth, this policy change also stemmed from persistent pressures from financial firms and corporate groups (*EIUCR-Taiwan*, 1st Quarter 1994: 18–19; *FEER*, 13 October 1988: 107). The KMT, which owned an increasing number of securities investment companies, had a stake in seeing taxes reduced (Kuo et al., 2000). Consequently, the capital gains tax was scrapped in 1991; the securities transaction tax was reduced to 0.3 per cent in 1993 and further halved a year later. In early 1996, KMT legislators foiled the attempt of the opposition to reimpose the capital gains tax (*EIUCR-Taiwan*, 1st Quarter 1996: 10, 23).

Official efforts to reduce the costs of share trading were also facilitated by the rapid deregulation of entry barriers in the securities industry and the strong regulatory capacity of CBC and MOF technocrats. The number and categories of securities-related firms multiplied in the late 1980s and 1990s. Apart from forty-seven integrated securities firms that were licensed to provide a full range of securities businesses, there had been more than 200 securities houses and nearly 180 brokerage companies by the mid-1990s (Liu, 1997: 838). This drove securities firms to compete fiercely for customers by keeping their commission and settlement fees low. Equally important, financial regulators who occupied a privileged position in the state apparatus and were widely respected for their technical competence had a demonstrated ability to force compliance with securities market rules. The manipulation of capital market rules for rent-seeking purposes was thus a long way from reaching Korea's level (Sheng, 2009: 173–86). As a direct result of the more competitive securities sector and more effective market regulation, the explicit and implicit costs of share trading were lower than those in Korea and many other East Asian economies (Table 11.3). This encouraged both individual and institutional investors to purchase and trade shares, contributing to an active and liquid stock market. In the late 1990s, more than 30 per cent of Taiwan's population owned shares (*Forbes*, 1998: 122), well above the level in Korea over the same period.

The weaknesses of bank-based financing exposed by the Asian crisis of 1997–8 and the looming domestic banking crisis in 1999–2000 heightened the importance of avoiding excessive reliance on bank credit and developing a more market-based corporate capital structure. There was a renewed consensus among key policymakers that a well-developed capital market would help Taiwan better cope with pressures created by globalization (Shen, 2005). The economic rationale for further market-oriented changes was reinforced by the desire of political leaders to promote the TSE as a foreign policy tool for boosting the international visibility and status of Taiwan. These considerations generated bipartisan interest in the further development of the stock market and rendered the ruling and opposition parties willing to cooperate on major reform policies designed to improve and strengthen market-oriented institutional changes.

Enhanced official interests in market-oriented reforms tied in strongly with the efforts of banks and securities firms to advance their own policy agenda. Following the financial crisis, private banks further scaled down their lending to the manufacturing sector. In another difference from their Korean counterparts, Taiwanese banks, both state owned and private, were under little pressure to extend massive policy loans to SMEs. As a result, their exposure to the sector remained much lower than that of Korean banks in the post-crisis period, as illustrated in Figure 11.2. Private financiers urged the government to bolster declining share prices and actively contributed to a stock market stabilization fund (*FEER*, 10 December 1998: 72; *TanXia*, 1 February 2001: 154). They took sides with financial technocrats against industrial and planning officials who were opposed to the launching of the fund and wanted to direct more funds to small firms (*EIUCR-Taiwan*, 1st Quarter 1999: 21).

As securities-related businesses became an increasingly important source of their incomes and profits, private financiers pressed for full access to the securities industry. Leaders of finance-based business groups had long craved to bring various banking, finance, and securities subsidiaries under centralized management and ownership controls. Under the DPP regime, the legislature was dominated by the opposition and the government was thus divided. This gave rise to stalemates and gridlocks in policymaking processes and bogged down important legislation. However, backed by powerful financial capitalists, the DPP government pushed through the financial bills that cleared the way for the establishment of financial holding companies in June 2001 (Brück and Sun, 2007; Wang et al., 2008). These companies were structured around leading banks and allowed their subsidiaries to operate right across the financial services spectrum.

Despite official and private efforts to boost share prices, the TSE remained largely depressed for more than a year after the Asian crisis, amid growing financial sector weaknesses, political uncertainties created by the electoral alternation of power, and global economic downturns. Given that a large proportion of Taiwan's population owned listed shares, the continued underperformance of the stock market had huge political consequences. The economic woes significantly undermined the credibility of the new government under the DPP with the general public (Wu, 2002). Up until the late 1990s,

Taiwan had operated a tightly controlled capital account and maintained extensive restrictions on foreign portfolio inflows, primarily because of policy-makers' concerns about the impact of foreign capital inflows on macroeco-nomic stability (Zhang, 2003). But when domestic investors shied away from the TSE due to market uncertainties and politicians were under strong political pressure to revitalize the stock market, the government had little choice but to turn to foreign investors.

Domestic pressures were sufficient to produce policy change, but this does not preclude a role for external forces. Following the financial crisis, foreign investors, many of whom had got their fingers severely burnt in the crisis, were hesitant to flock back. To revive their stock markets, many Asian states engaged in the competitive deregulation of restrictions on foreign portfolio inflows. This inter-country rivalry forced the Taiwanese government eventu-ally to abolish the system of only allowing qualified foreign institutional investors to buy shares and to scrap altogether the investment cap for foreign institutional investors in 2003. The policy shift prompted Morgan Stanley, a leading international investment bank, to increase the weighting of Taiwa-nese stocks in its regional stock indices that many global investors used as an investment guide (*WSJ*, 20 May 2004: 6). Foreign portfolio investment began to flow back in over 2001–2.

In parallel with their efforts to stabilize the demand side of the stock market, financial authorities moved to broaden the supply of trade shares. Trading in TSE-listed securities was traditionally concentrated narrowly on a small set of big companies, mainly because of the reluctance of major shareholders to trade their control shares away. In the early and mid-1990s, the government enforced stricter shareholding dispersal requirements, but these achieved a modicum of success. Frustrated in their attempts to open up closely held companies, policymakers turned to fiscal incentives as an alternative way to promote listings and increase tradable shares in the post-crisis period. In 1998, the MOF eliminated the taxation of company dividends paid to shareholders; this was followed by the integration of business taxes that removed the double taxation of shareholders and investors, as part of overall official efforts to boost investment activities.

However, there was a limit to the extent to which the government could resort to further tax cuts to promote listings, mainly due to Taiwan's rising budget deficits that got worse in the aftermath of the financial crisis and the ensuing recession. Consequently, securities market regulators explored the possibility of easing strict listing requirements and streamlining cumbersome application procedures for listings. The regulatory change also reflected the growing demands for the reforms of listing rules from high-profile Taiwanese companies that increasingly resorted to the capital market for long-term financing and from private financiers who stood to benefit from a broader market (*EUICR-Taiwan*, November 2000: 28; Shi and Chen, 2003). The relaxation of listing rules, combined with fiscal incentives, saw the number of listed companies increase more rapidly in the TSE than in the KSE, as shown in Figure 11.2.

The impact of fiscal incentives and listing deregulation on the breadth of stock trading was further magnified by the renewed efforts of the government to privatize SOEs. In late 1996, the bipartisan National Development Conference made a decision to accelerate the privatization process, with the view to broadening the capital market as well as to boosting the state offers and improving the declining competitiveness of the Taiwanese economy. Business groups that saw privatization as a good opportunity to expand the scope and size of their empires actively pushed for the rapid divestment of state assets (Chu, 2004). Despite its pro-labour stance, the DPP government stuck with the reform programme and saw through the privatization of many major SOEs in defiance of strong protests from trade unions (Wu, 2003). Between 1998 and 2004, the government transferred six large-scale manufacturing and transportation companies to private hands and sold its shares in nine financial institutions to the public, significantly increasing the market capitalization of the TSE (CEPD, 2005).

Institutional Changes and Complementarities

Financial transformations in Korea and Taiwan clearly illustrate the political dynamics of institutional changes under the impact of the dominant coalitions. Since the late 1980s, the well-entrenched, bank-centred institutions of financial governance have been reformed and significant structural changes have taken place. However, while financial market changes in Korea have centred on the development of banks, NBFIs, and corporate bond markets, those in Taiwan have been structured around finance-based groups and the stock market. As summarized in Table 11.2, this varied pattern of regulatory and market reforms has reflected cross-country variations in the composition, institutional parameters, and policy preferences of the dominant coalitions in Korea and Taiwan.

How do structural variations in the Korean and Taiwanese capital markets imply about the changing pattern of the overall financial system in the two economies? Have the structural transformations in financial structures run parallel to similar institutional changes in the other subspheres of the Korean and Taiwanese political economies? These are complicated issues, a detailed discussion of which cannot be accommodated here. This concluding section will provide a number of tentative observations on these issues in light of evidence presented in this and the other chapters of the volume and elsewhere.

As made clear in Chapter 1 of this volume, the financial system comprises three different yet interrelated institutional components—regulatory frameworks, market structures, and corporate governance patterns. Despite the increasing market orientation of the financial system in Taiwan and, to a lesser extent, in Korea, there are salient institutional differences that set the Korean and Taiwanese financial architectures apart from the liberal market economy (LME) model. In the first place, over the past decades and particularly since the Asian crisis of the late 1990s, the corporate sector of Korea and Taiwan has undergone significant institutional reforms (Liu, 2008; Zhang, 2010). However, the outsider model of corporate governance through the enforcement of shareholder rights and through the market for corporate control has not materialized in the two economies; controlling shareholders have tended to dominate the decision-making and power structure of Korean and Taiwanese firms (Gourevitch and Shinn, 2005; Liu, 2008; Walter, 2008). Furthermore, the LME model of financial market governance is based on securities regulation by independent agencies and accounting rules by private bodies. In both Korea and Taiwan, the key market regulatory agencies—the FSC and the Taiwanese Securities and Exchange Commission (SEC)—have operated under the direct influence of powerful state and societal actors who have attempted to harness capital market reforms to pursue their policy interests, as made clear in the foregoing analysis, despite the formal regulatory authority and independence of the FSC and the SEC.

If the overall financial market structure in Korea and Taiwan has not converged towards the LME model, institutional changes in the different subspheres of their political economies are far from complementary to each other. As posited in the VoC approach (Hall and Soskice, 2001), namely its theory of institutional complementarities, efforts to reform one sphere of the political economy may produce positive results if accompanied by parallel reforms in other spheres. Empirical evidence that supports this contention, particularly within the context of East Asia, seems mixed at best. In Korea, the less market-oriented changes in the capital market structure do not appear to have mirrored the more significant deregulation of the labour market and increasingly fluid industrial relations (Chapter 6; Yang, 2006) and the greater retreat of business–government ties from its dirigiste heritages (Chapter 4; Kalinowski, 2009). In Taiwan, the greater marketization of the financial structure has not been accompanied by similar changes in labour relations, business systems, and industrial policy regimes in which the role of non-market mechanisms seems to remain stronger and more persistent than in Korea (Chapter 4; Kong, 2006).

It is clear from the above that while both Korea and Taiwan have pursued neo-liberal reforms across the political economy, the process of institutional changes in various subspheres has been far from coherent and even. One possible reason for this is that the different subspheres of the political economy have been subject to differential systemic pressures and thus experienced varied changes. The uneven institutional reforms may also have reflected the different configurations of political structures, interests, and coalitions operating in different domains of the national political economy. Whatever the reasons, this may raise some questions about the impact of incoherent institutional changes on economic performance in Korea and Taiwan. Recent research (Campbell and Pedersen, 2007) conducted in the context of OECD countries suggests that a lack of complementarities or hybrid institutional arrangements may also yield economic successes. Further research needs to be done on why institutional changes across subspheres of the political economy have varied and how institutional heterogeneity shapes socioeconomic development in Korea, Taiwan, and beyond.

Part Five
Conclusion

12

Understanding Variations and Changes in East Asian Capitalism

Andrew Walter and Xiaoke Zhang

Chapter 1 of this volume set out three interrelated analytical objectives. First, it provided a typology of East Asian capitalism that identified key institutional domains for cross-national comparison and established guiding principles for categorizing political economies across the region. Second, it advanced an analytical framework for identifying observable institutional changes and illuminating the pathways of these changes both within and across the key institutional domains. Third, it developed theoretical propositions concerning the causes of institutional change and variation, focusing on the role of political coalitions, policy discourses, and state action and capacity.

The empirical chapters have shown how, since the 1980s, all of the major East Asian political economies have undergone important changes. The national institutions of capitalist development that were established in the post-war period have been reformed, transmuted, and in some cases dissolved. Institutional changes have been manifest across the key domains of socio-economic systems—business organizations, financial market structures, and labour relations. These changes have reflected national responses and readjustments to growing external market pressures unleashed by globalization. The increasingly frequent and severe financial crises and economic instability of the 1990s and 2000s intensified these pressures for policy, regulatory, and institutional reform. Systemic pressures aside, the reconfiguration of socio-economic class structures and legal–political institutions associated with sustained high growth and democratization processes has also heralded a remaking of East Asian capitalism (MacIntyre et al., 2008).

Nevertheless, the empirical chapters have also demonstrated that internal and external pressures have not dictated convergent transformative paths. In some cases, new organizational diversities within the region have emerged.

But the national systems of capitalism in the region remain both distinctively East Asian and retain important continuities with the past.

This concluding chapter is organized as follows. First, it summarizes the main patterns and trajectories of institutional change in national business organization, financial systems, and labour markets across the eight country cases over the past two decades. In doing so, it draws upon the empirical contributions in this volume as well as those in other prominent empirical studies on East Asia. Second, it investigates the causes of these institutional changes and persistent variations in East Asian capitalisms, deploying the analytical framework outlined in Chapter 1. Third, it addresses the implications of our findings for future research on the dynamics of capitalist development in East Asia and beyond.

Institutional Change: Patterns and Varieties

Our discussion of institutional changes focuses on the three analytical dimensions—business organizations, financial structures, and labour markets—identified at the outset as the core components of East Asian capitalisms and that have informed the preceding empirical chapters. We make three main arguments. First, new institutional diversities have emerged across these three dimensions of national political economies. Second, institutional reforms in these key institutional domains have demonstrated little complementarity with one another. Third, although the reforms taken as a whole constitute significant change, they have not yet been transformative. That is, they do not represent a shift to new modes of economic organization or a fundamental deviation from the key defining features of each of the four varieties of East Asian capitalism identified in Chapter 1.

Institutional Changes amidst Continuity

Consider first institutional changes in national business systems across the eight East Asian economies under review over the past two decades. As discussed in Chapter 1, business systems pertain to the ways in which intra-and inter-firm relations are coordinated. Following prominent studies on comparative business systems (Safarian and Dobson, 1996; Whitley, 1999; Redding, 2005), we have emphasized two key intra-firm relations—ownership structures and work management—and inter-firm alliances as the focal points for empirical analysis. Significant changes to the coordination of production and exchange would imply the alteration of the distribution of power between controlling shareholders, minority shareholders and managers, the forms of manager–employee interactions, and networks between firms from different industries.

In describing and analysing both spatial and temporal changes in the ownership structure of East Asian companies, we rely upon two sets of survey data compiled respectively by Claessens et al. (1999) and Nowland (2008). While different in the size of sample companies and the category of companies included in the surveys, both focused on public-traded companies and were designed to measure ownership concentration. For much of the post-war period, concentrated ownership by families and, in some cases, by states was a core organizational feature of East Asian companies. But there were significant cross-country variations in this pattern. More specifically, in Japan, corporate shares were generally widely held by various individuals and organizations. By contrast, the ownership of companies was heavily controlled by founding families in Indonesia, Malaysia, the Philippines, Taiwan, and Thailand, as illustrated in Table 12.1. Equally importantly, state ownership and control were significant in Indonesia, Korea, Malaysia, Singapore, and Thailand. Prior to the early 1990s, the ownership of Chinese industrial firms, particularly large and medium-sized ones, was predominantly concentrated in the hands of central and local government agencies.

Table 12.1. Corporate ownership structures in East Asia

	Widely held[a]	Family	State	Widely held companies[b]
Control of public-traded companies, percentages, 1996				
Hong Kong	7.0	71.5	4.8	10.8
Indonesia	6.6	67.3	15.2	8.4
Japan	85.5	4.1	7.3	1.6
Korea	51.1	24.6	19.9	4.3
Malaysia	16.2	42.6	34.8	5.3
The Philippines	28.5	46.4	3.2	13.7
Singapore	7.6	44.8	40.1	4.8
Taiwan	28.0	45.5	3.3	17.8
Thailand	8.2	51.9	24.1	9.5
	Family	Governments	Companies	Others[c]
Largest owners of listed companies, percentages, 2004				
Hong Kong	72.0	26	0	2
Indonesia	12	44	44	0
Korea	10	10	70	10
Malaysia	41	25	21	13
Singapore	29	38	24	9
Taiwan	65	6	14	15
Thailand	45	19	36	0

Sources: Claessens et al., 1999: table 4 and Nowland, 2008: table 2.

Notes: [a]Widely held companies are those in which no owner has significant control rights. [b]These are widely held companies and financial institutions (such as banks and insurance firms). [c]These owners include individuals, co-founders, and other organizations.

The concentration of corporate wealth was widely believed to have generated structural weaknesses and governance problems in the corporate sector of many East Asian economies and to have contributed to the regional financial crisis of the late 1990s. East Asian banks also exhibited concentrated ownership and were also controlled by families or by the state, but for a variety of reasons engaged in ineffective monitoring of their non-financial clients (Caprio et al., 2004; Walter, 2008). Following the crisis, many East Asian governments appeared bent on reducing ownership concentration through extensive legal and regulatory reforms. The results have been largely ineffective, however. As clearly shown in Table 12.1, corporate ownership has remained concentrated in and controlled by families across the region, particularly in Malaysia, Singapore, Taiwan, and Thailand. While founding families' control of company shares has declined in Indonesia and Korea, the stake owned by affiliated firms has significantly increased (Cho, 2003; Chang, 2006; Hanani, 2006). Increased cross-shareholdings have maintained the dominance of owner–managers and strengthened concentrated ownership structures.

In China, the control of large industrial firms and major banks has remained centralized in the hands of the state; various government agencies have controlled the majority of listed companies and typically owned more than 50 per cent of outstanding shares (Xu and Wang, 1999; Chen et al., 2009). The ownership structure of non-state or private firms has mirrored that of their state-owned counterparts and remained highly concentrated.

The main exception to this generalization is that in the major crisis-hit countries in which family-owned banks failed and were intervened by the state, there was a trend away from family control towards more dispersed ownership (after their re-privatization) (Walter, 2008). Nevertheless, state influence over the banking sector in many East Asian economies remains extensive, and more widely held banks have coexisted with family-controlled non-financial firms.

In terms of the second key aspect of business systems—work management, more specifically manager–employee interactions—crucial changes have run parallel to important institutional continuities. As noted in Chapter 1, significant variations characterized the post-war national patterns of manager–employee relations. Japanese companies traditionally exhibited very high levels of employer–employee interdependence that involved extensive consultations across departments and hierarchical levels and active participation on the part of workers (Whitley, 1992). While the erosion of long-term employment has weakened collective decision-making (Sako and Kotosaka, this volume), the consensus-driven approach has endured in many Japanese firms. By contrast, the extent of employee influence over work-organization decisions was more limited in Korean and Taiwanese firms than in their

Japanese counterparts, primarily reflecting the relatively short job tenures of Korean and Taiwanese employees. In recent years, increasingly non-regular and short-term employment contracts have further reduced incentives for both managers and employees to develop more interactive relationships in Korean and Taiwanese firms (Chen et al., 2003; Ee-Hwan Jung and Byung-you Cheon, 2006; Rowley et al., 2011).

In Southeast Asia, a top-down, non-participatory management structure was traditionally one of the key defining features of business organizations; relations between labour and management were either highly conflictual (as in Thai and Filipino firms) or largely arms-length (as in Malaysian and Indonesian firms). While this form of manager–employee relations was manifest across all Southeast Asian companies, it was particularly prevalent among ethnic Chinese business that dominated the corporate scene of the region (Redding, 1990; Lim 1996). The past decades have witnessed a gradual shift away from this highly personal and direct control over work processes and a move towards greater employer–employee interdependence, particularly among internationally oriented companies (Yeung, 2006) and in some large service sector firms (Abdul-Rahman and Rowley, 2008; Siengthai et al., 2008). However, more systematic studies (Ahlstrom et al., 2004) have shown that this change may have been the exception rather than the rule; the paternalistic and exclusive management structure typical of overseas Chinese enterprises in Southeast Asia has remained largely intact.

In China, the pattern of work management has changed little over the past two decades. From state-owned enterprises (SOEs) and collectives to private firms, the lack of close interaction between managers and workers has been a key organizational feature. Directors or owners have exercised strict control over decisions and information flow and often had complete discretion to command resources within the organization. There has been little delegation of authority to and little consultation with employees, as virtually all major decisions are often made by top management; not only ordinary workers but sometimes managers in the middle and upper-middle ranks have been excluded from involvement in basic corporate decision-making. Middle managers have generally acted as conduits of downward communication and as enforcers of disciplinary control over the workforce (Redding and Witt, 2007). This non-participatory management approach has been particularly dominant in non-state enterprises (Farh et al., 2006).

With regard to the third dimension of business systems examined in this volume, inter-firm alliances, institutional developments have been crucial and have varied considerably across different East Asian countries. But they have not been fundamentally discontinuous. In Japan, inter-firm partnerships appear to have undergone the most salient changes. Relationship banking has weakened, cross-shareholdings have begun to unwind in some firms, and purchase–supply networks have worn thin (Arikawa and Miyajima, 2007; Miyajima and Kuroki, 2007). Nevertheless, there is little evidence to suggest that the dense business networks underpinned by keiretsu have collapsed. The enduring long-term and reciprocal business relationships that have tied firms into business groups remain distinctive and resilient feature of Japanese manufacturing (Ahmadjian, 2006; McGuire and Dow, 2009).

In the other East Asian economies covered in this volume, the national patterns of inter-firm networks have remained largely unchanged. In Korea, the chaebols, being large and self-sufficient conglomerates, have been reluctant to network with firms outside the same chaebol families or from different industrial sectors. To the extent that they have recently strengthened their ties with smaller firms, these ties have tended to be exploitative and adversarial rather than reciprocal and cooperative (Park, 2007: 136–66). While inter-firm partnerships in Taiwan have often involved reciprocal commitments, these partnerships have been dependent upon personal contacts and trust; more often than not, inter-firm and intra-industry relations have been devoid of long-term, mutual obligations typical of business alliances in Japan (Kienzle and Shadur, 1997; Carney, 2005). The same can be said of the pattern of inter-firm networks among Southeast Asian firms in general and among ethnic Chinese businesses in particular (Hitt et al., 2002; Carney, 2005). In China, the reform era has witnessed the emergence of inter-firm and inter-sector networks, but such networks have been small in scale, low in density, and limited in institutional trust and have been primarily organized around interpersonal obligations and connections. These features are truer of SOEs than of private firms (Redding and Witt, 2007; Ren et al., 2009).

The institutional developments in the national configuration of business systems summarized above have evolved in parallel with their political underpinnings—state–business relations. One of the important changes that have reshaped the East Asian political economy has involved the erosion of close and stable ties between policymakers and firms. Two parallel and mutually reinforcing forces are crucial here. On the one hand, the sustained process of deregulation and privatization has deprived state actors of their traditional dirigiste means to control the allocation of resources and to influence the business decisions of firms. The consolidation of democracy in many East Asian countries, the decentralization of executive power, and the strengthening of competing sociopolitical groups have diminished the scope for symbiotic relationships between political and corporate interests (MacIntyre et al., 2008). On the other hand, sustained high growth and the global integration of national markets have broadened the scope of private firms' business and rendered their operations increasingly global. By dint of their growing economic power and organizational capabilities, private firms have now become less reliant on political–business alliances as their preferred business development strategies (Yeung, 2000, 2006).

This does not mean that East Asian political economies have been converging upon a common form of business–state interactions. The enduring desire of state actors to shape market outcomes can be seen in Chinese government protection and promotion of national champions in key industrial sectors as well as in the maintenance of control over finance (Breslin, this volume); in the endeavours of Japanese, Korean, and Taiwanese policymakers to nurture hi-tech firms and sectors (Weiss, 2004; Steinmo, 2010; Fields, this volume); and in the continuing propensity of Malaysian political leaders to shape corporate development (Gomez, this volume). But East Asian governments continue to differ dramatically in their abilities to orchestrate development patterns and in the means they deploy (Levy et al., 2006; Tipton, 2009). Differences in business–government relations and in the mode of state intervention have continued to define the institutional varieties of East Asian capitalism, as argued below.

More significant changes appear to have taken place in the second institutional domain that has informed the empirical analysis of East Asian capitalism in this volume—national financial systems. This has been truer of financial market structures than of corporate governance patterns. Carney, Pepinsky, and Zhang (this volume) show that bank-based financial systems predominated across the region for much of the post-war period. Banks functioned as the central institutions not only for allocating investment capital but also as a policy tool for managing development policies. Capital markets remained small in size; the main function of equity market trading was to determine market values for listed companies.

These macro features in the financial system translated into micro patterns in the corporate finance and governance of East Asian firms. The underdevelopment of capital markets in the region both derived from and enhanced the dominant position of banks as the most important external source of industrial financing. The bank-based mode of financial market governance also meant that a market for corporate control was virtually non-existent. The disciplinary function of takeovers played little role in East Asian capital markets and the insider pattern of corporate governance prevailed.[1]

However, the past two decades have witnessed significant changes in the national financial systems of East Asia. There has been a sustained shift towards a more market-oriented system in which capital markets in general and stock markets in particular have begun to play a linchpin role in financial

---

[1] Detailed reviews of the causal linkage between the bank-centred financial system and the insider pattern of corporate governance in East Asia can be found in Zhuang et al. (2000) and Claessens and Fan (2002).

Table 12.2. Financial market changes (percentages, yearly averages)

	1986–90	1991–5	1996–2000	2001–5	2006–9
Deposit money bank assets/GDP					
China	n.a.	n.a.	n.a.	n.a.	n.a.
Indonesia	30.26	48.81	51.45	39.18	30.88
Japan	217.9	238.6	236.3	163.0	152.1
Korea	48.50	49.99	63.69	90.67	111.1
Malaysia	128.1	101.2	144.6	123.7	104.9
The Philippines	21.91	31.15	55.26	48.14	34.33
Taiwan	88.02	143.5	163.9	160.3	158.9
Thailand	75.95	110.1	152.6	110.3	91.11
The United States	65.77	55.89	55.35	58.90	67.73
Stock market capitalization/GDP					
China	n.a.	5.632	22.43	35.55	96.24
Indonesia	1.213	15.54	29.66	19.96	50.15
Japan	132.2	73.14	72.21	70.21	103.9
Korea	31.86	34.84	37.04	52.18	111.8
Malaysia	69.79	198.7	179.8	137.5	170.4
The Philippines	12.21	49.92	60.11	41.17	70.28
Taiwan	67.06	69.91	95.54	110.6	193.8
Thailand	15.64	64.14	41.73	52.75	71.45
The United States	57.80	71.22	137.8	130.1	145.9
Private bond market capitalization/GDP					
China	3.362	2.962	4.950	8.744	15.65
Indonesia	n.a.	0.772	1.778	1.798	1.968
Japan	40.54	40.59	48.09	45.42	38.32
Korea	28.32	34.39	45.99	58.88	61.57
Malaysia	14.57	21.35	45.97	52.09	56.06
The Philippines	n.a.	0.135	0.232	0.524	1.078
Taiwan	13.63	14.71	24.75	25.99	24.45
Thailand	6.558	6.448	9.652	12.94	16.56
The United States	69.67	75.66	92.64	110.5	127.5
Stock and bond market capitalization/GDP to deposit money bank assets/GDP, per cent					
China	n.a.	n.a.	n.a.	n.a.	n.a.
Indonesia	n.a.	33.42	61.10	55.53	168.78
Japan	79.27	47.67	50.91	70.94	93.50
Korea	124.08	138.49	130.37	122.49	156.49
Malaysia	65.85	217.44	156.34	153.65	215.88
The Philippines	n.a.	160.69	109.20	86.61	207.86
Taiwan	91.67	58.97	73.39	85.21	137.35
Thailand	29.23	64.11	33.67	59.56	96.59
The United States	193.81	262.02	416.33	408.49	403.66

Sources: Authors' calculations based on data provided in Beck and Al-Hussainy (2010) and the Central Bank of China (*Financial Statistical Monthly*, various issues).

transactions. Table 12.2 shows that there have been general and sustained increases in the ratio of stock market capitalization to GDP and in the ratio of stock and bond market capitalization to deposit money bank assets (Table 12.2). While the role of banks has not been substantially eroded, securities markets of various kinds have increasingly complemented traditional bank finance. Market-oriented changes were well underway in many East Asian economies prior to the Asian financial crisis (AFC) of the late 1990s but have been consolidated and accelerated by post-crisis reforms that have further institutionalized market-oriented practices.

Nevertheless, the national financial systems of most East Asian economies still bear little structural resemblance to the financial architecture of the United States, a prototype of market-centred financial capitalism. Furthermore, despite the similar trajectory of financial market changes in the region, the eight economies we review have displayed striking differences in the size of capital markets, the market orientation of national finance, and the overall level of financial sector development. The capital markets in Malaysia and Taiwan stand out as the most developed. The financial systems in China, Indonesia, the Philippines, and, to a lesser extent, Thailand are less market oriented and developed. Indonesia and the Philippines only have a seemingly high ratio of stock and bond market capitalization to bank assets because they have poorly developed banking sectors. Japan and Korea continue to occupy intermediate positions.

There have been corresponding changes, at least with regard to the formal rules, in the overall patterns of corporate governance across many East Asian economies. The restructuring of the corporate sector was the linchpin of far-reaching economic reforms implemented in the wake of the AFC. The decade-long process of reforms has begun to alter the East Asian corporate landscape in terms of governance mechanisms. Legal changes have been introduced to lower the minimum requirements for minority shareholders to exercise their rights, for instance; the ability of institutional investors to monitor the management of invested firms has strengthened both through regulatory changes and through the growth of public and private equity funds; and important

Table 12.3. Rules on board independence, 2010

	Number of independent directors	Separation of chairmen from CEOs	Composition of auditing committees
China	One-third	Yes	Majority independent
Indonesia	30%[a]	Mandatory	Independent of directors
Japan	One independent director or statutory auditor[b]	No specific rule	No specific rule
Korea	25%	No specific rule	Majority independent
Malaysia	One-third	Yes	Majority independent
The Philippines	20%	Yes	No specific rule
Singapore	One-third	Yes	Majority independent
Taiwan	20%	Yes	No specific rule
Thailand	One-third	Yes	Majority independent

Source: ACGA (2010).

Notes: [a]In Indonesia, board data refer to the board of commissioners that supervises the board of directors. [b]Statutory auditors who are responsible for auditing a company's compliance with laws and regulations are permitted to attend board meetings but do not have a vote.

legal revisions have reduced powerful obstacles to hostile takeovers in many East Asian economies. One of the most potentially crucial regulatory reforms has been the mandatory introduction of independent directors. As shown in Table 12.3, all the eight East Asian economies had required by the late 2000s that at least 20 per cent of board members of listed companies be outsiders. This has begun to change the role of boards of directors as rubber stamps in corporate decision processes and generate constraining effects on controlling shareholders and managers (CLSA, various issues).

These legal and regulatory changes, while drastic and even unprecedented, are unlikely to eliminate the practices and structures of insider-oriented governance patterns characteristic of many East Asian firms. In the first place, some of the regulatory and institutional changes in national governance mechanisms have been cosmetic and superficial. Important empirical studies (Ho, 2005; Walter, 2008; Bhaskaran, 2009) have strongly suggested that changes in the formal rules and regulations have often not translated into changes in actual governance practices due to weak enforcement. Furthermore, the reform of corporate governance appears to have lost momentum in the mid- and late 2000s, as new and substantive reforms measures have become increasingly sporadic and

Table 12.4. Corporate governance patterns

	2001	2002	2003	2004	2005[b]	2007	2010
Rules and regulations[a]							
China	4.0	4.5	5.0	5.3	4.3	4.3	4.7
Indonesia	4.0	4.0	4.5	5.3	3.3	3.9	3.9
Japan	n.a.	n.a.	n.a.	n.a.	n.a.	4.3	4.5
Korea	5.0	6.0	7.0	6.1	5.1	4.5	4.3
Malaysia	8.0	9.0	9.0	7.1	5.9	4.4	4.9
The Philippines	5.0	6.0	6.5	5.8	5.3	3.9	3.5
Singapore	9.0	8.0	8.5	7.9	7.4	7.0	6.5
Taiwan	7.0	7.0	7.0	6.3	5.3	4.9	5.0
Thailand	7.0	7.5	7.5	6.1	5.8	5.8	5.6
Enforcement of rules and regulations							
China	2.0	3.0	4.0	4.2	4.0	3.3	3.6
Indonesia	2.0	1.0	1.5	2.7	2.9	2.2	2.8
Japan	n.a.	n.a.	n.a.	n.a.	n.a.	4.6	5.3
Korea	3.0	3.0	3.5	5.0	4.0	3.9	2.8
Malaysia	2.0	2.5	3.5	5.0	4.9	3.5	3.8
The Philippines	2.0	2.0	2.0	3.1	2.2	1.9	1.5
Singapore	7.0	7.0	7.5	6.5	5.6	5.0	6.0
Taiwan	4.0	5.0	5.0	4.6	4.9	4.7	4.7
Thailand	2.0	2.0	3.0	3.8	4.0	3.6	4.2

Source: CLSA Asia-Pacific Markets (*CG Watch*, various issues).

Notes: [a]The rules cover financial reporting standards, government efforts to improve securities laws, information disclosure, compliance with international best practices, independent board committees, and minority shareholder protection. The score ranges from 1 to 10, with 10 indicating the best. [b]The score trended downwards across all the countries from 2005, as a result of CLSA adopting a more rigorous ranking methodology.

Table 12.5. Trade union density, percentages

	1985	1990	1995	2000	2005
China	68.99	n.a.	69.76	61.56[a]	n.a.
Indonesia	n.a.	n.a.	n.a.	n.a.	6.50
Japan	28.75	25.37	23.97	22.18[b]	18.70
Korea	12.77	17.31	12.68	11.82	10.60[c]
Malaysia	n.a.	9.35	n.a.	n.a.	7.97
The Philippines	20.67	24.75	24.95	n.a.	n.a.
Singapore	20.60	16.88	15.58	17.99	n.a.
Taiwan	32.54	49.25	50.09	44.19[d]	36.95
Thailand	n.a.	n.a.	n.a.	2.58[e]	n.a.

Sources: Kuruvilla et al. (2002); Benson (2008); Isaac and Sitalaksmi (2008); Ramasamy and Rowley (2008); Rowley and Yoo (2008); Yukongdi (2008); and Zhu (2008).

Notes: [a]The figure is for 1999. [b]The figure is for 1999. [c]The figure is for 2004. [d]The figure is for 1999. [e]The figure is for 2001 and refers to union density in the private sector.

enforcement has further slackened (Table 12.4; Estrin and Prevezer, 2011; Jiang and Peng, 2011; Nakamura, 2011).

Perhaps the most fundamental changes bearing upon the East Asian political economy since the 1980s have involved labour market institutions. Regulatory and institutional changes have been so sustained and significant that they have reconfigured union organizational structures, employment relations, and, to a lesser extent, welfare provision systems—the three core analytical dimensions of labour market regimes highlighted in Chapter 1. While these changes may not have been strong and disruptive enough to lead to a complete rupture with the post-war labour market systems of East Asia, they have seriously eroded their basic institutional underpinnings.

In the first place, the organizational strength of trade unions in most of the eight East Asian countries covered in this volume has been declining over the past decades. This is primarily reflected in the across-the-board decrease in union density, as shown in Table 12.5. The weakening of union organization and influence has also been manifest in the dented ability of trade unions to represent their potential membership, as the coverage of collective bargaining agreements has been low and sagging in many East Asian economies. Cross-country comparative studies (Kuruvilla et al., 2002; Chor and Freeman, 2005) have provided ample evidence that the proportion of workforces covered by collective bargaining agreements in East Asia has not only decreased but also remained lower than that in most industrial countries. Union organization has become weaker against a broader backdrop of the sustained efforts of East Asian governments to encourage labour market flexibility and to allow market forces to determine employment conditions (Zhu and Benson, 2008; Deyo, Lee, and Sako and Kotosaka, this volume). Table 12.6 provides one indication that the national framework governing labour markets relations has often become increasingly market oriented. Shorter job tenures, the growth of

Table 12.6. The market orientation of labour market regulations

	1990	1995	2000	2005	2007	2008
China	3.16	4.54	4.66	4.98	4.90	4.82
Indonesia	n.a.	4.22	4.97	4.93	5.29	5.11
Japan	7.20	7.46	6.48	8.47	8.41	8.19
Korea	3.59	4.43	4.20	4.48	4.28	4.02
Malaysia	n.a.	n.a.	6.60	7.76	7.60	7.75
The Philippines	n.a.	6.82	6.06	5.95	5.86	5.93
Taiwan	4.73	5.22	4.51	4.43	4.30	4.36
Thailand	4.98	5.39	6.30	7.09	7.27	7.28

Source: Data are sourced from *The Economic Freedom of the World: 2010 Annual Report* compiled by Gwartney et al. (2010). Labour market regulations cover minimum wages, hiring and firing conditions, collective bargaining, worker dismissal, and conscription. Higher marks indicate freer or more market-oriented regulatory frameworks.

Table 12.7. Collective bargaining

	Centralization of collective bargaining[a]		Union involvement in collective bargaining		The level of collective bargaining	
	1990	2008	Late 1980s	Late 2000s	Late 1980s	Late 2000s
China	5.18	7.10	Medium	Low	Medium	Low
Indonesia	n.a.	6.20	Low	Low	Low	Low
Japan	7.93	8.02	High-medium	Medium-low	High	Medium-low
Korea	7.24	7.43	High-medium	Medium-low	High-medium	Low
Malaysia	n.a.	7.10	Low	Low	Low	Low
The Philippines	7.24	6.06	Medium	Low	Low	Low
Taiwan	7.93	8.02	High-medium	Low	Medium-low	Low
Thailand	5.93	6.28	Low	Low	Low	Low

Sources: McGuire (1999); Kuruvilla and Erickson (2002); Benson (2008); Isaac and Sitalaksmi (2008); Ramasamy and Rowley (2008); Rowley and Yoo (2008); Yukongdi (2008); Warner (2008); Zhu (2008); and Gwartney et al. (2010).

Note: [a]This examines whether wages are set by centralized bargaining processes or determined by individual companies; high marks indicate that wages are set more by employers than by centralized bargaining.

non-regular workers, and the enhancement of managerial power have all contributed to the declining level of union organization.

With the weakening of union organization, the level of collective bargaining has also decreased across all the eight East Asian economies under consideration despite continuing variation in its level of importance. Three changes are important here, as shown in Table 12.7.[2] First, wages have been increasingly decided by individual employers through firm-level bargaining rather than being set by centralized bargaining processes. For example, in Japan,

[2] In this and following tables, cross-country variations in the key institutional domains of the East Asian political economy are described on a five-point scale of: low, medium, medium-low, high-medium, and high. These reflect not so much the objective measurement of institutional variations and changes as the authors' subjective judgement based on key empirical studies cited in the sources of the tables.

where wage bargaining had long been informally coordinated nationally in the post-war period, the demise of *shunto* in the 1990s largely ended this system (Sako and Kotosaka, this volume). Second, declining organizational strength entailed weaker union involvement in collective bargaining at both firm and industry levels. Third and relatedly, the role of collective bargaining in influencing wages and working conditions has become more limited.

Furthermore, there have been parallel changes in employment relations across East Asian economies over the past two decades. In Japan, while lifetime employment that has underpinned highly developed internal labour markets in large firms has not been abandoned, its content and structure have been steadily modified by the shrinking core of lifetime jobs, the rapid growth of casual jobs, the introduction of merit-based pay systems, the partial delinking of skill levels from seniority pay, and the growing importance of external labour market functions (Jackson, 2007; Benson, 2011). In Korea and Taiwan, with employers facing ever-growing pressures to increase flexibility, companies have moved increasingly towards keeping core staff and hiring temporary workers for non-core jobs. This has not only increased the proportion of non-regular workers but also deepened polarization in the labour market (Chen et al., 2003; Jung and Cheon, 2006; Rowley et al., 2011; Deyo, this volume). Furthermore, the traditional reward practice that reflected more seniority than employee performance has gradually given way to competence-based systems (Jung and Cheon, 2006; Zhu et al., 2007).

In Southeast Asia, as in Japan, Korea, and Taiwan, companies have been driven by competitive pressures to push for greater employment and wage flexibility and to circumvent employee protection regulations, further reducing the already low tenures of workers and worsening job insecurity (Caraway, 2004; Ramasamy and Rowley, 2011; Deyo, this volume). Associated with increased labour market flexibility and fluidity has been the gradual replacement of seniority pay by performance and merit systems and group-based evaluation and reward mechanisms by more individualistic approaches (Abdul-Rahman and Rowley, 2008; Habir and Rajendran, 2008; Ofreneo, 2008; Siengthai et al., 2008). These changes have aggravated the long-existing problem of labour market segmentation in which a small and decreasing proportion of skilled employees work in the formal manufacturing and service sectors while a large and increasing majority of semi-skilled or unskilled workers are employed in the secondary labour force of the formal sectors or take irregular employment in the informal sectors. The former have better wages and working conditions and the latter receive lower wages, face poor job insecurity, and have lower entitlements (Kuruvilla and Erickson, 2002; Zhu and Benson, 2011).

Do these changes in labour market systems mean that it no longer makes sense to speak of East Asian varieties of capitalism (VoC) and that national

Table 12.8. The conditions of hiring and firing[a]

	2000	2005	2007	2008	All years
China	5.10	5.27	5.04	4.63	5.01
Indonesia	3.20	4.49	6.20	5.54	4.86
Japan	4.18	4.62	3.49	3.28	3.89
Korea	4.70	4.71	5.18	3.55	4.54
Malaysia	4.00	5.05	5.45	5.28	4.95
The Philippines	3.30	4.28	3.75	3.53	3.72
Taiwan	4.60	5.92	5.97	6.37	5.72
Thailand	4.60	4.75	5.63	5.70	5.17
The United States	6.65	7.01	7.28	7.27	7.05

Source: Gwartney et al. (2010).

Note: [a]The score ranges from 1 to 10, with 1 indicating that the hiring and firing of workers is heavily impeded by regulations and 10 indicating that the conditions of hiring and firing are flexibly determined by employers. Higher scores refer to greater freedom to hire and fire workers on the part of employers in line with market changes and conditions.

employment relations diverge only marginally from the liberal market economy (LME) version? If one fixates on the labour market changes currently taking place in East Asia, an affirmative answer to this question may seem appropriate. However, East Asian labour markets have remained much less market oriented than those of the Anglo-American economies. Nowhere has this been more manifest than in the plethora of legal, regulatory, and administrative rules that has rendered the conditions of hiring and firing significantly more rigid in most of the eight East Asian economies than in the United States (Table 12.8). Equally important, despite harmonizing pressures for labour market flexibility, they have differed significantly in terms of the key political, institutional, and managerial dimensions of employment relations, as demonstrated in Table 12.9. These differences serve as a strong reminder that institutional continuities in labour market practices have persisted over time and that the varieties of East Asian employment relations show how the institutional structures of the national political economy condition them.

Finally, East Asian economies have been attempting to balance changes in labour markets and social policy regimes, increasing employment flexibility but matching this with efforts to strengthen welfare provision. Table 12.10 shows that government spending on social security and welfare has increased across all the eight East Asian economies under review. Such spending appears to have increased more significantly in developing East Asian economies, albeit from a much lower level, than in developed ones like Japan, Korea, and Taiwan. While social welfare spending, even in more developed East Asian economies, is a long way from reaching the levels seen in European social democracies (as represented by Denmark and Sweden in Table 12.10), social welfare provision has strengthened in terms of both coverage and quality in many East Asian economies, particularly following the AFC of the late 1990s.

Table 12.9. Variations in employment relations, late 2000s

	Union influence	Union participation in board decisions	Role of worker councils at firm level	Individual pay and incentives	Merit-based evaluation	In-firm training
China	Medium	Medium	Medium	Medium-low	Medium	Medium
Indonesia	Low	Low	Low	Medium	Medium	Low
Japan	High	High-medium	High	Medium	Medium-low	High
Korea	High-medium	Medium	Medium	Medium	Medium	High-medium
Malaysia	Low	Low	Low	Medium	Medium	Medium
The Philippines	Low	Low	Low	Medium	Medium	Low
Taiwan	Medium	Medium	Medium	High	High	High-medium
Thailand	Low	Low	Low	Medium	Medium	Low

Sources: Zhu et al. (2007); Habir and Rajendran (2008); Ofreneo (2008); Siengthai et al. (2008); Zhu and Benson (2008); Benson (2011); and Rowley et al. (2011).

Table 12.10. Social welfare spending (as per cent of total central government expenditure, yearly averages)

	1985–90	1991–5	1996–2000	2001–5	2006–8
China					
Health	n.a.	n.a.	n.a.	n.a.	n.a.
Housing	3.63	n.a.	n.a.	n.a.	n.a.
Social security and welfare	1.62	1.75	3.37	7.45	9.74
Indonesia					
Health	3.22	2.75	2.30	1.41	n.a.
Housing	14.45	8.79	16.02	1.21	n.a.
Social security and welfare	n.a.	5.74	6.04	6.54	n.a.
Japan					
Health	20.25	20.78	20.57	22.15	22.30
Housing	1.38	1.43	1.34	1.21	1.03
Social security and welfare	33.52	35.22	36.93	37.73	38.24
Malaysia					
Health	4.61	5.55	6.28	7.07	6.58
Housing	1.00	0.66	1.52	1.69	1.55
Social security and welfare	2.18	3.56	3.77	4.46	3.87
The Philippines					
Health	3.06	2.68	2.57	1.68	1.51
Housing	0.57	0.46	0.82	0.24	0.66
Social security and welfare	0.65	1.36	3.79	4.93	4.91
South Korea					
Health	1.84	n.a.	0.83	0.59	1.00
Housing	6.96	0.89	6.98	5.31	6.66
Social security and welfare	7.10	9.01	11.54	15.53	19.50
Taiwan					
Health	2.36	0.63	0.53	1.19	1.45
Housing	0.85	2.19	1.67	3.07	2.34
Social security and welfare	15.43	20.69	25.18	22.87	24.82
Thailand					
Health	6.94	7.34	7.04	7.85	8.62
Housing	2.24	3.47	4.75	2.92	1.63
Social security and welfare	3.65	3.57	3.78	9.36	7.56
Denmark					
Health	1.17	1.05	0.65	0.87	n.a.
Housing	1.14	1.87	1.69	1.59	n.a.
Social security and welfare	38.24	41.33	41.44	40.39	n.a.
Sweden					
Health	1.09	0.51	1.39	4.54	n.a.
Housing	3.21	4.74	2.41	0.63	n.a.
Social security and welfare	47.67	49.59	45.96	47.43	n.a.

Source: Authors' calculations based on data provided in ADB (*Key Indicators of Developing Asian and Pacific Countries*, various issues; *Key Indicators for Asia and the Pacific*, various issues), IMF (*Government Finance Statistics*, various issues).

To what extent has this development changed the core institutions of East Asian social policy regimes? More specifically, have we witnessed any salient alterations in the post-war social welfare system in which social policy was subordinated to development imperatives, the state acted more as a regulator of social welfare than as a provider, and selectivity rather than social inclusion characterized welfare provision?

This is a highly complicated issue, a detailed and effective discussion of which cannot be accommodated here. Focusing on labour welfare practices and drawing upon recent empirical studies, we make three key observations. First, the broadened coverage and increased quality of welfare provision have indicated that while East Asian governments may continue to see social policy in instrumentalist terms, some of them have begun to appreciate and even embrace the intrinsic value of social protection (Wilding, 2008; Kwon, 2009). Second, some East Asian economies appear to have deviated from the conservative welfare system in which the state contribution to the broad welfare mix is marginal. While the role of families in welfare provision has remained crucial, the state has increasingly become a provider as much as a regulator. This has been particularly the case in Japan, Korea, and Taiwan (Kwon, 2005a; Haggard and Kaufman, 2008; Choi, 2009). Third, some East Asian economies have shifted away from the selective mode of welfare provision that prioritized workers in SOEs and large firms towards a more universal and socially inclusive approach (Croissant, 2004; Gough, 2004; Kwon, 2009). Whether these changes have represented a rupture with the productivist welfare regime is a moot point.[3] But it is safe to argue that social policy in East Asia has undergone subtle yet crucial changes over the past decades, particularly since the AFC. Welfare regimes in the region have varied more systematically across countries, as summarized in Table 12.11, than allowed for by the productivist welfare model (Holliday, 2000; Holliday and Wilding, 2003).

Enduring Varieties of East Asian Capitalism

It is clear from the foregoing analysis that a steady but uneven process of institutional change in business organization, financial market structures, and especially labour relations systems has altered East Asian capitalisms. These changes have led some analysts to conclude that the cohesion and distinctiveness of East Asian capitalisms have been undermined so significantly that they all have hybridized business, financial, and labour market systems (Yeung, 2000; Zhu et al., 2007; Wilding, 2008). In our view, this claim conceals as much as reveals the changing dynamics of capitalist institutions in the

---

[3] For recent debates on this issue, see Holliday (2005); Kwon (2005b, 2009); and Wilding (2008).

Table 12.11. Variations in welfare provision regimes, mid-2000s

	Subordination of social policy to development imperatives	Role of the state in welfare provision	Social inclusiveness of welfare provision
China	High	Medium-low	Low
Indonesia	High-medium	Low	Low
Japan	Medium	High-medium	Medium
Korea	Medium	High-medium	Medium
Malaysia	High	Low	Low
The Philippines	High-medium	Low	Low
Taiwan	Medium	High-medium	Medium
Thailand	Medium	Medium-low	Medium-low

Sources: Hort and Kuhnle (2000); Croissant (2004); Gough (2004); Haggard and Kaufman (2008); and Kwon (2009).

Table 12.12. State organization of the economy

	State enterprises and investment[a]		State regulation of credit, labour, and business[b]		State control of trade unions and business associations	
	1980s	Late 2000s	1980s	Late 2000s	1980s	Late 2000s
China	0.00	0.00	3.12	5.56	High	High
Indonesia	2.67	7.00	4.53	6.04	High-medium	Low
Japan	7.67	9.33	6.43	7.91	Low	Low
Korea	7.00	8.00	5.36	6.60	High-medium	Medium-low
Malaysia	3.33	2.00	6.44	7.62	High-medium	High-medium
The Philippines	7.00	8.00	5.87	6.67	Medium-low	Low
Taiwan	2.00	6.67	4.99	6.57	High-medium	Medium-low
Thailand	5.33	6.67	5.66	7.38	Medium-low	Low

Sources: MacIntyre, 1994; Gomez, 2002; Gwartney et al., 2010; Benson and Zhu, 2008, 2011; MacIntyre et al., 2008. *Notes*: [a]The score ranges from 0 to 10; the higher the score, the less extensive state participation in the economy. For instance, a score of 10 is given to countries where there are few SOEs and government investment is generally less than 15 per cent of total investment; a score of 0 is assigned when the economy is dominated by SOEs and government investment normally exceeds 50 per cent of total investment. For details, see Gwartney et al. (2010: 219). [b]The higher scores mean weaker government regulations of financial, labour, and product markets. See Gwartney et al. (2010: 226–9) for a more detailed discussion of the scoring methods and data sources.

region. Our starting point is the framework we provided in Chapter 1, which focuses on two key dimensions: the vertical dimension of state organization and the horizontal dimension of social coordination of economic activity (Table 1.3), producing four main East Asian VoC (Table 1.4).

Table 12.12 summarizes the temporal and spatial evolution of state organization of the economy for our eight countries along three key dimensions: state participation in the economy as the owner of and investor in industries; state regulation of product, financial, and labour markets through legal, administrative, and other means; and state control of social organizations, specifically trade unions and business associations. It shows that although the state organization of the economy has weakened across the region, important continuities have characterized the core dimensions of this governance mechanism. Indonesia seems to be the only exception, where state intervention has declined dramatically across the three indicators.

In terms of the social coordination of economic action, we summarize outcomes in terms of three key measures: the extent to which social actors and groups (mainly labour and business) make long-term commitments to each other through institutionalized and credible mechanisms; the strength of social networking across firms and trade unions; and the ability of labour and business to facilitate collaboration through autonomous, semi-autonomous, or state-sponsored social associations. Table 12.13 shows that the temporal changes have not been as discontinuous as to lead to alterations in the basic contours of social coordination and to render the cross-country variations in these governance mechanisms any less significant.

Table 12.14 reproduces the four different ways in which the state organization and social coordination of economic action have interacted with each other, incorporating the changes as well as the continuities outlined above. In Korea and Taiwan, the basic mode of organizing economic activity has remained co-governed (Cell I). While state participation in the economy has declined and government regulations of market activities have weakened, the ability of state actors to shape development strategies and trajectories has been stronger than most of their East Asian counterparts (Wong, 2004a; Thurbon and Weiss, 2006; Fields, this volume). By the same token, while labour organization at the national level has become weaker, the unity of peak trade unions has remained higher and their ability to coordinate collective action stronger in Korea and Taiwan than in Southeast Asia (Rowley and Yoo, 2008; Zhu, 2008). Equally importantly, the role of industrial associations, particularly those representing the interests of large firms, in maintaining business

Table 12.13. Social coordination of economic activity

	Long-term commitments to each other		Strength of social networking		Ability to facilitate collaboration	
	Late 1980s	Late 2000s	Late 1980s	Late 2000s	Late 1980s	Late 2000s
China	Low	Low	Low	Low	Low	Low
Indonesia	Low	Low	Low	Low	Low	Medium-low
Japan	High	High-medium	High	High-medium	High	High
Korea	High-medium	Medium-low	Medium-low	Medium-low	Medium-low	Medium-low
Malaysia	Low	Low	Medium-low	Low	Low	Low
The Philippines	Low	Low	Low	Low	Low	Low
Taiwan	High-medium	High-medium	High-medium	High-medium	High-medium	Medium-low
Thailand	Medium-low	Low	Medium-low	Low	Medium-low	Low

Sources: MacIntyre, 1994b; Campos and Root, 1996; Orru et al. 1997; Gomez, 2002b; Yeung, 2007; Benson and Zhu, 2008, 2011.

Table 12.14. Variations in economic governance, late 2000s

		Social coordination of economic action	
		Strong	Weak
State organization of the economy	Extensive	I Co-governed (−51%) Korea Taiwan	II State led (+1%) China Malaysia
	Modest	III Networked (−98%) Japan	IV Personalized (+127%) Indonesia The Philippines Thailand

Note: The figures in parentheses are the average unweighted percentage change in growth performance (measured as growth in GDP per capita) between the decade averages in the 1980s and in the 2000s (*Source*: IMF, *World Economic Outlook database*, April 2010).

networks and influence has been important. Business partnerships have often involved reciprocalities, particularly in Taiwan. In Korea and Taiwan, economic activity has thus continued to be organized through the negotiated or co-governed relationship between a relatively strong state and largely well-organized social groups, although the balance of power has clearly tilted in favour of business.

In China and Malaysia (Cell II), the basic approach to economic management has remained more state led than that in all the other East Asian economies under review for two key reasons. First, while government regulation of market activities has loosened in both, the share of industrial output produced by SOEs and government investment as a share of total investment have remained high and even increased (see Table 12.12). Second, state control of labour and business organizations has remained as tight as ever. Trade unions in China and Malaysia have continued to operate under the aegis of the government; despite relatively high unionization rates, particularly in China, unions and their peak organizations have lacked the independent ability to articulate and promote their interests. Similarly, not only have business associations been kept on a short leash but they have also remained poorly organized and fragmented along industrial, regional, or (in the case of Malaysia) ethnic lines (Hahn and Lee, 2006; Tipton, 2009). The combination of the strong role of the state in economic organization and relatively weak and weakly organized social groups has kept in place the top-down governance structure in which multiple socio-economic actors and institutions have been connected hierarchically by centralized authority.

Japan has continued to be the only country in our study in which state and societal actors and groups govern economic activity in a networked manner (Cell III). The past two decades have witnessed the further decline of state intervention in the economy, both as an owner of industries and as a market regulator (see Table 12.12). At the same time, the role of well-organized social groups in coordinating market behaviour, activities, and processes has remained crucial. As suggested in the foregoing analysis, business alliances and firms' long-term commitments to each other have become weaker and the organizational cohesion and capabilities of trade unions, particularly at the national and industrial levels, have declined. However, the overall pattern of economic governance in Japan, as compared to that in many other East Asian economies, has remained strongly based on a multiplicity of socio-economic networks among a broad array of organizational stakeholders—firms, unions, banks, and state agencies. Such networks have continued to be shaped as much by informal norms of reciprocity as by formal relations permeating business, financial, and labour institutions. These networks have been a fundamental barrier to liberal market reforms.

The remaining three Southeast Asian economies under discussion here—Indonesia, the Philippines, and Thailand—fall under the mode of personalized governance (Cell IV). State intervention, always relatively weak in these three countries, has further weakened in recent decades. The checked yet sustained process of democratization in these countries has been accompanied by a significant loosening of state control of civic organizations. Relatively low state strength and capacity have continued to limit the ability of the state to organize market activities (MacIntyre, 1994; Tipton, 2009). Deregulation and shrinking state intervention have been most marked in Indonesia (Table 12.12). In all three cases, weakening state intervention has not been accompanied by a strengthening of the social coordination of market activities. Institutional trust, reciprocal commitments, and social networks that are essential to the effective coordination of economic action have traditionally been poorly developed in Indonesia and the Philippines (Root, 1996; Ikeda and Kobayashi, 2007). In Thailand, social capital was relatively strong in the post-war period but has dissipated rapidly in recent years (Unger, 1998; Doner, 2009). The resultant lack of organizing and coordinating capabilities on the part of state actors and key social groups has allowed powerful individuals and families to continue to control the commanding heights of the economy. The atomistic, fluid, or individualized patterns of governance have continued to feature prominently in the overall structure of economic organization in these countries.

In line with each of these four modes of economic governance, the three institutional domains—business organizations, financial market structures, and labour relations systems—have continued to differ systematically across our eight cases. This means there is substantial continuity in the core institutional contours of each of the four VoC, as detailed in Table 12.15.

Table 12.15. Changes and continuities in the varieties of East Asian capitalism, late 2000s

	Core changes	Key continuities
Business organization		
Co-governed	Reduced family ownership (particularly in Korea)	Strong group affiliation; non-participatory work management; weak inter-firm alliances; personally based business partnerships
State led	No significant change (except in a small number of hybrid and cluster firms)	Ownership concentrations in SOEs and private firms; top-down and highly hierarchical manager–employee relations; thin inter-firm networks
Networked	Weakened relational banking, cross-shareholding, or buyer–supplier ties in some (particularly relatively independent and well-performing) firms	Relatively strong relational finance and cross-shareholdings in group-affiliated firms; strong manager–employee interactions; reciprocal business alliances among keiretsu
Personalized	Reduced family ownership (particularly in Indonesia)	High ownership concentration in families or group-affiliated firms; non-participatory employee relations; poorly institutionalized and largely ephemeral inter-firm and cross-sector relations
Financial system		
Co-governed	Increasingly market-oriented structures; significantly marketized corporate finance in large firms; crucial reforms of corporate governance rules	Important roles of banks; largely insider-dominated governance practices
State led	Rapid growth of capital markets, particularly in Malaysia; market-oriented changes in formal corporate governance rules	Banks as central institutions; highly bureaucratized governance structures in SOEs; extensive insider practices in private firms
Networked	Important reforms of corporate governance rules; increased market finance, board independence, and transparency in some firms	Largely bank-based financial market structure; strong insider-based governance practices most traditional firms
Personalized	No significant change	Poorly developed capital markets and financial sectors (with partial exception of Thailand); largely bank-based corporate finance; strong insider-controlled governance patterns despite reforms of formal rules
Labour relations regime		
Co-governed	Increased labour market flexibility; declining union density; more inclusive social policy	Relatively strong union influence at the firm level; lingering elements of productivism in welfare provision; relatively strong in-firm training
State led	Increased employment flexibility and declining union influence (particularly in Malaysia)	Relatively strong but tightly controlled unions in SOEs; weak and fragmented union organization in private firms; strong productivist social policy; relatively strong training in SOEs but weak in private firms
Networked	Shrinking core of lifetime employment; declining union organizational strength; merit-based pay in some firms	Relatively rigid hiring and firing conditions; extensive union influence over wage bargaining at the firm level; strong employee participation in management; relatively strong vocational and firm-specific training

	Core changes	Key continuities
Personalized	Increased employment flexibility and job insecurity; further weakening of unions	Fragmented and weak union structures; ineffective collective bargaining, even at the firm level; little in-firm training (particularly in private and small firms); selective and poorly public-funded welfare programmes (with partial exception of Thailand)

China and Malaysia have demonstrated strong state-oriented tendencies in the changing process of economic governance over the past decades, although they have differed in the trajectory of capitalist development. In the two countries, corporate wealth in SOEs has remained concentrated in the hands of state agencies. The ownership structure of privately owned firms has strongly mirrored that of their SOE counterparts. In both SOEs and private firms that have featured top-down patterns of work organization, employees and low and mid-ranking managers have had little participation in and influence over corporate decision processes. While business partnerships have emerged in certain industrial sectors, inter-firm alliances among SOEs and private firms have remained sporadic and thin. The rapid growth of the capital markets, particularly in Malaysia, has reflected not so much market forces as the political and policy considerations of state elites (Cooper, 2007; Zhang, 2009). Corporate governance in SOEs has been dictated by socio-political considerations other than wealth maximization, whereas corporate governance in private firms has been imbued with insider practices. In China, while SOE unions may have dense memberships, they are more an instrument of state policy than a promoter of workers' interests (Lee, this volume). By the same token, Malaysian unions that have operated under the tight oversight of the state have not become an independent sociopolitical force in their own right. As with the poorly organized private business sector, unions in Chinese and Malaysian private firms have been fragmented and lacked any effective workplace organization. In association with their efforts to encourage labour market flexibility, the Chinese and Malaysian governments have increasingly relied upon the market for welfare provision. As a result, the social policy regimes of the two countries have been no less productivist and selective than they were in the 1980s. They have continued to be driven by the imperatives of development and regime legitimation and give priority to government employees and workers in large, often state-owned, enterprises (Haggard and Kaufman, 2008; London, 2008).

In Japan, for all the institutional changes in business organizations, corporate governance, and labour market systems, the networked variety of capitalism has remained closely associated with mutually dependent intra-firm and inter-firm relations, insider-oriented corporate management, and a stakeholder model of employment. With the considerable increase in non-bank financing and arms-length foreign and domestic investment, relational banking and cross-shareholdings characteristic of keiretsu ownership structure have been weakened. However, this outcome has not been uniform across all firms; financial ties have been relatively stable and resilient among group-affiliated firms. While corporate finance has become more market oriented, the overall financial structure has been much less so, and is less market oriented than that in Korea, Malaysia, Taiwan, and even Thailand (Table 12.2). Recent corporate governance reforms have stressed board independence and information disclosure, but they have not led to a radical shift towards the outsider pattern typical of LMEs. Similarly, while the market for corporate control has grown in importance, hostile takeovers have remained rare. Finally, despite increased labour market flexibility and reduced lifetime jobs, employment relations in major firms have demonstrated more continuity, particularly in terms of hiring and firing conditions, union influence over wage bargaining at the firm level, and employee participation in corporate management.

Among all the East Asian economies examined in this volume, Indonesia, the Philippines, and Thailand have displayed more continuities than changes in their main capitalist institutions. These institutions have featured highly personalized intra-firm relations, generally low employee involvement in decision-making, sporadic inter-firm coordination, low human capital formation, and (with the partial exception of Thailand) poorly developed financial systems. Despite government attempts to improve the coverage and quality of welfare provision, the overall structure of social policy regimes has also remained highly selective and poorly funded in Indonesia and the Philippines. While Thailand extended the social policy reach of the state, particularly with regard to health and unemployment, it has faced administrative and political problems in implementation (Haggard and Kaufman, 2008).

Growing Institutional Diversity within East Asian Capitalism

While each of the four national models of capitalism in East Asia has retained the core aspects of dominant institutional practices across business, financial, and labour market systems, not all organizations and firms have conformed to these dominant practices. Indeed, as alluded to in the foregoing analysis, the enduring varieties of East Asian capitalism have been coterminous with increasing internal diversity within each of the four national models of capitalism, particularly at the firm level. Some internal diversity has always existed along regional, sectoral, and corporate lines in different East Asian political economies (Safarian and Dobson, 1996; Orrù et al., 1997), but the degree of internal diversity has recently grown in intensity and scope against the backdrop of sustained global market pressures, policy liberalization, and institutional realignments. The growing heterogeneity of internal institutional practices in East Asia, as in many European coordinated market economies (CMEs) (Deeg, 2009; Lane and Wood, 2009; Streeck, 2009), has raised a whole range of new conceptual and empirical questions about the multifaceted nature of institutional changes. Space limitations do not allow for a detailed discussion of these questions. Drawing upon recent empirical studies, we briefly describe the major internal variations within key East Asian economies.

As already noted, Japan's networked capitalist system has demonstrated significant institutional resilience that has prevented outright convergence upon an LME model. However, once the unit of analysis shifts from the national level and moves towards the sectoral and firm level, the nationally distinctive model of networked capitalism becomes more variable and displays greater organizational heterogeneity (Jackson and Miyajima, 2007; Sako and Kotosaka, this volume). For example, Jackson (2009) has found that there have been three different types of firms in Japan, each of which has differed from the others in terms of ownership structure, corporate finance, governance practices, or employment relations. The first involves traditional Japanese firms that have depended primarily on banks for much of their industrial financing and retained extensive cross-shareholdings. Equally importantly, these firms have had insider-dominated boards, low information disclosure, and weak orientation towards shareholder value. In line with these core features of networked capitalism, these firms have maintained lifetime employment norms and have not moved towards performance-based pay systems. Coexisting with these traditional firms have been two other types of hybrid firms. One has combined market-based finance and relatively arm's length inter-firm relations with lifetime employment practices and extensive manager–employee interactions, whereas the other has interposed low levels of lifetime employment and unionization upon bank-based corporate financing and extensive inter-firm shareholdings.

Similarly, in Korea and Taiwan, substantial internal diversity has emerged, particularly with respect to the patterns of corporate finance and governance. Institutional variations have traditionally existed between large firms and small and medium-sized enterprises (SMEs), with the former being far more internationally oriented and relying upon market finance for a growing proportion of external financing and the latter being largely domestically based and maintaining their traditional national, bank-centred patterns of finance. In recent years, greater diversity has emerged even within large and small firms. In Korea, while the large corporate sector has been generally imbued with insider governance practices, a small number of chaebol firms, newly privatized enterprises, and banks have developed a more independent board system, achieved greater decision-making transparency, and had lower levels of group affiliation (Kim and Kim, 2008; Walter, 2008; Zhang, 2010). In Taiwan, the rise of mini multinationals—small and medium-sized export-oriented and hi-tech firms—has generated salient organizational fissures and diversities in the corporate sector. Unlike traditional family-owned enterprises, most mini multinationals, created by returned Silicon Valley professionals, have operated with more dispersed ownership structures, developed more market-based financing patterns, pursued a greater shareholder value orientation, and adopted higher accounting and disclosure standards (Zhang, 2009).

In Southeast Asia, the continued process of global market integration has also given rise to a different cluster of firms that have been more internationally oriented in their operations and managerial approaches (the following draws on Yeung, 2006; Steier, 2009; Terjesen and Hessels, 2009). While their ownership and authority structures have remained concentrated, these export-oriented and professionally managed enterprises have broken through the constraints of relational financing and actively sought market-based, international sources of investment funds. Furthermore, these firms have begun to move away from the traditional top-down decision-making structure that has inhibited information flows and creativity and shifted towards a more consultative and cooperative approach to managing employee relations. Finally, these firms have employed more flexible wage compensation schemes that have allowed managers to tie individual rewards more closely to performance and productivity and to incentivize value-added activities by employees. The emergence of these hybrid firms whose managerial and governance practices are more isomorphic with global expectations and standards has created important internal variations in the otherwise institutionally monolithic business system of Southeast Asia.

In China, scholars have long emphasized the varied forms of Chinese business organizations in terms of ownership, location, and size.[4] Even if one focuses on the mode of economic governance, at least two other types of firms have emerged and developed alongside state-led enterprises during the reform era. One involves hybrid firms jointly owned or controlled by state, private, and foreign individuals and organizations. Mostly operating in the capital-intensive and hi-tech sectors, these firms have typically featured more dispersed ownership structures, stronger boards of directors, and more market-driven behaviour of managers. While employment contracts in these firms have tended to be shorter than those in SOEs, trade unions have been more

---

[4] There are voluminous studies on these varied forms. For those that focus on ownership-based diversity, see Guthrie and Wang (2006) and Redding and Witt (2007); for those that emphasize location-oriented variations, see Koo and Yeh (1999) and Tsai (2007); and for those that prioritize size-centred differences, see Huchet and Richet (2002) and Ernst and Naughton (2007).

independent from the Party-State and in-house training has been of higher quality (Jing and Tylecote, 2005; Ernst and Naughton, 2007). The other involves firms in locally embedded specialized industrial clusters that often operate in the labour-intensive sectors. What has primarily differentiated them from hierarchically structured and relatively free-standing SOEs is that their core principle of economic organization has comprised formal and informal norms of reciprocity. Within the industrial clusters, inter-firm and buyer–supplier relations are underpinned by cooperative, long-term, and mutually committed networks that are in turn facilitated and maintained by local state-sponsored, semi-autonomous or autonomous industrial associations (Shi and Ganne, 2006; Nee and Opper, 2010).

Patterns of business organization, corporate governance, and employment relations within each East Asian political economy vary along more institutional dimensions than can be easily and parsimoniously captured here. More systematic research needs to be done not only to identify the trajectories and properties of internal diversity but also to explore the impact of rising heterogeneity on the organizational cohesiveness of the national systems of economic governance. Growing diversity within East Asian VoC suggests that judging the extent of institutional evolution depends in part on the level of analysis. However, we argue that internal institutional variations between different firms and organizations should not be taken to imply that the four distinctive models of East Asian capitalisms are necessarily adaptable, erratic, or even elusive. The national institutions that have underpinned each of the four modes of governing economic action discussed in the previous section have never been fully constraining. Rather, they have impacted the strategic choices of firms highly unevenly and allowed them to respond differently to comparable pressures and challenges. In this sense, internal diversity and hybridity may help to buttress the existing order of economic governance by infusing it with institutional dynamism and allowing it to adapt incrementally to pressures for change (Lane and Wood, 2009).

Explaining Capitalist Evolution and Diversity

It would be an impossible task within the confines of this section to attempt to explain the great diversity of the institutional forms of capitalism in East Asia discussed above. Instead, we focus on accounting for three broad outcomes: the general resilience of the different VoC in the region, the finding that there has been more change in some dimensions of capitalist organization than in others, and the tendency towards a greater degree of intra-national variation in organizational practices over time. In addressing each of these three questions, we reprise the main explanatory variables outlined in Chapter 1, focusing on the respective roles of change coalitions, state action and capacity, and policy discourses. We draw on the evidence reviewed above, but our intention is primarily to be illustrative rather than comprehensive. We argue that fundamental institutional change in the region has not occurred so far because all three explanatory drivers have not pushed strongly in the same direction. As a result, change in East Asia in recent decades has been uneven, incremental, and partial. This helps to understand why, as described above, we see a paradoxical combination of limited convergence and greater intra-variety diversity.

What explains the resilience of the four main varieties of East Asian capitalism that we have argued characterized the region about two decades ago? First, this outcome provides broad support for the view that institutional change is generally path dependent and that although change is not impossible, it is more likely to be of an incremental kind than characterized by sudden, sharp ruptures with the past. Remarkably, even the crisis of the late 1990s, the most important challenge to East Asian political economies in the past half-century, did not fundamentally reshape the political economies of the region. Second, as already noted, we argue that more fundamental change has not occurred so far because change coalitions, state action and capacity, and policy discourses have not generally pushed strongly and simultaneously in the direction of radical reform. Korea since the late 1980s offers a good illustration of this. From this time, Korean governments embraced the rhetoric of globalization at the level of national strategy, as did important parts of the corporate sector. But the constituency for change was much more limited than this suggested: the major chaebol were keen to finance diversification and foreign expansion but without jeopardizing the oligopolistic structure of domestic industries, family control of corporate assets, or their often privileged relationships with policymakers. Labour, a much weaker social partner than business, often suspected that globalization rhetoric was a lever that would be used to entrench further the dominant position of business. As a result, a comprehensive change coalition was not forthcoming; state action and policy discourses were often marked by internal conflicts. Even after the crisis of 1997–8, the reformist government of Kim Dae-Jung found it difficult to achieve its declared aim of reducing the political and economic power of the major chaebol. In some of its actions—notably the 'big deal' of early 1998 and in its countenancing of regulatory forbearance to support distressed major firms in the dot.com recession of 2001–2—it oversaw corporate consolidation and stepped back from the strict implementation of neo-liberal reforms (Graham, 2003; Walter, 2008). Although the political leadership may have been convinced of the need for change and aligned itself more thoroughly than before with the rhetoric of globalization and of importing Western-style regulation (Pirie, 2006), the powerful business sector and associated corporate families were far less convinced and were often able to protect and even to consolidate their existing position and privileges.

We can see a similar pattern in some other countries in the region, though often in a context in which the capacity for effective state action relative to entrenched private sector elites has been much weaker than in Korea (Indonesia and Thailand are examples, but so too is Japan). In China, where state capacity was much greater and where the boundary between the business sector and the state remains much more blurred, the strong preference of the political leadership has been to pursue gradualism, with the overriding objective of maintaining the political monopoly enjoyed by the Party. As Breslin (this volume) points out, although the leadership has countenanced a massive shift of ownership in the economy from the public to the private sector, it has been very careful to retain key levers of state control, notably through the financial sector, through residual ownership of strategic business sectors, through limits on the entry of foreign capital, and limits on the media and in politics generally.

Nevertheless, even in state-led China, the very success of the strategy of embracing (albeit partially) globalization has rendered the government highly dependent on the continued success of key parts of the business sector and their ability to generate new jobs. Generally, the strong policy emphasis on export competitiveness in the region favours the interests of business in policy discourses, especially those of large and internationalized business groups. This phenomenon seems relatively independent of political regime type, from authoritarian China through the intermediate political regimes of Singapore and Malaysia to the more democratic systems of Indonesia, Korea, Japan, and Taiwan. In Korea, partisan politics has been more important than in most other countries, with centre-left governments attempting to constrain business influence since the late 1990s and centre-right governments retaining a pro-business stance (as with the government of Lee Myung-bak since late 2007).

One important development in recent decades is the rise in levels of economic inequality in the region. Whereas East Asian developing countries had been characterized by relatively low levels of income inequality by comparison with those in other regions, since the 1990s increasing income inequality has been particularly marked in China, though it seems to be common to most countries in the region, with Thailand a possible exception (ADB, 2007: 6–7). Without delving into the underlying causes of this trend, it would seem to be consistent with the finding of relative stability in business–government relations in the region and greater change in financial sector and especially labour market systems.[5] It also creates a potential political problem for

---

[5] Evidence from advanced countries, particularly the United States, has shown a strong correlation between financial deregulation and 'excess wages' for financial sector employees (Philippon and Reshef, 2009).

incumbent governments: rising inequality can fuel popular discontent and lead to increasing demands for redistribution.

As we have seen, there are signs that governments have responded to these pressures by increasing social welfare spending—including in relatively authoritarian countries like China, where the leadership has spoken explicitly of its concerns about rising economic inequality and its determination to address it, in part by increasing social welfare spending. China in particular, but East Asian countries with large current account surpluses more generally, has also come under growing external pressure to raise levels of consumption and to reduce saving. Thus, both domestic and international pressures have converged to encourage a different stance towards social welfare policies in parts of the region. In some countries, successful electoral strategies have involved pro-poor policy platforms. In Thailand, the Shinawatras have attracted rural votes by promising welfare handouts for the relatively poor. In Korea, centre-left governments have also been more open to pro-welfare arguments. Korean policymakers, like China, have also been subject to international pressure to move in this direction, including via peer reviews in the OECD (OECD, 2011). This outcome could provide some support for the 'compensation hypothesis' at the regional level, that globalization produces rising domestic demand for social welfare policies. It also reflects the pressures of aging populations in countries like Japan and the shift to democracy in countries such as Korea and Taiwan. Nevertheless, overall levels of social welfare expenditure in the region remain low even by the standards of other countries at similar levels of development. This reflects in part the continuing weakness of organized labour and associated political parties of the centre-left compared to business coalitions.

The continuity of a privileged position for business in East Asian political economies also helps to explain the second broad outcome we have identified, that institutional change has been greater in labour market systems and least in the area of business–government relations, with the evolution of financial systems occupying an intermediate position. In countries such as Japan and Korea, in which labour protection was among the highest in the region, governments have increasingly tolerated the emergence of dual labour markets, which have permitted new businesses to deploy labour more flexibly whilst avoiding a general backlash of labour that more Thatcherite policies might have produced. That this phenomenon is also apparent in other advanced economies associated with the CME model such as Germany (Streeck, 2009) provides support for the view that governments in more coordinated economies have increasingly favoured organized business coalitions rather than organized labour. However, in comparison to Europe, the position of organized labour has eroded more sharply in the East Asian region.

This, it should be noted, has occurred in the context of very rapid growth. As Lee (this volume) points out, the position of labour has not markedly improved despite decades of high growth.

For similar reasons, there has been more change in finance than in business–government systems as the needs of an expanding corporate sector have continued to grow. In addition, however, governments also came to recognize that the previous heavy reliance on bank-based finance in a policy environment in which prudential regulation was generally weak was a major source of vulnerability (Woo-Cumings, 1999). After the Asian crisis of the late 1990s, many major banks and highly leveraged firms in Asia were in no position to resist change and often were subject to government intervention or (in the case of banks) foreign takeovers. The dominant prevailing policy discourse also favoured the development of capital markets and the importation of managerial and regulatory practices from the major Western countries. Reformist political elites from Jakarta to Tokyo and Beijing saw advantages in hitching a ride on this particular policy discourse. As the global financial crisis of 2008–9 indicated, most Asian banks were relatively highly capitalized and much less dependent on risky securitization businesses than their Western counterparts.

Even so, the extent of general improvement in financial regulation in the Asian region since the 1990s should not be exaggerated. East Asian financial systems collectively were also protected in the latest global crisis by the large foreign exchange reserves and fiscal resources available to major governments in the region. Even these resources were not wholly sufficient, however, as demonstrated by the participation of Korea and Singapore in the emergency swaps of dollar liquidity provided during the crisis by the US Federal Reserve. The significant variations in financial openness, development, and in political relations with the United States continue to shape the comparative vulnerabilities of Asian financial systems to serious disruptions. So too do domestic coalitions. In the wake of the Asian crises of the late 1990s, powerful domestic business coalitions mobilized to prevent proposed changes in the structure and governance of the financial sector from generating pressure for change in the rest of the political economy. As mentioned above, these business interests and their political allies ensured that during times of significant financial and corporate distress, favourable access to bank finance prevailed at the cost of setting aside new prudential regulatory rules. This phenomenon can be seen in Korea at the beginning of the 2000s and in China during the global crisis of 2008–9, though they were far from alone. Similarly, business elites who have deployed a variety of techniques—from packing boards with directors who are independent in name only to lobbying in favour of weak implementation of new securities market rules—to ensure that the promotion of capital markets has not substantially reduced the degree of control over key assets enjoyed by many of the region's powerful corporate families. Such techniques have been easiest to deploy in countries in which highly personalized networks predominate, such as Indonesia and Thailand. Even in highly developed Japan, networked relationships between banks, firms, and politicians have posed significant barriers to the full implementation of financial regulatory reform (Walter, 2006). More state-led systems such as those in Singapore and Malaysia have sometimes been more able to deflect private sector pressures to resist the enhancement of prudential regulation. However, as the Chinese case demonstrates, policymaking elites who prefer to maintain bank-based systems as key elements of state control have relied more upon more direct forms of intervention at the expense of promoting better private sector risk management.

Finally, what accounts for the increased diversity of practices *within* the main varieties of East Asian capitalism? In part, the answer to this question lies in the contrast between the formal regulation of capitalism in the region, which has expanded significantly in recent years, and the continuing large enforcement gap that characterizes most countries (Singapore being an exception). Weak enforcement, itself an indication of the continuing influence of business and political interests in the economic policymaking process, has allowed many corporate families to continue practices at odds with the intent of reformers. In countries with extensive state intervention in the economy, lead policymakers have also sometimes weakened enforcement at critical junctures. But one consequence of more extensively regulated capitalism is that weaker and less well connected firms have been subject to greater compliance pressure. During the Thaksin era in Thailand, the enforcement of securities rules was least effective concerning the business activities of his own family, but securities regulators were able to achieve some victories over less connected business interests. Despite significant improvements in Indonesia under President Yudhoyono since 2004, personalized policymaking remains an important constraint on the consistency of policymaking. In the co-governed systems of Korea and Taiwan, more effective states and growing pressure from civil society has delivered greater rule of law, but the ability of business to deflect neo-liberal reforms remains considerable. State-led systems exhibit greater variation in respect of the enforcement gap. In China, as Lee (this volume) documents, the gap between formal labour rights and business practice has grown substantially in recent decades.

Weaknesses in enforcement have provided opportunities for some firms within the region who have perceived a reputational and business advantage in distinguishing themselves from the norm by pursuing internal governance reforms. For example, even within countries that perform very poorly on corporate governance overall there are firms that approach international best practice, including TSMC (Taiwan); LG Electronics, Shinhan Financial, and Posco (Korea); Telcom Indonesia and Astra International (Indonesia); and ICBC (China) (CLSA Asia-pacific Markets, 2010: 4). As these examples suggest, firms that are relatively globalized in their sales, production, or financing are also more likely to engage in better corporate governance practices. Similar considerations apply to the growing diversity of corporate practices with respect to labour, where firms reliant on the supply of relatively skilled and mobile labour have been more likely to offer improved working conditions. Generally, some firms have taken increasing advantage of the financial, production, marketing, and learning opportunities provided by globalization to break the mould within particular economies. This means that the continuing integration of East Asian economies into the global economy contributes to the growing diversity of practice within particular countries, by weakening the position of some actors in domestic political economies and strengthening that of others. The Asian crisis of the late 1990s contributed to this growing diversity by generally increasing both the degree of openness of economies and the reputational advantages for some firms of signalling their divergence from general domestic practices. In the major crisis-hit economies, the failure of many large banks significantly increased the level of foreign participation in and in some cases control of banking firms. These firms have often been among those approaching best practice in corporate governance. We have argued that globalization has certainly not yet produced convergence of capitalist institutions within Asia, but through these kinds of mechanism it can have potentially significant long-term consequences for governance practices within particular firms and states. This underlines the point made by Mahoney and Thelen that incremental change is more common than radical ruptures, and that such change may eventually accumulate to produce a tipping point that few expect.

What are the Implications of Our Analysis for Future Research?

We have argued that the recent evolution of East Asian VoC has been characterized more by incremental, partial change within existing VoC than by fundamental ruptures with the past. Inevitably, there is a difficulty in judging the extent of incremental change. Whereas we judge the glass to be still less than half empty, others will be inclined to see it as already more than half full and to argue that there have been more fundamental shifts than we have claimed. If continued incremental evolution is the most likely outcome in most of the region, we need to know more about the point at which incremental change can add up to a more fundamental shift of capitalist paradigm. We have insufficient knowledge about the triggers or tipping points of such fundamental change. The deep financial and economic crises of the late 1990s were often insufficient, at least so far, to produce this kind of change.

Nor have wholesale political regime changes—including apparently successful transitions from authoritarianism to democracy in Indonesia, Korea, the Philippines, and Taiwan—produced radical changes in VoC in the way that some might have expected. Whether political regime change in a country like China would produce similar outcomes also remains highly uncertain.

There is also considerable remaining uncertainty about the extent to which uneven change across the different institutional dimensions of capitalism can continue, and the point at which this could create serious dysfunctionalities or ruptures. What, for example, could mobilize labour organizations to play a greater role in social, economic, and political processes of the kind that sociologists such as Karl Polanyi (1944) thought inevitable? Are such mobilizations impossible under current circumstances of increasingly globalized corporate networks, which seem in general to have contributed to the weakening of labour movements? The answer to such questions are of course linked to the nature of political systems, although a continuing weak voice for labour has continued to characterize a wide variety of political regimes in the Asian region.

This also brings us back full circle to the question of institutional complementarities and modes of governance. As a region, East Asian economies have continued to outperform the rest of the world, though as noted in Chapter 1 there has been a growing dispersion of economic performance in the region. Given the substantial variations in the nature of capitalist organization across the region, this makes it very difficult to generalize about institutional complementarities. It is often claimed, especially since 2008, that those countries characterized by more extensive state intervention have generally outperformed those characterized by weaker state intervention. Some see the contrast between the economic performance of the region's two major economies, China and Japan, as most revealing in this regard and as evidence of the economic benefits of strong, authoritarian states (Halper, 2010). Substantial growth decelerations have also occurred in the co-governed systems of Korea and Taiwan, which have combined democratization with still considerable state intervention (Table 12.14). Our own view is that it is far too early to reach such definitive conclusions in respect of a global crisis that is far from over. It is also notable that the largest percentage improvements in growth outcomes have occurred in the personalized model of capitalism, notably in the Philippines and Indonesia. The same point could be made about democratic India, about which this book has been able to say very little. Of course, the improvements in the Philippines and Indonesia came from a relatively low base, but they may indicate that even modest policy reforms can improve growth prospects in such political economies.

References

Abdul-Rahman, Saaidah and Chris Rowley. 2008. 'The Changing Face of Human Resource Management in Malaysia.' In Chris Rowley and Saaidah Abdul-Rahman, eds. *The Changing Face of Management in South East Asia*. London: Routledge, 59–96.

Acharya, Amitav. 2009. *Whose Ideas Matter? Agency and Power in Asian Regionalism*. Ithaca, NY: Cornell University Press.

Agnblad, J., E. Berglof, P. Hogfeldt and H. Svancar. 2001. 'Ownership and Control in Sweden: Strong Owners, Weak Minorities and Social Control.' In F. Barca and M. Becht, eds. *The Control of Corporate Europe*. Oxford: Oxford University Press.

Ahlstrom, David, Michael N. Young, Eunice C. Chan and Garry D. Bruton. 2004. 'Facing Constraints to Growth?' *Asia Pacific Journal of Management* 21 (2): 263–85.

Ahmadjian, Christina L. 2006. 'Japanese Business Groups.' In Sea-Jin Chang, ed. *Business Groups in East Asia*. Oxford: Oxford University Press, 29–51.

—— Gregory E. Robbins. 2005. 'A Clash of Capitalisms: Foreign Shareholders and Corporate Restructuring in 1990s Japan.' *American Sociological Review* 70 (3): 451–71.

Akhand, Hafiz and Kanhaya Gupta. 2005. *Economic Development in Pacific Asia*. London: Routledge.

Alfaro, L., Y. Huang and M. Kalochoritis. 2001. 'Power to the States: "Fiscal Wars" for FDI in Brazil.' *Harvard Business School Case 701-079*.

Allen, Franklin and Douglas Gale. 2000. *Comparing Financial Systems*. Cambridge, MA: MIT Press.

Amable, Bruno. 2003. *The Diversity of Modern Capitalism*. Oxford: Oxford University.

Amsden, A. 1989. *Asia's Next Giant: South Korea and Late Industrialisation*. New York: Oxford University Press.

Amyx, Jennifer. 2004. *Japan's Financial Crisis: Institutional Rigidity and Reluctant Change*. Princeton: Princeton University Press.

—— Harukata Takenaka and A. Maria Toyoda. 2005. 'The Politics of Postal Savings Reform in Japan.' *Asian Perspective* 29: 23–48.

Aoki, M., ed. 1984. *The Economic Analysis of the Japanese Firms*. Amsterdam: North Holland.

—— 2001. *Towards A Comparative Institutional Analysis*. Cambridge, MA: MIT Press.

—— Y. Hayami, eds. 2001. *Communities and Markets in Economic Development*. Oxford: Oxford University Press.

—— H. Kim, eds. 1995. *Corporate Governance in Transitional Economies; Insider Control and the Role of Banks*. Washington, DC: World Bank.

References

—— H. Patrick, eds. 1994. *The Japanese Main Bank System: Its Relevance for Developing and Transforming Economies*. Oxford: Oxford University Press.

—— G. Saxonhouse, eds. 2000. *Finance, Governance, and Competiveness in Japan*. Oxford: Oxford University Press.

Aoki, M., H. Kim and M. Okuno-Fujiwara, eds. 1997. *The Role of Government in East Asian Economic Development: Comparative Institutional Analysis*. Oxford: Oxford University Press.

—— G. Jackson and H. Miyajima, eds. 2007. *Corporate Governance in Japan: Institutional Change and Organizational Diversity*. Oxford: Oxford University Press.

Arikawa, Yasuhiro and Hideaki Miyajima. 2007. 'Relationship Banking in Post-bubble Japan.' In Masahiko Aoki, Gregory Jackson and Hideaki Miyajima, eds. *Corporate Governance in Japan*. Oxford: Oxford University Press, 51–78.

Ash, Robert. 1988. 'The Evolution of Agricultural Policy.' *The China Quarterly* 116: 529–55.

Asian Corporate Governance Association (ACGA). 2010. *Rules and Recommendations on the Number of Independent Directors in Asia*. Hong Kong: ACGA.

Asian Development Bank (ADB). 'Labor Markets in Asia.' In *Key Indicators for Asia and the Pacific 2005*. Manila: ADB.

—— 2007. *Inequality in Asia: Key Indicators for Asia and the Pacific 2007, Special Chapter: Highlights*. Manila: ADB.

Aspalter, Christian. 2006. 'The East Asian Welfare Model.' *International Journal of Social Welfare* 15 (3): 290–301.

Athukorala, Prema-Chandra, Chris Mannang and Piyasiri Wichramasekara. 2000. *Growth, Employment, and Migration. Structural Change in the Greater Mekong Countries*. Cheltenham. Edward Elgar.

Australian Stock Exchange (ASX). 2005. *International Share Ownership*. Sydney: ASX.

—— 2009. *Australian Share Ownership Study*. Sydney: ASX.

Bachman, David. 1986. 'Differing Visions of China's Post-Mao Economy: The Ideas of Chen Yun, Deng Xiaoping, and Zhao Ziyang.' *Asian Survey* March, 292–321.

Bai, C., Q. Liu, J. Lu, F. Song and J. Zhang. 2004. 'Corporate Governance and Market Valuation in China.' *Journal of Comparative Economics* 32 (4): 599–616.

Balassa, Bela. 1981. *The Newly Industrialising Countries in the World Economy*. New York: Pergamon Press.

Bamber, Greg and Russell D. Lansbury, eds. 1998. *International and Comparative Employment Relations*. London: Sage.

Bank of Japan. 2010. *Financial System Report*. March, http://www.boj.or.jp/en/research/brp/fsr/fsr10a.htm/

Bank of Korea (BOK). Various issues. *Economics Statistics Yearbook*. Seoul: Bank of Korea.

Bao, Yujun. 2010. 'Fitting in The Private Sector.' *Caixin*, 20 April. http://english.caing.com/2010-04-20/100137074.html

Bartley, T. 2007. 'How Foundations Shape Social Movements: The Construction of an Organizational Field and the Rise of Forest Certification.' *Social Problems* 54 (3): 229–55.

Bautista, Romeo M. and Mario B. Lamberte. 1996. 'The Philippines: Economic Developments and Prospects.' *Asian-Pacific Economic Literature* 10 (2): 16–31.

Baye, M., D. Kovenock and C. de Vries. 2012. 'Contests with Rank-Order Spillovers.' *Economic Theory*, forthcoming.

Beck, Thorsten and Ed Al-Hussainy. 2010. *A New Database on Financial Development and Structure*. Washington, DC: World Bank.

—— Asli Demirgüç-Kunt and Ross Levine. 2000. 'A New Database on Financial Development and Structure.' *World Bank Economic Review* 14 (3): 597–605.

Beeson, Mark. 1999. *Competing Capitalisms: Australia, Japan and Economic Competition in the Asia Pacific*. London: Macmillan.

—— 2009. 'Developmental States in East Asia: A Comparison of the Japanese and Chinese Experiences.' *Asian Perspective* 33: 5–39.

Bell, S. and H. Feng. 2009. 'Reforming China's Stock Market: Institutional Change Chinese Style. *Political Studies* 57 (1): 117–40.

Benson, John. 2008. 'Trade Unions in Japan.' In John Benson and Ying Zhu, eds. *Trade Unions in Asia*. London: Routledge, 24–42.

—— 2011. 'Labour Markets in Japan.' In John Benson and Ying Zhu, eds. *The Dynamics of Asian Labour Markets*. London: Routledge, 33–60.

——Ying Zhu. 2008. *Trade Unions in Asia*. London: Routledge.

—— —— eds. 2011. *The Dynamics of Asian Labour Markets*. London: Routledge.

Berkman, H., R. A. Cole and J. Fu. 2009. 'Expropriation through Loan Guarantees to Related Parties: Evidence from China.' *Journal of Banking and Finance* 33 (1): 141–56.

Bhaskaran, Manu. 2009. 'The Asian Financial Crisis Ten Years Later—Lessons Learnt: The Private Sector Perspective.' In Richard Carney, ed. *Lessons from the Asian Financial Crisis*. London: Routledge, 112–34.

Birdsall, Nancy and Stephan Haggard. 2002. 'After the Crisis: The Social Contract and the Middle Class in East Asia.' In Ethan Kapstein and Brouko Milanovic, eds. *When Markets Fail: Social Policy and Economic Reform*. New York: Russell Sage Foundation.

Blyth, Mark. 2002. *Great Transformations Economic Ideas and Institutional Change in the Twentieth Century*. Cambridge: Cambridge University Press.

Boyd, Richard and Tak-Wing Ngo, eds. 2005. *Asian States*. London: Routledge.

Boyer, Robert. 2005. 'How and Why Capitalisms Differ.' *Economy and Society* 34 (4): 509–57.

Bradsher, Keith. 2010. 'Foreign Companies Chafe at China's Restrictions.' *New York Times*, 16 May.

Brenner, R. 1998. 'The Economics of Global Turbulence.' *New Left Review*, 229.

Breslin, Shaun. 2006. 'Foreign Direct Investment in the People's Republic of China: Preferences, Policies and Performance.' *Policy and Society* 25 (1): 9–38.

Brookfield, Jonathan. 2007. 'Firm Clustering and Specialization: A Study of Taiwan's Machine Tool Industry.' *Small Business Economics* 30: 405–22.

Brown, Earl, Jr. 2003. 'Thailand: Labour and the Law.' In Asia Monitor Resource Center, *Asia Pacific Labour Law Review*. Hong Kong: Asia Monitor Resource Center, 258–9.

Brown, Andrew. 2004. *Labour, Politics, and the State in Industrializing Thailand*. London: Routledge/Curzon.

Brück, Sebastian and Laixiang Sun. 2007. 'Achieving Effective Government under Divided Government and Private Interest Group Pressure.' *Journal of Contemporary China* 16 (53): 655–80.

References

Business Korea (BK). Various years. Seoul: *Business Korea*.

Cai, Yongshun. 2002a. 'The Resistance of Chinese Laid-off Workers in the Reform Period.' *The China Quarterly* 170: 327–44.

—— 2002b. 'Relaxing the Constraints from Above: Politics of Privatizing Public Enterprises in China.' *Asian Journal of Political Science* 10 (2): 94–121.

Calder, K. 1993. *Strategic Capitalism*. Princeton: Princeton University Press.

Calder, Kent E. 1997. 'Assault on the Banker's Kingdom: Politics, Markets, and the Liberalization of Japanese Industrial Finance.' In Micheal Loriaux et al. eds. *Capital Ungoverned: Liberalizing Finance in Interventionist States*. Ithaca: Cornell University Press, 17–56.

Callen, T. and P. Reynolds. 1997. 'Capital Market Development and the Monetary Market Mechanism in Malaysia and Thailand.' In J. Hicklin, D. Robinson and A. Singh, eds. *Macroeconomic Issues Facing ASEAN Countries*. Washington, DC: International Monetary Fund, 184–230.

Calmfors, L. and J. Driffil. 1988. 'Bargaining Structure, Corporatism, and Macroeconomic Performance.' *Economic Policy* 6: 13–61.

Campbell, John L. and Ove K. Pedersen. 2007. 'The Varieties of Capitalism and Hybrid Success.' *Comparative Political Studies* 40 (3): 307–320.

Capital IQ. 2010. *Capital IQ Markets*. http://www.capitaliq.com

Caprio, Gerard, Jonathan L. Fiechter, Robert E. Litan and Michael Pomerleano, eds. 2004. *The Future of State-Owned Financial Institutions*. Washington, DC: Brookings Institution Press.

Caraway, Teri L. 2004. 'Protective Repression, International Pressure, and Institutional Design: Explaining Labour Reform in Indonesia.' *Studies in Comparative International Development* 39 (3): 28–49.

—— 2007. *Assembling Women*. Ithaca: Cornell University Press.

Carney, Michael. 2005. 'Globalisation and the Renewal of Asian Business Networks.' *Asia Pacific Journal of Management* 22 (3): 337–54.

—— Eric Gedajlovic and Xiaohua Yang. 2009a. 'Varieties of Asian Capitalism.' *Asia Pacific Journal of Management* 26 (3): 361–80.

———— 2009b. 'Varieties of Asian Capitalism: Toward an institutional theory of Asia enterprise.' *Asia Pacific Journal of Management* 26 (September): 361–80.

Carney, R. W. 2009. 'Chinese Capitalism in the OECD Mirror.' *New Political Economy* 14 (1): 71–99.

—— 2010. *Contested Capitalism*. London: Routledge.

Central Bank of China (CBC). Various issues. *Financial Statistics Monthly*. Taipei: CBC.

—— Various issues. *Financial Statistics*. Taipei: CBC.

—— Various issues. *Loans by Domestic Banks to SMEs*. Taipei: CBC.

Chan, A. 1993. 'Revolution or Corporatism? Workers and Trade Unions in Post-Mao China.' *The Australian Journal of Chinese Affairs* 29: 31–61.

—— 2001. *China's Workers Under Assault: The Exploitation of Labor in a Globalizing Economy*. Armonk, NY: M.E. Sharpe.

Chan, J. W.-l. 2006. 'Chinese Women Workers Organize in the Export Zone.' *New Labor Forum* 15 (1): 19–27.

—— 2009. 'Meaningful Progress or Illusory Reform? Analyzing China's Labor Contract Law.' *New Labor Forum* 18 (2): 43–51.

Chandler, A. 1962. *Strategy and Structure: Chapters in the History of the American Industrial Enterprise*. Cambridge, MA: MIT Press.

—— 1977. *The Visible Hand: The Managerial Revolution in American Business*. Cambridge, MA: Harvard University Press.

—— 1990. *Scale and Scope: The Dynamics of Industrial Capitalism*. Cambridge, MA: Harvard University Press.

—— 1997. 'The United States: Engines of Economic Growth in the Capital-Intensive and Knowledge-Intensive Industries.' In A. Chandler, F. Amatori and T. Hikino, eds. *Big Business and the Wealth of Nations*. Cambridge: Cambridge University Press, 63–101.

—— F. Amatori and T. Hikino, eds. 1997. *Big Business and the Wealth of Nations*. Cambridge: Cambridge University Press.

Chang, Ha-Joon. 1998. 'Korea: The Misunderstood Crisis.' *World Development* 26 (August): 1555–61.

—— 2002. 'The East Asian Model of Economic Policy.' In Evelyn Huber ed. *Models of Capitalism: Lessons for Latin America*. University Park, PA: The Pennsylvania State University Press: 197–235.

—— Hong-Jae Park and Chul Gyue Yoo. 1998. 'Interpreting the Korean Crisis: Financial Liberalisation, Industrial Policy and Corporate Governance.' *Cambridge Journal of Economics* 22: 735–46.

Chang, Sea-Jin. 2006. 'Business Groups in East Asia: Post-crisis Restructuring and New Growth.' *Asia Pacific Journal of Management* 23: 407–17.

—— 2006. 'Korean Business Groups.' In Sea-Jin Chang, ed. *Business Groups in East Asia*. Oxford: Oxford University Press, 52–69.

—— 2006. *Business Groups in East Asia*. Oxford: Oxford University Press.

Chaudhry, Kiren Aziz. 1993. 'The Myths of the Market and the Common History of Late Developers.' *Politics & Society* 21 (3): 245–74.

Che, Jiahua and Yingyi Qian. 1998. 'Institutional Environment, Community Government, and Corporate Governance: Understanding China's Township-Village Enterprises.' *Journal of Law, Economics, and Organization* 14 (1): 1–23.

Chen, An. 2003. 'Rising Class Politics and its Impact on China's Path to Democracy' *Democratization* 10 (2): 141–62.

Chen, Edward. 1979. *Hyper-Growth in Asian Economies*. New York: Holmes & Meier.

Chen, F. 2000. 'Subsistence Crises, Managerial Corruption and Labour Protests in China.' *The China Journal* 44: 41–63.

—— 2003. 'Between the State and Labour: The Conflict of Chinese Trade Unions' Double Identity in Market Reform.' *The China Quarterly* 176: 1006–28.

—— 2004. 'Legal Mobilization by Trade Unions: The Case of Shanghai.' *The China Journal* 52: 27–45.

—— 2007. 'Individual Rights and Collective Rights: Labor's Predicament in China.' *Communist and Post-Communist Studies* 40: 59–79.

—— 2009. 'Union Power in China: Source, Operation, and Constraints.' *Modern China* 35: 662–89.

Chen, Gongmeng, Michael Firth and Liping Xu. 2009. 'Does the Type of Ownership Control Matter? Evidence from China's listed Companies.' *Journal of Banking and Finance* 33 (1): 171–81.

Chen, John. 2003. 'Reflections on Labour Law in China.' In Asia Monitor Resource Center, *Asia Pacific Labour Law Review* 2003.

—— S. C. Thomas. 2003. 'The Ups and Downs of the PRC Securities Market.' *China Business Review* 30 (1): 36–40.

Chen, K. 2004. 'China's Party Line is Capital; Market-Based Blueprint would Continue Tough Approach.' *Wall Street Journal* (Eastern Edition), 12 February, C. 20.

Chen, Lan and Bao-qin Hou. 2008. 'China: Economic Transition, Employment Flexibility and Security.' In Sangheon Lee and Francois Eyraud, eds. *Globalization, Flexibilization and Working Conditions in Asia and the Pacific.* Oxford: Chandos Publishing and Geneva, International Labour Office.

Chen, S. 2009. 'dui "laodong hetong fa" shishi guocheng zhong ruogan wenti de sikao' (On some issues in the implementation of the Labor Contract Law). *hunan sheng gonghui ganbu xuexiao* 23 (3): 30–2.

Chen, Shyh-Jer, Jyh-Jer Roger Ko and John Lawler. 2003. 'Changing Patterns of Industrial Relations in Taiwan.' *Industrial Relations* 42 (3): 315–40.

Chen, Y., H. Li and L.A. Zhou. 2005. 'Relative Performance Evaluation and the Turnover of Provincial Leaders in China.' *Economics Letters* 88 (3): 421–5.

Chen, Z. and P. Xiong. 2001. 'Discounts on Illiquid Stocks: Evidence from China.' *Yale ICF Working Paper* No. 00-56.

Cheng, Joseph Yu-shek. 1985. 'Reform of the Economic Structure and "One Country, Two Systems".' *The Australian Journal of Chinese Affairs* 13: 109–20.

Cheng, T. J. 1990. 'Political Regimes and Developmental Strategies: South Korea and Taiwan.' In Gary Gerreffi and Donald L. Wyman, eds. *Manufacturing Miracles: Paths of Industrialization in Latin America and East Asia.* San Diego: Center for U.S.–Mexican Studies.

China Banking Regulatory Commission (CBRC). 2007. *Annual Report 2006.* Beijing: CBRC.

China Daily. 2006. 'China Defines Key National Economic Sectors.' *China Daily,* 18 December.

Chiu, B. and M. Lewis. 2006. *Reforming China's State-owned Enterprises and Banks.* Northanpton, MA: Edward Elgar.

Cho, Myeong-Hyeon. 2003. 'Reform of Corporate Governance.' In Stephan Haggard, Wonhyuk Lim and Eusung Kim, eds. *Economic Crisis and Corporate Restructuring in Korea.* Cambridge: Cambridge University Press, 286–306.

Choi, Young Jun. 2009. 'From Developmental Regimes to Post-developmental Regimes.' In Ka Ho Mok and Ray Forrest, eds. *Changing Governance and Public Policy in East Asia.* London: Routledge, 206–27.

Chor, Davin and Richard Freeman. 2005. 'The 2004 Global Labour Survey.' *NBER Working Paper* No. 11598. Cambridge, MA: National Bureau of Economic Research.

Chou, K. P. 2006. 'Downsizing Administrative Licensing System and Private Sector Development in China: A Preliminary Assessment.' Asian Development Bank Institute (Tokyo) *Discussion Paper* No. 52.

Chu Yun-han. 2002. 'Re-engineering the Developmental State in an Age of Globalization: Taiwan in Defiance of Neo-liberalism.' *The China Review* 2 (Spring): 29–59.

—— 2007. 'Taiwan in 2006: A Year of Political Turmoil' *Asian Survey* 47 (January): 44–51.

Chu, Wan-wen. 2004. 'A Re-examination of Privatisation in the Post-authoritarian Era.' *Social Studies Quarterly* 53: 29–59. (In Chinese.)

Chubu, Sanseiken. 2004. *Rodoryoku Tayouka no nakade no Atarashii Hatarakikata* (New Modes of Working in the midst of Labour Force Diversification: Co-existence with Non-standard Workers). Toyota City: Chubu Sanseiken.

Chun, Jennifer Jihye. 2009. *Organizing at the Margins: The Symbolic Politics of Labour in South Korea and the United States*. Ithaca, NY: Cornell University Press.

Chung, Chi-Nien and Ishtiaq P. Mahmood. 2006. 'Taiwanese Business Groups.' In Sea-Jin Chang, ed. *Business Groups in East Asia*. Oxford: Oxford University Press, 70–92.

Chung, Kyuil. 2009. 'Household Debt, the Savings Rate and Monetary Policy.' *BIS Papers* No. 46: 83–94.

Claessens, Stijn and Joseph P. H. Fan. 2002. 'Corporate Governance in Asia: A Survey.' *International Review of Finance* 3 (2): 71–103.

—— Simeon Djankov and Larry H. P. Lang. 1999. 'Who Controls East Asian Corporations?' *Policy Research Working Paper* 2054. The World Bank.

Clark, Cal and K. C. Roy. 1997. *Comparing Development Patterns in Asia*. Boulder: Lynne Rienner.

CLSA Asia-Pacific Markets. Various issues. *Corporate Governance Watch*. Hong Kong: CLSA.

Coke Concerned Student Group. 2009. *Hangzhou kekoukele zhuangpingchang diaocha baogao* (Investigative Report on Hangzhou Coca-Cola Bottling Plant). Hangzhou: Coke Concerned Student Group.

Conyon, M. and L. He. 2008. 'Executive Compensation and CEO Equity Incentives in China's Listed Firms.' Available at SSRN: http://ssrn.com/abstract=1261911

Cooney, S., S. Biddulph, K. Li and Y. Zhu. 2007. 'China's New Labor Contract Law: Responding to the Growing Complexity of Labour Relations in the PRC.' *University of New South Wales Law Journal* 30: 786–801.

Cooper, John F. 2009. 'The Devolution of Taiwan's Democracy during the Chen Shui-bian Era.' *Journal of Contemporary China* 18 (60): 463–78.

Cooper, Mary C. 2007. 'Capital Markets and Regime Type in East Asia.' Paper presented to the annual meeting of the American Political Science Association, Chicago, 26–30 August.

Cortell, Andrew P. and James W. Davis, Jr. 2000. 'Understanding the Domestic Impact of International Norms: A Research Agenda.' *International Studies Review* 2 (1): 65–87.

Council for Economic Planning and Development (CEPD). 2005. *Privatisation of SOEs in Taiwan*. Taipei: CEPD.

Croissant, Aurel. 2004. 'Changing Welfare Regimes in East and Southeast Asia.' *Social Policy and Administration* 38 (5): 504–24.

Crouch, Colin. 1993. *Industrial Relations and European State Traditions*. Oxford: Clarendon Press.

—— 2005. *Capitalist Diversity and Change: Recombinant Governance and Institutional Entrepreneurs*. Oxford: Oxford University Press.

Culpepper, Pepper D. 2005. 'Institutional Change in Contemporary Capitalism.' *World Politics* 57 (2): 173–99.

Dahrendorf, Ralf. 1968. *Essays in the Theory of Society*. Palo Alto, CA: Stanford Univeristy Press.

de Dios, Emmanuel S. and Paul D. Hutchcroft. 2003. 'Political Economy.' In Arsenio M. Balisacan and Hal Hill, eds. *The Philippine Economy: Development, Policies, and Challenges*. New York: Oxford University Press, 45–73.

Deeg, Richard. 2009. 'The Rise of Internal Capitalist Diversity?' *Economy and Society* 38 (4): 552–79.

—— Gregory Jackson. 2007. 'Towards a More Dynamic Theory of Capitalist Variety.' *Socio-Economic Review* 5 (2): 149–79.

Demirgüç-Kunt, Asli and Harry Huizinga. 1999. 'Determinants of Commercial Bank Interest Margins and Profitability: Some International Evidence.' *World Bank Economic Review* 113 (2): 379–408.

Deyo, F. C. 1987. *The Political Economy of the New Asian Industrialisation*. Ithaca: Cornell University Press.

—— 1989. *Beneath the Miracle*. Berkeley: University of California Press.

—— 2012. *Reforming Asian Labor Systems: Reregulation and Social Accommodation*. Ithaca: Cornell University Press.

Dickson, Bruce. 2003. *Red Capitalists in China: The Party, Private Entrepreneurs, and Prospects for Political Change*. Cambridge: Cambridge University Press.

Ding, D. Z., K. Goodall and M. Warner. 2002. 'The Impact of Economic Reform on the Role of Trade Unions in Chinese Enterprises.' *International Journal of Human Resource Management* 13 (3): 431–49.

Ding, Xueliang. 2000. 'The Illicit Asset Stripping of China's State Firms.' *China Journal* 43: 1–28.

Dittmer, Lowell. 1990. 'Patterns of Elite Strife and Succession in Chinese Politics.' *The China Quarterly* 123: 405–30.

Dodgson, Mark. 2009. 'Asia's National Innovation Systems: Institutional Adaptability and Rigidity in the Face of Global Innovation Challenges.' *Asia Pacific Journal of Management* 26: 589–609.

Doner, Richard F. 1992. 'Limits of State Strength.' *World Politics* 44 (3): 398–431.

Doner, Richard F. 2009. *The Politics of Uneven Development: Thailand's Economic Growth in Comparative Perspective*. Cambridge: Cambridge University Press.

—— Daniel Unger. 1993. 'The Politics of Finance in Thai Economic Development.' In Stephan Haggard, Chung H. Lee and Sylvia Maxfield, eds. *The Politics of Finance in Developing Countries*. Ithaca: Cornell University Press, 93–122.

Dore, R. 1973. *British Factory: Japanese Factory: The Origin of National Diversity in Industrial Relations*. Berkeley: University of California Press.

—— 2000. *Stock Market Capitalism: Welfare Capitalism: Japan and Germany versus the Anglo-Saxons*. Oxford: Oxford University Press.

Dyer, Geoff. 2008. 'Beijing Offers Just Quarter of Stimulus Funds.' *Financial Times*, 14 November.

Eastern Centre for Legal Culture, ed. 2008. *The Dispatching of Services*. Shanghai: Renmin Publishing House. (In Chinese.)

Economic News (Taipei). 2010. 'Legislature Enacts Statute for Industrial Innovation.' 19 April.

Economist. 2010. 'The Global Revival of Industrial Policy.' 5 August.

—— 2011. 'Huawei: The Long March of the Invisible Mr Ren.' 2 June.

Ehrhardt, George. 2009. 'Administrative Reform in East Asia.' *Asian Survey* 49 (July/August): 625–46.

Elder, Mark. 2003. 'METI and Industrial Policy in Japan.' In Ulrike Schaede and William Grimes, eds. *Japan's Managed Globalization: Adapting to the Twenty-first Century*. Armonk, NY: M.E. Sharpe.

Ernst, Dieter and Barry Naughton. 2007. 'China's Emerging Industrial Economy: Insights from the IT Industry.' In Christopher A. McNally, ed. *China's Emergent Political Economy*. London: Routledge, 39–59.

Esping-Andersen, Gøsta. 1990. *The Three Worlds of Welfare Capitalism*. Cambridge: Polity.

Estrin, Saul and Martha Prevezer. 2011. 'The Role of Informal Institutions in Corporate Governance.' *Asia Pacific Journal of Management* 28 (1): 41–67.

Evans, P. 1995. *Embedded Autonomy: States and Industrial Transformation*. Princeton: Princeton University Press.

—— S. Staveteig. 2009. 'The Changing Structure of Employment in Contemporary China.' In D. Davis and F. Wang, eds. *Creating Wealth and Poverty in Postsocialist China*. Stanford: Stanford University Press, 69–84.

EVCA. 2007. *European Private Equity and Venture Capital Association Yearbook*. Brussels: EVCA.

Fan, Gang. 2000. '论体制转轨的动态过程 Lun Tizhi Zhuangui de Dongtai Guocheng' (On Dynamic Process of Institutional Transition). *Jingji Yanjiu* (Economic Review) January, 11–21.

Fan, J. P. H., T. J. Wong and T. Zhang. 2005. 'The Emergence of Corporate Pyramids in China.' *CEI Working Paper Series* 2006-3.

Farh, Jiing-Lih, Bor-Shiuan Cheng, Li-Fang Chou and Xiao-Ping Chu. 2006. 'Authority and Benevolence: Employees' Responses to Paternalistic Leadership in China.' In Anne S. Tsui, Yanjie Bian and Leonard Cheng, eds. *China's Domestic Private Firms*. New York: M.E. Sharpe, 230–60.

Farrell, D., S. Lund, J. Rosenfeld, F. Morin, N. Gupta and E. Greenberg. 2006. *Putting China's Capital to Work: The Value of Financial System Reform*. New York: McKinsey, May.

Feldmann, Magnus. 2007. 'The Origins of Varieties of Capitalism: Lessons from Post-Socialist Transition in Estonia and Slovenia.' In Hancké, Rhodes and Thatcher (2007a), 328–50.

Fields, Karl. 1995. *Enterprise and the State in Korea and Taiwan*. Ithaca: Cornell University Press.

—— 1997. 'Strong States and Business Organization in Korea and Taiwan.' In Ben Schneider and Sylvia Maxfield, eds. *The Elusive Embrace: Business-State Collaboration in Developing Countries*. Ithaca: Cornell University Press.

Financial Supervisory Commission (FSC). Various issues. *Bank Management Statistics*. Seoul: FSC.

References

Foot, Rosemary and Andrew Walter. 2011. *China, the United States, and Global Order.* New York: Cambridge University Press.

Francis, Bill, Iftekhar Hasan and Xian Sun. 2009. 'Political Connections and the Process of Going Public: Evidence from China.' *Journal of International Money and Finance* 28 (4): 696–719.

Frenkel, Stephen and David Peetz. 1998. 'Globalisation and Industrial Relations in East Asia.' *Industrial Relations* 37 (3): 282–310.

—— Sarosh Kuruvilla. 2002. 'Logics of Action, Globalisation, and Changing Employment Relations in China, India, Malaysia, and the Philippines.' *Industrial and Labour Relations Review* 55 (3): 387–412.

Friedman, E. 2009. 'External Pressure and Local Mobilization: Transnational Activism and the Emergence of the Chinese Labor Movement.' *Mobilization: An International Journal* 14 (2): 199–218.

Fruin, W. Mark, ed. 1999. *Networks, Markets and the Pacific Rim.* Oxford: Oxford University Press.

Gabriele, Alberto. 2009. 'The Role of the State in China's Industrial Development: A Reassessment.' *MPRA Paper* No. 1455.

Gaelle Pierre and Stefano Scarpetta. 2004. 'How Labor Market Policy Can Combine Workers' Protection and Job Creation.' Background Paper, partially reproduced in The World Bank, *World Development Report* 2005, 145 and 147.

Gallagher, M. 2004. 'Time is Money, Efficiency is Life: The Transformation of Labor Relations in China.' *Studies in Comparative International Development* 39 (2): 11–44.

—— 2005. *Contagious Capitalism: Globalization and the Politics of Labor in China.* Princeton: Princeton University Press.

Gamble, Andrew, Steve Ludlam, Andrew Taylor and Stephen Wood, eds. *Labour, the State Social Movements and the Challenge of Neo-Liberal Globalisation.* Manchester: Manchester University Press.

Gao, B. 2001. *Japan's Economic Dilemma: The Institutional Origins of Prosperity and Stagnation.* Cambridge: Cambridge University Press.

—— 2002. *Economic Ideology and Japanese Industrial Policy: Developmentalism from 1931 to 1965.* Cambridge: Cambridge University Press.

Garnaut, Ross, Ligang Song and Yang Yao. 2006. 'Impact and Significance of State-Owned Enterprise Restructuring.' *The China Journal* 55: 35–63.

Gerschenkron, Alexander. 1962. *Economic Backwardness in Historical Perspective.* New York: Praeger.

Ghosh, Swati R. 2006. *East Asian Finance.* New York: World Bank.

Giles, John, John Park and Fang Cai. 2003. 'How has Economic Restructuring Affected China's Urban Workers?' http://www.msu.edu/~gilesj/jilesparkcai.pdf

Gold, Thomas B. 2010. 'Eroding Landslide.' *Asian Survey* 50: 65–75.

Gomez, E. T. 1999. *Chinese Business in Malaysia: Accumulation, Ascendance, Accommodation.* Honolulu: University of Hawai'i Press.

—— 2002a. 'Political Business in Malaysia: Party Factionalism, Corporate Development and Economic Crisis.' In Edmund Terence Gomez, ed. *Political Business in East Asia.* London: Routledge, 82–114.

—— 2002b. *Political Business in East Asia.* London: Routledge.

—— 2004. 'Paradoxes of Governance: Ownership and Control of Corporate Malaysia.' In Ferdinand A. Gul and Judy S. L. Tsui, eds. *The Governance of East Asian Corporations: Post Asian Financial Crisis*. Basingstoke: Palgrave Macmillan.

—— 2009. 'The Rise and Fall of Capital: Corporate Malaysia in Historical Perspective.' *Journal of Contemporary Asia* 39 (3): 345–81.

—— K. S. Jomo. 1997. *Malaysia's Political Economy: Politics, Patronage, and Profits*. New York: Cambridge University Press.

—————— 1999. *Malaysia's Political Economy: Politics, Patronage and Profits*. Cambridge: Cambridge University Press.

Gompers, Paul and Josh Lerner. 1999. *The Venture Capital Cycle*. Cambridge, MA: MIT Press.

Gough, Ian. 2004. 'East Asia: The Limits of Productivist Regimes.' In Ian Gough and Geof Wood, eds. *Insecurity and Welfare Regimes in Asia, Africa and Latin America*. Cambridge: Cambridge University Press, 169–201.

Gourevitch, Peter A. and James Shinn. 2005. *Political Power and Corporate Control*. Princeton: Princeton University Press.

Graham, Edward M. 2003. *Reforming Korea's Industrial Conglomerates*. Washington, DC: Institute for International Economics.

Green, S. 2003. 'China's Stock Market: Eight Myths and Some Reasons to be Optimistic.' *The Royal Institute of International Affairs*. Cambridge: Cambridge University Press.

—— 2004. *The Development of China's Stock Market, 1984–2002: Equity Politics and Market Institutions*. London: RoutledgeCurzon.

Greenwood, Royston and C. R. Hinings. 1996. 'Understanding Radical Organizational Change: Bringing Together the Old and the New Institutionalism.' *Academy of Management Review* 21 (4): 1022.

Guo, Sujian. 1998. 'Enigma of All Enigmas: Capitalist Takeover? Assessment of the Post-Mao Economic Transformation.' *Journal of Chinese Political Science* 4 (1): 33–72.

Guthrie, Doug and Junmin Wang. 2006. 'Business Organisations in China.' In Henry Wai-chung Yeung, ed. *Handbook of Research on Asian Business*. Cheltenham: Edward Elgar, 99–121.

Gwartney, James, Joshua Hall and Robert Lawson. 2010. *The Economic Freedom of the World: 2010 Annual Report*. Vancouver: Fraser Institute.

Ha, Yong-Chool and Wang Hwi Lee. 2007. 'The Politics of Economic Reform in South Korea: Crony Capitalism after Ten Years.' *Asian Survey* 47 (6): 894–914.

Habir, Ahmad D. and Krishnan Rajendran. 2008. 'The Changing Face of Human Resource Management in Indonesia.' In Chris Rowley and Saaidah Abdul-Rahman, eds. *The Changing Face of Management in South East Asia*. London: Routledge, 30–58.

Haggard, Stephan. 1994. 'Business, Politics and Policy in Northeast and Southeast Asia.' In Andrew MacIntyre, ed. *Business and Government in Industrialising Asia*. St Leonards: Allen & Unwin, 268–301.

—— 2000. *The Political Economy of the Asian Financial Crisis*. Washington, DC: Institute for International Economics.

—— 2004. 'Institutions and Growth in East Asia.' *Studies in Comparative International Development* 38 (4): 53–81.

—— Robert R. Kaufman. 2008. *Development, Democracy and Welfare States*. Princeton: Princeton University Press.

—— Chung H. Lee, eds. 1995. *Financial Systems and Economic Policy in Developing Countries*. Ithaca: Cornell University Press.

———— Sylvia Maxfield, eds. 1993. *The Politics of Finance in Developing Countries*. Ithaca: Cornell University Press.

Hahm, Joon-Ho. 2003. 'The Government, the Chaebol and Financial Institutions before the Economic Crisis.' In Stephan Haggard, Wonhyuk Lim and Euysung Kim, eds. *Economic Crisis and Corporate Restructuring in Korea*. Cambridge: Cambridge University Press, 79–101.

—— 2007. 'Ten Years after the Crisis: Financial System Transition in Korea.' Paper presented to the Conference on Ten Years after the Korean Crisis, Seoul, 19–21 September.

Hahn, Donghoon and Keun Lee. 2006. 'Chinese Business Groups.' In Sea-Jin Chang, ed. *Business Groups in East Asia*. Oxford: Oxford University Press, 207–31.

Hall, Peter A. 1994. 'Keynes in Political Science.' *History of Political Economy* 26 (1): 137–53.

—— 2010. 'Historical Institutionalism in Rationalist and Sociological Perspectives.' In Mahoney and Thelen (2010), 204–23.

—— David Soskice., eds. 2001. *Varieties of Capitalism: The Institutional Foundations of Comparative Advantage*. Oxford: Oxford University Press.

———— 2001. 'An Introduction to Varieties of Capitalism.' In Peter A. Hall and David Soskice, eds. *Varieties of Capitalism*. Oxford: Oxford University Press, 1–70.

—— Daniel W. Gingerich. 2009. 'Varieties of Capitalism and Institutional Complementarities in the Political Economy.' *British Journal of Political Science* 39 (3): 449–82.

Hall, Michael G. 2006. 'Coalition Formation and Models of Capitalism.' *Business and Politics* 8 (3): 1–37.

Halper, Stefan. 2010. *The Beijing Consensus: How China's Authoritarian Model will Dominate the Twenty-First Century*. New York: Basic Books.

Hamilton-Hart, Natasha. 2002. *Asian States, Asian Bankers: Central Banking in Southeast Asia*. Ithaca: Cornell University Press.

Hamilton-Hart, Natasha. 2008. 'Banking Systems a Decade After the Crisis.' In Andrew J. MacIntyre, T. J. Pempel and John Ravenhill, eds. *Crisis as Catalyst: Asia's Dynamic Political Economy*. Ithaca: Cornell University Press, 45–69.

Hamrin, Carol. 1984. 'Competing Policy Packages in Post-Mao China.' *Asian Survey* March, 487–518.

—— 1990. *China and the Challenge of the Future*. Boulder, CO: Westview Press.

Han, Deqiang. 2000. 碰撞：全球化陷阱与中国现实选择 *Pengzhuang: Quanqiuhua Xianjing yu Zhongguo Xianshí Xuanze* (Collision: The Globalisation Trap and China's Real Choice). Beijing: Economic Management Press.

Hanani, Alberto D. 2006. 'Indonesian Business Groups.' In Sea-Jin Chang, ed. *Business Groups in East Asia*. Oxford: Oxford University Press, 179–206.

Hancké, Bob, Martin Rhodes and Mark Thatcher, eds. 2007a. *Beyond Varieties of Capitalism: Conflict, Contradictions, and Complementarities in the European Economy*. Oxford: Oxford University Press.

———— 2007b. 'Introduction.' In Hancké, Rhodes and Thatcher (2007a), 3–38.

Haque, Irfan ul. 2007. 'Rethinking Industrial Policy.' *United Nations Conference on Trade and Development Discussion Papers* No. 183.

Harvey, David. 2005. *A Brief History of Neoliberalism*. Oxford: Oxford University Press.

Hattori, M., H. S. Shin and W. Takahashi. 2009. 'A Financial System Perspective on Japan's Experience in the Late 1980s.' *IMES Discussion Paper* No. 2009-E-19, Institute for Monetary and Economic Studies, Bank of Japan.

Hay, Colin. 2005. 'Two can Play at that Game ... or can They?' In David Coates, ed. *Varieties of Capitalism, Varieties of Approaches*. London: Palgrave Macmillan, 106–21.

Hayami, Y. and M. Aoki. 1998. *The Institutional Foundations of East Asian Economic Development*. London: Macmillan.

Hayashi, F. and E. C. Prescott. 2002. 'The 1990s in Japan: A Lost Decade.' *Review of Economic Dynamics* 5 (1): 206–35.

Heilmann, Sebastian. 2009. 'Maximum Tinkering under Uncertainty: Unorthodox Lessons from China.' *Modern China* 35 (4): 450–62.

Hellmann, T., K. Murdock and J. Stiglitz. 1997. 'Financial Restraint: Toward a New Paradigm.' In Aoki, Kim, and Okuno-Fujiwara (1997), 163–207.

Helmke, Gretchen and Steven Levitsky. 2004. 'Informal Institutions and Comparative Politics: A Research Agenda.' *Perspectives on Politics* 2 (4): 725–40.

Henderson, Jeff. 2011. *The East Asian Transformation*. London: Routledge.

Hernandez, Zenaida. 2004. 'Industrial Policy in East Asia: In Search for Lessons.' Paper prepared for *World Development Report 2005: A Better Investment Climate for Everyone*. Washington, DC: World Bank.

Heston, Alan, Robert Summers and Bettina Aten. 2009. Penn World Tables, Version 6.3. Philadelphia: Center for International Comparisons of Production, Income and Prices, University of Pennsylvania.

Hewison, Kevin. 2005. 'Neo-liberalism and Domestic Capital: The Political Outcomes of the Economic Crisis in Thailand.' *Journal of Development Studies* 41 (2): 310–30.

Hitt, Michael A., Ho-Uk Lee and Emre Yucel. 2002. 'The Importance of Social Capital to the Management of Multinational Enterprises.' *Asia Pacific Journal of Management* 19 (4): 353–72.

Ho, Khai Leong, ed. 2005. *Reforming Corporate Governance in Southeast Asia*. Singapore: Institute of Southeast Asian Studies.

Hogan, Judith R. and Yuichi Abiko. 1996. 'Financing Capital Market Intermediaries in Korea.' In Hal S. Scott and Philip A. Wellons, eds. *Financing Capital Market Intermediaries in East and Southeast Asia*. The Hague: Kluwer, 123–57.

Holliday, Ian. 2000. 'Productivist Welfare Capitalism.' *Political Studies* 48 (4): 706–23.

Holliday, Ian. 2005. 'East Asian Social Policy in the Wake of the Financial Crisis.' *Policy and Politics* 33 (1): 145–62.

—— P. Wilding, eds. 2003a. *Welfare Capitalism in East Asia: Social Policy in the Tiger Economies*. Houndmills: Palgrave Macmillan.

——— 2003b. 'Welfare Capitalism in the Tiger Economies of East and Southeast Asia.' In Holliday and Wilding (2003), 1–17.

Hollingsworth, Rogers and Robert Boyer, eds. 1997. *Contemporary Capitalism: The Embeddedness of Institutions*. Cambridge: Cambridge University Press.

Holmstrom, B. and P. Milgrom. 1991. 'Multitask Principal-Agent Analyses: Incentive Contract, Asset Ownership, and Job Design.' *Journal of Law, Economics and Organization* 7 (special issue): 24–52.

Hölzl, Werner. 2006. 'Convergence of Financial Systems.' *Journal of Institutional Economics* 2 (1): 67–90.

Höpner, Martin. 2007. 'Coordination and Organization: The Two Dimensions of Non-liberal Capitalism.' *MPIfG Working Paper* 07/12.

Hort, Sven E. O. and Stein Kuhnle. 2000. 'The Coming of East and Southeast Asian Welfare States.' *Journal of European Social Policy* 10 (2): 162–84.

Hoshi, T. 1995. 'Cleaning up the Balance Sheet: Japanese Experience in the Post War Reconstruction Period.' In Aoki and Kim (1995), 303–59.

—— A. Kashyap. 1999. 'The Japanese Banking Crisis: Where did it Come from and How will it End?' *NBER Working Paper* No. 7250.

———— D. Sharfstein. 1993. 'The Role of Banks in Reducing Costs of Financial Distress in Japan.' *Journal of Financial Economics* 27: 67–88.

Howell, Chris. 2003. 'Varieties of Capitalism and then there was One?' *Comparative Politics* 36 (1): 103–24.

Howell, J. 2003. 'Trade Unionism in China: Sinking or Swimming?' *Journal of Communist Studies and Transition Politics* 19 (1): 102–22.

—— 2008. 'All-China Federation of Trade Unions beyond Reform? The Slow March of Direct Elections.' *China Quarterly* 196: 845–63.

Hsing, You-tien. 2010. *The Great Urban Transformation: Politics of Land and Property in China*. Oxford: Oxford University Press.

Huang, Yasheng. 2008. 'Zhejiang Province: A Free-Market Success Story.' *Business Week*, 20 October.

—— 2011. 'Rethinking the Beijing Consensus.' *Asia Policy* 11: 1–26.

Huber, Evelyne, ed. 2003. *Models of Capitalism*. Pennsylvania: Pennsylvania State University Press.

Huchet, Jean-Francois and Xavier Richet. 2002. 'Between Bureaucracy and Market: Chinese Industrial Groups in Search of New Forms of Corporate Governance.' *Post-Communist Economies* 14 (2): 169–201.

Hundt, David. 2009. *Korea's Developmental Alliance*. London: Routledge.

Hung, Mingyi, T. J. Wong and Tianyu Zhang. 2008. 'Political Relations and Overseas Stock Exchange Listing: Evidence from Chinese State Owned Enterprises.' https://www.bschool.nus.edu.sg/Departments/FinanceNAccounting/seminars/Papers/mingyi%20hung.pdf

Hurst, W. 2004. 'Understanding Contentious Collective Action by Chinese Laid-Off Workers: The Importance of Regional Political Economy.' *Studies in Comparative International Development* 39 (2): 94–120.

—— 2009. *The Chinese Worker after Socialism*. Cambridge: Cambridge University Press.

Hutchcroft, Paul D. 1993. 'Selective Squander: The Politics of Preferential Credit Allocation in the Philippines.' In Stephan Haggard, Chung H. Lee and Sylvia Maxfield, eds. *The Politics of Finance in Developing Countries*. Ithaca: Cornell University Press, 165–200.

—— 1998. *Booty Capitalism: The Politics of Banking in the Philippines*. Ithaca: Cornell University Press.

—— 1999. 'Neither Dynamo nor Domino: Reforms and Crises in the Philippine Political Economy.' In T. J. Pempel, ed. *The Politics of the Asian Economic Crisis*. Ithaca: Cornell University Press, 163–83.

Hutchison, Jane. 2006. 'Poverty of Politics in the Philippines.' In Garry Rodan, Kevin Hewison and Richard Robison, eds. *The Political Economy of South-East Asia: Markets, Power, and Contestation.* New York: Oxford University Press, 39–73.

Ikeda, Ken'ichi and Tetsuro Kobayashi. 2007. 'The Influence of Social Capital on Political Participation in the Cultural Context of Asia.' *Working Paper* No. 37. Taipei: Asian Barometer Project Office, National Taiwan University.

Isaac, Joe and Sari Sitalaksmi. 2008. 'Trade Unions in Indonesia.' In John Benson and Ying Zhu, eds. *Trade Unions in Asia.* London: Routledge, 236–55.

Islam, Iyanatul and Anis Chowdhury. 2000. *The Political Economy of East Asia.* Melbourne: Oxford University Press.

Jabko, Nicolas. 2006. *Playing the Market: A Political Strategy for Uniting Europe, 1985–2005.* Ithaca, NY: Cornell University Press.

Jackson, Gregory. 2005. 'Contested Boundaries: Ambiguity and Creativity in the Evolution of German Codetermination.' In Streeck and Thelen (2005).

—— 2007. 'Employment Adjustment and Distributional Conflict in Japanese Firms.' In Masahiko Aoki, Gregory Jackson and Hideaki Miyajima, eds. *Corporate Governance in Japan.* Oxford: Oxford University Press, 282–309.

—— 2009. 'The Japanese Firm and its Diversity.' *Economy and Society* 38 (4): 606–29.

—— Richard Deeg. 2008. 'From Comparing Capitalisms to the Politics of Institutional Change.' *Review of International Political Economy* 15 (4): 680–709.

—— Hideaki Miyajima. 2007. 'Introduction: The Diversity and Change of Corporate Governance in Japan.' In Masahiko Aoki, Gregory Jackson and Hideaki Miyajima, eds. *Corporate Governance in Japan.* Oxford: Oxford University Press, 1–50.

Jacobson, G. 2004. *The Politics of Congressional Elections.* New York: Pearson Longman.

Japan Institute of Labour Policy and Training (JILPT). 2010. *Japanese Working Life Profile.* Tokyo: JILPT.

Jayasuriya, Kanishka. 2006. *Statecraft, Welfare and the Politics of Inclusion.* Houndmills: Palgrave Macmillan.

Jiang, Yi and Mike W. Peng. 2011. 'Are Family Ownership and Control in Large Firms Good, Bad, or Irrelevant?' *Asia Pacific Journal of Management* 28 (1): 15–39.

Jin, Dal Yong. 2006. 'Political and Economic Processes in the Privatisation of the Korean Telecommunications Industry.' *Telecommunications Policy* 30 (1): 3–13.

Jing, Cai and Andrew Tylecote. 2005. 'A Healthy Hybrid: The Technological Dynamism of Minority-State-Owned Firms in China.' *Technology Analysis and Strategic Management* 17 (3): 257–77.

Johnson, C. A. 1982. *MITI and the Japanese Miracle: The Growth of Industrial Policy, 1925–1975.* Stanford, CA: Stanford University Press.

—— 1987. 'Political Institutions and Economic Performance: The Government-Business Relationship in Japan, South Korea, and Taiwan.' In Frederic Deyo, ed. *The Political Economy of the New Asian Industrialism.* Ithaca, NY: Cornell University Press.

—— 1998. 'Economic Crisis in East Asia.' *Cambridge Journal of Economics* 22 (4): 653–61.

Johnson, S., L. P. Rafael, F. Lopez-de-Silanes and A. Shleifer. 2000. 'Tunnelling.' *American Economic Review* 90 (2): 22–7.

Jomo K. S. 1997. 'A Specific Idiom of Chinese Capitalism in Southeast Asia: Sino-Malaysian Capital Accumulation in the Face of State Hostility.' In D. Chirot and

A. Reid, eds. *Essential Outsiders: Chinese and Jews in the Modern transformation of Southeast Asia and Central Europe*. Seattle: University of Washington Press, 237–57.

—— 2001. *Southeast Asia's Industrialisation*. London: Macmillan.

—— E. T. Gomez. 2000. 'The Malaysian Development Dilemma.' In Mushtaq H. Khan and K. S. Jomo, eds. *Rents, Rent-Seeking and Economic Development: Theory and Evidence in Asia*. Cambridge: Cambridge University Press, 274–303.

—— Patricia Todd. 1994. *Trade Unions and the State in Peninsular Malaysia*. Kuala Lumpur: Oxford University Press.

Jung, Ee-Hwan and Byung-you Cheon. 2006. 'Economic Crisis and Changes in Employment Relations in Japan and Korea.' *Asian Survey* 46 (3): 457–76.

Kalinowski, Thomas. 2008. 'Korea's Recovery since the 1997/98 Financial Crisis: The Last Stage of the Developmental State.' *New Political Economy* 13 (December): 447–62.

—— 2009. 'The Politics of Market Reforms: Korea's Path from Chaebol Republic to Market Democracy and Back.' *Contemporary Politics* 15 (3): 287–304.

Kang, Soon-Hie, Jaeho Keum, Dong-Heon Kim and Donggyun Shin. 2001. 'Korea: Labor Market Outcomes and Policy Responses after the Crisis.' In Gordon Betcherman and Rizwanul Islam, eds. *East Asian Labor Markets and the Economic Crisis*. Washington, DC: The World Bank, and Geneva: The International Labour Office, 97–139.

Kang, Y., L. Shi and E. Brown. 2008. 'Chinese Corporate Governance: History and Institutional Framework.' Los Angeles: Rand Corporation.

Katz, R. 1998. *Japan: The System that Soured*. New York: M.E. Sharpe.

Kenworthy, L. 2006. 'Institutional Coherence and Macroeconomic Performance.' *Socio-Economic Review* 4 (1): 69–91.

Khanna, T. and K. Palepu. 2000. 'Is Group Membership Profitable in Emerging Markets? An Analysis of Diversified Indian Business Groups.' *The Journal of Finance* 55 (2): 867–91.

Kienzle, Rene and Mark Shadur. 1997. 'Developments in Business Networks in East Asia.' *Management Decision* 35 (1): 23–32.

Kim, Dong-One, Johngseok Bae and Changwon Lee. 2000. 'Globalization and Labour Rights: The Case of Korea.' In Chris Rowley and John Benson, eds. *Globalization and Labour in the Asia Pacific Region*. London: Frank Cass.

Kim, E. Han and Woochan Kim. 2008. 'Changes in Korean Corporate Governance: A Response to Crisis.' *Journal of Applied Corporate Finance* 20 (1): 47–58.

Kim, Hee Min. 1995. 'The Formation of the Grand Conservative Coalition.' In Hee Min Kim and Woosang Kim, eds. *Rationality and Politics in the Korean Peninsula*. Osaka: International Society for Korean Studies.

Kim, Hong-Bum and Chung H. Lee. 2006. 'Financial Reform, Institutional Interdependence, and Supervisory Failure in Post-crisis Korea.' *Journal of East Asian Studies* 6 (3): 409–31.

Kim, Son Bae. 2008. 'Regional Production Networks and Reconfiguration of Regional Division of Labor among the Core Economic Regions of Northeast Asia.' *KIEP Working Paper* (August). Korea Institute for International Economic Policy.

Kim, Sungmin. 2004. 'Boom and Bust Cycles of the Korean Corporate Bond Market.' *Korea's Economy* 20: 20–32.

Kim, Yun Tae. 2005. 'DJnomics and the Transformation of the Developmental State.' *Journal of Contemporary Asia* 35: 471–84.

Kimura, Takumna, Yoshihide Sano, et al. 2004. 'Seizo Bunya ni okeru Ukeoi Kigyo no Jigyo Senryaku to Jinzai Kanri no Kadai' (Business Strategy and Human Resource Management for Onsite Sub-contracting Service in Manufacturing Industry). *Nihon Rodo Kyokai Zasshi* 46 (5): 16–30.

King, Lawrence P. 2007. 'Central European Capitalism in Comparative Perspective.' In Hancké, Rhodes and Thatcher (2007a), 307–27.

King, J. and Y.-M. Lin. 2007. 'The Decline of Township-and-Village Enterprises in China's Economic Transition.' *World Development* 35 (4): 569–84.

King, Desmond and Stewart Wood. 1999. 'The Political Economy of Neoliberalism: Britain and the United States in the 1980s.' In H. Kitschelt, P. Lange, G. Marks and J. Stephens, eds. *Continuity and Change in Contemporary Capitalism*. New York: Cambridge University Press, 371–97.

Koike, K. 1984. 'Skill Formation Systems in the U.S. and Japan: Comparative Study.' In Aoki (1984), 47–76.

Kondoh, Hisahiro. 2002. 'Policy Networks in South Korea and Taiwan During the Democratic Era.' *The Pacific Review* 15: 225–44.

Kong, Tat Yan. 2006. 'Globalisation and Labour Market Reform: Patterns of Response in Northeast Asia.' *British Journal of Political Science* 36 (2): 359–83.

Koo, Hagen. 2001. *Korean Workers: The Culture and Politics of Class Formation*. Ithaca: Cornell University Press.

Koo, Anthony Y. C. and K. C. Yeh. 1999. 'The Impact of Township, Village, and Private Enterprises' Growth on State Enterprises Reform.' In Orville Schell and David Shambaugh, eds. *The China Reader*. New York: Vintage Books, 321–35.

Korea Herald (*KH*). Various years. Seoul: *Koera Herald*.

Korea Times (*KT*). Various years. Seoul: *Koera Herald*.

Korean National Statistical Office (KNSO). 2005. *Yearbook of Labor Statistics*. Seoul: KNSO.

Kroeber, Arthur and Rosealea Yao. 2008. 'Large and in Charge.' *Financial Times*, 14 July.

Kudrna, Z. 2007. 'Banking Reform in China: Driven by International Standards and Chinese Specifics.' *Transformation, Integration and Globalization Economic Research Working Paper Series* 109.

Kung, James, Kai-xing and Yi-min Lin. 2007. 'The Decline of Township-and-Village Enterprises in China's Economic Transition.' *World Development* 35 (4): 569–84.

Kuo, Chengtian, Shangmao Chen and Zhonghao Huang. 2000. 'Money up for Grabs?' In Yun-han Chu and Zhonghe Bao, eds. *Democratic Transition and Economic Conflicts*. Taipei: Laureate Book, 75–111 (in Chinese).

Kuruvilla, Sarosh and Christopher L. Erickson. 2002. 'Change and Transformation in Asian Industrial Relations.' *Industrial Relations* 41 (2): 171–227.

—— Subesh Das, Hyunji Kwon and Soonwon Kwon. 2002. 'Trade Union Growth and Decline in Asia.' *British Journal of Industrial Relations* 40 (3): 431–61.

Kwon, Huck-ju. 2005a. 'An Overview of the Study: The Developmental Welfare State and Policy Reforms in East Asia.' In Huck-ju Kwon, ed. *Transforming the Developmental Welfare State in East Asia*. New York: Palgrave Macmillan, 1–23.

—— 2005b. 'Transforming the Developmental Welfare State in East Asia.' *Development and Change* 36 (3): 477–97.

References

—— 2009. 'The Reform of the Developmental Welfare State in East Asia.' *International Journal of Social Welfare* 18 (1): 12–21.

Laeven, Luc. 2002. 'Financial Constraints on Investments and Credit Policy in Korea.' *Journal of Asian Economics* 13 (4): 251–69.

Lamper, D. and M. Sullivan. 2008. 'Chinese Accounting Lagging but Improving.' *Forbes*, 20 November.

Lampton D. M. and K. Lieberthal, eds. 1992. *Bureaucracy, Politics, and Decision Making in Post-Mao China*. Berkeley, CA: University of California Press.

Lane, Christel and Geoffrey Wood. 2009. 'Capitalist Diversity and Diversity within Capitalism.' *Economy and Society* 38 (4): 531–51.

Lane, David and Martin Myant, eds. 2007. *Varieties of Capitalism in Post-Communist Countries*. London: Palgrave Macmillan.

Lardy, Nicholas R. 1998. *China's Unfinished Economic Revolution*. Washington, DC: Brookings Institution Press.

—— 2008. 'Financial Repression in China.' *Peterson Institute Policy Brief*, No. PB08-8, September.

Lau, Lawrence, Yingyi Qian and Gerard Roland. 2000. 'Reform without Losers: An Interpretation of China's Dual Track Approach to Transition.' *Journal of Political Economy* 108 (1): 120–63.

Lau, R. W. K. 2001. 'Socio-political Control in Urban China: Changes and Crisis.' *British Journal of Sociology* 52 (4): 605–20.

—— 2003. 'The Habitus and "Logic of Practice" of China's Trade Unionists.' *Issues & Studies* 39 (3): 75–103.

Lawler, John J. and Chokechai Suttawet. 2000. 'Labour Unions, Globalization, and Deregulation in Thailand.' In Chris Rowley and John Benson, eds. *Globalization and Labour in the Asia Pacific Region*. London: Frank Cass, 214–38.

Lazear, E. and S. Rosen. 1981. 'Rank-Order Tournaments as Optimum Labor Contract.' *The Journal of Political Economy* 89 (5): 841–64.

Lazonick, W. 1991. *Business Organization and the Myth of the Market Economy*. Cambridge: Cambridge University Press.

—— 2003. 'The Theory of the Market Economy and the Social Foundation of Innovative Enterprise.' *Economic and Industrial Democracy* 24 (1): 9–44.

Lee, C. K. 1998. *Gender and the South China Miracle*. Berkeley, CA: University of California Press, 1998.

—— 2000. 'The 'Revenge of History': Collective Memories and Labor Protests in North-Eastern China.' *Ethnography* 1 (2): 217–37.

—— 2002. 'From the Specter of Mao to the Spirit of the Law: Labor Insurgency in China.' *Theory and Society* 31: 189–228.

—— 2007. *Against the Law: Labour Protests in China's Rustbelt and Sunbelt*. Berkeley, CA: University of California Press.

—— 2010. 'Pathways of Labour Activism.' In Elizabeth Perry and Mark Selden, eds. *Chinese Society: Change, Conflict, and Resistance*. London: RoutledgeCurzon, 57–79.

Lee, Chung H., Keun Lee and Kangkook Lee. 2002. 'Chaebols, Financial Liberalisation and Economic Crisis.' *Asian Economic Journal* 16 (1): 17–35.

Lee, Pei-shan and Yun-han Chu. 2008. 'The new political economy after regime turn-over in Taiwan.' In Steven M. Goldstein and Julian Chang, eds. *Presidential Politics in Taiwan*. Norwalk: EastBridge, 143–70.

Leutert, H. G. and R. Sudhoff. 1999. 'Technology Capacity Building in the Malaysian Automotive Industry.' In K. S. Jomo, G. Felker and R. Rasiah, eds. *Industrial Technology Development in Malaysia: Industry and Firm Studies*. London: Routledge.

Levine, Ross. 1997. 'Financial Development and Economic Growth: Views and Agenda.' *Journal of Economic Literature* 35 (2): 688–726.

Levy, Jonah D., Mari Mirua and Gene Park. 2006. 'Existing Étatisme? New Directions in State Policy in France and Japan.' In Jonah D. Levy, ed. *The State after Statism*. Cambridge, MA: Harvard University Press, 93–137.

Li, H. 2005. 'fazhan yu yinyou: woguo laowu paiqian xianzhuang zhi wojian' (Development and Hidden Dangers: My Views on the Current Conditions for Chinese Dispatch Labor). *shengli youtian dangxiao xuebao* 18 (5): 46–9.

—— L-A. Zhou. 2005. 'Political Turnover and Economic Performance: The Incentive Role of Personnel Control in China.' *Journal of Public Economics* 89 (9–10): 1743–62.

Li, Hongbin and Scott Rozelle. 2003. 'Privatizing Rural China: Insider Privatization, Innovative Contracts and the Performance of Township Enterprises.' *The China Quarterly* 176: 981–1005.

—— Lingsheng Meng, Qian Wang and Li-An Zhou. 2008. 'Political Connections, Financing and Firm Performance: Evidence from Chinese Private Firms.' *Journal of Development Economics* 87 (2): 283–99.

Li, Linda. 2007. 'Moving Towards More Effective Public Service Delivery in Rural China?—Township public service unit reform in Hubei.' Paper presented at International Conference on the State Capacity of China in the 21st Century, Hong Kong, April.

Li, T. 2009. 'China's Nonperforming Loans: A $540 Billion Problem Unsolved.' In J. Barth, J. Tatom and G. Yago, eds. *China's Emerging Financial Markets: Challenges and Opportunities*. New York: Springer, 403–22.

Liao, Guomin and Wei Liu. 2005. 'Banking Institution, Bankruptcy Cost and Government Guarantee: An Analytical Framework for the Formation of NPLs at State-Owned Banks.' *Management World*, 3.

Lieberthal, K. and M. Oksenberg. 1988. *Policy Making in China: Leaders, Structures, and Processes*. Princeton, NJ: Princeton University Press.

Lim M. H. 1981. *Ownership and Control of the One Hundred Largest Corporations in Malaysia*. Kuala Lumpur: Oxford University Press.

Lim, Linda. 1996. 'Southeast Asian Business Systems.' In A. E. Safarian and Wendy Dobson, eds. *East Asian Capitalism: Diversity and Dynamism*. Toronto: University of Toronto Press, 91–117.

Lim, Wonhyuk. 2003. *Public Enterprise Reform and Privatisation in Korea*. Seoul: Korea Development Institute.

Lim, Young-il, Dae-sook Kim and Young-Lee Kim. 2003. 'South Korea.' In Stephen Frost, Omana George and Ed Shephard, eds. *Asia Pacific Labour Law Review: Workers Rights for the New Century*. Hong Kong. Asia Monitor Resource Centre, 313–26.

Lin, Chun. 2008a. 'Against Privatization in China: A Historical and Empirical Argument.' *Journal of Chinese Political Science* 13 (1): 1–27.

References

—— 2008b. 'China: Changing the Rules of the Game.' *Soundings* 39: 7–19.

Lincoln, Edward J. 2001. *Arthritic Japan: The Slow Pace of Economic Reform*. Washington, DC: Brookings Institution Press.

Little, Ian, Tibor Scitovsky and Maurice Scott. 1970. *Industry and Trade in some Developing Countries*. Oxford: Oxford University Press.

Liu, Alan. 1992. 'The Wenzhou Model of Development and China's Modernization.' *Asian Survey* 32 (8): 696–711.

Liu, Lawrence S. 1997. 'Law and Political Economy of Capital Market Regulation in the Republic of China on Taiwan.' *Law and Policy in International Business* 28 (3): 813–56.

—— 2008. 'The Politics of Corporate Governance in Taiwan.' In Hideki Kanda, Kon-Sik Kim and Curtis J. Milhaupt, eds. *Transforming Corporate Governance in East Asia*. London: Routledge, 255–77.

Liu, Q. 2006. 'Corporate Governance in China: Current Practices, Economic Effects and Institutional Determinants.' *CESifo Economic Studies* 52 (2): 415–53.

Liu, Y. 2009. 'cong tonggongtongchou kan paiqiangong laodong pingdeng wenti' (Looking at the Problem of Equality for Dispatch Labor From the Perspective of Equal Pay for Equal Work). *hunan xingzheng xueyuan xuebao* 2 (56): 49–51.

Liu, T., M. Zhong and J. Xing. 2005. 'Industrial Accidents: Challenges for China's Economic and Social Development.' *Safety Science* 43: 503–22.

London, Jonathan. 2008. 'Welfare Regimes in the Wake of State Socialism.' Paper presented at the Conference on East Asian Social Policy, Taipei, 3–4 November.

Longstaff, F. 1995. 'How Much can Marketability Affect Securities Values?' *The Journal of Finance* 50 (5): 1767–74.

Luong, P. J. and E. Weinthal. 1999. 'The NGO Paradox: Democratic Goals and Non-democratic Outcomes in Kazakhstan.' *Europe-Asia Studies* 51 (7): 1267–84.

MacIntyre, Andrew. 1994. 'Business, Government and Development: Northeast and Southeast Asian Comparisons.' In Andrew MacIntyre, ed. *Business and Government in Industrialising Asia*. Sydney: Allen and Unwin, 1–28.

—— ed. 1994. *Business and Government in Industrialising Asia*. St Leonards: Allen & Unwin.

—— T. J. Pempel and John Ravenhill. 2008. 'Conclusion: The Political Economy of East Asia: Directions for the Next Decade.' In Andrew MacIntyre, T. J. Pempel and John Ravenhill, eds. *Crisis as Catalyst*. Ithaca: Cornell University Press, 271–92.

Mahathir, Mohamad. 2002. 'The New Malay Dilemma.' Speech delivered at the Harvard Club of Malaysia, 27 July.

Mahoney, James and Kathleen Thelen, eds. 2010. *Explaining Institutional Change: Ambiguity, Agency, and Power*. New York: Cambridge University Press.

Malaysia. 1996. *Seventh Malaysia Plan, 1996–2000*. Kuala Lumpur: Government Printers.

—— 2006. *Ninth Malaysia Plan, 2006–2010*. Kuala Lumpur: Government Printers.

—— 2008. *Mid-Term Review of the Ninth Malaysia Plan, 2006–2010*. Kuala Lumpur: Government Printers.

—— 2010a. *Government Transformation Plan*. Kuala Lumpur: Government Printers.

—— 2010b. *New Economic Model for Malaysia, Part I*. Putrajaya: National Economic Advisory Council.

—— 2010c. *Tenth Malaysia Plan, 2011–2015*. Kuala Lumpur: Percetakan Nasional Malaysia Berhad.

Marx, Karl. 1867. ' "Preface" to *Capital*.' In Robert Tucker, ed. 1978. *The Marx-Engels Reader*. New York: WW Norton.

Mattlin, Mikael. 2009. 'Chinese Strategic State-Owned Enterprises and Ownership Control.' *Brussels Institute of Contemporary China Studies Asia Paper*, 4 (6).

Mayhew, D. 1974. *Congress: The Electoral Connection*. New Haven: Yale University Press.

McCubbins, M. and T. Sullivan, eds. 1987. *Congress: Structure and Policy*. New York: Cambridge University Press.

McGuinness, P. and K. Keasey. 2009. 'The Listing of Chinese State-Owned Banks and their Path to Banking and Ownership Reform.' *The China Quarterly* 201: 125–55.

McGuire, James W. 1999. 'Labour Union Strength and Human Development in East Asia and Latin America.' *Studies in Comparative International Development* 34 (1): 3–34.

McGuire, Jean and Sandra Dow. 2009. 'Japanese Keiretsu: Past, Present and Future.' *Asia Pacific Journal of Management* 26 (3): 333–51.

McKay, Steven. 2006. *Satanic Mills or Silicon Islands: The Politics of High-Tech Production in the Philippines*. Ithaca: ILR Press/Cornell University Press.

McNally, Christopher A. 2007. 'China's Capitalist Transition.' In Lars Mjøset and Tommy H. Clausen, eds. *Capitalisms Compared*. Amsterdam: Elsevier, 177–203.

McVey, Ruth, ed. 1992. *Southeast Asian Capitalists*. Ithaca: Cornell University Southeast Asian Programme.

Mertha, Andrew. 2010. *China's Water Warriors: Citizen Action and Policy Change*. Ithaca, NY: Cornell University Press.

Metcalf, D. and J. Li. 2005. 'Chinese Unions: Nugatory or Transforming?—An Alice Analysis.' Center for Economic Performance, London School of Economics and Political Science.

METI. 2008. *Venture Kigyo no Soshutsu-Seicho ni Kansuru Kenkyu-kai Salsya hokoku syo 30/04/2008*. Tokyo: METI.

MHLW. Various years. *Chinage no Jittai* (Report on Wage Increases). Tokyo: Okurasho Insatsukyoku.

—— 2009a. *Heisei 21 nen minkan shuyou kigyo shunki chinage claketsu jyoukyou ni tusite 10/09/2009*. Tokyo: MHLW.

—— 2009b. *Heisei 20 nen chingin hikiage tou no Jittai ni Kansuru chousa 12/2009*. Tokyo: MHLW'.

Mikuni, Akio and Murphy, R. Taggart. 2002. *Japan's Policy Trap: Dollars, Deflation, and the Crisis of Japanese Finance*. Washington, DC: Brookings Institution.

Ministry of Finance. 2011. 'guanyu 2010 zhongyang he difang yusuan zhixing qing-kuang yu 2011 nian zhongyang he difang yusuan can'an de baogao' (Report on the Implementation of the 2010 Central and Local Budget and the Draft Budget for 2011). Report to the National People's Congress, 5 March, published 17 March. http://www.mof.gov.cn/zhengwuxinxi/caizhengxinwen/201103/t20110317_505087.html

Minns, John. 2001. 'Of Miracles and Models: The Rise and Decline of the Developmental State in South Korea.' *Third World Quarterly* 22: 1025–43.

Miura, Mari. 2003. *The New Politics of Labour: Shifting Veto Points and Representing the Unorganized*. Tokyo: Mimeo, Institute of Social Science, University of Tokyo.

Miyajima, Hideaki and Fumiaki Kuroki. 2007. 'The Unwinding of Cross-shareholding in Japan.' In Masahiko Aoki, Gregory Jackson and Hideaki Miyajima, eds. *Corporate Governance in Japan*. Oxford: Oxford University Press, 79–123.

Mo, Jongryn and Daniel I. Okimoto, eds. 2006. *From Crisis to Opportunity*. Stanford: Walter H. Shorenstein Asia-Pacific Research Centre.

Momoko K. 2007. 'The Rise of Taiwanese Family-owned Business Groups in the Telecommunications Industry.' In A. E. Fernandez Jilberto and B. Hogenboom, eds. *Big Business and Economic Development: Conglomerates and Economic Groups in Developing Countries and Transition Economies under Globalisation*. London: Routledge, 86–108.

Montinola, G., Y. Qian and B. Weinhast. 1995. 'Federalism, Chinese Style: The Political Basis for Economic Success in China.' *World Politics* 48 (1): 50–81.

Moran, Michael. 1990. 'Financial Markets.' In James Simmie and Roger King, eds. *The State in Action*. London: Pinter, 43–56.

Morck, R. and M. Nakamura. 2003. 'Been There, Done That: The History of Corporate Ownership in Japan.' *European Institute of Corporate Governance Finance Working Paper* No. 20/2003.

Morgan, G. et al., eds. 2010. *The Oxford Handbook of Comparative Institutional Analysis*. Oxford: Oxford University Press.

Muscat, Robert J. 1995. 'Thailand.' In Stephan Haggard and Chung H. Lee, eds. *Financial Systems and Economic Policy in Developing Countries*. Ithaca: Cornell University Press, 113–39.

Mykhnenko, Vlad. 2007. 'Strengths and Weaknesses of 'Weak' Coordination: Economic Institutions, Revealed Comparative Advantages, and Socio-Economic Performance of Mixed Market Economies in Poland and Ukraine.' In Hancké, Rhodes and Thatcher (2007a), 351–78.

Myrdal, Gunnar. 1968. *Asian Drama*. London: Penguin Press.

Nakamura, Keisuke. 2009. 'The Process of Formulating Policy in Labor Matters: Derailment or Transformation?' *Japan Labor Review* 6 (2): 76–90.

Nakamura, Masao. 2011. 'Adoption and Policy Implications of Japan's New Corporate Governance Practices after the Reform.' *Asia Pacific Journal of Management* 28 (1): 187–213.

NAO. 2011. 'quanguo difang zhengfu xing shenji jieguo' (The Result of the Audit of the Nature of Local Government Debt). *PRC National Audit Office Audit Report Announcement*, No. 2011/35. http://www.audit.gov.cn/n1992130/n1992150/n1992500/2752208.html

National Bureau of Statistics of China (NBSC). 1996. *China Labour Statistical Yearbook*. Beijing: NBSC.

Naughton, Barry. 1985. 'False Starts and Second Wind: Financial Reforms in China's Industrial System.' In E. Perry and C. Wong, eds. *The Political Economy of Reform in Post-Mao China*. Cambridge: Harvard University Press, 223–52.

—— 2003. 'The Emergence of Wen Jiabao.' *China Leadership Monitor*, No. 6.

—— 2005. 'SASAC Rising.' *China Leadership Monitor*, No. 15.

Naughton, Barry. 2006. 'Top-Down Control: SASAC and the Persistence of State Ownership in China.' http://www.nottingham.ac.uk/gep/documents/conferences/2006/june2006conf/naughton-june2006.pdf

—— 2007a. 'Strengthening the Center, and Premier Wen Jiabao.' *China Leadership Monitor*, No. 21.

—— 2007b. *The Chinese Economy: Transitions and Growth*. Cambridge, MA: MIT Press.

—— 2009a. 'Market Economy, Hierarchy and Single Party Rule.' In J. Kornai and Y. Qian, eds. *Market and Socialism Reconsidered (with Particular Reference to China and Vietnam)*. London: Macmillan, for the International Economic Association, 135–61.

—— 2009b. 'China: Economic Transformation Before and After 1989.' http://www.democ.uci.edu/research/conferences/documents/naughton.pdf

—— 2010. 'The Turning Point in Housing.' *China Leadership Monitor*, No. 33.

Nee, Victor and Sonja Opper. 2010. 'Endogenous Institutional Change and Dynamic Capitalism.' *Centre for the Study of Economy and Society Working Paper* No. 54, Cornell University.

Nezu, Risabura. 2007. 'Industrial Policy in Japan.' *Journal of Industry, Competition and Trade* 7: 229–43.

Ngok, K. 2008. 'The Changes of Chinese Labor Policy and Labor Legislation in the Context of Market Transition.' *International Labor and Working-Class History* 73: 45–64.

Noguchi, Y. 1995. *1940-nen taisei (The 1940 System)*. Tokyo: Toyo Keizai Shimposha.

—— 1998. 'The 1940 System Japan under the Wartime Economy.' *American Economic Review* 88: 404–16.

Nölke, Andreas and Arjan Vliegenthart. 2009. 'Enlarging the Varieties of Capitalism.' *World Politics* 61 (4): 670–702.

Nowland, John. 2008. 'Are East Asian Companies Benefiting from Western Board Practices?' *Journal of Business Ethics* 79 (2): 133–50.

NVCA. Various years. *National Venture Capital Association Yearbook*. Arlington, VA: NVCA.

OANDA. 2010. *OANDA Historical Exchange Rates*. http://www.oanda.com/currency/historical-rates/

OECD (Organisation for Economic Co-operation and Development). 2011. *A Framework for Growth and Social Coherence in Korea*. Paris: OECD.

Ofreneo, Rene E. 2008. 'The Changing face of Human Resource Management in the Philippines.' In Chris Rowley and Saaidah Abdul-Rahman, eds. *The Changing Face of Management in South East Asia*. London: Routledge, 97–128.

Ogura, Kazuya. 2005. 'International Comparison of Atypical Employment: Differing Concepts and Realities in Industrialized Countries.' *Japan Labor Review* 2 (2): 5–29.

Oi, Jean. 2005. 'Patterns of Corporate Restructuring in China: Political Constraints on Privatization.' *The China Journal* 53: 115–36.

Okazaki, T. and M. Okuno-Fujiwara. 1998. 'Evolution of Economic System: The Case of Japan.' In Hayami and Aoki (1998), 482–521.

———— eds. 1999. *Japanese Economic System and Its Historical Origins*. New York: Oxford University Press.

Okazaki, K., M. Hattori and W. Takahashi. 2011. 'The Challenges Confronting the Banking System Reform in China: An Analysis in Light of Japan's Experience of Financial Liberalization.' *IMES Discussion Paper* No. 2011-E-6. Institute for Monetary and Economic Studies, Bank of Japan.

References

Oliver, Christine. 1992. 'The Antecedents of Deinstitutionalization.' *Organization Studies* 13 (4): 563–88.

Olson, M. 1965. *The Logic of Collective Action*. Cambridge, MA: Harvard University Press.

Olson, Mancur. 1982. *The Rise and Decline of Nations: Economic Growth, Stagflation and Social Rigidities*. New Haven: Yale University Press.

Onis, Ziya. 1991. 'The Logic of the Developmental State.' *Comparative Politics* 24 (October): 109–21.

Orrù, Marco, Nicole Woolsey Biggart and Gary G. Hamilton. 1997. *The Economic Organisation of East Asian Capitalism*. London: Sage.

Osugi, K. 1990. 'Japan's Experience of Financial Deregulation Since 1984 in an International Perspective.' *BIS Working Papers* No. 26, January.

Overholt, William. 2002. 'Japan's Economy, at War with Itself.' *Foreign Affairs* (January/ February): 134–47.

Park, Hun Joo. 2007. *Diseased Dirigisme: The Political Sources of Financial Policy toward Small Business in Korea*. Berkeley: Institute of East Asian Studies, University of California.

Park, Jin. 2009. 'Lessons from SOE Management and Privatisation in Korea.' *KDI School of Public Policy and Management Working Paper* No. 09-10, Seoul.

Park, Kyung Suh. 2003. 'Bank-led Corporate Restructuring.' In Stephan Haggard, Won-hyuk Lim and Euysung Kim, eds. *Economic Crisis and Corporate Restructuring in Korea*. Cambridge: Cambridge University Press, 181–206.

Park, Sang Yong. 1999. 'Financial Reform and its Impact on Corporate Organisation in Korea.' In Gordon de Brouwer and Wisarn Pupphavesa, eds. *Asia Pacific Financial Deregulation*. London: Routledge, 207–31.

Park, Albert and Fang Cai. 2007. 'The Informalisation of the Chinese Labour Market.' Unpublished manuscript.

Pasuk, Phongpaichit and Chris Baker. 2002. *Thailand: Economy and Politics*. New York: Oxford University Press.

People's Bank of China (PBOC). 2011. '2010 nian zhongguo quyu jinrong yunxing baogao' (Report on 2010 Regional Finance Development). Beijing: People's Bank of China.

Peerenboom, R. 2002. *China's Long March toward Rule of Law*. New York: Cambridge University Press.

Pekkanen, Robert. 2004. 'After the Developmental State: Civil Society in Japan.' *Journal of East Asian Studies* 4: 363–88.

Pempel, T. J. 1998. *Regime Shift: Comparative Dynamics of the Japanese Political Economy*. Ithaca, NY: Cornell University Press.

—— 1999a. 'The Developmental Regime in a Changing World Economy.' In Meredith Woo-Cumings, ed. *The Developmental State*. Ithaca: Cornell University Press, 137–81.

—— ed. 1999b. *Politics of the Asian Economic Crisis*. Ithaca: Cornell University Press.

—— 2002. 'Labour Exclusion and Privatised Welfare.' In Evelyne Huber, ed. *Models of Capitalism*. Pennsylvania: Pennsylvania State University Press, 277–300.

—— 2010. 'Between Pork and Productivity: The Collapse of the Liberal Democratic Party.' *The Journal of Japanese Studies* 36 (Summer): 227–54.

Peng, Ito and Joseph Wong. 2008. 'Institutions and Institutional Purpose.' *Politics and Society* 36 (1): 61–88.

Penrose, E. T. 1980. *The Theory of the Growth of the Firm*. Oxford: Basil Blackwell.

People's Daily. 2005. 'China has Socialist Market Economy in Place.' (Online edition), *People's Daily*, 13 July.

Pepinsky, Thomas B. 2009. *Economic Crises and the Breakdown of Authoritarian Regimes: Indonesia and Malaysia in Comparative Perspective*. New York: Cambridge University Press.

Persson, T. and G. Tabellini. 2002. *Political Economics*. Cambridge, MA: The MIT Press.

Philion, Stephen. 2007. 'Workers' Democracy vs. Privatization in China.' *Socialism and Democracy* 21 (2): 37–55.

Philippon, Thomas and Ariell Reshef. 2009. 'Wages and Human Capital in the US Financial Industry: 1909–2006.' *NBER Working Paper* No. 14644, January.

Pirie, Iain. 2006. 'Economic Crisis and the Construction of a Neo-Liberal Regulatory Regime in Korea.' *Competition & Change* 10 (March): 49–71.

Polanyi, Karl. 1944. *The Great Transformation*. Boston: Beacon Press.

Pun, N. 2005. *Made in China: Women Factory Workers in a Global Workplace*. Durham, NC: Duke University Press.

Puthucheary, J. J. 1960. *Ownership and Control in the Malayan Economy*. Singapore: Eastern Universities Press.

Pye, Lucian W. 1967. *Southeast Asia's Political Systems*. New Jersey: Prentice-Hall.

Qian, Y. 2003. 'How Reform Worked in China.' In D. Rodrik, ed. *In Search of Prosperity: Analytic Narratives on Economic Growth*. Princeton, NJ: Princeton University Press, 297–333.

Qiao, Jian. 2009. 'The New Labour Contract Law and Labour Conditions in 2008.' In Y. Xin, X. Y. Lu and L. Li eds. *Society of China: Analysis and Forecast*. Beijing: Social Science Academic Press, 312–27. (In Chinese.)

Quah, Danny. 2010. 'The Global Economy's Shifting Centre of Gravity.' London School of Economics, August. http://econ.lse.ac.uk/staff/dquah/p/GE_Shifting_-CG-DQ.pdf

Quintos, Paul L. 2003. 'A Century of Labour Rights and Wrongs in the Philippines.' In Asia Monitor Resource Center, *Asia Pacific Labour Law Review* (2003), 277–91.

Rae, Keith. 2008. 'Foreign Investment & Australia—Counting the Cost of Regulation.' *AOIF Paper* 2. http://www.ipa.org.au/library/publication/1229298979_document_rae.pdf 13.

Rajan, Raghuram G. and Luigi Zingales. 1998. 'Which Capitalism? Lessons from the East Asian Crisis.' *Journal of Applied Corporate Finance* 11 (3): 40–8.

——— 2003a. 'The Great Reversals: The Politics of Financial Development in the Twentieth Century.' *Journal of Financial Economics* 69 (1): 5–50.

——— 2003b. *Saving Capitalism from the Capitalists*. London: Random House Business Books.

Ramasamy, Nagiah and Chris Rowley. 2011. 'Trade Unions in Malaysia.' In John Benson and Ying Zhu, eds. *Trade Unions in Asia*. London: Routledge, 121–39.

Ramesh, M. 2000. *Welfare Capitalism in Southeast Asia*. London: Palgrave Macmillan.

Ramesh, Mishra. 2003. 'Globalization and Social Security Expansion in East Asia.' In Linda Weiss, ed. *States in the Global Economy: Beinging Domestic Institutions Back In*. Cambridge: Cambridge University Press, 83–100.

Redding, Gordon. 1990. *The Spirit of Chinese Capitalism*. New York: de Gruyter.

—— 2002. 'The Capitalist Business System of China and its Rationale.' *Asia Pacific Journal of Management* 19 (2): 221–49.

—— 2005. 'The Thick Description and Comparison of Societal Systems of Capitalism.' *Journal of International Business Studies* 36 (2): 123–55.

—— Michael A. Witt. 2007. *The Future of Chinese Capitalism*. Oxford: Oxford University Press.

Ren, Bing, Kevin Y. Au and Thomas A. Birtch. 2009. 'China's Business Network Structure during Institutional Transitions.' *Asia Pacific Journal of Management* 26 (3): 219–40.

Rhodes, Martin and Richard Higgott. 2000. 'Introduction: Asian Crises and the Myth of Capitalist Convergence.' *Pacific Review* 13 (1): 1–19.

Rodan, Garry, Kevin Hewison and Richard Robison, eds. 2005. *The Political Economy of South-East Asia: Markets, Power and Contestation*. Melbourne: Oxford University Press.

Roland Berger. 2010. *Overcapacity in China*. Beijing: Roland Berger Strategy Consultants for the European Union Chamber of Commerce in China.

Root, Hilton L. 1996. *Small Countries, Big Lessons: Governance and the Rise of East Asia*. Hong Kong: Oxford University Press.

—— 2006. *Capital and Conclusion*. Princeton: Princeton University Press.

Rowley, Chris and John Benson, eds. 2000. *Globalisation and Labour in the Asia Pacific Region*. London: Frank Cass.

—— Kil-Sang Yoo. 2008. 'Trade Unions in South Korea.' In John Benson and Ying Zhu, eds. *Trade Unions in Asia*. London: Routledge, 43–62.

—— —— Dong-Heon Kim. 2011. 'Labour Markets in South Korea.' In John Benson and Ying Zhu, eds. *The Dynamics of Asian Labour Markets*. London: Routledge, 61–82.

Safarian, A. E. and Wendy Dobson, eds. 1996. *East Asian Capitalism: Diversity and Dynamism*. Toronto: University of Toronto Press.

Sakakibara, E. 1995. *Beyond Capitalism; The Japanese Model of Market Economies*. Lenham, MD: University Press of America.

—— Y. Noguchi. 1977. 'Okurasho-nichigin ocho no bunseki' (An Analysis of the Dynasty of the Ministry of Finance and the Bank of Japan). *Chuuo koron* 8. (In Japanese.)

Sako, Mari. 1992. 'Training, Productivity, and Quality Control in Japanese Multinational Companies.' In Aoki and Dore (1992), 84–116.

—— 1997. 'Shunto: The Role of Employer and Union Co-ordination.' Chapter 10 in Mari Sako and H. Sato, eds. *Japanese Labour and Management in Transition*. London: Routledge.

—— 2003. 'Between Bit Valley and Silicon Valley: Hybrid Forms of Business Governance in the Japanese Internet Economy.' In B. M. Kogut, ed. *The Global Internet Economy*. Cambridge. MA: MIT Press, 291–326.

—— 2005. 'Does Embeddedness Imply Limits to Within-Country Diversity?' *British Journal of Industrial Relations* 43 (4): 585–92.

—— 2006. *Shifting Boundaries of the Firm: Japanese Company—Japanese Labour*. Oxford: Oxford University Press.

—— 2007. 'Organizational Diversity and Institutional Change: From Financial and Labour Markets in Japan.' In M. Aoki, G. Jackson and H. Miyajima, eds. *Corporate Governance in Japan: Institutional Change and Organizational Diversity*. Oxford: Oxford University Press.

—— Gregory Jackson. 2006. 'Strategy Meets Institutions: The Transformation of Labor-Management Relations at Deutsche Telekom and NTT.' *Industrial and Labor Relations Review* 59 (3): 347–66.

Sato, Hiroki, Yoshihide Sano, et al. 2003. *Dai ikkai Seisan Genba ni okeru Jonai Ukeoi no Katsuyo ni kansuru Chosa* (*First Survey on the Use of Inside Contractors on the Production Shopfloor*). Tokyo: SSJ Data Archive Research Paper Series, Institute of Social Science, University of Tokyo.

———— et al. 2004. *Seisan Genba ni okeru Gaibu Jinzai no Katsuyou to Jinzai Bijinesu* (Human Resource Management and the Staffing Business at Japanese Manufacturing Site Volume 1). Tokyo: Institute of Social Science, University of Tokyo.

Sato, Yuri. 2005. 'Bank Restructuring and Financial Institution Reform in Indonesia.' *The Developing Economies* 43 (1): 91–120.

Schaede, Ulrike. 1995. 'The "Old Boy" Network and Government-Business Relation-ships.' Mimeo.

—— 2004. 'What Happened to the Japanese Model?' *Review of International Economics* 12 (2): 277–94.

Schmidt, Vivien A. 2009. 'Putting the Political Back into Political Economy by Bringing the State Back in Yet Again.' *World Politics* 61 (3): 516–46.

Schneider, Ben Ross. 2009. 'Hierarchical Market Economies and Varieties of Capitalism in Latin America.' *Journal of Latin American Studies* 41 (4): 553–75.

Scott, Richard W. 2001. *Institutions and Organizations*. Thousand Oaks: Sage Publications.

Searle, P. 1999. *The Riddle of Malaysian Capitalism: Rent-Seekers or Real Capitalists*. Honolulu: University of Hawai'i Press.

Semkow, Brian Wallace. 1994. *Taiwan's Capital Market Reform*. Oxford: Clarendon Press.

Shea, Jia-Dong. 1995. 'Financial Development and Policies in Taipei, China.' In Shahid N. Zahid, ed. *Financial Sector Development in Asia*. Manila: Asian Development Bank, 81–161.

Sheard, P. 1994. 'Main Bank and the Governance of Financial Distress.' In Aoki and Patrick (1994), 188–230.

Shen, Zhong-Hua. 2005. 'Launching the Second Financial Reform.' *Taiwan Economic Forum* 3 (4): 1–25 (in Chinese).

Sheng, Andrew. 2009. *From Asian to Global Financial Crisis*. Cambridge: Cambridge University Press.

Shi, Lu and Bernard Ganne. 2006. 'Understanding the Zhejiang Industrial Clusters.' Paper presented to the International Workshop on Asian Industrial Clusters, Lyon, 29–30 November.

Shi, Yan and Yi-Duan Chen. 2003. 'The Development of a Multidimensional Financial System.' *CBC Quarterly* 25 (4): 23–9. (In Chinese.)

Shih, Vector. 2008. *Factions and Finance in China: Elite Conflict and Inflation*. New York: Cambridge University Press.

—— 2011. 'Guest Post: China's Local Debt Problem is Bigger Than it Looks.' *Financial Times Online Blog*, 28 June.

Shirk, Susan. 2007. *China: Fragile Superpower*. New York: Oxford University Press.

Shoufield, Andrew. 1965. *Modern Capitalism: The Changing Balance of Public and Private Power*. Oxford: Oxford University Press.

Sibal, Jorge V. and Maragtas S. V. Amante. 2008. 'The Philippines: Changes at the Workplace.' In Sangheon Lee and Francois Eyraud, eds. *Globalization, Flexibilization and Working Conditions in Asia and the Pacific*. Oxford: Chandos Publishing and Geneva: International Labour Office, 279–312.

Siengthai, Sununta. 2008. 'Thailand: Globalization and Unprotected Workers.' In Sangheon Lee and Francois Eyraud, eds. *Globalization, Flexibilization and Working Conditions in Asia and the Pacific*. Oxford: Chandos Publishing and Geneva: International Labour Office, 313–42.

—— Uthai Tanlamai and Chris Rowley. 2008. 'The Changing Face of Human Resource Management in Thailand.' In Chris Rowley and Saaidah Abdul-Rahman, eds. *The Changing Face of Management in South East Asia*. London: Routledge, 155–84.

Sloane, P. 1999. *Islam, Modernity and Entrepreneurship Among the Malays*. Basingstoke: Macmillan.

Soesastro, M. Hadi. 1989. 'The Political Economy of Deregulation in Indonesia.' *Asian Survey* 29 (9): 853–69.

Solinger, Dorothy. 1999. *Contesting Citizenship in Urban China: Peasant Migrants, the State, and the Logic of Market*. Berkeley: University of California Press.

Soskice, David. 1999. 'Divergent Production Regimes.' In Herbert Kitschelt, Peter Lange, Gary Marks and John D. Stephens, eds. *Continuity and Change in Contemporary Capitalism*. Cambridge: Cambridge University Press, 101–34.

State Council Research Office Team. 2006. *China's Migrant Workers Survey Report*. Beijing: China Yanshi Publishing House. (In Chinese.)

Steier, Lloyd P. 2009. 'Familial Capitalism in Global Institutional Contexts.' *Asia Pacific Journal of Management* 26 (3): 513–35.

Steinmo, Sven. 2010. *The Evolution of Modern States*. Cambridge: Cambridge University Press.

Stiglitz, Joseph E. and Shahid Yusuf, eds. 2001. *Rethinking the East Asian Miracle*. Oxford: Oxford University Press.

Streeck, Wolfgang. 2009. *Re-Forming Capitalism: Institutional Change in the German Political Economy*. Oxford: Oxford University Press.

—— Kathleen Thelen, eds. 2005. *Beyond Continuity: Institutional Change in Advanced Political Economies*. Oxford: Oxford University Press.

Sun, Liping. 2008. 'Societal Transition: New Issues in the Field of the Sociology of Development.' *Modern China* 34 (1): 88–113.

Sun, F. 2009. 'laowu paiqian yonggong fangshi xia laozi sanfang xingwei de boyi fenxi' [An Analysis of Tripartite Labor-Capital Activities under the System of Dispatch Labor]. *fazhi yu shehui* 243.

Tai, K. and C. Wong. 2003. *Standard & Poor's Country Governance Study: Corporate Governance in China*. http://www.acga- asia.org/loadfile.cfm? SITE_FILE_ID=187

Taipei Stock Exchange (TSE). 1999. *Fact Book*. Taipei: TSE.

Takahashi, W. 2003. 'The East Asian Economies after the Financial Crisis: A Role for the Japanese Yen?' In H. Dobson and G. Hook, eds. *Japan and Britain in the Contemporary World: Response to Common Issues*. London: Routledge Curzon.

—— S. Kobayakawa. 2003. 'Globalization: Role of Institution Building in the Japanese Financial Sector.' *Bank of Japan Working Paper* No. 03-E-7, Bank of Japan.

Tan T. W. 1982. *Income Distribution and Determination in West Malaysia*. Kuala Lumpur: Oxford University Press.

Tashiro, Yutaka and David Osman. 1996. 'Financing Capital Market Intermediaries in Taiwan.' In Hal S. Scott and Philip A. Wellons, eds. *Financing Capital Market Intermediaries in East and Southeast Asia*. The Hague: Kluwer, 247–67.

Taylor, B. and Q. Li. 2007. 'Is the ACFTU a Union and Does it Matter?' *Journal of Industrial Relations* 49 (5): 701–15.

Tenev, S., C. Zhang and L. Brefort. 2002. *Corporate Governance and Enterprise Reform in China*. Washington, DC: World Bank and the International Finance Corporation.

Teranishi, J. 1990. 'Financial Systems and Industrialization of Japan: 1900–1970.' *Banca Nazionale del Lavoro Quarterly Review* 174: 309–41.

—— 1994. 'Loan Syndication in War-Time Japan and Origins of the Main Bank System.' In Aoki and Patrick (1994), 51–88.

—— 1997. 'Sectorial Resource Transfer, Conflict, and Macrostability.' In Aoki, Kim and Okuno-Fujiwara, eds. *Economic Development: A Comparative Analysis*, 279–322.

—— 2000. 'The Fall of Taisho Economic System.' In Aoki and Saxonhouse (2000), 43–63.

Terjesen, Siri and Jolanda Hessels. 2009. 'Varieties of Export-Oriented Entrepreneurship in Asia.' *Asia Pacific Journal of Management* 26 (3): 537–61.

Tett, Gillian. 2009. *Fool's Gold: How Unrestrained Greed Corrupted a Dream, Shattered Global Markets and Unleashed a Catastrophe*. London: Little, Brown.

Thelen, Kathleen. 2004. *How Institutions Evolve*. Cambridge: Cambridge University Press.

Thurbon, Elizabeth. 2001. 'Two Paths to Financial Liberalization: South Korea and Taiwan.' *The Pacific Review* 14: 241–67.

—— Linda Weiss. 2006. 'Investing in Openness: The Evolution of FDI Strategy in South Korea and Taiwan.' *New Political Economy* 11 (1): 1–22.

Tipton, Frank B. 2009. 'Southeast Asian Capitalism: History, Institutions, States, and Firms.' *Asia Pacific Journal of Management* 26 (3): 401–34.

Toya, T. 2000. 'The Political Economy of the Japanese Financial Big Bang: Institutional Change in Finance and Public Policy Making.' Ph.D. thesis, Stanford University.

Tsai, Ming-Chang. 2001. 'Dependency, the State and Class in the Neoliberal Transition of Taiwan.' *Third World Quarterly* 22: 359–79.

Tsai, Kellee. 2007. *Capitalism without Democracy*. Ithaca, NY: Cornell University Press.

Tung, An-Chi. 2001. 'Taiwan's Semiconductor Industry: What the State Did and Did Not.' *Review of Development Economics* 5: 266–88.

Underhill, Geoffrey R. D. and Xiaoke Zhang. 2005. 'The Changing State-Market Condominium in East Asia.' *New Political Economy* 10 (1): 1–24.

Unger, Daniel. 1998. *Building Social Capital in Thailand*. Cambridge: Cambridge University Press.

Unirule. 2011. 'Guoyou Qingye de Xingxhi, Baoxian yu Gaige' (The Nature, Performance, and Reform of State-owned Enterprises). Tianze (Unirule) Economic Research Institute Discussion Group, 12 April. http://www.unirule.org.cn/xiazai/2011/20110412.pdf

U.S. Department of Labor. 2003. *Foreign Labor Trends, Korea*. Washington, DC: Department of Labor.

VEC (Venture Enterprise Centre). Annual, various years. *Annual Survey of Japanese Venture Capita Investments* Tokyo: VEC.

Vogel, E. F. 1979. *Japan as Number One: Lessons for America*. Cambridge, MA: Harvard University Press.

Vogel, Steven K. 2006. *Japan Remodeled: How Government and Industry are Reforming Japanese Capitalism*. Ithaca: Cornell University Press.

Wade, Robert. 1998. 'From "Miracle" to "Cronyism": Explaining the Great Asian Slump.' *Cambridge Journal of Economics* 22: 693–706.

Wain, B. 2009. *Malaysian Maverick: Mahathir Mohamad in Turbulent Times*. Basingstoke: Palgrave Macmillan.

Walder, Andrew. 1986. *Communist Neo-Traditionalism: Work and Authority in Chinese Industry*. Berkeley: University of California Press.

—— 2002. 'Privatization and Elite Mobility: Rural China, 1979–1996.' *Stanford Institute for International Studies A/PARC Working Paper*.

Waldner, David. 1999. *State Building and Late Development*. Ithaca: Cornell University Press.

Walker, Alan and Chack-kie Wong, eds. 2005. *East Asian Welfare Regimes in Transition*. Bristol: Policy Press.

Walter, Andrew. 2006. 'From Developmental to Regulatory State? Japan's New Financial Regulatory System.' *The Pacific Review* 19: 405–28.

—— 2008. *Governing Finance: East Asia's Adoption of International Standards*. Ithaca: Cornell University Press.

Wang, Hui. 2004. 'The Year 1989 and the Historical Roots of Neoliberalism in China.' *Positions: East Asia Cultures Critique* 12 (1): 7–70.

Wang, B. S. and Q. Z. Cui. 2006. *Principles on China's Company Law*. Beijing: China Social Sciences Academic Press.

Wang, Jen-Hwan. 2007. 'From Technological Catch-up to Innovation-based Economic Growth: South Korea and Taiwan Compared.' *Journal of Developmental Studies* 43: 1084–104.

Wang, Xinyuan. 2010. 'Local Government Debt Balloons.' *Global Times*, 7 April. http://business.globaltimes.cn/china-economy/2010-04/519528.html

Wang, H., R. P. Appelbaum, F. Degiuli and N. Lichtenstein. 2009. 'China's New Labour Contract Law: Is China Moving Towards Increased Power for Workers?' *Third World Quarterly* 30 (3): 485–501.

Wang, Jane-Sue, Jing-Twen Chen and Pin-Huang Chou. 2008. 'Market Reactions to the Passage of the Financial Holding Company Act in Taiwan.' *Pacific Economic Review* 13 (4): 453–72.

Wank, David. 1998. *Commodifying Chinese Communism: Business, Trust, and Politics in a South Coast City*. Cambridge: Cambridge University Press.

Warner, Malcolm. 2002. 'Globalisation, Labour Markets and Human Resources in Asia-Pacific Economies.' *International Journal of Human Resource Management* 13 (3): 384–98.

—— 2008. 'Trade unions in China.' In John Benson and Ying Zhu, eds. *Trade Unions in Asia*. London: Routledge, 142–56.

Watts, J. 2005. 'Democracy in China: Civil Rights: Protests Surge as Reforms Fail to Match Rising Hopes.' *Guardian International*, 11 October, 17.

Weiss, Linda. 1998. *The Myth of the Powerless State: Governing the Economy in a Global Era*. Cambridge: Polity Press.

—— 2000. 'Developmental States in Transition: Adapting, Dismantling, Innovating, not "Normalizing.' *The Pacific Review* 13: 21–55.

—— ed. 2003. *States in the Global Economy*. Cambridge: Cambridge University Press.

—— 2004. 'Developmental States before and after the Asian Crisis.' In Jonathan Perraton and Ben Clift, eds. *Where are National Capitalism Now?* Basingstoke: Palgrave Macmillan, 154–68.

White, Gordon. 1984. 'Changing Relations Between State and Enterprise in Contemporary China: Expanding Enterprise Autonomy.' In N. Maxwell and B. McFarlane, eds. *China's Changed Road to Development*. Oxford: Pergamon, 43–60.

Whitley, Richard. 1992. *Business Systems in East Asia: Firms, Markets and Societies*. London: Sage.

—— 1999. *Divergent Capitalisms*. Oxford: Oxford University Press.

—— 2007. *Business Systems and Organisational Capabilities*. Oxford: Oxford University Press.

Whyte, M. K. 2010. *D. Chinese Citizens Want the Government to do More?* New York: Routledge.

Widmaier, Wesley W., Mark Blyth and Leonard Seabrooke. 2007. 'Exogenous Shocks or Endogenous Constructions? The Meanings of Wars and Crises.' *International Studies Quarterly* 51 (4): 747–59.

Wildau, Gabriel. 2008. 'Enterprise Reform: Albatross turns Phoenix.' *China Economic Quarterly* 12 (2): 27–33.

Wilding, Paul. 2008. 'Is the East Asian Welfare Model Still Productive?' *Journal of Asian Public Policy* 1 (1): 18–31.

Williamson, Oliver E. 1975. *Markets and Hierarchies: Analysis and Antitrust Implications*. New York: Free Press.

Winters, Jeffrey A. 1994. 'Power and the Control of Capital.' *World Politics* 46 (3): 419–52.

Womack, J. P., D. Roos and D. Jones. 1990. *The Machine That Changed the World*. New York: Rawson Associates.

Wong, Joseph. 2004a. 'The Adaptive Developmental State in East Asia.' *Journal of Asian Studies* 4 (3): 345–63.

—— 2004b. 'From Learning to Creating: Biotechnology and the Postindustrial Developmental State in Korea.' *Journal of East Asian Studies* 4: 491–517.

Woo, Wing Thye and Liang-Yn Liu. 1994. 'Taiwan's Persistent Trade Surpluses.' In Joel D. Aberbach, David Dollar and Kenneth L. Sokoloff, eds. *The Role of the State in Taiwan's Development*. New York: M.E. Sharpe, 90–112.

—— Sachs, Jeffrey D. and Claus Schwab, eds. 2000. *The Asian Financial Crisis: Lessons for a Resilient Asia*. Cambridge: The MIT Press.

Woo-Cumings, M., ed. 1999. *The Developmental State*. Ithaca: Cornell University Press.

World Bank. 1993. *The East Asian Miracle*. Oxford: Oxford University Press.

—— 1997. *China's Management of Enterprise Assets: The State as Shareholder*. Washington, DC: World Bank.

—— 2006. *Doing Business 2007: How to Reform*. Washington, DC: World Bank.

References

Wright, T. 2004. 'The Political Economy of Coal Mine Disasters in China: Your Rice Bowl or Your Life.' *The China Quarterly* 179: 629–46.

Wu, Yu-Shan. 2002. 'Taiwan in 2001.' *Asian Survey* 42 (1): 29–38.

—— 2007. 'Taiwan's Developmental State: After the Economic and Political Turmoil.' *Asian Survey* 47 (November/December): 977–1001.

Wu, Xue-Liang. 2003. 'The Road to Liberalization.' *Taiwan Economic Forum* 1 (7): 39–61.

Wu, Yongping. 2004. 'Rethinking the Taiwanese Developmental State.' *The China Quarterly* 77 (May): 91–114.

Wuttke, Joerg. 2010. 'China is Beginning to Frustrate Foreign Business.' *The Financial Times*, 7 April.

Xiao, Geng. 1998. 'Reforming the Governance Structure of China's State-Owned Enterprises.' *Public Administration and Development* 18 (3): 273–80.

—— Yang, Xiuke and Janus, Anna. 2009. 'State-owned Enterprises in China: Reform Dynamics and Impacts.' In Ross Garnaut, Ligang Song and Wing Thye Woo, eds. *China's New Place In A World In Crisis: Economic, Geopolitical and Environmental Dimensions*. Canberra: ANU Press.

Xie, Weiqun. 2010. 'Binggou shi jiangjin ruotui erfei guojin mintui' (Mergers and Acquisitions are the Strong Expanding and the Weak Retreating, not the State Expanding and the Private retreating). *People's Daily*, 5 March.

Xin, Dingding. 2010. 'City Workers Lacking Social Welfare.' *China Daily*, 30 March.

Xinhua News. 2004. 'Shenzhen Exchange Launches SME Board.' 28 May.

Xu, Xiaonian and Yan Wang. 1999. 'Ownership Structure and Corporate Governance in Chinese Stock Companies.' *China Economic Review* 10 (1): 75–98.

Yang, D. 2004. *Remaking the Chinese Leviathan: Market Transition and the Politics of Governance in China*. Stanford, CA: Stanford University Press.

Yang, Jae-jin. 2006. 'Corporate Unionism and Labour Market Flexibility in South Korea.' *Journal of East Asian Studies* 6 (2): 205–31.

—— Chung-in Moon. 2005. 'South Korea: Globalization, Neoliberal Labor Reform, and the Trilemma of an Emerging Welfare State.' In Joseph S. Tulchin and Gary Bland, eds. *Getting Globalization Right: The Dilemmas of Inequality*. Boulder: Lynne Rienner Publishers, 71–91.

Yao, Yang. 2004. 'Government Commitment and the Outcome of Privatization.' In Takatoshi Ito and Anne O. Krueger, eds. *Governance, Regulation, and Privatization in the Asia-Pacific Region*. Chicago: University of Chicago Press, 251–78.

Yep, Ray. 2004. 'Can "Tax-for Fee" Reform Reduce Rural Tension in China? The Process, Progress and Limitations.' *China Quarterly* 177: 42–70.

Yeung, Henry Wai-chung. 2000. 'The Dynamics of Asian Business Systems in a Globalising Era.' *Review of International Political Economy* 7 (3): 399–433.

—— 2006. 'Change and Continuity in Southeast Asian Ethnic Chinese Business.' *Asia Pacific Journal of Management* 23 (2): 229–54.

Yin, G. and M. Yang. 2009. 'shenzhen laogong yu shenzhen laogong feizhengfu zuzhi' (Shenzhen's Labor and Shenzhen's Labor NGOs). *chongqing gongxueyuan xuebao (shehui kexue)* 23 (6).

Yoshihara Kunio. 1988. *The Rise of Ersatz Capitalism in Southeast Asia*. New York: Oxford University Press.

Yoshimatsu, Hidetaka. 2003. 'Japanese Policy in the Asian Economic Crisis and the Developmental State Concept.' *Journal of the Asia Pacific Economy* 8: 102–25.

Yu, Hairong. 2011. 'Economist: China's Market-Oriented Reforms in Retreat.' *Caixin*. http://english.caing.com/2011-07-05/100275974.html

Yu, T. T., M. M. Zhang and S. Qi. 2005. 'Government Intervention and Market Distortion: The Case of the Chinese Stock Market.' *Journal of American Academy of Business* 6 (2): 32–6.

Yue, J. 2007. 'feizhengfu zuzhi yu nongmingong quanyi de weihu—yi panyu dagongzu wenshu chuli fuwubu wei ge'an' (NGO and the Protection of Peasant Workers: A Case Study of Panyu Service Department for Peasant Workers). *zhongshan daxue xuebao* 47 (3): 80–5.

Yukongdi, Vimolwan. 2008. 'Trade unions in Thailand.' In John Benson and Ying Zhu, eds. *Trade Unions in Asia*. London: Routledge, 216–35.

Yusuf, S. and K. Nabeshima. 2009. *Tiger Economies Under Threat*. Washington, DC: World Bank.

Zhang, Xiaoke. 2003. 'Political Structures and Financial Liberalisation in Pre-crisis East Asia.' *Studies in Comparative International Development* 38 (1): 64–91.

—— 2007. 'Political Parties and Financial Development: Evidence from Malaysia and Thailand.' *Journal of Public Policy* 27 (3): 341–74.

—— 2009. 'From Banks to Markets: Malaysian and Taiwanese Finance in Transition.' *Review of International Political Economy* 16 (3): 382–408.

—— 2010. 'Global Forces and Corporate Reforms in Korea.' *International Political Science Review* 31 (1): 59–76.

Zhang, L. 2008. 'Lean Production and Labor Controls in the Chinese Automobile Industry in an Age of Globalization.' *International Labor and Working-Class History* 73 (1): 1–21.

Zhang, O. 2009. 'ladong hetongfa banbu beijing xia dui laowu paiqiangong daiyu wenti de yanjiu yu sikao.' *zhiye jishu* 106: 78.

Zhao, Xiao. 1999. 'Jingzheng, Gonggong Xuanze yu Zhidu Bianqian' (Competition, Public Choice and System Change). *Beijing University China Centre for Economic Research Working Paper* No. C1999025.

Zheng Yongnian. 1999. 'Political Incrementalism: Political Lessons from China's 20 Years of Reform.' *Third World Quarterly* 20 (6): 1157–77.

—— 2007. *De Facto Federalism in China: Reforms and Dynamics Of Central-Local Relations*. Singapore: World Scientific.

Zhu, Ying. 2008. 'Trade Unions in Taiwan.' In John Benson and Ying Zhu, eds. *Trade Unions in Asia*. London: Routledge, 63–80.

—— John Benson. 2008. 'Trade Unions in Asia: A Comparative Analysis.' In John Benson and Ying Zhu, eds. *Trade Unions in Asia*. London: Routledge, 256–66.

—— —— 2011. 'Labour Markets in Asia.' In John Benson and Ying Zhu, eds. *The Dynamics of Asian Labour Markets*. London: Routledge, 224–42.

—— Malcolm Warner and Chris Rowley. 2007. 'Human Resource Management with "Asian" Characteristics.' *International Journal of Human Resource Management* 18 (5): 745–68.

References

Zhuang, Juzhong, David Edwards, David Webb and Ma. Virginita A. Capulong. 2000. *Corporate Governance and Finance in East Asia*. Manila: Asian Development Bank.

Zweig, David. 1997. *Freeing China's Farmers: Rural Restructuring in the Reform Era*. Armonk: M.E. Sharpe.

Zysman, J. 1984. *Governments, Markets and Growth: Finance and the Politics of Industrial Change*. Ithaca: Cornell University Press.

Index

Nissan Oppama Factory 149
'Nixon Shock' 210
Noguchi, Y. 204
Nölke, A. 5, 8, 14
norms:
  behavioural 20, 23
  formal 273
  informal 16, 20, 267, 273
  lifetime employment 271
  neoliberal 66
  sociocultural 49
  see also social norms
North Atlantic-centrism 8
North Korea 22, 55 n.
Northeast Asia 223–43
Nowland, J. 249
NPLs (nonperforming loans) 161, 162, 165,
  166, 168, 169, 173, 176, 215
  problems with 159, 167, 171, 177, 219

ODR (official discount rate) 208
OECD countries 229, 243, 276
OEM (original equipment manufacturing) 50, 57
oil shocks 147, 209
Okazaki, T. 203, 221
Okuno-Fujiwara, M. 203
Oliver, C. 136
Olson, M. 146, 160
Osaka Stock Exchange 137
OSS (outsourcing and shared services) 79

Park Hun Joo 252
PBOC (People's Bank of China) 43, 167,
  169 n., 171
Pearl River Delta 122
  see also Dongguan; Foshan; Guangzhou;
  Hong Kong; Shenzhen
Peetz, D. 12
Pekkanen, R. 53, 61, 63, 64
PEMANDU (Malaysian Performance
  Management and Delivery Unit) 80
Pempel, T. J. 195
Penrose, E. T. 69 n.
pension funds 141, 142, 235, 236
People's Liberation Army (China) 39
Pepinsky, T. B. 160, 188, 195, 253
Perodua 77, 78
PEZA (Philippine Economic Zone
  Authority) 100
Philippines 6, 101, 106, 180–1, 195,
  270, 280
  banking system 182–3, 184, 255
  deregulation 108, 193
  equity markets 180, 183, 192
  financial development 197, 198, 199
  financial system 179, 255
  labour market changes 98–100

ownership of companies controlled by
  founding families 249
mediocre growth outcomes 4
personalism/clientelism 91, 188, 190, 267, 280
policy-making subservient to interests of
  oligarchs 188–9
political instability 190, 195, 197
small, family-based firms 98, 104
state interference in allocation of credit 198
growth 179
transition from authoritarianism to
  democracy 279
weakening of labour's political efficacy 200
see also Labor Code; Marcos; Ramos
Pierre, G. 94 n.
Pirie, I. 47 n., 55, 62, 65, 274
planned economy 203
Plaza Accord (1985) 40, 213
PNB Equity Resource Corporation 78
POEA (Philippine Overseas Employment
  Administration) 100
Polanyi, K. 21, 116, 187
politics:
  conflict 3–4, 65
  hierarchy 160–5
  instability 4, 190, 195, 197
  labour 103–4
POSCO 85, 278
PPB Group 82
Prescott, E. C. 215
price controls 44, 54
private banks:
  establishment of 54, 58, 64
  scaled down lending to manufacturing
    sector 239
privatization 29, 33, 35, 36, 40, 45, 51, 52, 55,
  66, 72, 74, 100, 105, 114, 193, 197, 201,
  230, 231, 235, 250, 271
  acceleration of 119, 241
  consequence of 195
  business interests rewarded by 194
  collusive deals 59 n.
  persistence of 80
  endorsement of 70
  gradual 58
  introduction (mid-1990s) 32
  opposition to 31
  partial 54, 70–1
  politicized 59, 63
  promotion of 71, 76, 85
  renationalized major projects 75
  sustained 252
  trade union protests against 241
  widespread 31
  worker protest slowing down 119–20
Pro-democracy Movement (China 1989) 126–7
profitability 35, 39, 167, 173, 211, 215, 228

Index